Django 1.1 Testing and Debugging

Building rigorously tested and bug-free Django applications

Karen M. Tracey

PUBLISHING

BIRMINGHAM - MUMBAI

Django 1.1 Testing and Debugging

First published: April 2010

Production Reference: 1120410

Published by Packt Publishing Ltd.
32 Lincoln Road
Olton
Birmingham, B27 6PA, UK.

ISBN 978-1-847197-56-6

www.packtpub.com

Cover Image by Raj Kataria (rajkataria17@gmail.com)

Credits

Author
Karen M. Tracey

Reviewer
Benjamin A. Slavin

Acquisition Editor
Steven Wilding

Development Editor
Neha Patwari

Technical Editor
Conrad Sardinha

Indexers
Hemangini Bari
Rekha Nair

Editorial Team Leader
Mithun Sehgal

Project Team Leader
Priya Mukherji

Project Coordinator
Leena Purkait

Proofreader
Aaron Nash

Production Coordinator
Shantanu Zagade

Cover Work
Shantanu Zagade

About the Author

Karen has a PhD in Electrical/Computer Engineering from the University of Notre Dame. Her research there focused on distributed operating systems, which led to work in an industry centered on communications protocols and middleware. Outside of work she has an interest in puzzles, which led her to take up crossword construction. She has published nearly 100 puzzles in the New York Times, the Los Angeles Times syndicate, the New York Sun, and USA Today. She amassed a database of thousands of puzzles to aid in constructing and cluing her own puzzles. The desire to put a web frontend on this database is what led her to Django. She was impressed by the framework and its community, and became an active core framework contributor. Karen is one of the most prolific posters on the django-users mailing list. Her experience in helping hundreds of people there guided her in choosing the best and most useful material to include in this book.

Many thanks to Steven Wilding and the entire Packt Publishing team for making this book possible.

I'd also like to thank the Django community. The community is too large to name everyone individually, but Jacob Kaplan-Moss, Adrian Holovaty, Malcolm Tredinnick, and Russell Keith-Magee deserve special mention. I very much appreciate the tremendous amount of work you all have done to create an excellent framework and foster a helpful and welcoming community.

Finally thanks to my parents, brothers, and many friends who supported me throughout the writing process. Your encouraging words have been very helpful and much appreciated.

About the Reviewer

BEN SLAVIN is an entrepreneur, technology strategist, and developer, focused on high performance web applications. He has been using Django to build scalable, reliable websites and applications since 2006. As a Director of Technology and a CTO, Ben has successfully integrated Django into multiple businesses' operations, reducing technology costs and improving productivity.

Residing in Washington, DC, Ben has built and operates the Heliograph Network, designed to improve the performance and reliability of web applications. You can find him online at `http://benslavin.net`.

In memory of Mello and Haley

Table of Contents

Preface

Bugs are a time consuming burden during software development. Django's built-in test framework and debugging support help lessen this burden. This book will teach you quick and efficient techniques for using Django and Python tools to eradicate bugs and ensure your Django application works correctly.

This book will walk you step-by-step through the development of a complete sample Django application. You will learn how best to test and debug models, views, URL configuration, templates, and template tags. This book will help you integrate with and make use of the rich external environment of testing and debugging tools for Python and Django applications.

This book starts with a basic overview of testing. It will highlight areas to look out for while testing. You will learn about the different kinds of tests available, the pros and cons of each, and details of test extensions provided by Django that simplify the task of testing Django applications. You will see an illustration of how external tools that provide even more sophisticated testing features can be integrated into Django's framework.

On the debugging front, the book illustrates how to interpret the extensive debugging information provided by Django's debug error pages, and how to utilize logging and other external tools to learn what code is doing.

This book is a step-by-step guide to running tests using Django's test support and making best use of Django and Python debugging tools.

What this book covers

In *Chapter 1, Django Testing Overview*, we begin development of a sample Django survey application. The example tests automatically generated by Django are described and run. All of the options available for running tests are covered.

In *Chapter 2, Does This Code Work? Doctests in Depth*, the models used by the sample application are developed. Using doctests to test models is illustrated by example. The pros and cons of doctests are discussed. Specific caveats for using doctests with Django applications are presented.

In *Chapter 3, Testing 1, 2, 3: Basic Unit Testing*, the doctests implemented in the previous chapter are re-implemented as unit tests and assessed in light of the pros, cons, and caveats of doctests discussed in the previous chapter. Additional tests are developed that need to make use of test data. Using fixture files to load such data is demonstrated. In addition, some tests where fixture files are inappropriate for test data are developed.

In *Chapter 4, Getting Fancier: Django Unit Test Extensions*, we begin to write the views that serve up web pages for the application. The number of tests is starting to become significant, so this chapter begins by showing how to replace use of a single tests.py file for tests with a tests directory, so that tests may be kept well-organized. Then, tests for views are developed that illustrate how unit test extensions provided by Django simplify the task of testing web applications. Testing form behavior is demonstrated by development of a test for an admin customization made in this chapter.

Chapter 5, Filling in the Blanks: Integrating Django and Other Test Tools, shows how Django supports integration of other test tools into its framework. Two examples are presented. The first illustrates how an add-on application can be used to generate test coverage information while the second demonstrates how use of the twill test tool (which allows for much easier testing of form behavior) can be integrated into Django application tests.

Chapter 6, Django Debugging Overview, provides an introduction to the topic of debugging Django applications. All of the settings relevant for debugging are described. Debug error pages are introduced. The database query history maintained by Django when debugging is turned on is described, as well as features of the development server that aid in debugging. Finally, the handling of errors that occur during production (when debug is off) is detailed, and all the settings necessary to ensure that information about such errors is captured and sent to the appropriate people are mentioned.

In *Chapter 7, When the Wheels Fall Off: Understanding a Django Debug Page*, development of the sample application continues, making some typical mistakes along the way. These mistakes result in Django debug pages. All of the information available on these pages is described, and guidance on what pieces are likely most helpful to look at in what situations is given. Several different kinds of debug pages are encountered and discussed in depth.

Chapter 8, When Problems Hide: Getting More Information, focuses on how to get more information about how code is behaving in cases where a problem doesn't result in a debug error page. It walks through the development of a template tag to embed the query history for a view in the rendered page, and then shows how the Django debug toolbar can be used to get the same information, in addition to much more. Finally, some logging utilities are developed.

Chapter 9, When You Don't Even Know What to Log: Using Debuggers, walks through examples of using the Python debugger (pdb) to track down what is going wrong in cases where no debug page appears and even logging isn't helpful. All of the most useful pdb commands are illustrated by example. In addition, we see how pdb can be used to ensure correct code behavior for code that is subject to multi-process race conditions.

Chapter 10, When All Else Fails: Getting Outside Help, describes what to do when none of the techniques covered so far have solved a problem. Possibly, it is a bug in external code: tips are given on how to search to see if others have experienced the same and if there are any fixes available. Possibly it's a bug in our code or a misunderstanding about how some things work; avenues for asking questions and tips on writing good questions are included.

In *Chapter 11, When it's Time to Go Live: Moving to Production*, we move the sample application into production, using Apache and mod_wsgi instead of the development server. Several of the most common problems encountered during this step are covered. In addition, the option of using Apache with mod_wsgi during development is discussed.

What you need for this book

You will need a computer running a Django 1.1 release—the latest 1.1.X release is recommended. You will also need an editor to edit code files and a web browser. You may choose to use whatever operating system, editing, and browsing tools you are most comfortable with, so long as you choose an operating system that can run Django. For more information on Django's requirements, consult http://docs.djangoproject.com/en/1.1/intro/install/.

For your reference, the example console output and screenshots in this book are all taken from a machine running:

- Ubuntu 8.10
- Python 2.5.2
- Django 1.1 (early in the book) and 1.1.1 (later in the book)
- Firefox 3.5.7

You can use any database supported by Django. For illustration purposes, different databases (SQLite, MySQL, PostgreSQL) are used at different points in the book. You will likely prefer to choose one to use throughout.

Additional software is used at specific points in the book. Wherever a software package is introduced, notes on where to obtain it for installation are included. For your reference, the following is a list of additional software packages and the versions used in the book:

- *Chapter 5, Filling in the Blanks: Integrating Django and Other Test Tools*, uses:
  - ○ coverage 3.2
  - ○ django_coverage 1.0.1
  - ○ twill 0.9 (and latest development level)
- *Chapter 8, When Problems Hide: Getting More Information*, uses:
  - ○ django-debug-toolbar 0.8.0
- *Chapter 9, When You Don't Even Know What to Log: Using Debuggers*, uses:
  - ○ pygooglechart 0.2.0
  - ○ matplotlib 0.98.3
- *Chapter 11, When it's Time to Go Live: Moving to Production*, uses:
  - ○ Apache 2.2
  - ○ mod_wsgi 2.3
  - ○ siege 2.6.6

Note that you do not need to have any of these additional packages installed when you start working through this book, they can each be added at the specific point where you want to start using them. The versions listed are those used for the output shown in the book; it is expected that later versions will work as well, though the output produced may be slightly different if you use a newer version.

Who this book is for

If you are a Django application developer who wants to create robust applications quickly that work well and are easy to maintain in the long term, this book is for you. This book is the right pick if you want to be smartly tutored to make best use of Django's rich testing and debugging support and make development an effortless task.

Basic knowledge of Python, Django, and the overall structure of a database-driven web application is assumed. However, the code samples are fully explained so that even beginners who are new to the area can learn a great deal from this book. If you are new to Django, it is recommended that you work through the online Django tutorial before beginning this book.

Conventions

In this book, you will find a number of styles of text that distinguish between different kinds of information. Here are some examples of these styles, and an explanation of their meaning.

Code words in text are shown as follows: "Now we have the basic skeleton of a Django project and application: A `settings.py` file, a `urls.py` file, the `manage.py` utility, and a `survey` directory containing `.py` files for models, views, and tests."

A block of code is set as follows:

```
__test__ = {"doctest": """
Another way to test that 1 + 1 is equal to 2.

>>> 1 + 1 == 2
True
"""}
```

When we wish to draw your attention to a particular part of a code block, the relevant lines or items are set in bold:

```
urlpatterns = patterns('',
    # Example:
    # (r'^marketr/', include('marketr.foo.urls')),

    # Uncomment the admin/doc line below and add
    # 'django.contrib.admindocs'
    # to INSTALLED_APPS to enable admin documentation:
    # (r'^admin/doc/', include('django.contrib.admindocs.urls')),
```

```
    # Uncomment the next line to enable the admin:
    (r'^admin/', include(admin.site.urls)),
    (r'', include('survey.urls')),
)
```

Any command-line input or output is written as follows:

```
kmt@lbox:/dj_projects$ django-admin.py startproject marketr
```

New terms and **important words** are shown in bold. Words that you see on the screen, in menus or dialog boxes for example, appear in the text like this: "This drop-down box contains a full list of the ticket attributes we could search on, such as **Reporter**, **Owner**, **Status**, and **Component**."

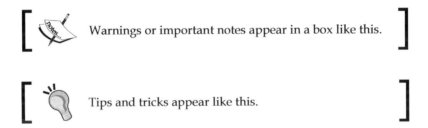

Warnings or important notes appear in a box like this.

Tips and tricks appear like this.

Reader feedback

Feedback from our readers is always welcome. Let us know what you think about this book—what you liked or may have disliked. Reader feedback is important for us to develop titles that you really get the most out of.

To send us general feedback, simply send an e-mail to feedback@packtpub.com, and mention the book title via the subject of your message.

If there is a book that you need and would like to see us publish, please send us a note in the **SUGGEST A TITLE** form on www.packtpub.com or e-mail suggest@packtpub.com.

If there is a topic that you have expertise in and you are interested in either writing or contributing to a book on, see our author guide on www.packtpub.com/authors.

Customer support

Now that you are the proud owner of a Packt book, we have a number of things to help you to get the most from your purchase.

Downloading the example code for the book

Visit `http://www.packtpub.com/files/code/7566_Code.zip` to directly download the example code.

The downloadable files contain instructions on how to use them.

Errata

Although we have taken every care to ensure the accuracy of our content, mistakes do happen. If you find a mistake in one of our books—maybe a mistake in the text or the code—we would be grateful if you would report this to us. By doing so, you can save other readers from frustration and help us improve subsequent versions of this book. If you find any errata, please report them by visiting `http://www.packtpub.com/support`, selecting your book, clicking on the **let us know** link, and entering the details of your errata. Once your errata are verified, your submission will be accepted and the errata will be uploaded on our website, or added to any list of existing errata, under the Errata section of that title. Any existing errata can be viewed by selecting your title from `http://www.packtpub.com/support`.

Piracy

Piracy of copyright material on the Internet is an ongoing problem across all media. At Packt, we take the protection of our copyright and licenses very seriously. If you come across any illegal copies of our works, in any form, on the Internet, please provide us with the location address or website name immediately so that we can pursue a remedy.

Please contact us at `copyright@packtpub.com` with a link to the suspected pirated material.

We appreciate your help in protecting our authors, and our ability to bring you valuable content.

Questions

You can contact us at `questions@packtpub.com` if you are having a problem with any aspect of the book, and we will do our best to address it.

1
Django Testing Overview

How do you know when code you have written is working as intended? Well, you test it. But how? For a web application, you can test the code by manually bringing up the pages of your application in a web browser and verifying that they are correct. This involves more than a quick glance to see whether they have the correct content, as you must also ensure, for example, that all the links work and that any forms work properly. As you can imagine, this sort of manual testing quickly becomes impossible to rely on as an application grows beyond a few simple pages. For any non-trivial application, automated testing is essential.

Automated testing of Django applications makes use of the fundamental test support built-in to the Python language: doctests and unit tests. When you create a new Django application with `manage.py startapp`, one of the generated files contains a sample doctest and unit test, intended to jump-start your own test writing. In this chapter, we will begin our study of testing Django applications. Specifically, we will:

- Examine in detail the contents of the sample `tests.py` file, reviewing the fundamentals of Python's test support as we do so

- See how to use Django utilities to run the tests contained in `tests.py`

- Learn how to interpret the output of the tests, both when the tests succeed and when they fail

- Review the effects of the various command-line options that can be used when testing

Getting started: Creating a new application

Let's get started by creating a new Django project and application. Just so we have something consistent to work with throughout this book, let's assume we are setting out to create a new market-research type website. At this point, we don't need to decide much about this site except some names for the Django project and at least one application that it will include. As `market_research` is a bit long, let's shorten that to `marketr` for the project name. We can use `django-admin.py` to create a new Django project:

kmt@lbox:/dj_projects$ django-admin.py startproject marketr

Then, from within the new `marketr` directory, we can create a new Django application using the `manage.py` utility. One of the core applications for our market research project will be a survey application, so we will start by creating it:

kmt@lbox:/dj_projects/marketr$ python manage.py startapp survey

Now we have the basic skeleton of a Django project and application: a `settings.py` file, a `urls.py` file, the `manage.py` utility, and a `survey` directory containing `.py` files for models, views, and tests. There is nothing of substance placed in the auto-generated models and views files, but in the `tests.py` file there are two sample tests: one unit test and one doctest. We will examine each in detail next.

Understanding the sample unit test

The unit test is the first test contained in `tests.py`, which begins:

```
"""
This file demonstrates two different styles of tests (one doctest and
one unittest). These will both pass when you run "manage.py test".

Replace these with more appropriate tests for your application.
"""

from django.test import TestCase

class SimpleTest(TestCase):
    def test_basic_addition(self):
        """
        Tests that 1 + 1 always equals 2.
        """
        self.failUnlessEqual(1 + 1, 2)
```

The unit test starts by importing `TestCase` from `django.test`. The `django.test`. `TestCase` class is based on Python's `unittest.TestCase`, so it provides everything from the underlying Python `unittest.TestCase` plus features useful for testing Django applications. These Django extensions to `unittest.TestCase` will be covered in detail in *Chapter 3, Testing 1, 2, 3: Basic Unit Testing* and *Chapter 4, Getting Fancier: Django Unit Test Extensions*. The sample unit test here doesn't actually need any of that support, but it does not hurt to base the sample test case on the Django class anyway.

The sample unit test then declares a `SimpleTest` class based on Django's `TestCase`, and defines a test method named `test_basic_addition` within that class. That method contains a single statement:

```
self.failUnlessEqual(1 + 1, 2)
```

As you might expect, that statement will cause the test case to report a failure unless the two provided arguments are equal. As coded, we'd expect that test to succeed. We'll verify that later in this chapter, when we get to actually running the tests. But first, let's take a closer look at the sample doctest.

Understanding the sample doctest

The doctest portion of the sample `tests.py` is:

```
__test__ = {"doctest": """
Another way to test that 1 + 1 is equal to 2.

>>> 1 + 1 == 2
True
"""}
```

That looks a bit more mysterious than the unit test half. For the sample doctest, a special variable, `__test__`, is declared. This variable is set to be a dictionary containing one key, `doctest`. This key is set to a string value that resembles a docstring containing a comment followed by what looks like a snippet from an interactive Python shell session.

The part that looks like an interactive Python shell session is what makes up the doctest. That is, lines that start with `>>>` will be executed (minus the `>>>` prefix) during the test, and the actual output produced will be compared to the expected output found in the doctest below the line that starts with `>>>`. If any actual output fails to match the expected output, the test fails. For this sample test, we would expect entering `1 + 1 == 2` in an interactive Python shell session to result in the interpreter producing the output `True`, so again it looks like this sample test should pass.

Note that doctests do not have to be defined by using this special __test__ dictionary. In fact, Python's doctest test runner looks for doctests within all the docstrings found in the file. In Python, a docstring is a string literal that is the first statement in a module, function, class, or method definition. Given that, you'd expect snippets from an interactive Python shell session found in the comment at the very top of this tests.py file to also be run as a doctest. This is another thing we can experiment with once we start running these tests, which we'll do next.

Running the sample tests

The comment at the top of the sample tests.py file states that the two tests: will both pass when you run "manage.py test". So let's see what happens if we try that:

```
kmt@lbox:/dj_projects/marketr$ python manage.py test

Creating test database...

Traceback (most recent call last):

  File "manage.py", line 11, in <module>

    execute_manager(settings)

  File "/usr/lib/python2.5/site-packages/django/core/management/__init__
.py", line 362, in execute_manager

    utility.execute()

  File "/usr/lib/python2.5/site-packages/django/core/management/__init__
.py", line 303, in execute

    self.fetch_command(subcommand).run_from_argv(self.argv)

  File "/usr/lib/python2.5/site-packages/django/core/management/base.py",
line 195, in run_from_argv

    self.execute(*args, **options.__dict__)

  File "/usr/lib/python2.5/site-packages/django/core/management/base.py",
line 222, in execute

    output = self.handle(*args, **options)

  File "/usr/lib/python2.5/site-packages/django/core/management/commands/
test.py", line 23, in handle

    failures = test_runner(test_labels, verbosity=verbosity, interactive=
interactive)

  File "/usr/lib/python2.5/site-packages/django/test/simple.py", line
191, in run_tests

    connection.creation.create_test_db(verbosity, autoclobber=not
interactive)

  File "/usr/lib/python2.5/site-packages/django/db/backends/creation.py",
line 327, in create_test_db
```

```
    test_database_name = self._create_test_db(verbosity, autoclobber)
  File "/usr/lib/python2.5/site-packages/django/db/backends/creation.py",
line 363, in _create_test_db
    cursor = self.connection.cursor()
  File "/usr/lib/python2.5/site-packages/django/db/backends/dummy/base.
py", line 15, in complain
    raise ImproperlyConfigured, "You haven't set the DATABASE_ENGINE
setting yet."
django.core.exceptions.ImproperlyConfigured: You haven't set the
DATABASE_ENGINE setting yet.
```

Oops, we seem to have gotten ahead of ourselves here. We created our new Django project and application, but never edited the settings file to specify any database information. Clearly we need to do that in order to run the tests.

But will the tests use the production database we specify in settings.py? That could be worrisome, since we might at some point code something in our tests that we wouldn't necessarily want to do to our production data. Fortunately, it's not a problem. The Django test runner creates an entirely new database for running the tests, uses it for the duration of the tests, and deletes it at the end of the test run. The name of this database is test_ followed by DATABASE_NAME specified in settings. py. So running tests will not interfere with production data.

In order to run the sample tests.py file, we need to first set appropriate values for DATABASE_ENGINE, DATABASE_NAME, and whatever else may be required for the database we are using in settings.py. Now would also be a good time to add our survey application and django.contrib.admin to INSTALLED_APPS, as we will need both of those as we proceed. Once those changes have been made to settings. py, manage.py test works better:

```
kmt@lbox:/dj_projects/marketr$ python manage.py test
Creating test database...
Creating table auth_permission
Creating table auth_group
Creating table auth_user
Creating table auth_message
Creating table django_content_type
Creating table django_session
Creating table django_site
Creating table django_admin_log
Installing index for auth.Permission model
Installing index for auth.Message model
```

```
Installing index for admin.LogEntry model
..................................
---------------------------------------------------------------------
Ran 35 tests in 2.012s

OK
Destroying test database...
```

That looks good. But what exactly got tested? Towards the end it says `Ran 35 tests`, so there were certainly more tests run than the two tests in our simple `tests.py` file. The other 33 tests are from the other applications listed by default in `settings.py`: auth, content types, sessions, and sites. These Django "contrib" applications ship with their own tests, and by default, `manage.py test` runs the tests for all applications listed in `INSTALLED_APPS`.

> Note that if you do not add `django.contrib.admin` to the `INSTALLED_APPS` list in `settings.py`, then `manage.py test` may report some test failures. With Django 1.1, some of the tests for `django.contrib.auth` rely on `django.contrib.admin` also being included in `INSTALLED_APPS` in order for the tests to pass. That inter-dependence may be fixed in the future, but for now it is easiest to avoid the possible errors by including `django.contrib.admin` in `INTALLED_APPS` from the start. We will want to use it soon enough anyway.

It is possible to run just the tests for certain applications. To do this, specify the application names on the command line. For example, to run only the `survey` application tests:

```
kmt@lbox:/dj_projects/marketr$ python manage.py test survey
Creating test database...
Creating table auth_permission
Creating table auth_group
Creating table auth_user
Creating table auth_message
Creating table django_content_type
Creating table django_session
Creating table django_site
Creating table django_admin_log
Installing index for auth.Permission model
Installing index for auth.Message model
Installing index for admin.LogEntry model
..
```

```
- - - - - - - - - - - - - - - - - - - - - - - - - - - - - - - - - - - - - - - - - - - -
Ran 2 tests in 0.039s

OK
Destroying test database...
```

There—`Ran 2 tests` looks right for our sample `tests.py` file. But what about all those messages about tables being created and indexes being installed? Why were the tables for these applications created when their tests were not going to be run? The reason for this is that the test runner does not know what dependencies may exist between the application(s) that are going to be tested and others listed in `INSTALLED_APPS` that are not going to be tested.

For example, our survey application could have a model with a `ForeignKey` to the `django.contrib.auth` User model, and tests for the survey application may rely on being able to add and query `User` entries. This would not work if the test runner neglected to create tables for the applications excluded from testing. Therefore, the test runner creates the tables for all applications listed in `INSTALLED_APPS`, even those for which tests are not going to be run.

We now know how to run tests, how to limit the testing to just the application(s) we are interested in, and what a successful test run looks like. But, what about test failures? We're likely to encounter a fair number of those in real work, so it would be good to make sure we understand the test output when they occur. In the next section, then, we will introduce some deliberate breakage so that we can explore what failures look like and ensure that when we encounter real ones, we will know how to properly interpret what the test run is reporting.

Breaking things on purpose

Let's start by introducing a single, simple failure. Change the unit test to expect that adding 1 + 1 will result in 3 instead of 2. That is, change the single statement in the unit test to be: `self.failUnlessEqual(1 + 1, 3)`.

Now when we run the tests, we will get a failure:

```
kmt@lbox:/dj_projects/marketr$ python manage.py test
Creating test database...
Creating table auth_permission
Creating table auth_group
Creating table auth_user
Creating table auth_message
```

```
Creating table django_content_type
Creating table django_session
Creating table django_site
Creating table django_admin_log
Installing index for auth.Permission model
Installing index for auth.Message model
Installing index for admin.LogEntry model
.........................F.......
======================================================================
FAIL: test_basic_addition (survey.tests.SimpleTest)
----------------------------------------------------------------------
Traceback (most recent call last):
  File "/dj_projects/marketr/survey/tests.py", line 15, in test_basic_
addition
    self.failUnlessEqual(1 + 1, 3)
AssertionError: 2 != 3


----------------------------------------------------------------------
Ran 35 tests in 2.759s

FAILED (failures=1)
Destroying test database...
```

That looks pretty straightforward. The failure has produced a block of output
starting with a line of equal signs and then the specifics of the test that has failed.
The failing method is identified, as well as the class containing it. There is a
`Traceback` that shows the exact line of code that has generated the failure,
and the `AssertionError` shows details of the cause of the failure.

Notice the line above the equal signs—it contains a bunch of dots and one F. What
does that mean? This is a line we overlooked in the earlier test output listings. If you
go back and look at them now, you'll see there has always been a line with some
number of dots after the last `Installing index` message. This line is generated as
the tests are run, and what is printed depends on the test results. F means a test has
failed, dot means a test passed. When there are enough tests that they take a while
to run, this real-time progress update can be useful to get a sense of how the run is
going while it is in progress.

Finally at the end of the test output, we see `FAILED (failures=1)` instead of the `OK`
we had seen previously. Any test failures make the overall test run outcome a failure
instead of a success.

Next, let's see what a failing doctest looks like. If we restore the unit test back to its original form and change the doctest to expect the Python interpreter to respond `True` to `1 + 1 == 3`, running the tests (restricting the tests to only the `survey` application this time) will then produce this output:

```
kmt@lbox:/dj_projects/marketr$ python manage.py test survey
Creating test database...
Creating table auth_permission
Creating table auth_group
Creating table auth_user
Creating table auth_message
Creating table django_content_type
Creating table django_session
Creating table django_site
Creating table django_admin_log
Installing index for auth.Permission model
Installing index for auth.Message model
Installing index for admin.LogEntry model
.F
======================================================================
FAIL: Doctest: survey.tests.__test__.doctest
----------------------------------------------------------------------
Traceback (most recent call last):
  File "/usr/lib/python2.5/site-packages/django/test/_doctest.py", line
2180, in runTest
    raise self.failureException(self.format_failure(new.getvalue()))
AssertionError: Failed doctest test for survey.tests.__test__.doctest
  File "/dj_projects/marketr/survey/tests.py", line unknown line number,
in doctest


----------------------------------------------------------------------
File "/dj_projects/marketr/survey/tests.py", line ?, in survey.tests.__
test__.doctest
Failed example:
    1 + 1 == 3
Expected:
    True
Got:
```

```
    False


----------------------------------------------------------------

Ran 2 tests in 0.054s

FAILED (failures=1)
Destroying test database...
```

The output from the failing doctest is a little more verbose and a bit less straightforward to interpret than the unit test failure. The failing doctest is identified as `survey.tests.__test__.doctest` — this means the key `doctest` in the `__test__` dictionary defined within the `survey/tests.py` file. The `Traceback` portion of the output is not as useful as it was in the unit test case as the `AssertionError` simply notes that the doctest failed. Fortunately, details of what caused the failure are then provided, and you can see the content of the line that caused the failure, what output was expected, and what output was actually produced by executing the failing line.

Note, though, that the test runner does not pinpoint the line number within `tests.py` where the failure occurred. It reports `unknown line number` and `line ?` in different portions of the output. Is this a general problem with doctests or perhaps a result of the way in which this particular doctest is defined, as part of the `__test__` dictionary? We can answer that question by putting a test in the docstring at the top of `tests.py`. Let's restore the sample doctest to its original state and change the top of the file to look like this:

```
    """
    This file demonstrates two different styles of tests (one doctest and
    one unittest). These will both pass when you run "manage.py test".

    Replace these with more appropriate tests for your application.

    >>> 1 + 1 == 3
    True
    """
```

Then when we run the tests we get:

```
kmt@lbox:/dj_projects/marketr$ python manage.py test survey
Creating test database...
Creating table auth_permission
Creating table auth_group
Creating table auth_user
```

```
Creating table auth_message
Creating table django_content_type
Creating table django_session
Creating table django_site
Creating table django_admin_log
Installing index for auth.Permission model
Installing index for auth.Message model
Installing index for admin.LogEntry model
.F.
======================================================================
FAIL: Doctest: survey.tests
----------------------------------------------------------------------
Traceback (most recent call last):
  File "/usr/lib/python2.5/site-packages/django/test/_doctest.py", line
2180, in runTest
    raise self.failureException(self.format_failure(new.getvalue()))
AssertionError: Failed doctest test for survey.tests
  File "/dj_projects/marketr/survey/tests.py", line 0, in tests

----------------------------------------------------------------------
File "/dj_projects/marketr/survey/tests.py", line 7, in survey.tests
Failed example:
    1 + 1 == 3
Expected:
    True
Got:
    False



----------------------------------------------------------------------
Ran 3 tests in 0.052s

FAILED (failures=1)
Destroying test database...
```

Here line numbers are provided. The `Traceback` portion apparently identifies the line above the line where the docstring containing the failing test line begins (the docstring starts on `line 1` while the traceback reports `line 0`). The detailed failure output identifies the actual line in the file that causes the failure, in this case `line 7`.

The inability to pinpoint line numbers is thus a side-effect of defining the doctest within the `__test__` dictionary. While it doesn't cause much of a problem here, as it is trivial to see what line is causing the problem in our simple test, it's something to keep in mind when writing more substantial doctests to be placed in the `__test__` dictionary. If multiple lines in the test are identical and one of them causes a failure, it may be difficult to identify which exact line is causing the problem, as the failure output won't identify the specific line number where the failure occurred.

So far all of the mistakes we have introduced into the sample tests have involved expected output not matching actual results. These are reported as test failures. In addition to test failures, we may sometimes encounter test errors. These are described next.

Test errors versus test failures

To see what a test error looks like, let's remove the failing doctest introduced in the previous section and introduce a different kind of mistake into our sample unit test. Let's assume that instead of wanting to test that 1 + 1 equals the literal 2, we want to test that it equals the result of a function, `sum_args`, that is supposed to return the sum of its arguments. But we're going to make a mistake and forget to import that function. So change `self.failUnlessEqual` to:

```
self.failUnlessEqual(1 + 1, sum_args(1, 1))
```

Now when the tests are run we see:

```
kmt@lbox:/dj_projects/marketr$ python manage.py test survey
Creating test database...
Creating table auth_permission
Creating table auth_group
Creating table auth_user
Creating table auth_message
Creating table django_content_type
Creating table django_session
Creating table django_site
Creating table django_admin_log
Installing index for auth.Permission model
Installing index for auth.Message model
```

```
Installing index for admin.LogEntry model
E.
======================================================================
ERROR: test_basic_addition (survey.tests.SimpleTest)
----------------------------------------------------------------------
Traceback (most recent call last):
  File "/dj_projects/marketr/survey/tests.py", line 15, in test_basic_
addition
    self.failUnlessEqual(1 + 1, sum_args(1, 1))
NameError: global name 'sum_args' is not defined


----------------------------------------------------------------------
Ran 2 tests in 0.041s


FAILED (errors=1)
Destroying test database...
```

The test runner encountered an exception before it even got to the point where it could compare 1 + 1 to the return value of sum_args, as sum_args was not imported. In this case, the error is in the test itself, but it would still have been reported as an error, not a failure, if the code in sum_args was what caused a problem. Failures mean actual results didn't match what was expected, whereas errors mean some other problem (exception) was encountered during the test run. Errors may imply a mistake in the test itself, but don't necessarily have to imply that.

Note that a similar error made in a doctest is reported as a failure, not an error. For example, we can change the doctest 1 + 1 line to:

```
    >>> 1 + 1 == sum_args(1, 1)
```

If we then run the tests, the output will be:

```
kmt@lbox:/dj_projects/marketr$ python manage.py test survey
Creating test database...
Creating table auth_permission
Creating table auth_group
Creating table auth_user
Creating table auth_message
Creating table django_content_type
Creating table django_session
```

```
Creating table django_site

Creating table django_admin_log

Installing index for auth.Permission model

Installing index for auth.Message model

Installing index for admin.LogEntry model

EF

======================================================================

ERROR: test_basic_addition (survey.tests.SimpleTest)

----------------------------------------------------------------------

Traceback (most recent call last):

  File "/dj_projects/marketr/survey/tests.py", line 15, in test_basic_
addition

    self.failUnlessEqual(1 + 1, sum_args(1, 1))

NameError: global name 'sum_args' is not defined


======================================================================

FAIL: Doctest: survey.tests.__test__.doctest

----------------------------------------------------------------------

Traceback (most recent call last):

  File "/usr/lib/python2.5/site-packages/django/test/_doctest.py", line
2180, in runTest

    raise self.failureException(self.format_failure(new.getvalue()))

AssertionError: Failed doctest test for survey.tests.__test__.doctest

 File "/dj_projects/marketr/survey/tests.py", line unknown line number,
in doctest


----------------------------------------------------------------------

File "/dj_projects/marketr/survey/tests.py", line ?, in survey.tests.__
test__.doctest

Failed example:

    1 + 1 == sum_args(1, 1)

Exception raised:

    Traceback (most recent call last):

      File "/usr/lib/python2.5/site-packages/django/test/_doctest.py",
line 1267, in __run

        compileflags, 1) in test.globs

      File "<doctest survey.tests.__test__.doctest[0]>", line 1, in
<module>
```

```
    1 + 1 == sum_args(1, 1)
  NameError: name 'sum_args' is not defined



----------------------------------------------------------------

Ran 2 tests in 0.044s


FAILED (failures=1, errors=1)
Destroying test database...
```

Thus, the error versus failure distinction made for unit tests does not necessarily apply to doctests. So, if your tests include doctests, the summary of failure and error counts printed at the end doesn't necessarily reflect how many tests produced unexpected results (unit test failure count) or had some other error (unit test error count). However, in any case, neither failures nor errors are desired. The ultimate goal is to have zero for both, so if the difference between them is a bit fuzzy at times that's not such a big deal. It can be useful though, to understand under what circumstances one is reported instead of the other.

We have now seen how to run tests, and what the results look like for both overall success and a few failures and errors. Next we will examine the various command line options supported by the manage.py test command.

Command line options for running tests

Beyond specifying the exact applications to test on the command line, what other options are there for controlling the behavior of manage.py test? The easiest way to find out is to try running the command with the option --help:

```
kmt@lbox:/dj_projects/marketr$ python manage.py test --help
Usage: manage.py test [options] [appname ...]


Runs the test suite for the specified applications, or the entire site if
no apps are specified.


Options:
  -v VERBOSITY, --verbosity=VERBOSITY
                    Verbosity level; 0=minimal output, 1=normal output,
                    2=all output
```

```
--settings=SETTINGS      The Python path to a settings module, e.g.
                         "myproject.settings.main". If this isn't
                         provided, the
                         DJANGO_SETTINGS_MODULE environment variable will
                         be used.
--pythonpath=PYTHONPATH
                         A directory to add to the Python path, e.g.
                         "/home/djangoprojects/myproject".
--traceback              Print traceback on exception
--noinput                Tells Django to NOT prompt the user for input of
                         any kind.
--version                show program's version number and exit
-h, --help               show this help message and exit
```

Let's consider each of these in turn (excepting help, as we've already seen what it does):

Verbosity

Verbosity is a numeric value between 0 and 2. It controls how much output the tests produce. The default value is 1, so the output we have seen so far corresponds to specifying -v 1 or --verbosity=1. Setting verbosity to 0 suppresses all of the messages about creating the test database and tables, but not summary, failure, or error information. If we correct the last doctest failure introduced in the previous section and re-run the tests specifying -v0, we will see:

```
kmt@lbox:/dj_projects/marketr$ python manage.py test survey -v0

======================================================================
ERROR: test_basic_addition (survey.tests.SimpleTest)
----------------------------------------------------------------------
Traceback (most recent call last):
  File "/dj_projects/marketr/survey/tests.py", line 15, in test_basic_
addition
    self.failUnlessEqual(1 + 1, sum_args(1, 1))
NameError: global name 'sum_args' is not defined

----------------------------------------------------------------------
Ran 2 tests in 0.008s

FAILED (errors=1)
```

Setting verbosity to 2 produces a great deal more output. If we fix this remaining error and run the tests with verbosity set to its highest level, we will see:

```
kmt@lbox:/dj_projects/marketr$ python manage.py test survey --verbosity=2
Creating test database...
Processing auth.Permission model
Creating table auth_permission
Processing auth.Group model
Creating table auth_group

[...more snipped...]

Creating many-to-many tables for auth.Group model
Creating many-to-many tables for auth.User model
Running post-sync handlers for application auth
Adding permission 'auth | permission | Can add permission'
Adding permission 'auth | permission | Can change permission'

[...more snipped...]

No custom SQL for auth.Permission model
No custom SQL for auth.Group model

[...more snipped...]

Installing index for auth.Permission model
Installing index for auth.Message model
Installing index for admin.LogEntry model
Loading 'initial_data' fixtures...
Checking '/usr/lib/python2.5/site-packages/django/contrib/auth/fixtures'
for fixtures...
Trying '/usr/lib/python2.5/site-packages/django/contrib/auth/fixtures'
for initial_data.xml fixture 'initial_data'...
No xml fixture 'initial_data' in '/usr/lib/python2.5/site-packages/
django/contrib/auth/fixtures'.

[....much more snipped...]
```

```
No fixtures found.
test_basic_addition (survey.tests.SimpleTest) ... ok
Doctest: survey.tests.__test__.doctest ... ok


----------------------------------------------------------------------

Ran 2 tests in 0.004s


OK
Destroying test database...
```

As you can see, at this level of verbosity the command reports in excruciating detail all of what it is doing to set up the test database. In addition to the creation of database tables and indexes that we saw earlier, we now see that the database setup phase includes:

1. Running `post-syncdb` signal handlers. The `django.contrib.auth` application, for example, uses this signal to automatically add permissions for models as each application is installed. Thus you see messages about permissions being created as the `post-syncdb` signal is sent for each application listed in INSTALLED_APPS.

2. Running custom SQL for each model that has been created in the database. Based on the output, it does not look like any of the applications in INSTALLED_APPS use custom SQL.

3. Loading `initial_data` fixtures. Initial data fixtures are a way to automatically pre-populate the database with some constant data. None of the applications we have listed in INSTALLED_APPS make use of this feature, but a great deal of output is produced as the test runner looks for initial data fixtures, which may be found under any of several different names. There are messages for each possible file that is checked and for whether anything was found. This output might come in handy at some point if we run into trouble with the test runner finding an initial data fixture (we'll cover fixtures in detail in *Chapter 3*), but for now this output is not very interesting.

Once the test runner finishes initializing the database, it settles down to running the tests. At verbosity level 2, the line of dots, Fs, and Es we saw previously is replaced by a more detailed report of each test as it is run. The name of the test is printed, followed by three dots, then the test result, which will either be ok, ERROR, or FAIL. If there are any errors or failures, the detailed information about why they occurred will be printed at the end of the test run. So as you watch a long test run proceeding with verbosity set to 2, you will be able to see what tests are running into problems, but you will not get the details of the reasons why they occurred until the run completes.

Settings

You can pass the settings option to the `test` command to specify a settings file to use instead of the project default one. This can come in handy if you want to run tests using a database that's different from the one you normally use (either for speed of testing or to verify your code runs correctly on different databases), for example.

Note the help text for this option states that the DJANGO_SETTINGS_MODULE environment variable will be used to locate the settings file if the settings option is not specified on the command line. This is only accurate when the `test` command is being run via the `django-admin.py` utility. When using `manage.py test`, the `manage.py` utility takes care of setting this environment variable to specify the `settings.py` file in the current directory.

Pythonpath

This option allows you to append an additional directory to the Python path used during the test run. It's primarily of use when using `django-admin.py`, where it is often necessary to add the project path to the standard Python path. The `manage.py` utility takes care of adding the project path to the Python path, so this option is not generally needed when using `manage.py test`.

Traceback

This option is not actually used by the `test` command. It is inherited as one of the default options supported by all `django-admin.py` (and `manage.py`) commands, but the `test` command never checks for it. Thus you can specify it, but it will have no effect.

Noinput

This option causes the test runner to not prompt for user input, which raises the question: When would the test runner require user input? We haven't encountered that so far. The test runner prompts for input during the test database creation if a database with the test database name already exists. For example, if you hit *Ctrl + C* during a test run, the test database may not be destroyed and you may encounter a message like this the next time you attempt to run tests:

```
kmt@lbox:/dj_projects/marketr$ python manage.py test
Creating test database...
Got an error creating the test database: (1007, "Can't create database
'test_marketr'; database exists")
Type 'yes' if you would like to try deleting the test database 'test_
marketr', or 'no' to cancel:
```

If `--noinput` is passed on the command line, the prompt is not printed and the test runner proceeds as if the user had entered 'yes' in response. This is useful if you want to run the tests from an unattended script and ensure that the script does not hang while waiting for user input that will never be entered.

Version

This option reports the version of Django in use and then exits. Thus when using `--version` with `manage.py` or `django-admin.py`, you do not actually need to specify a subcommand such as `test`. In fact, due to a bug in the way Django processes command options, at the time of writing this book, if you do specify both `--version` and a subcommand, the version will get printed twice. That will likely get fixed at some point.

Summary

The overview of Django testing is now complete. In this chapter, we:

- Looked in detail at the sample `tests.py` file generated when a new Django application is created
- Learned how to run the provided sample tests
- Experimented with introducing deliberate mistakes into the tests in order to see and understand what information is provided when tests fail or encounter errors
- Finally, we examined all of the command line options that may be used with `manage.py test`

We will continue to build on this knowledge in the next chapter, as we focus on doctests in depth.

2

Does This Code Work?
Doctests in Depth

In the first chapter, we learned how to run the sample tests created by `manage.py`
`startapp`. Although we used a Django utility to run the tests, there was nothing
specific to Django about the sample tests themselves. In this chapter, we will start
getting into details of how to write tests for a Django application. We will:

- Begin writing the market research project created in the first chapter by
  developing some basic models that will be used by the project
- Experiment with adding doctests to one of the models
- Begin to learn the kinds of tests that are useful, and the kinds that just add
  clutter to the code
- Discover some of the advantages and disadvantages of doctests

While the previous chapter mentioned both doctests and unit tests, the focus for this
chapter will be on doctests exclusively. Developing unit tests for Django applications
will be the focus of *Chapter 3, Testing 1, 2, 3: Basic Unit Testing* and *Chapter 4, Getting
Fancier: Django Unit Test Extensions*.

The Survey application models

A common place to start development of a new Django application is with the
models: the basic building blocks of data that are going to be manipulated and stored
by the application. A cornerstone model for our example market research `survey`
application will be the `Survey` model.

A Survey is going to be similar to the Django tutorial Poll model, except that:

- Where the tutorial Poll only contains one question, a Survey will have multiple questions.

- A Survey will have a title for reference purposes. For the tutorial Poll, a single question could be used for this.

- A Survey will only be open for responses for a limited (and variable, depending on the Survey instance) time. While the Poll model has a pub_date field, it is not used for anything other than ordering Polls on the index page. Thus, Survey will need two date fields where Poll has only one, and the Survey date fields will be used more than the Poll pub_date field is used.

Given just these few simple requirements for Survey, we can start developing a Django model for it. Specifically, we can capture those requirements in code by adding the following to the auto-generated models.py file for our survey application:

```
class Survey(models.Model):
    title = models.CharField(max_length=60)
    opens = models.DateField()
    closes = models.DateField()
```

Note that since a Survey may have several questions, it does not have a question field. Instead there is a separate model, Question, to hold questions along with the Survey instance they are related to:

```
class Question(models.Model):
    question = models.CharField(max_length=200)
    survey = models.ForeignKey(Survey)
```

The final model we need (at least to start with) is one to hold the possible answers to each question, and to track how many times each answer is chosen by a survey respondent. This model, Answer, is much like the tutorial Choice model, except it is related to a Question, not a Poll:

```
class Answer(models.Model):
    answer = models.CharField(max_length=200)
    question = models.ForeignKey(Question)
    votes = models.IntegerField(default=0)
```

Testing the Survey model

If you are at all like me, at this point you might want to start verifying that what you've got so far is correct. True, there is not much code yet, but particularly when just starting out on a project I like to make sure, early and often, that what I've got so far is valid. So, how do we start testing at this point? First, we can verify that we've got no syntax errors by running `manage.py syncdb`, which will also let us start experimenting with these models in a Python shell. Let's do that. Since this is the first time we've run `syncdb` for this project, we'll get messages about creating tables for the other applications listed in `INSTALLED_APPS`, and we'll be asked if we want to create a superuser, which we may as well go ahead and do also.

Testing Survey model creation

Now, what might we do with these models to test them in a Python shell? Really, not much beyond creating each, perhaps verifying that if we don't specify one of the fields we get an error, or the correct default value is assigned, and verifying whether we can traverse the relationships between the models. If we focus first on the `Survey` model and what we might do in order to test the creation of it, a Python shell session for that might look something like this:

```
kmt@lbox:/dj_projects/marketr$ python manage.py shell
Python 2.5.2 (r252:60911, Oct  5 2008, 19:24:49)
[GCC 4.3.2] on linux2
Type "help", "copyright", "credits" or "license" for more information.
(InteractiveConsole)
>>> from survey.models import Survey
>>> import datetime
>>> t = 'First!'
>>> d = datetime.date.today()
>>> s = Survey.objects.create(title=t, opens=d, closes=d)
>>>
```

Here we started by importing our `Survey` model and the Python `datetime` module, then created a variable `t` to hold a title string and a variable `d` to hold a date value, and used those values to create a `Survey` instance. No error was reported, so that looks good.

If we then wanted to verify whether we'd get an error if we tried to create a Survey with no close date, we would proceed with:

```
>>> s = Survey.objects.create(title=t, opens=d, closes=None)
  File "<console>", line 1, in <module>
  File "/usr/lib/python2.5/site-packages/django/db/models/manager.py",
line 126, in create
    return self.get_query_set().create(**kwargs)
  File "/usr/lib/python2.5/site-packages/django/db/models/query.py", line
315, in create
    obj.save(force_insert=True)
  File "/usr/lib/python2.5/site-packages/django/db/models/base.py", line
410, in save
    self.save_base(force_insert=force_insert, force_update=force_update)
  File "/usr/lib/python2.5/site-packages/django/db/models/base.py", line
495, in save_base
    result = manager._insert(values, return_id=update_pk)
  File "/usr/lib/python2.5/site-packages/django/db/models/manager.py",
line 177, in _insert
    return insert_query(self.model, values, **kwargs)
  File "/usr/lib/python2.5/site-packages/django/db/models/query.py", line
1087, in insert_query
    return query.execute_sql(return_id)
  File "/usr/lib/python2.5/site-packages/django/db/models/sql/subqueries.
py", line 320, in execute_sql
    cursor = super(InsertQuery, self).execute_sql(None)
  File "/usr/lib/python2.5/site-packages/django/db/models/sql/query.py",
line 2369, in execute_sql
    cursor.execute(sql, params)
  File "/usr/lib/python2.5/site-packages/django/db/backends/util.py",
line 19, in execute
    return self.cursor.execute(sql, params)
  File "/usr/lib/python2.5/site-packages/django/db/backends/sqlite3/base.
py", line 193, in execute
    return Database.Cursor.execute(self, query, params)
IntegrityError: survey_survey.closes may not be NULL
```

Here all we did differently with the `Survey` instance creation attempt was specify `None` for the `closes` value instead of passing in our date variable `d`. The result was an error ending in a message reporting an `IntegrityError`, since the closes column of the survey table cannot be null. This confirms our expectation of what should happen, so all is good so far. We could then perform similar tests for the other fields, and see identical tracebacks reporting an `IntegrityError` for the other columns.

If we wanted to, we could then make these tests a permanent part of our model definition by cutting-and-pasting them from our shell session directly in our `survey/models.py` file, like so:

```
import datetime
from django.db import models

class Survey(models.Model):
    """
    >>> t = 'First!'
    >>> d = datetime.date.today()
    >>> s = Survey.objects.create(title=t, opens=d, closes=d)
    >>> s = Survey.objects.create(title=t, opens=d, closes=None)
    Traceback (most recent call last):
    ...
    IntegrityError: survey_survey.closes may not be NULL
    >>> s = Survey.objects.create(title=t, opens=None, closes=d)
    Traceback (most recent call last):
    ...
    IntegrityError: survey_survey.opens may not be NULL
    >>> s = Survey.objects.create(title=None, opens=d, closes=d)
    Traceback (most recent call last):
    ...
    IntegrityError: survey_survey.title may not be NULL
    """
    title = models.CharField(max_length=60)
    opens = models.DateField()
    closes = models.DateField()
```

You probably noticed that the results shown are not a direct cut-and-paste from the shell session. Differences include:

- The `import datetime` was moved out of the doctest and made part of the code in the `models.py` file. This wasn't strictly necessary—it would have worked fine as part of the doctest, but it is not necessary in the doctest if the import is in the main code. As the code in `models.py` will likely need to use `datetime` functions later on, putting the import in the main code now reduces duplication and clutter later, when the main code needs the import.

- • The call stack portion of the tracebacks, that is everything except the first and last lines, were removed and replaced with lines containing three dots. This too was not strictly necessary and was done simply to remove clutter and highlight the important bits of the result. The doctest runner ignores the contents of the call stack (if present in the expected output) when deciding on test success or failure. So you can leave a call stack in the test if it has some explanatory value. However, for the most part, it is best to remove call stacks since they produce a lot of clutter without providing much in the way of useful information.

If we now run `manage.py test survey -v2`, the tail end of the output will be:

```
No fixtures found.
test_basic_addition (survey.tests.SimpleTest) ... ok
Doctest: survey.models.Survey ... ok
Doctest: survey.tests.__test__.doctest ... ok


----------------------------------------------------------------------

Ran 3 tests in 0.030s


OK
Destroying test database...
```

We've still got our sample tests in `tests.py` running, and now we can also see our `survey.models.Survey` doctest listed as being run, and passing.

Is that test useful?

But wait; is that test we just added useful? What is it actually testing? Nothing really, beyond verifying that basic Django functions work as advertised. It tests whether we can create an instance of a model we've defined, and that the fields we specified as required in the model definition are in fact required in the associated database table. It seems that this test is testing the underlying Django code more than our application. Testing Django itself is not necessary in our application: Django has its own test suite we can run if we want to test it (though it is pretty safe to assume basic functions work correctly in any released version of Django).

It could be argued that this test validates that the correct and intended options have been specified for each field in the model, and so it is a test of the application and not just the underlying Django functions. However, testing things that are obvious by inspection (to anyone with a basic knowledge of Django) strikes me as going a bit overboard. This is not a test I would generally include in a project I was writing.

That is not to say I would not try out things like this in a Python shell during development: I would, and I do. But not everything experimented with in the shell during development needs to become a permanent test in the application. The kinds of tests you want to include in the application are those that exercise behavior that is unique to the application. So let's start developing some survey application code and experiment with testing it in the Python shell. When we have the code working, we can assess what tests from the shell session are useful to keep.

Developing a custom Survey save method

To begin writing some application-specific code, consider that for the Survey model we may want to allow for the `closes` field to assume a default value of a week after `opens`, if `closes` is not specified when the model instance is created. We cannot use the Django model field default option for this, as the value we want to assign is dependent on another field in the model. Therefore, we would typically do this by overriding the model's save method. A first attempt at implementing this might be:

```
import datetime
from django.db import models

class Survey(models.Model):
    title = models.CharField(max_length=60)
    opens = models.DateField()
    closes = models.DateField()

    def save(self, **kwargs):
        if not self.pk and not self.closes:
            self.closes = self.opens + datetime.timedelta(7)
        super(Survey, self).save(**kwargs)
```

That is, in the case where `save` is called and the model instance does not have a primary key assigned yet (and so this is the first save to the database), and `closes` has not been specified, we assign `closes` a value that is a week later than `opens` before calling the superclass `save` method. We could then test if this works properly by experimenting in a Python shell:

```
kmt@lbox:/dj_projects/marketr$ python manage.py shell
Python 2.5.2 (r252:60911, Oct  5 2008, 19:24:49)
[GCC 4.3.2] on linux2
Type "help", "copyright", "credits" or "license" for more information.
(InteractiveConsole)
>>> from survey.models import Survey
>>> import datetime
```

```
>>> t = "New Year's Resolutions"
>>> sd = datetime.date(2009, 12, 28)
>>> s = Survey.objects.create(title=t, opens=sd)
>>> s.closes
datetime.date(2010, 1, 4)
>>>
```

This is very similar to our earlier tests except we chose a specific date to assign to opens rather than using today's date, and after creating the Survey instance without specifying a value for closes, we checked the value that was assigned to it. The value displayed is a week later than opens, so that looks good.

Note the choice of an opens date where the week-later value would be in the next month and year was deliberate. Testing boundary values is always a good idea and a good habit to get into, even when (as here) there is nothing in the code we are writing that is responsible for getting the answer right for the boundary case.

Next we might want to make sure that if we do specify a value for closes, it is honored and not overridden by a week-later default date:

```
>>> s = Survey.objects.create(title=t, opens=sd, closes=sd)
>>> s.opens
datetime.date(2009, 12, 28)
>>> s.closes
datetime.date(2009, 12, 28)
>>>
```

All looks good there, opens and closes are displayed as having the same value, as we specified on the create call. We can also verify that if we reset closes to None after the model has already been saved, and try to save again, we'll get an error. Resetting closes to None on an existing model instance would be an error in the code that does that. So what we are testing here is that our save method override does not hide that error by quietly re-assigning a value to closes. In our shell session, we proceed like so and see:

```
>>> s.closes = None
>>> s.save()
Traceback (most recent call last):
  File "<console>", line 1, in <module>
  File "/dj_projects/marketr/survey/models.py", line 12, in save
    super(Survey, self).save(**kwargs)
```

```
    File "/usr/lib/python2.5/site-packages/django/db/models/base.py", line
410, in save
      self.save_base(force_insert=force_insert, force_update=force_update)
    File "/usr/lib/python2.5/site-packages/django/db/models/base.py", line
474, in save_base
      rows = manager.filter(pk=pk_val)._update(values)
    File "/usr/lib/python2.5/site-packages/django/db/models/query.py", line
444, in _update
      return query.execute_sql(None)
    File "/usr/lib/python2.5/site-packages/django/db/models/sql/subqueries.
py", line 120, in execute_sql
      cursor = super(UpdateQuery, self).execute_sql(result_type)
    File "/usr/lib/python2.5/site-packages/django/db/models/sql/query.py",
line 2369, in execute_sql
      cursor.execute(sql, params)
    File "/usr/lib/python2.5/site-packages/django/db/backends/util.py",
line 19, in execute
      return self.cursor.execute(sql, params)
    File "/usr/lib/python2.5/site-packages/django/db/backends/sqlite3/base.
py", line 193, in execute
      return Database.Cursor.execute(self, query, params)
IntegrityError: survey_survey.closes may not be NULL
>>>
```

Again, that looks good since it is the result we expect. Finally, since we have inserted some of our own code into the basic model save processing, we should verify that we have not broken anything for the other expected failure cases where no `title` or no `opens` field is specified on `create`. If we do that, we will see that the case of no `title` specified works correctly (we get the expected `IntegrityError` on the database title column), but if neither `opens` nor `closes` is specified we get an unexpected error:

```
>>> s = Survey.objects.create(title=t)
Traceback (most recent call last):
  File "<console>", line 1, in <module>
    File "/usr/lib/python2.5/site-packages/django/db/models/manager.py",
line 126, in create
      return self.get_query_set().create(**kwargs)
    File "/usr/lib/python2.5/site-packages/django/db/models/query.py", line
315, in create
      obj.save(force_insert=True)
```

```
   File "/dj_projects/marketr/survey/models.py", line 11, in save
      self.closes = self.opens + datetime.timedelta(7)
TypeError: unsupported operand type(s) for +: 'NoneType' and 'datetime.
timedelta'

>>>
```

Here we have traded a reasonably clear error message reporting that we have left a required value unspecified for a rather more obscure message complaining about unsupported operand types—that's not good. The problem is we did not check if opens had a value before attempting to use it in our save method override. In order to get the correct (clearer) error for this case, our save method should be modified to look like this:

```
def save(self, **kwargs):
    if not self.pk and self.opens and not self.closes:
        self.closes = self.opens + datetime.timedelta(7)
    super(Survey, self).save(**kwargs)
```

That is, we should not attempt to set closes if opens has not been specified. Rather, in this case we forward the save call directly to the superclass and let the normal error path report the problem. Then, when we try to create a Survey without specifying an opens or closes value, we will see:

```
>>> s = Survey.objects.create(title=t)
Traceback (most recent call last):
  File "<console>", line 1, in <module>
  File "/usr/lib/python2.5/site-packages/django/db/models/manager.py",
line 126, in create
    return self.get_query_set().create(**kwargs)
  File "/usr/lib/python2.5/site-packages/django/db/models/query.py", line
315, in create
    obj.save(force_insert=True)
  File "/dj_projects/marketr/survey/models.py", line 12, in save
    super(Survey, self).save(**kwargs)
  File "/usr/lib/python2.5/site-packages/django/db/models/base.py", line
410, in save
    self.save_base(force_insert=force_insert, force_update=force_update)
  File "/usr/lib/python2.5/site-packages/django/db/models/base.py", line
495, in save_base
    result = manager._insert(values, return_id=update_pk)
  File "/usr/lib/python2.5/site-packages/django/db/models/manager.py",
line 177, in _insert
```

```
    return insert_query(self.model, values, **kwargs)
  File "/usr/lib/python2.5/site-packages/django/db/models/query.py", line
1087, in insert_query
    return query.execute_sql(return_id)
  File "/usr/lib/python2.5/site-packages/django/db/models/sql/subqueries.
py", line 320, in execute_sql
    cursor = super(InsertQuery, self).execute_sql(None)
  File "/usr/lib/python2.5/site-packages/django/db/models/sql/query.py",
line 2369, in execute_sql
    cursor.execute(sql, params)
  File "/usr/lib/python2.5/site-packages/django/db/backends/util.py",
line 19, in execute
    return self.cursor.execute(sql, params)
  File "/usr/lib/python2.5/site-packages/django/db/backends/sqlite3/base.
py", line 193, in execute
    return Database.Cursor.execute(self, query, params)
IntegrityError: survey_survey.opens may not be NULL
>>>
```

That is much better, since the reported error directly indicates what the problem is.

Deciding what to test

At this point we are reasonably certain our `save` override is working the way we intended. Of all the tests we ran in the Python shell for verification purposes, which ones make sense to include in the code permanently? The answer to that question involves a judgment call, and reasonable people may have different answers. Personally, I would tend to include:

- All tests involving the parameter(s) directly affected by the code
- Any tests that I ran across while doing initial testing of the code that did not work in the original version of the code I had written

So, my `save` override function, including doctests with comments to explain them, might look something like this:

```
def save(self, **kwargs):
    """
    save override to allow for Survey instances to be created
    without explicitly specifying a closes date. If not
    specified, closes will be set to 7 days after opens.
```

```
>>> t = "New Year's Resolutions"
>>> sd = datetime.date(2009, 12, 28)
>>> s = Survey.objects.create(title=t, opens=sd)
>>> s.closes
datetime.date(2010, 1, 4)

If closes is specified, it will be honored and not auto-set.

>>> s = Survey.objects.create(title=t, opens=sd, closes=sd)
>>> s.closes
datetime.date(2009, 12, 28)

Any changes to closes after initial creation need to be
explicit. Changing closes to None on an existing instance will
not result in closes being reset to 7 days after opens.

>>> s.closes = None
>>> s.save()
Traceback (most recent call last):
    ...
IntegrityError: survey_survey.closes may not be NULL

Making the mistake of specifying neither opens nor closes
results in the expected IntegrityError for opens, not any
exception in the code here.

>>> s = Survey.objects.create(title=t)
Traceback (most recent call last):
    ...
IntegrityError: survey_survey.opens may not be NULL
"""
if not self.pk and self.opens and not self.closes:
    self.closes = self.opens + datetime.timedelta(7)
super(Survey, self).save(**kwargs)
```

Some pros and cons of doctests so far

Even with the experience of just this one example method we have studied, we can begin to see some of the pros and cons of doctests. Clearly, it is easy to re-use work done in Python shell sessions (work that is likely already being done as part of coding) for permanent test purposes. This makes it both more likely that tests will be written for the code, and that the tests themselves will not need to be debugged. Those are two nice advantages of doctests.

A third is that doctests provide unambiguous documentation of how the code is expected to behave. Prose descriptions can be fuzzy while code examples in the form of tests are impossible to misinterpret. Furthermore, the fact that the tests are part of the docstrings makes them accessible to all Python tools that use docstrings to auto-generate help and documentation.

Including tests here helps to make this documentation complete. For example, the behavior after resetting `closes` to `None` is one where the intended behavior might not be obvious—an equally valid design would have been to say that in this case `closes` would be reset to a week-later date during `save`. This sort of detail can easily be forgotten when writing documentation. Thus having the intended behavior spelled out in a doctest is helpful, as it is then automatically documented.

However, this tests-doubling-as-documentation feature also has a down side: some of the testing you may want to include may not really be appropriate as documentation, and you may wind up with an overwhelming amount of documentation for rather simple code. Consider the `save` override case we developed. It has four lines of code and a more than 30 line docstring. That ratio may be appropriate for some complicated functions with many parameters, or parameters that interact in non-obvious ways, but nearly ten times as much documentation as code seems excessive for this straightforward method.

Let's consider the individual tests in `save`, focusing on their usefulness as documentation:

- The first test, which shows creating a `Survey` with `title` and `opens` but no `closes`, and verifies that the correct value is assigned to `closes` after creation, is an example of what the `save` override allows a caller to do. This is the specific call pattern enabled by the added code, and is therefore useful as documentation, even though it largely duplicates the prose description.

- The second test, which shows that `closes` is honored if specified, is not particularly useful as documentation. Any programmer would expect that if `closes` is specified, it should be honored. This behavior may be good to test, but is not necessary to document.

- The third test, which illustrates the expected behavior of `save` after resetting `closes` to `None` on an existing `Survey` instance, is useful as documentation, for the previously-mentioned reasons.

- The fourth and final test illustrates that the added code will not cause an unexpected exception to be generated in the error case where neither `opens` nor `closes` is specified. This is another example of something that is good to test, but not necessary to document, as the right behavior is obvious.

Having half of our docstring classified as not useful for documentation purposes is not good. People tend to stop reading when they encounter obvious, redundant, or unhelpful information. We can address this problem without giving up some of the advantages of doctests by moving such tests from the docstring method into our `tests.py` file. If we take this approach, we might change the `__test__` dictionary in `tests.py` to look like this:

```
__test__ = {"survey_save": """

Tests for the Survey save override method.

>>> import datetime
>>> from survey.models import Survey
>>> t = "New Year's Resolutions"
>>> sd = datetime.date(2009, 12, 28)

If closes is specified, it will be honored and not auto-set.

>>> s = Survey.objects.create(title=t, opens=sd, closes=sd)
>>> s.closes
datetime.date(2009, 12, 28)

Making the mistake of specifying neither opens nor closes results
in the expected IntegrityError for opens, not any exception in the
save override code itself.

>>> s = Survey.objects.create(title=t)
Traceback (most recent call last):
   ...
IntegrityError: survey_survey.opens may not be NULL
"""}
```

Here we changed the key for the test from the generic `doctest` to `survey_save`, so that the reported test name in any test output will give a hint as to what is being tested. Then we just moved the "non-documentation" tests (along with some of the variable setup code that now needs to be in both places) from our `save` override docstring into the key value here, adding a general comment at the top noting what the tests are for.

What remains in the docstring for the `save` method itself are the tests that do have some value as documentation:

```
def save(self, **kwargs):
    """
    save override to allow for Survey instances to be created
    without explicitly specifying a closes date. If not
    specified, closes will be set to 7 days after opens.
```

```
>>> t = "New Year's Resolutions"
>>> sd = datetime.date(2009, 12, 28)
>>> s = Survey.objects.create(title=t, opens=sd)
>>> s.closes
datetime.date(2010, 1, 4)

Any changes to closes after initial creation need to be
explicit. Changing closes to None on an existing instance will
not result in closes being reset to 7 days after opens.

>>> s.closes = None
>>> s.save()
Traceback (most recent call last):
  ...
IntegrityError: survey_survey.closes may not be NULL

"""
if not self.pk and self.opens and not self.closes:
    self.closes = self.opens + datetime.timedelta(7)
super(Survey, self).save(**kwargs)
```

That is certainly a much more manageable docstring for the function, and is no longer likely to overwhelm someone typing help(Survey.save) in a Python shell.

This approach, though, does also have its down side. The tests for the code are no longer all in one place, making it hard to know or easily determine how completely the code is tested. Anyone who ran across the test in tests.py, without knowing there were additional tests in the method's docstring, might well wonder why only these two edge cases were tested and why a straightforward test of the basic function added was omitted.

Also, when adding tests, it may not be clear (especially to programmers new to the project) where exactly the new tests should go. So even if a project starts out with a nice clean split of "tests that make for good documentation" in the docstring tests and "tests that are necessary but not good documentation" in the tests.py file, this distinction may easily become blurred over time.

Test choice and placement thus involves a tradeoff. There is not necessarily a "right" answer for every project. Adopting a consistent approach, though, is best. When choosing that approach, each project team should take into account the answers to questions such as:

- **What is the expected audience for auto-generated docstring-based documentation**?

  If other documentation exists (or is being written) that is expected to be the main source for "consumers" of the code, then it may not be a problem to have doctests that do not serve the documentation function very well.

- **How many people will likely be working on the code**?

  If it is a relatively small and constant number, it may not be much of an issue to get everyone to remember about tests split between two places. For a larger project or if there is high developer turnover, educating developers about this sort of split may become more of an issue and it may be harder to maintain consistent code.

Additional doctest caveats

Doctests have some additional disadvantages that we haven't necessarily run into or noticed yet. Some of these are just things we need to watch out for if we want to make sure our doctests will work properly in a wide variety of environments and as code surrounding our code changes. Others are more serious issues that are most easily solved by switching to unit tests instead of doctests for at least the affected tests. In this section, we will list many of the additional doctest issues to watch out for, and give guidance on what to do to avoid or overcome them.

Beware of environmental dependence

It is very easy for doctests to be unintentionally dependent on implementation details of code other than the code that is actually being tested. We have some of this already in the `save` override tests, though we have not tripped over it yet. The dependence we have is actually a very specific form of environmental dependence—database dependence. As database dependence is a fairly big issue on its own, it will be discussed in detail in the next section. However, we'll first cover some other minor environmental dependencies we might easily run into and see how to avoid including them in our tests.

An extremely common form of environmental dependence that creeps into doctests is relying on the printed representation of objects. For example, a __unicode__ method is a common method to be implemented in a model class first. It was omitted from the earlier `Survey` model discussion since it wasn't necessary at that time, but in reality we probably would have implemented __unicode__ before the `save` override. A first pass at a __unicode__ method for `Survey` may have looked something like this:

```
def __unicode__(self):
    return u'%s (Opens %s, closes %s)' % (self.title, self.opens,
                                          self.closes)
```

Here we have decided that the printed representation of a `Survey` instance will consist of the title value followed by a parenthesized note about when this survey opens and closes. Given that method definition, our shell session for testing the proper setting of `closes` when it is not specified during creation may have looked something like this:

```
>>> from survey.models import Survey
>>> import datetime
>>> sd = datetime.date(2009, 12, 28)
>>> t = "New Year's Resolutions"
>>> s = Survey.objects.create(title=t, opens=sd)
>>> s
<Survey: New Year's Resolutions (Opens 2009-12-28, closes 2010-01-04)>
>>>
```

That is, instead of specifically checking the value assigned to `closes`, we may have just displayed the printed representation of the created instance, since it includes the `closes` value. When experimenting in a shell session, it's natural to perform checking this way rather than interrogating the attribute in question directly. For one thing, it's shorter (`s` is a good bit easier to type than `s.closes`). In addition, it often displays more information than the specific piece we may be testing, which is helpful when we are experimenting.

However, if we had cut and pasted directly from that shell session into our
save override doctest, we would have made that doctest dependent on the
implementation details of __unicode__. We might subsequently decide we didn't
want to include all of that information in the printable representation of a Survey,
or even just that it would look better if the "o" in "Opens" was not capitalized. So we
make a minor change to the __unicode__ method implementation and suddenly a
doctest for an unrelated method begins to fail:

```
======================================================================
FAIL: Doctest: survey.models.Survey.save
----------------------------------------------------------------------
Traceback (most recent call last):
  File "/usr/lib/python2.5/site-packages/django/test/_doctest.py", line
2189, in runTest
    raise self.failureException(self.format_failure(new.getvalue()))
AssertionError: Failed doctest test for survey.models.Survey.save
  File "/dj_projects/marketr/survey/models.py", line 9, in save


----------------------------------------------------------------------
File "/dj_projects/marketr/survey/models.py", line 32, in survey.models.
Survey.save
Failed example:
    s
Expected:
    <Survey: New Year's Resolutions (Opens 2009-12-28, closes 2010-01-
04)>
Got:
    <Survey: New Year's Resolutions (opens 2009-12-28, closes 2010-01-
04)>


----------------------------------------------------------------------
Ran 3 tests in 0.076s


FAILED (failures=1)
Destroying test database...
```

Thus when creating doctests from shell sessions, it's good to carefully consider whether the session relied on implementation details of any code other than that specifically being tested, and if so make adjustments to remove the dependence. In this case, using `s.closes` to test what value has been assigned to `closes` removes the dependence on how the `Survey` model `__unicode__` method happens to be implemented.

There are many other cases of environmental dependence that may arise in doctests, including:

- Any test that relies on the printed representation of a file path can run afoul of the fact that on Unix-based operating systems path components are separated by a forward slash where Windows uses a backslash. If you need to include doctests that rely on file path values, it may be necessary to use a utility function to normalize file path representations across different operating systems.

- Any test that relies on dictionary keys being printed in a specific order can run afoul of the fact that this order may be different for different operating systems or Python implementations. Thus to make such tests robust across different platforms, it may be necessary to specifically interrogate dictionary key values instead of simply printing the entire dictionary contents, or use a utility function that applies a consistent order to the keys for the printed representation.

There is nothing particularly specific to Django about these kinds of environmental dependence issues that often arise in doctests. There is, however, one type of environmental dependence that is particularly likely to arise in a Django application: database dependence. This issue is discussed next.

Beware of database dependence

The Django **object-relational manager** (**ORM**) goes through considerable trouble to shield application code from differences in the underlying databases. However, it is not feasible for Django to make all of the different supported databases look exactly the same under all circumstances. Thus it is possible to observe database-specific differences at the application level. These differences may then easily find their way into doctests, making the tests dependent on a specific database backend in order to pass.

This sort of dependence is already present in the `save` override tests developed earlier in this chapter. Because SQLite is the easiest database to use (since it requires no installation or configuration), so far the example code and tests have been developed using a setting of `DATABASE_ENGINE = 'sqlite3'` in `settings.py`. If we switch to using MySQL (`DATABASE_ENGINE = 'mysql'`) for the database instead, and attempt to run our `survey` application tests, we will see failures. There are two failures, but we will first focus only on the last one in the test output:

```
======================================================================
FAIL: Doctest: survey.tests.__test__.survey_save
----------------------------------------------------------------------
Traceback (most recent call last):
  File "/usr/lib/python2.5/site-packages/django/test/_doctest.py", line
2189, in runTest
    raise self.failureException(self.format_failure(new.getvalue()))
AssertionError: Failed doctest test for survey.tests.__test__.survey_save
  File "/dj_projects/marketr/survey/tests.py", line unknown line number,
in survey_save

----------------------------------------------------------------------
File "/dj_projects/marketr/survey/tests.py", line ?, in survey.tests.__
test__.survey_save
Failed example:
    s = Survey.objects.create(title=t)
Expected:
    Traceback (most recent call last):
      ...
    IntegrityError: survey_survey.opens may not be NULL
Got:
    Traceback (most recent call last):
        File "/usr/lib/python2.5/site-packages/django/test/_doctest.py",
line 1274, in __run
        compileflags, 1) in test.globs
        File "<doctest survey.tests.__test__.survey_save[6]>", line 1, in
<module>
        s = Survey.objects.create(title=t)
        File "/usr/lib/python2.5/site-packages/django/db/models/manager.
py", line 126, in create
        return self.get_query_set().create(**kwargs)
```

```
      File "/usr/lib/python2.5/site-packages/django/db/models/query.py",
line 315, in create
        obj.save(force_insert=True)
      File "/dj_projects/marketr/survey/models.py", line 34, in save
        super(Survey, self).save(**kwargs)
      File "/usr/lib/python2.5/site-packages/django/db/models/base.py",
line 410, in save
        self.save_base(force_insert=force_insert, force_update=force_
update)
      File "/usr/lib/python2.5/site-packages/django/db/models/base.py",
line 495, in save_base
        result = manager._insert(values, return_id=update_pk)
      File "/usr/lib/python2.5/site-packages/django/db/models/manager.
py", line 177, in _insert
        return insert_query(self.model, values, **kwargs)
      File "/usr/lib/python2.5/site-packages/django/db/models/query.py",
line 1087, in insert_query
        return query.execute_sql(return_id)
      File "/usr/lib/python2.5/site-packages/django/db/models/sql/
subqueries.py", line 320, in execute_sql
        cursor = super(InsertQuery, self).execute_sql(None)
      File "/usr/lib/python2.5/site-packages/django/db/models/sql/query.
py", line 2369, in execute_sql
        cursor.execute(sql, params)
      File "/usr/lib/python2.5/site-packages/django/db/backends/mysql/
base.py", line 89, in execute
        raise Database.IntegrityError(tuple(e))
    IntegrityError: (1048, "Column 'opens' cannot be null")


----------------------------------------------------------------
Ran 3 tests in 0.434s


FAILED (failures=2)
Destroying test database...
```

What's the problem here? For the `save` call in the doctest in `tests.py` where no value for `opens` was specified, an `IntegrityError` was expected, and an `IntegrityError` was produced, but the details of the `IntegrityError` message are different. The SQLite database returns:

```
IntegrityError: survey_survey.opens may not be NULL
```

MySQL says the same thing somewhat differently:

```
IntegrityError: (1048, "Column 'opens' cannot be null")
```

There are two simple ways to fix this. One is to use the doctest directive `IGNORE_EXCEPTION_DETAIL` on the failing test. With this option, the doctest runner will only consider the type of exception (in this case, `IntegrityError`) when determining whether the expected result matches the actual result. So differences in the exact exception messages produced by the different databases will not cause the test to fail.

Doctest directives are specified for individual tests by placing them as comments on the line containing the test. The comment starts with `doctest:` and is followed by one or more directive names preceded either by + to turn the option on or – to turn the option off. So in this case, we would change the failing test line in `tests.py` to be (note that though this line wraps to a second line on this page, it needs to be kept on a single line in the test):

```
>>> s = Survey.objects.create(title=t) # doctest: +IGNORE_EXCEPTION_
DETAIL
```

The other way to fix this is to replace the detailed message portion of the expected output in the test with three dots, which is an ellipsis marker. That is, change the test to be:

```
>>> s = Survey.objects.create(title=t)
Traceback (most recent call last):
  ...
IntegrityError: ...
```

This is an alternate way to tell the doctest runner to ignore the specifics of the exception message. It relies on the doctest option `ELLIPSIS` being enabled for the doctest run. While this option is not enabled by default by Python, it is enabled by the doctest runner that Django uses, so you do not need to do anything in your test code to enable use of ellipsis markers in expected output. Also note that `ELLIPSIS` is not specific to exception message details; it's a more general method that lets you indicate portions of doctest output that may differ from run to run without resulting in test failure.

If you read the Python documentation for `ELLIPSIS`, you may notice that it was introduced in Python 2.4. You may expect, then, if you are running Python 2.3 (which is still supported by Django 1.1), that you would not be able to use the ellipsis marker technique in your Django application's doctests. However, Django 1.0 and 1.1 ship with a customized doctest runner that is used when you run your application's doctests. This customized runner is based on the doctest module that is shipped with Python 2.4. Thus you can use doctest options, such as `ELLIPSIS`, from Python 2.4 even if you are running an earlier Python version.

Note, though, the flip side of Django using its own customized doctest runner: if you are running a more recent Python version than 2.4, you cannot use doctest options added later than 2.4 in your application's doctests. For example, Python added the `SKIP` option in Python 2.5. Until Django updates the version of its customized doctest module, you will not be able to use this new option in your Django application doctests.

Recall that there were two test failures and we only looked at the output from one (the other most likely scrolled off the screen too quickly to read). Given what the one failure we examined was, though, we might expect the other one would be the same, since we have a very similar test for an `IntegrityError` in the doctest in `models.py`:

```
>>> s.closes = None
>>> s.save()
Traceback (most recent call last):
  ...
IntegrityError: survey_survey.closes may not be NULL
```

This will certainly also need to be fixed to ignore the exception detail, so we may as well do both at the same time and perhaps correct both test failures. And in fact, when we run the tests again after changing both expected `IntegrityErrors` to include an ellipsis marker instead of a specific error message, the tests all pass.

Note that for some configurations of MySQL, this second test failure will not be corrected by ignoring the exception details. Specifically, if the MySQL server is configured to run in "non-strict" mode, attempting to update a row to contain a NULL value in a column declared as NOT NULL does not raise an error. Rather, the value is set to the implicit default value for the column's type and a warning is issued.

Most likely if you are using MySQL, you will want to configure it to run in "strict mode". However, if for some reason you cannot, and you need to have a test like this in your application, and you need the test to pass on multiple databases, you would have to account for that difference in database behavior in your test. It can be done, but it is much more easily done in a unit test than a doctest, so we will not cover how to fix the doctest for this case.

Now that we have gotten our tests to pass on two different database backends, we may think we are set and would likely get a clean test run on all databases that Django supports. We'd be wrong, as we will discover when we attempt to run these same tests using PostgreSQL as the database. The database difference we encounter with PostgreSQL highlights the next item to beware of when writing doctests, and is covered in the next section.

Beware of test interdependence

We get a very curious result if we now try running our tests using PostgreSQL as the database (specify DATABASE_ENGINE = 'postgresql_psycopg2' in settings.py). From the tail end of the output of manage.py test survey -v2, we see:

```
No fixtures found.
test_basic_addition (survey.tests.SimpleTest) ... ok
Doctest: survey.models.Survey.save ... ok
Doctest: survey.tests.__test__.survey_save ... FAIL
```

The sample unit test we still have in tests.py runs and passes, then the doctest from models.py also passes, but the doctest we added to tests.py fails. The failure details are:

```
======================================================================
FAIL: Doctest: survey.tests.__test__.survey_save
----------------------------------------------------------------------
Traceback (most recent call last):
```

```
    File "/usr/lib/python2.5/site-packages/django/test/_doctest.py", line
2189, in runTest

        raise self.failureException(self.format_failure(new.getvalue()))

AssertionError: Failed doctest test for survey.tests.__test__.survey_save

    File "/dj_projects/marketr/survey/tests.py", line unknown line number,
in survey_save


----------------------------------------------------------------------

File "/dj_projects/marketr/survey/tests.py", line ?, in survey.tests.__
test__.survey_save

Failed example:
    s = Survey.objects.create(title=t, opens=sd, closes=sd)

Exception raised:
    Traceback (most recent call last):
        File "/usr/lib/python2.5/site-packages/django/test/_doctest.py",
line 1274, in __run
            compileflags, 1) in test.globs
        File "<doctest survey.tests.__test__.survey_save[4]>", line 1, in
<module>
            s = Survey.objects.create(title=t, opens=sd, closes=sd)
        File "/usr/lib/python2.5/site-packages/django/db/models/manager.
py", line 126, in create
            return self.get_query_set().create(**kwargs)
        File "/usr/lib/python2.5/site-packages/django/db/models/query.py",
line 315, in create
            obj.save(force_insert=True)
        File "/dj_projects/marketr/survey/models.py", line 34, in save
            super(Survey, self).save(**kwargs)
        File "/usr/lib/python2.5/site-packages/django/db/models/base.py",
line 410, in save
            self.save_base(force_insert=force_insert, force_update=force_
update)
        File "/usr/lib/python2.5/site-packages/django/db/models/base.py",
line 495, in save_base
            result = manager._insert(values, return_id=update_pk)
        File "/usr/lib/python2.5/site-packages/django/db/models/manager.
py", line 177, in _insert
            return insert_query(self.model, values, **kwargs)
```

```
    File "/usr/lib/python2.5/site-packages/django/db/models/query.py",
line 1087, in insert_query
      return query.execute_sql(return_id)
    File "/usr/lib/python2.5/site-packages/django/db/models/sql/
subqueries.py", line 320, in execute_sql
      cursor = super(InsertQuery, self).execute_sql(None)
    File "/usr/lib/python2.5/site-packages/django/db/models/sql/query.
py", line 2369, in execute_sql
      cursor.execute(sql, params)
  InternalError: current transaction is aborted, commands ignored until
end of transaction block


----------------------------------------------------------------------
File "/dj_projects/marketr/survey/tests.py", line ?, in survey.tests.__
test__.survey_save
Failed example:
  s.closes
Exception raised:
    Traceback (most recent call last):
      File "/usr/lib/python2.5/site-packages/django/test/_doctest.py",
line 1274, in __run
        compileflags, 1) in test.globs
      File "<doctest survey.tests.__test__.survey_save[5]>", line 1, in
<module>
        s.closes
    NameError: name 's' is not defined



----------------------------------------------------------------------
Ran 3 tests in 0.807s


FAILED (failures=1)
Destroying test database...
```

This time we need to examine the reported errors in order as the second error is resulting from the first. Such chaining of errors is common, so it is good to keep in mind that while it may be tempting to start by looking at the last failure, since it is the easiest one to see at the end of the test run, that may not be the most productive route. If it isn't immediately obvious what is causing the last failure, it's usually best to start at the beginning and figure out what is causing the first failure. The reason for subsequent failures may then become obvious. For reference, the beginning of the test that is failing is:

```
>>> import datetime
>>> from survey.models import Survey
>>> t = "New Year's Resolutions"
>>> sd = datetime.date(2009, 12, 28)

If closes is specified, it will be honored and not auto-set.

>>> s = Survey.objects.create(title=t, opens=sd, closes=sd)
>>> s.closes
datetime.date(2009, 12, 28)
```

Thus, based on the test output, the very first attempt to access the database—that is the attempt to create a `Survey` instance—in this test results in an error:

InternalError: current transaction is aborted, commands ignored until end of transaction block

Then the next line of the test also results in an error as it uses the variable s that was supposed to be assigned in the previous line. However, that line did not complete execution, so the variable s is not defined when the test attempts to use it. So the second error makes sense given the first, but why did the first database access in this test result in an error?

In order to understand the explanation for that, we have to look back at the test that ran immediately preceding this one. We can see from the test output that the test immediately preceding this one was the doctest in `models.py`. The end of that test is:

```
>>> s.closes = None
>>> s.save()
Traceback (most recent call last):
  ...
IntegrityError: ...
"""
```

The last thing that test did was something that was expected to raise a database error. A side-effect of this, on PostgreSQL, is that the database connection enters a state where the only commands it will allow are ones that end the transaction block. So this test ended leaving the database connection in a broken state, and it was still broken when the next doctest began running, causing the next doctest to fail as soon as it attempted any database access.

This problem illustrates that there is no database isolation between doctests. What one doctest does to the database can be observed by subsequent ones that run. This includes problems such as the one seen here, in addition to creation, updates, or deletion of rows in the database tables. This particular problem can be solved by adding a call to rollback the current transaction following the code that deliberately caused a database error:

```
>>> s.closes = None
>>> s.save()
Traceback (most recent call last):
  ...
IntegrityError: ...
>>> from django.db import transaction
>>> transaction.rollback()
"""
```

This will allow the tests to pass on PostgreSQL and will be harmless on the other database backends. Thus one way to deal with no database isolation in doctests is to code them so that they clean up after themselves. That may be an acceptable approach for problems such as this one, but if a test has added, modified, or deleted objects in the database, it may be difficult to put everything back the way it was originally at the end.

A second approach is to reset the database to a known state on entry to every doctest. Django does not do this for you, but you can do it manually by calling the management command to synchronize the database. I would not recommend this approach in general because it becomes extremely time-consuming as your application grows.

A third approach is to make doctests reasonably tolerant of database state, so that they will be likely to run properly regardless of whether other tests may or may not have run before them. Techniques to use here include:

- Create all objects needed by the test in the test itself. That is, do not rely on the existence of objects created by any previously-run tests since that test may change, or be removed, or the order in which tests run may change at some time.

- When creating objects, guard against collisions with similar objects that may be created by other tests. For example, if a test needs to create a User instance with the is_superuser field set to True in order to test certain behavior for users that have that attribute, it might seem natural to give the User instance a username of "superuser". However, if two doctests did that, then whichever one was unlucky enough to run second would encounter an error because the username field of the User model is declared to be unique, so the second attempt to create a User with this username would fail. Thus it is best to use values for unique fields in shared models that are unlikely to have been used by other tests.

All of these approaches and techniques have their disadvantages. For this particular issue, unit tests are a much better solution, as they automatically provide database isolation without incurring a performance cost to reset the database (so long as you run them on a database that supports transactions). Thus if you start encountering a lot of test interdependence issues with doctests, I'd strongly suggest considering unit tests as a solution instead of relying on any of the approaches listed here.

Beware of Unicode

The final issue we will cover in doctest caveats is Unicode. If you have done much work with Django (or even just Python) using data from languages with character sets broader than English, you've likely run into UnicodeDecodeError or UnicodeEncodeError once or twice. As a result, you may have gotten into the habit of routinely including some non-ASCII characters in your tests to ensure that everything is going to work properly for all languages, not just English. That's a good habit, but unfortunately testing with Unicode values in doctests has some unexpected glitches that need to be overcome.

The previously mentioned __unicode__ method of Survey would be a likely place we would want to test for proper behavior in the face of non-ASCII characters. A first pass at a test for this might be:

```
def __unicode__(self):
    """
    >>> t = u'¿Como está usted?'
    >>> sd = datetime.date(2009, 12, 28)
    >>> s = Survey.objects.create(title=t, opens=sd)
    >>> print s
    ¿Como está usted? (opens 2009-12-28, closes 2010-01-04)
    """
    return u'%s (opens %s, closes %s)' % (self.title, self.opens,
                                          self.closes)
```

This test is similar to many of the save override tests in that it first creates a Survey instance. The significant parameter in this case is the title, which is specified as a Unicode literal string and contains non-ASCII characters. After the Survey instance is created, a call is made to print it in order to verify that the non-ASCII characters are displayed correctly in the printed representation of the instance, and that no Unicode exceptions are raised.

How well does this test work? Not so well. Attempting to run the survey tests after adding that code will result in an error:

```
kmt@lbox:/dj_projects/marketr$ python manage.py test survey
Traceback (most recent call last):
  File "manage.py", line 11, in <module>
    execute_manager(settings)
  File "/usr/lib/python2.5/site-packages/django/core/management/__init__
.py", line 362, in execute_manager
    utility.execute()
  File "/usr/lib/python2.5/site-packages/django/core/management/__init__
.py", line 303, in execute
    self.fetch_command(subcommand).run_from_argv(self.argv)
  File "/usr/lib/python2.5/site-packages/django/core/management/base.py",
line 195, in run_from_argv
    self.execute(*args, **options.__dict__)
  File "/usr/lib/python2.5/site-packages/django/core/management/base.py",
line 222, in execute
    output = self.handle(*args, **options)
  File "/usr/lib/python2.5/site-packages/django/core/management/commands/
test.py", line 23, in handle
    failures = test_runner(test_labels, verbosity=verbosity, interactive=
interactive)
  File "/usr/lib/python2.5/site-packages/django/test/simple.py", line
178, in run_tests
    app = get_app(label)
  File "/usr/lib/python2.5/site-packages/django/db/models/loading.py",
line 114, in get_app
    self._populate()
  File "/usr/lib/python2.5/site-packages/django/db/models/loading.py",
line 58, in _populate
    self.load_app(app_name, True)
  File "/usr/lib/python2.5/site-packages/django/db/models/loading.py",
line 74, in load_app
```

```
    models = import_module('.models', app_name)
  File "/usr/lib/python2.5/site-packages/django/utils/importlib.py", line
35, in import_module
    __import__(name)
  File "/dj_projects/marketr/survey/models.py", line 40
SyntaxError: Non-ASCII character '\xc2' in file /dj_projects/marketr/
survey/models.py on line 41, but no encoding declared; see http://www.
python.org/peps/pep-0263.html for details
```

This one is easy to fix; we simply forgot to declare the encoding for our Python source file. To do that, we need to add a comment line to the top of the file specifying the encoding used by the file. Let's assume we are using UTF-8 encoding, so we should add the following as the first line of our `models.py` file:

```
    # -*- encoding: utf-8 -*-
```

Now will the new test work? Not yet, we still get a failure:

```
======================================================================
FAIL: Doctest: survey.models.Survey.__unicode__
----------------------------------------------------------------------
Traceback (most recent call last):
  File "/usr/lib/python2.5/site-packages/django/test/_doctest.py", line
2180, in runTest
    raise self.failureException(self.format_failure(new.getvalue()))
AssertionError: Failed doctest test for survey.models.Survey.__unicode__
  File "/dj_projects/marketr/survey/models.py", line 39, in __unicode__

----------------------------------------------------------------------
File "/dj_projects/marketr/survey/models.py", line 44, in survey.models.
Survey.__unicode__
Failed example:
    print s
Expected:
    ¿Como está usted? (opens 2009-12-28, closes 2010-01-04)
Got:
    Â¿Como estÃ¡ usted? (opens 2009-12-28, closes 2010-01-04)


----------------------------------------------------------------------
Ran 4 tests in 0.084s

FAILED (failures=1)
Destroying test database...
```

This one is a bit puzzling. Though we specified the title as a Unicode literal string `u'¿Como está usted?'` in our test, it is apparently coming back as **Â¿Como estÃ¡ usted?** when printed. Data corruption like this is a telltale sign that the wrong encoding has been used at some point to transform a bytestring into a Unicode string. In fact the specific nature of the corruption here, where each non-ASCII character in the original string has been replaced by two (or more) characters in the corrupted version, is the characteristic of a string which is actually encoded in UTF-8 being interpreted as if it were encoded in ISO-8859-1 (also called Latin-1). But how could that happen here, as we specified UTF-8 as our Python file encoding declaration? Why would this string be interpreted using any other encoding?

At this point, we might go and carefully read the web page referenced in the first error message we got, and learn that the encoding declaration we have added only has an effect on how Unicode literal strings are constructed by the Python interpreter from the source file. We may then notice that though our title is a Unicode literal string, the doctest it is contained in is not. So perhaps this odd result is because we neglected to make the docstring containing the doctest a Unicode literal. Our next version of the test, then, might be to specify the whole docstring as a Unicode literal.

Unfortunately this too would be unsuccessful, due to problems with Unicode literal docstrings. First the doctest runner cannot correctly compare expected output (now Unicode, since the docstring itself is a Unicode literal) with actual output that is a bytestring containing non-ASCII characters. Such a bytestring must be converted to Unicode in order to perform the comparison. Python will automatically perform this conversion when necessary, but the problem is that it does not know the actual encoding of the bytestring it is converting. Thus it assumes ASCII, and fails to perform the conversion if the bytestring contains any non-ASCII characters.

This failure in conversion will lead to an assumed failure of the comparison involving the bytestring, which in turn will lead to the test being reported as failing. Even if the expected and received outputs were identical, if only the right encoding were assumed for the bytestring, there is no way to get the proper encoding to be used, so the test will fail. For the `Survey` model `__unicode__` doctest, this problem will cause the test to fail when attempting to compare the actual output of `print s` (which will be a UTF-8 encoded bytestring) to the expected output.

A second problem with Unicode literal docstrings involves reporting of output that contains non-ASCII characters, such as this failure that will occur with the `Survey` model `__unicode__` doctest. The doctest runner will attempt to display a message showing the expected and received outputs. However, it will run into the same problem as encountered during the comparison when it attempts to combine the expected and received outputs into a single message for display. Thus instead of generating a message that would at least reveal where the test is running into trouble, the doctest runner itself generates a `UnicodeDecodeError`.

There is an open Python issue in Python's bug tracker that reports these problems: `http://bugs.python.org/issue1293741`. Until it is fixed, it is probably best to avoid using Unicode literal docstrings for doctests.

Is there any way, then, to include some testing of non-ASCII data in doctests? Yes, it is possible. The key to making such tests work is to avoid using Unicode literals within the docstring. Instead, explicitly decode strings to Unicode objects. For example:

```
def __unicode__(self):
    """
    >>> t = '¿Como está usted?'.decode('utf-8')
    >>> sd = datetime.date(2009, 12, 28)
    >>> s = Survey.objects.create(title=t, opens=sd)
    >>> print s
    ¿Como está usted? (opens 2009-12-28, closes 2010-01-04)
    """
    return u'%s (opens %s, closes %s)' % (self.title, self.opens,
                                            self.closes)
```

That is, replace the Unicode literal title string with a bytestring that is explicitly decoded using UTF-8 to create a Unicode string.

Does that work? Running `manage.py test survey -v2` now, we see the following at the tail end of the output:

```
No fixtures found.
test_basic_addition (survey.tests.SimpleTest) ... ok
Doctest: survey.models.Survey.__unicode__ ... ok
Doctest: survey.models.Survey.save ... ok
Doctest: survey.tests.__test__.survey_save ... ok


----------------------------------------------------------------------

Ran 4 tests in 0.046s


OK
Destroying test database...
```

Success! It is possible, then, to correctly test with non-ASCII data in doctests. Some care must simply be taken to avoid running into existing problems related to using Unicode literal docstrings or embedding Unicode literal strings within a doctest.

Summary

Our exploration of doctests for Django applications is now complete. In this chapter, we:

- Began to develop some models for our Django `survey` application
- Experimented with adding doctests to one of these models—the `Survey` model
- Learned what sorts of doctests are useful and which simply add clutter to the code
- Experienced some of the advantages of doctests, namely the easy re-use of Python shell session work and convenient use of doctests as documentation
- Ran afoul of many of the disadvantages of doctests, and learned how to avoid or overcome them

In the next chapter, we will begin to explore unit tests. While unit tests may not offer some of the easy re-use features of doctests, they also do not suffer from many of the disadvantages of doctests. Furthermore, the overall unit test framework allows Django to provide convenient support specifically useful for web applications, which will be covered in detail in *Chapter 4*.

3
Testing 1, 2, 3: Basic Unit Testing

In the previous chapter, we began learning about testing Django applications by writing some doctests for the `Survey` model. In the process, we experienced some of the advantages and disadvantages of doctests. When discussing some of the disadvantages, unit tests were mentioned as an alternative test approach that avoids some doctest pitfalls. In this chapter, we will start to learn about unit tests in detail. Specifically, we will:

- Re-implement the `Survey` doctests as unit tests

- Assess how the equivalent unit test version compares to the doctests in terms of ease of implementation and susceptibility to the doctest caveats discussed in the previous chapter

- Begin learning some of the additional capabilities of unit tests as we extend the existing tests to cover additional functions

Unit tests for the Survey save override method

Recall in the previous chapter that we ultimately implemented four individual tests of the `Survey` save override function:

- A straightforward test of the added capability, which verifies that if `closes` is not specified when a `Survey` is created, it is auto-set to a week after `opens`

- A test that verifies that this auto-set operation is not performed if `closes` is explicitly specified during creation

- A test that verifies that `closes` is only auto-set if its value is missing during initial creation, not while saving an existing instance
- A test that verifies that the `save` override function does not introduce an unexpected exception in the error case where neither `opens` nor `closes` is specified during creation

To implement these as unit tests instead of doctests, create a `TestCase` within the `suvery/tests.py` file, replacing the sample `SimpleTest`. Within the new `TestCase` class, define each individual test as a separate test method in that `TestCase`, like so:

```
import datetime
from django.test import TestCase
from django.db import IntegrityError
from survey.models import Survey

class SurveySaveTest(TestCase):
    t = "New Year's Resolutions"
    sd = datetime.date(2009, 12, 28)

    def testClosesAutoset(self):
        s = Survey.objects.create(title=self.t, opens=self.sd)
        self.assertEqual(s.closes, datetime.date(2010, 1, 4))

    def testClosesHonored(self):
        s = Survey.objects.create(title=self.t, opens=self.sd,
                                  closes=self.sd)
        self.assertEqual(s.closes, self.sd)

    def testClosesReset(self):
        s = Survey.objects.create(title=self.t, opens=self.sd)
        s.closes = None
        self.assertRaises(IntegrityError, s.save)

    def testTitleOnly(self):
        self.assertRaises(IntegrityError, Survey.objects.create,
                          title=self.t)
```

This is more difficult to implement than the doctest version, isn't it? It is not possible to use a direct cut-and-paste from a shell session, and there is a fair amount of code overhead—code that does not appear anywhere in the shell session—that needs to be added. We can still use cut-and-paste from our shell session as a starting point, but we must edit the code after pasting it, in order to turn the pasted code into a proper unit test. Though not difficult, this can be tedious.

Most of the extra work consists of choosing names for the individual test methods, minor editing of cut-and-pasted code to refer to class variables such as `t` and `sd` correctly, and creating the appropriate test assertions to verify the expected result. The first of these requires the most brainpower (choosing good names can be hard), the second is trivial, and the third is fairly mechanical. For example, in a shell session where we had:

```
>>> s.closes
datetime.date(2010, 1, 4)
>>>
```

In the unit test, we instead have an `assertEqual`:

```
    self.assertEqual(s.closes, datetime.date(2010, 1, 4))
```

Expected exceptions are similar, but use `assertRaises`. For example, where in a shell session we had:

```
>>> s = Survey.objects.create(title=t)
Traceback (most recent call last):
  [ traceback details snipped ]
IntegrityError: survey_survey.opens may not be NULL
>>>
```

In the unit test, this is:

```
    self.assertRaises(IntegrityError, Survey.objects.create, title=self.t)
```

Note we do not actually call the `create` routine in our unit test code, but rather leave that up to the code within `assertRaises`. The first parameter passed to `assertRaises` is the expected exception, followed by the callable expected to raise the exception, followed by any parameters that need to be passed to the callable when calling it.

Pros of the unit test version

What do we get from this additional work? Right off the bat, we get a little more feedback from the test runner, when running at the highest verbosity level. For the doctest version, the output of `manage.py test survey -v2` was simply:

```
Doctest: survey.models.Survey.save ... ok
```

For the unit test version, we get individual results reported for each test method:

```
testClosesAutoset (survey.tests.SurveySaveTest) ... ok

testClosesHonored (survey.tests.SurveySaveTest) ... ok

testClosesReset (survey.tests.SurveySaveTest) ... ok

testTitleOnly (survey.tests.SurveySaveTest) ... ok
```

If we take a little more effort and provide single-line docstrings for our test methods, we can get even more descriptive results from the test runner. For example, if we add docstrings like so:

```python
class SurveySaveTest(TestCase):
    """Tests for the Survey save override method"""
    t = "New Year's Resolutions"
    sd = datetime.date(2009, 12, 28)

    def testClosesAutoset(self):
        """Verify closes is autoset correctly"""
        s = Survey.objects.create(title=self.t, opens=self.sd)
        self.assertEqual(s.closes, datetime.date(2010, 1, 4))

    def testClosesHonored(self):
        """Verify closes is honored if specified"""
        s = Survey.objects.create(title=self.t, opens=self.sd,
                                  closes=self.sd)
        self.assertEqual(s.closes, self.sd)

    def testClosesReset(self):
        """Verify closes is only autoset during initial create"""
        s = Survey.objects.create(title=self.t, opens=self.sd)
        s.closes = None
        self.assertRaises(IntegrityError, s.save)

    def testTitleOnly(self):
        """Verify correct exception is raised in error case"""
        self.assertRaises(IntegrityError, Survey.objects.create,
                          title=self.t)
```

The test runner output for this test will then be:

```
Verify closes is autoset correctly ... ok

Verify closes is honored if specified ... ok

Verify closes is only autoset during initial create ... ok

Verify correct exception is raised in error case ... ok
```

This additional descriptive detail may not be that important when all tests pass, but when they fail, it can be very helpful as a clue to what the test is trying to accomplish.

For example, let's assume we have broken the `save` override method by neglecting to add seven days to `opens`, so that if `closes` is not specified, it is auto-set to the same value as `opens`. With the doctest version of the test, the failure would be reported as:

```
======================================================================
FAIL: Doctest: survey.models.Survey.save
----------------------------------------------------------------------
Traceback (most recent call last):
  File "/usr/lib/python2.5/site-packages/django/test/_doctest.py", line
2180, in runTest
    raise self.failureException(self.format_failure(new.getvalue()))
AssertionError: Failed doctest test for survey.models.Survey.save
  File "/dj_projects/marketr/survey/models.py", line 10, in save


----------------------------------------------------------------------
File "/dj_projects/marketr/survey/models.py", line 19, in survey.models.
Survey.save
Failed example:
    s.closes
Expected:
    datetime.date(2010, 1, 4)
Got:
    datetime.date(2009, 12, 28)
```

That doesn't give much information on what has gone wrong, and you really have to go read the full test code to see what is even being tested. The same failure reported by the unit test is a bit more descriptive, as the FAIL header includes the test docstring, so we immediately know the problem has something to do with `closes` being auto-set:

```
======================================================================
FAIL: Verify closes is autoset correctly
----------------------------------------------------------------------
Traceback (most recent call last):
  File "/dj_projects/marketr/survey/tests.py", line 20, in
testClosesAutoset
    self.assertEqual(s.closes, datetime.date(2010, 1, 4))
AssertionError: datetime.date(2009, 12, 28) != datetime.date(2010, 1, 4)
```

We can take this one step further and make the error message a bit friendlier by specifying our own error message on the call to assertEqual:

```
def testClosesAutoset(self):
    """Verify closes is autoset correctly"""
    s = Survey.objects.create(title=self.t, opens=self.sd)
    self.assertEqual(s.closes, datetime.date(2010, 1, 4),
        "closes not autoset to 7 days after opens, expected %s, "
        "actually %s" %
        (datetime.date(2010, 1, 4), s.closes))
```

The reported failure would then be:

```
======================================================================
FAIL: Verify closes is autoset correctly
----------------------------------------------------------------------
Traceback (most recent call last):
  File "/dj_projects/marketr/survey/tests.py", line 22, in
testClosesAutoset
    (datetime.date(2010, 1, 4), s.closes))
AssertionError: closes not autoset to 7 days after opens, expected 2010-
01-04, actually 2009-12-28
```

In this case, the custom error message may not be much more useful than the default one, since what the save override is supposed to do here is quite simple. However, such custom error messages can be valuable for more complicated test assertions to help explain what is being tested, and the "why" behind the expected result.

Another benefit of unit tests is that they allow for more selective test execution than doctests. On the manage.py test command line, one or more unit tests to be executed can be identified by TestCase name. You can even specify that only particular methods in a TestCase should be run. For example:

python manage.py test survey.SurveySaveTest.testClosesAutoset

Here we are indicating that we only want to run the testClosesAutoset test method in the SurveySaveTest unit test found in the survey application. Being able to run just a single method or a single test case is a very convenient time saver when developing tests.

Cons of the unit test version

Has anything been lost by switching to unit tests? A bit. First, there is the ease of implementation that has already been mentioned: unit tests require more work to implement than doctests. Though generally not difficult work, it can be tedious. It is also work where errors can be made, resulting in a need to debug the test code. This increased implementation burden can serve to discourage writing comprehensive tests.

We've also lost the nice property of having tests right there with the code. This was mentioned in the previous chapter as one negative effect of moving some doctests out of docstrings and into the `__test__` dictionary in `tests.py`. The effect is worse with unit tests since all unit tests are usually kept in files separate from the code being tested. Thus there are usually no tests to be seen right near the code, which again may discourage writing tests. With unit tests, unless a methodology such as a test-driven development is employed, the "out of sight, out of mind" effect may easily result in test-writing becoming an afterthought.

Finally, we've lost the built-in documentation of the doctest version. This is more than just the potential for automatically-generated documentation from docstrings. Doctests are often more readable than unit tests, where extraneous code that is just test overhead can obscure what the test is intending to test. Note though, that using unit tests does not imply that you have to throw away doctests; it is perfectly fine to use both kinds of tests in your application. Each has their strengths, thus for many projects it is probably best to have a good mixture of unit tests and doctests rather than relying on a single type for all testing.

Revisiting the doctest caveats

In the previous chapter, we developed a list of things to watch out for when writing doctests. When discussing these, unit tests were sometimes mentioned as an alternative that did not suffer from the same problems. But are unit tests really immune to these problems, or do they just make the problems easier to avoid or address? In this section, we revisit the doctest caveats and consider how susceptible unit tests are to the same or similar issues.

Environmental dependence

The first doctest caveat discussed was environmental dependence: relying on the implementation details of code other than the code actually being tested. Though this type of dependence can happen with unit tests, it is less likely to occur. This is because a very common way for this type of dependence to creep into doctests is due to reliance on the printed representation of objects, as they are displayed in a Python shell session. Unit tests are far removed from the Python shell. It requires some coding effort to get an object's printed representation in a unit test, thus it is rare for this form of environmental dependence to creep into a unit test.

One common form of environmental dependence mentioned in *Chapter 2* that also afflicts unit tests involves file pathnames. Unit tests, just as doctests, need to take care that differences in file pathname conventions across operating systems do not cause bogus test failures when a test is run on an operating system different from the one where it was originally written. Thus, though unit tests are less prone to the problem of environmental dependence, they are not entirely immune.

Database dependence

Database dependence is a specific form of environmental dependence that is particularly common for Django applications to encounter. In the doctests, we saw that the initial implementation of the tests was dependent on the specifics of the message that accompanied an `IntegrityError`. In order to make the doctests pass on multiple different databases, we needed to modify the initial tests to ignore the details of this message.

We do not have this same problem with the unit test version. The `assertRaises` used to check for an expected exception already does not consider the exception message detail. For example:

```
self.assertRaises(IntegrityError, s.save)
```

There are no message specifics included there, so we don't need to do anything to ignore differences in messages from different database implementations.

In addition, unit tests make it easier to deal with even more wide-reaching differences than message details. It was noted in the previous chapter that for some configurations of MySQL, ignoring the message detail is not enough to allow all the tests to pass. The test that has a problem here is the one that ensures `closes` is only auto-set during initial model creation. The unit test version of this test is:

```
def testClosesReset(self):
    """Verify closes is only autoset during initial create"""
```

```
        s = Survey.objects.create(title=self.t, opens=self.sd)
        s.closes = None
        self.assertRaises(IntegrityError, s.save)
```

This test fails if it is run on a MySQL server that is running in non-strict mode. In this mode, MySQL does not raise an `IntegrityError` on an attempt to update a row to contain a `NULL` value in a column declared to be `NOT NULL`. Rather, the value is set to an implicit default value, and a warning is issued. Thus, we see a test error when we run this test on a MySQL server configured to run in non-strict mode:

```
======================================================================
ERROR: Verify closes is only autoset during initial create
----------------------------------------------------------------------
Traceback (most recent call last):
  File "/dj_projects/marketr/survey/tests.py", line 35, in
testClosesReset
    self.assertRaises(IntegrityError, s.save)
  File "/usr/lib/python2.5/unittest.py", line 320, in failUnlessRaises
    callableObj(*args, **kwargs)
  File "/dj_projects/marketr/survey/models.py", line 38, in save
    super(Survey, self).save(**kwargs)
  File "/usr/lib/python2.5/site-packages/django/db/models/base.py", line
410, in save
    self.save_base(force_insert=force_insert, force_update=force_update)
  File "/usr/lib/python2.5/site-packages/django/db/models/base.py", line
474, in save_base
    rows = manager.filter(pk=pk_val)._update(values)
  File "/usr/lib/python2.5/site-packages/django/db/models/query.py", line
444, in _update
    return query.execute_sql(None)
  File "/usr/lib/python2.5/site-packages/django/db/models/sql/subqueries.
py", line 120, in execute_sql
    cursor = super(UpdateQuery, self).execute_sql(result_type)
  File "/usr/lib/python2.5/site-packages/django/db/models/sql/query.py",
line 2369, in execute_sql
    cursor.execute(sql, params)
  File "/usr/lib/python2.5/site-packages/django/db/backends/mysql/base.
py", line 84, in execute
    return self.cursor.execute(query, args)
```

```
    File "/var/lib/python-support/python2.5/MySQLdb/cursors.py", line 168,
in execute
    if not self._defer_warnings: self._warning_check()
    File "/var/lib/python-support/python2.5/MySQLdb/cursors.py", line 82,
in _warning_check
    warn(w[-1], self.Warning, 3)
  File "/usr/lib/python2.5/warnings.py", line 62, in warn
    globals)
  File "/usr/lib/python2.5/warnings.py", line 102, in warn_explicit
    raise message
Warning: Column 'closes' cannot be null
```

Here we see that the warning issued by MySQL causes a simple `Exception` to be raised, not an `IntegrityError`, so the test reports an error.

There is also an additional wrinkle to consider here: This behavior of raising an `Exception` when MySQL issues a warning is dependent on the Django `DEBUG` setting. MySQL warnings are turned into raised `Exceptions` only when `DEBUG` is `True` (as it was for the previously run test). If we set `DEBUG` to `False` in `settings.py`, we see yet a different form of test failure:

```
======================================================================
FAIL: Verify closes is only autoset during initial create
----------------------------------------------------------------------
Traceback (most recent call last):
  File "/dj_projects/marketr/survey/tests.py", line 35, in
testClosesReset
    self.assertRaises(IntegrityError, s.save)
AssertionError: IntegrityError not raised
```

In this case, MySQL allowed the save, and since `DEBUG` was not turned on Django did not transform the warning issued by MySQL into an `Exception`, so the save simply worked.

At this point, we may seriously question whether it is even worth the effort to get this test to run properly in all these different situations, given the wildly divergent observed behaviors. Perhaps we should just require that if the code is run on MySQL, the server must be configured to run in strict mode. Then the test would be fine as it is, since the previous failures would both signal a server configuration problem. However, let's assume we do need to support running on MySQL, yet we cannot impose any particular configuration requirement on MySQL, and we still need to verify whether our code is behaving properly for this test. How do we do that?

Note what we are attempting to verify in this test is that our code does not auto-set `closes` to some value during save if it has been reset to `None` after initial creation. At first, it seemed that this was easily done by just checking for an `IntegrityError` on an attempted save. However, we've found a database configuration where we don't get an `IntegrityError`. Also, depending on the `DEBUG` setting, we may not get any error reported at all, even if our code behaves properly and leaves `closes` set to `None` during an attempted save. Can we write the test so that it reports the proper result—that is, whether our code behaves properly—in all these situations?

The answer is yes, so long as we can determine in our test code what database is in use, how it is configured, and what the `DEBUG` setting is. Then all we need to do is change the expected results based on the environment the test is running in. In fact, we can test for all these things with a bit of work:

```
def testClosesReset(self):
    """Verify closes is only autoset during initial create"""
    s = Survey.objects.create(title=self.t, opens=self.sd)
    s.closes = None

    strict = True
    debug = False
    from django.conf import settings
    if settings.DATABASE_ENGINE == 'mysql':
        from django.db import connection
        c = connection.cursor()
        c.execute('SELECT @@SESSION.sql_mode')
        mode = c.fetchone()[0]
        if 'STRICT' not in mode:
            strict = False;
            from django.utils import importlib
            debug = importlib.import_module(
                settings.SETTINGS_MODULE).DEBUG

    if strict:
        self.assertRaises(IntegrityError, s.save)
    elif debug:
        self.assertRaises(Exception, s.save)
    else:
        s.save()
        self.assertEqual(s.closes, None)
```

The test code starts by assuming that we are running on a database that is operating in strict mode, and set the local variable `strict` to `True`. We also assume DEBUG is `False` and set a local variable to reflect that. Then, if the database in use is MySQL (determined by checking the value of `settings.DATABASE_ENGINE`), we need to perform some further checking to see how it is configured. Consulting the MySQL documentation shows that the way to do this is to `SELECT` the session's `sql_mode` variable. If the returned value contains the string `STRICT`, then MySQL is operating in strict mode, otherwise it is not. We issue this query and obtain the result using Django's support for sending raw SQL to the database. If we determine that MySQL is not configured to run in strict mode, we update our local variable `strict` to be `False`.

If we get to the point where we set strict to `False`, that is also when the DEBUG value in settings becomes important, since it is in this case that MySQL will issue a warning instead of raising an `IntegrityError` for the case we are testing here. If DEBUG is `True` in the settings file, then warnings from MySQL will be turned into `Exceptions` by Django's MySQL backend. This is done by the backend using Python's `warnings` module. When the backend is loaded, if DEBUG is `True`, then a `warnings.filterwarnings` call is issued to force all database warnings to be turned into `Exceptions`.

Unfortunately, at some point after the database backend is loaded and before our test code runs, the test runner will change the in-memory settings so that DEBUG is set to `False`. This is done so that the behavior of test code matches as closely as possible what will happen in production. However, it means that we cannot just test the value of `settings.DEBUG` during the test to see if DEBUG was `True` when the database backend was loaded. Rather, we have to re-load the settings module and check the value in the newly loaded version. We do this using the `import_module` function of `django.utils.importlib` (this is a function from Python 2.7 that was backported to be used by Django 1.1).

Finally, we know what to look for when we run our test code. If we have determined that we are running a database operating in strict mode, we assert that attempting to save our model instance with `closes` set to `None` should raise an `IntegrityError`. Else, if we are running in non-strict mode, but DEBUG is `True` in the settings file, then the attempted save should result in an `Exception` being raised. Otherwise the save should work, and we test the correct behavior of our code by ensuring that `closes` is still set to `None` even after the model instance has been saved.

All of that may seem like rather a lot of trouble to go through for a pretty minor test, but it illustrates how unit tests can be written to accommodate significant differences in expected behavior in different environments. Doing the same for the doctest version is not so straightforward. Thus, while unit tests clearly do not eliminate the problem of dealing with database dependence in the tests, they make it easier to write tests that account for such differences.

Test interdependence

The next doctest caveat encountered in the last chapter was test interdependence. When the doctests were run on PostgreSQL, an error was encountered in the test following the first one that intentionally triggered a database error, since that error caused the database connection to enter a state where it would accept no further commands, except ones that terminated the transaction. The fix for that was to remember to "clean up" after the intentionally triggered error by including a transaction rollback after any test step that causes such an error.

Django unit tests do not suffer from this problem. The Django test case class, `django.test.TestCase`, ensures that the database is reset to a clean state before each test method is called. Thus, even though the `testClosesReset` method ends by attempting a model save that triggers an `IntegrityError`, no error is seen by the next test method that runs, because the database connection is reset in the interim by the `django.test.TestCase` code. It is not just this error situation that is cleaned up, either. Any database rows that are added, deleted, or modified by a test case method are reset to their original states before the next method is run. (Note that on most databases, the test runner can use a transaction rollback call to accomplish this very efficiently.) Thus Django unit test methods are fully isolated from any database changes that may have been performed by tests that ran before them.

Unicode

The final doctest caveat discussed in the previous chapter concerned using Unicode literals within doctests. These were observed to not work properly, due to underlying open issues in Python related to Unicode docstrings and Unicode literals within docstrings.

Unit tests do not have this problem. A straightforward unit test for the behavior of the `Survey` model `__unicode__` method works:

```
class SurveyUnicodeTest(TestCase):
    def testUnicode(self):
        t = u'¿Como está usted?'
        sd = datetime.date(2009, 12, 28)
        s = Survey.objects.create(title=t, opens=sd)
        self.assertEqual(unicode(s),
            u'¿Como está usted? (opens 2009-12-28, closes 2010-01-04)')
```

Note that it is necessary to add the encoding declaration to the top of `survey/tests.py`, just as we did in the previous chapter for `survey/models.py`, but it is not necessary to do any manual decoding of bytestring literals to construct Unicode objects as needed to be done in the doctest version. We just need to set our variables as we normally would, create the `Survey` instance, and assert that the result of calling `unicode` on that instance produces the string we expect. Thus testing with non-ASCII data is much more straightforward when using unit tests than it is with doctests.

Providing data for unit tests

Besides not suffering from some of the disadvantages of doctests, unit tests provide some additional useful features for Django applications. One of these features is the ability to load the database with test data prior to the test run. There are a few different ways this can be done; each is discussed in detail in the following sections.

Providing data in test fixtures

The first way to provide test data for unit tests is to load them from files, called fixtures. We will cover this method by first developing an example test that can benefit from pre-loaded test data, then showing how to create a fixture file, and finally describing how to ensure that the fixture file is loaded as part of the test.

Example test that needs test data

Before jumping into the details of how to provide a test with pre-loaded data, it would help to have an example of a test that could use this feature. So far our simple tests have gotten by pretty easily by just creating the data they need as they go along. However, as we begin to test more advanced functions, we quickly run into cases were it would become burdensome for the test itself to have to create all of the data needed for a good test.

For example, consider the `Question` model:

```
class Question(models.Model):
    question = models.CharField(max_length=200)
    survey = models.ForeignKey(Survey)

    def __unicode__(self):
        return u'%s: %s' % (self.survey, self.question)
```

(Note that we have added a __unicode__ method to this model. This will come in handy later in the chapter when we begin to use the admin interface to create some survey application data.)

Recall that the allowed answers for a given Question instance are stored in a separate model, Answer, which is linked to Question using a ForeignKey:

```
class Answer(models.Model):
    answer = models.CharField(max_length=200)
    question = models.ForeignKey(Question)
    votes = models.IntegerField(default=0)
```

This Answer model also tracks how many times each answer has been chosen, in its votes field. (We have not added a __unicode__ method to this model yet, since given the way we will configure admin later in the chapter, it is not yet needed.)

Now, when analyzing survey results, one of the things we will want to know about a given Question is which of its Answers was chosen most often. That is, one of the functions that a Question model will need to support is one which returns the "winning answer" for that Question. If we think about this a bit, we realize there may not be a single winning answer. There could be a tie with multiple answers getting the same number of votes. So, this winning answer method should be flexible enough to return more than one answer. Similarly, if there were no responses to the question, it would be better to return no winning answers than the whole set of allowed answers, none of which were ever chosen. Since this method (let's call it winning_answers) may return zero, one, or more results, it's probably best for consistency's sake for it to always return something like a list.

Before even starting to implement this function, then, we have a sense of the different situations it will need to handle, and what sort of test data will be useful to have in place when developing the function itself and tests for it. A good test of this routine will require at least three different questions, each with a set of answers:

- One question that has a clear winner among the answers, that is one answer with more votes than all of the others, so that winning_answers returns a single answer
- One question that has a tie among the answers, so that winning_answers returns multiple answers
- One question that gets no responses at all, so that winning_answers returns no answers

In addition, we should test with a `Question` that has no answers linked to it. This is an edge case, certainly, but we should ensure that the `winning_answers` function operates properly even when it seems that the data hasn't been fully set up for analysis of which answer was most popular. So, really there should be four questions in the test data, three with a set of answers and one with no answers.

Using the admin application to create test data

Creating four questions, three with several answers, in a shell session or even a program is pretty tedious, so let's use the Django admin application instead. Back in the first chapter we included `django.contrib.admin` in `INSTALLED_APPS`, so it is already loaded. Also, when we ran `manage.py syncdb`, the tables needed for admin were created. However, we still need to un-comment the admin-related lines in our `urls.py` file. When we do that `urls.py` should look like this:

```
from django.conf.urls.defaults import *

# Uncomment the next two lines to enable the admin:
from django.contrib import admin
admin.autodiscover()

urlpatterns = patterns('',
    # Example:
    # (r'^marketr/', include('marketr.foo.urls')),

    # Uncomment the admin/doc line below and add
    # 'django.contrib.admindocs'
    # to INSTALLED_APPS to enable admin documentation:
    # (r'^admin/doc/', include('django.contrib.admindocs.urls')),

    # Uncomment the next line to enable the admin:
    (r'^admin/', include(admin.site.urls)),
)
```

Finally, we need to provide some admin definitions for our survey application models, and register them with the admin application so that we can edit our models in the admin. Thus, we need to create a `survey/admin.py` file that looks something like this:

```
from django.contrib import admin
from survey.models import Survey, Question, Answer

class QuestionsInline(admin.TabularInline):
    model = Question
    extra = 4

class AnswersInline(admin.TabularInline):
    model = Answer

class SurveyAdmin(admin.ModelAdmin):
    inlines = [QuestionsInline]

class QuestionAdmin(admin.ModelAdmin):
    inlines = [AnswersInline]

admin.site.register(Survey, SurveyAdmin)
admin.site.register(Question, QuestionAdmin)
```

Here we have mostly used the admin defaults for everything, except that we have defined and specified some admin inline classes to make it easier to edit multiple things on a single page. The way we have set up the inlines here allows us to edit `Questions` on the same page as the `Survey` they belong to, and similarly edit `Answers` on the same page as the `Questions` they are associated with. We've also specified that we want four extra empty `Questions` when they appear inline. The default for this value is three, but we know we want to set up four questions and we might as well set things up so we can add all four at one time.

Now, we can start the development server by running `python manage.py runserver` in a command prompt, and access the admin application by navigating to `http://localhost:8000/admin/` from a browser on the same machine. After logging in as the superuser we created back in the first chapter, we'll be shown the admin main page. From there, we can click on the link to add a `Survey`. The **Add survey** page will let us create a survey with our four `Questions`:

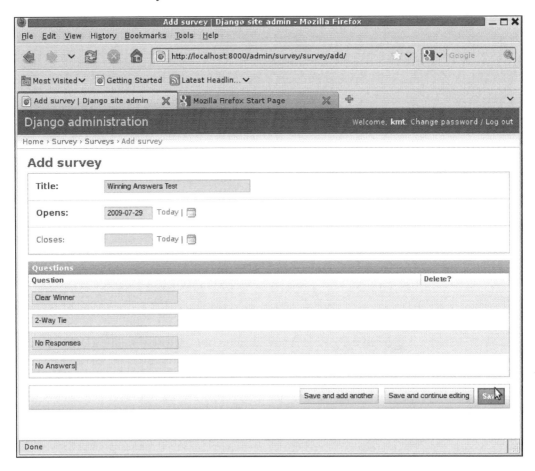

Here we've assigned our `Question` instances `question` values that are not so much questions as indications of what we are going to use each one to test. Notice this page also reflects a slight change made to the `Survey` model: `blank=True` has been added to the `closes` field specification. Without this change, admin would require a value to be specified here for `closes`. With this change, the admin application allows the field to be left blank, so that the automatic assignment done by the save override method can be used.

Once we have saved this survey, we can navigate to the change page for the first question, **Clear Winner**, and add some answers:

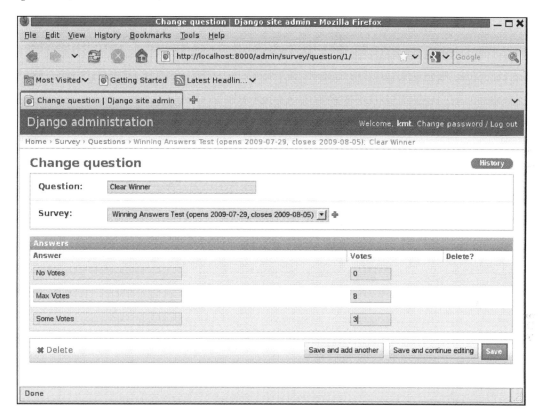

Thus, we set up the **Clear Winner** question to have one answer (**Max Votes**) that has more votes than all of the other answers. Similarly, we can set up the **2-Way Tie** question to have two answers that have the same number of votes:

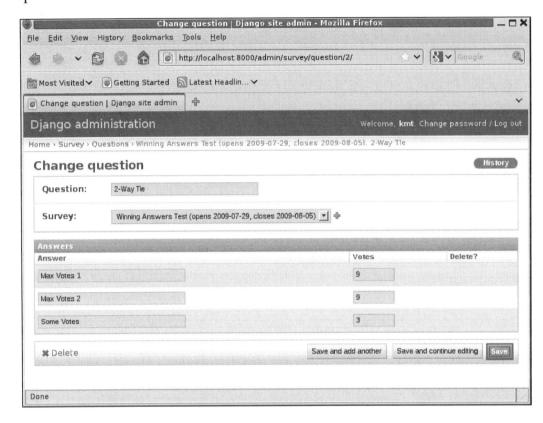

And finally, we set up the answers for **No Responses** so that we can test the situation where none of the answers to a `Question` have received any votes:

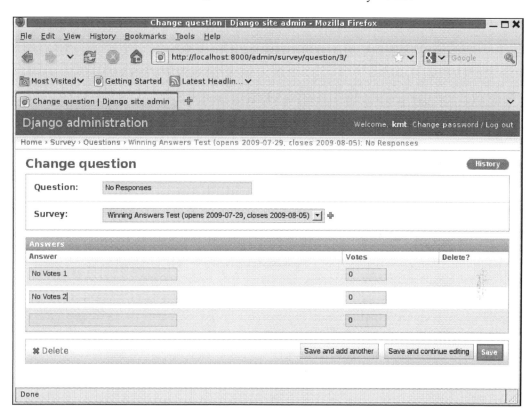

We do not need to do anything further with the **No Answers** question since that one is going to be used to test the case where the answer set for the question is empty, as it is when it is first created.

Writing the function itself

Now that we have our database set up with test data, we can experiment in the shell with the best way to implement the `winning_answers` function. As a result, we might come up with something like:

```
from django.db.models import Max

class Question(models.Model):
    question = models.CharField(max_length=200)
    survey = models.ForeignKey(Survey)
```

```
def winning_answers(self):
    rv = []
    max_votes = self.answer_set.aggregate(Max('votes')).values()[0]
    if max_votes and max_votes > 0:
        rv = self.answer_set.filter(votes=max_votes)
    return rv
```

The method starts by initializing a local variable `rv` (return value) to an empty list. Then, it uses the aggregation `Max` function to retrieve the maximum value for `votes` that exists in the set of `Answer` instances associated with this `Question` instance. That one line of code does several things in order to come up with the answer, so it may bear some more explanation. To see how it works, take a look at what each piece in turn returns in a shell session:

```
>>> from survey.models import Question
>>> q = Question.objects.get(question='Clear Winner')
>>> from django.db.models import Max
>>> q.answer_set.aggregate(Max('votes'))
{'votes__max': 8}
```

Here we see that applying the aggregate function `Max` to the `votes` field of the `answer_set` associated with a given `Question` returns a dictionary containing a single key-value pair. We're only interested in the value, so we retrieve just the values from the dictionary using `.values()`:

```
>>> q.answer_set.aggregate(Max('votes')).values()
[8]
```

However, `values()` returns a list and we want the single item in the list, so we retrieve it by requesting the item at index zero in the list:

```
>>> q.answer_set.aggregate(Max('votes')).values()[0]
8
```

Next the code tests for whether `max_votes` exists and if it is greater than zero (at least one answer was chosen at least once). If so, `rv` is reset to be the set of answers filtered down to only those that have that maximum number of votes.

But when would `max_votes` not exist, since it was just set in the previous line? This can happen in the edge case where there are no answers linked to a question. In that case, the aggregate `Max` function is going to return `None` for the maximum votes value, not zero:

```
>>> q = Question.objects.get(question='No Answers')
>>> q.answer_set.aggregate(Max('votes'))
{'votes__max': None}
```

Thus in this edge case, `max_votes` may be set to `None`, so it's best to test for that and avoid trying to compare `None` to `0`. While that comparison will actually work and return what seems like a sensible answer (`None` is not greater than `0`) in Python 2.x, the attempted comparison will return a `TypeError` beginning with Python 3.0. It's wise to avoid such comparisons now so as to limit problems if and when the code needs to be ported to run under Python 3.

Finally, the function returns `rv`, at this point hopefully set to the correct value. (Yes, there's a bug in this function. It's more entertaining to write tests that catch bugs now and then.)

Writing a test that uses the test data

Now that we have an implementation of `winning_answers`, and data to test it with, we can start writing our test for the `winning_answers` method. We might start by adding the following test to `tests.py`, testing the case where there is a clear winner among the answers:

```
from survey.models import Question
class QuestionWinningAnswersTest(TestCase):
    def testClearWinner(self):
        q = Question.objects.get(question='Clear Winner')
        wa_qs = q.winning_answers()
        self.assertEqual(wa_qs.count(), 1)
        winner = wa_qs[0]
        self.assertEqual(winner.answer, 'Max Votes')
```

The test starts by retrieving the `Question` that has its `question` value set to `'Clear Winner'`. Then, it calls `winning_answers` on that `Question` instance to retrieve the query set of answers for the question that received the most number of votes. Since this question is supposed to have a single winner, the test asserts that there is one element in the returned query set. It then does some further checking by retrieving the winning answer itself and verifying that its answer value is `'Max Votes'`. If all that succeeds, we can be pretty sure that `winning_answers` returns the correct result for the case where there is a single "winner" among the answers.

Extracting the test data from the database

Now, how do we run that test against the test data we loaded via the admin application into our database? When we run the tests, they are not going to use our production database, but rather create and use an initially empty test database. This is where fixtures come in. Fixtures are just files containing data that can be loaded into the database.

The first task, then, is to extract the test data that we loaded into our production database into a fixture file. We can do this by using the `manage.py` dumpdata command:

```
python manage.py dumpdata survey --indent 4 >test_winning_answers.json
```

Beyond the dumpdata command itself, the various things specified there are:

- survey: This limits the dumped data to the survey application. By default, dumpdata will output data for all installed applications, but the winning answers test does not need data from any application other than survey, so we can limit the fixture file to contain only data from the survey application.

- --indent 4: This makes the data output easier to read and edit. By default, dumpdata will output the data all on a single line, which is difficult to deal with if you ever need to examine or edit the result. Specifying indent 4 makes dumpdata format the data on multiple lines, with four-space indentation making the hierarchy of structures clear. (You can specify whatever number you like for the indent value, it does not have to be 4.)

- >test_winning_answers.json: This redirects the output from the command to a file. The default output format for dumpdata is JSON, so we use .json as the file extension so that when the fixture is loaded its format will be interpreted correctly.

When dumpdata completes, we will have a test_winning_answers.json file, which contains a serialized version of our test data. Besides loading it as part of our test (which will be covered next), what might we do with this or any fixture file?

First, we can load fixtures using the `manage.py` loaddata command. Thus dumpdata and loaddata together provide a way to move data from one database to another. Second, we might have or write programs that process the serialized data in some way: it can sometimes be easier to perform analysis on data contained in a flat file instead of a database. Finally, the `manage.py` testserver command supports loading fixtures (specified on the command line) into a test database and then running the development server. This can come in handy in situations where you'd like to experiment with how a real server behaves given this test data, instead of being limited to the results of the tests written to use the data.

Getting the test data loaded during the test run

Returning to our task at hand: how do we get this fixture we just created loaded when running the tests? An easy way to do this is to rename it to `initial_data.json` and place it in a `fixtures` subdirectory of our survey application directory. If we do that and run the tests, we will see that the fixture file is loaded, and our test for the clear winner case runs successfully:

```
kmt@lbox:/dj_projects/marketr$ python manage.py test survey
Creating test database...
Creating table auth_permission
Creating table auth_group
Creating table auth_user
Creating table auth_message
Creating table django_content_type
Creating table django_session
Creating table django_site
Creating table django_admin_log
Creating table survey_survey
Creating table survey_question
Creating table survey_answer
Installing index for auth.Permission model
Installing index for auth.Message model
Installing index for admin.LogEntry model
Installing index for survey.Question model
Installing index for survey.Answer model
Installing json fixture 'initial_data' from '/dj_projects/marketr/survey/
fixtures'.
Installed 13 object(s) from 1 fixture(s)
.........
----------------------------------------------------------------------
Ran 9 tests in 0.079s

OK
Destroying test database...
```

However, that is not really the right way to get this particular fixture data loaded. Initial data fixtures are meant for constant application data that should always be there as part of the application, and this data does not fall into that category. Rather, it is specific to this particular test, and needs to be loaded only for this test. To do that, place it in the survey/fixtures directory with the original name, test_winning_answers.json. Then, update the test case code to specify that this fixture should be loaded for this test by including the file name in a fixtures class attribute of the test case:

```
class QuestionWinningAnswersTest(TestCase):

    fixtures = ['test_winning_answers.json']

    def testClearWinner(self):
        q = Question.objects.get(question='Clear Winner')
        wa_qs = q.winning_answers()
        self.assertEqual(wa_qs.count(), 1)
        winner = wa_qs[0]
        self.assertEqual(winner.answer, 'Max Votes')
```

Note that manage.py test, at least as of Django 1.1, does not provide as much feedback for the loading of test fixtures specified this way as it does for loading initial data fixtures. In the previous test output, where the fixture was loaded as initial data, there are messages about the initial data fixture being loaded and 13 objects being installed. There are no messages like that when the fixture is loaded as part of the TestCase.

Furthermore there is no error indication if you make a mistake and specify the wrong filename in your TestCase fixtures value. For example, if you mistakenly leave the ending s off of test_winning_answers, the only indication of the problem will be that the test case fails:

```
kmt@lbox:/dj_projects/marketr$ python manage.py test survey
Creating test database...
Creating table auth_permission
Creating table auth_group
Creating table auth_user
Creating table auth_message
Creating table django_content_type
Creating table django_session
Creating table django_site
Creating table django_admin_log
```

```
Creating table survey_survey
Creating table survey_question
Creating table survey_answer
Installing index for auth.Permission model
Installing index for auth.Message model
Installing index for admin.LogEntry model
Installing index for survey.Question model
Installing index for survey.Answer model
E........
======================================================================
ERROR: testClearWinner (survey.tests.QuestionWinningAnswersTest)
----------------------------------------------------------------------
Traceback (most recent call last):
  File "/dj_projects/marketr/survey/tests.py", line 67, in
testClearWinner
    q = Question.objects.get(question='Clear Winner')
  File "/usr/lib/python2.5/site-packages/django/db/models/manager.py",
line 120, in get
    return self.get_query_set().get(*args, **kwargs)
  File "/usr/lib/python2.5/site-packages/django/db/models/query.py", line
305, in get
    % self.model._meta.object_name)
DoesNotExist: Question matching query does not exist.


----------------------------------------------------------------------
Ran 9 tests in 0.066s


FAILED (errors=1)
Destroying test database...
```

Possibly the diagnostics provided for this error case may be improved in the future, but in the meantime it's best to keep in mind that mysterious errors such as that DoesNotExist above are likely due to the proper test fixture not being loaded rather than some error in the test code or the code being tested.

Now that we've got the test fixture loaded and the first test method working properly, we can add the tests for the three other cases: the one where there is a two-way tie among the answers, the one where no responses were received to a question, and the one where no answers are linked to a question. These can be written to be very similar to the existing method that tests the clear winner case:

```
def testTwoWayTie(self):
    q = Question.objects.get(question='2-Way Tie')
    wa_qs = q.winning_answers()
    self.assertEqual(wa_qs.count(), 2)
    for winner in wa_qs:
        self.assert_(winner.answer.startswith('Max Votes'))

def testNoResponses(self):
    q = Question.objects.get(question='No Responses')
    wa_qs = q.winning_answers()
    self.assertEqual(wa_qs.count(), 0)

def testNoAnswers(self):
    q = Question.objects.get(question='No Answers')
    wa_qs = q.winning_answers()
    self.assertEqual(wa_qs.count(), 0)
```

Differences are in the names of the `Questions` retrieved from the database, and how the specific results are tested. In the case of the `2-Way Tie`, the test verifies that `winning_answers` returns two answers, and that both have `answer` values that start with `'Max Votes'`. In the case of no responses, and no answers, all the tests have to do is verify that there are no items in the query set returned by `winning_answers`.

If we now run the tests, we will find the bug that was mentioned earlier, since our last two tests fail:

```
======================================================================
ERROR: testNoAnswers (survey.tests.QuestionWinningAnswersTest)
----------------------------------------------------------------------
Traceback (most recent call last):
  File "/dj_projects/marketr/survey/tests.py", line 88, in testNoAnswers
    self.assertEqual(wa_qs.count(), 0)
TypeError: count() takes exactly one argument (0 given)


======================================================================
ERROR: testNoResponses (survey.tests.QuestionWinningAnswersTest)
----------------------------------------------------------------------
```

```
Traceback (most recent call last):
  File "/dj_projects/marketr/survey/tests.py", line 83, in
testNoResponses
    self.assertEqual(wa_qs.count(), 0)
TypeError: count() takes exactly one argument (0 given)
```

The problem here is that `winning_answers` is inconsistent in what it returns:

```
def winning_answers(self):
    rv = []
    max_votes = self.answer_set.aggregate(Max('votes')).values()[0]
    if max_votes and max_votes > 0:
        rv = self.answer_set.filter(votes=max_votes)
    return rv
```

The return value `rv` is initialized to a list in the first line of the function, but then when it is set in the case where there are answers that received votes, it is set to be the return value from a `filter` call, which returns a `QuerySet`, not a list. The test methods, since they use `count()` with no arguments on the return value of `winning_answers`, are expecting a `QuerySet`.

Which is more appropriate for `winning_answers` to return: a list or a `QuerySet`? Probably a `QuerySet`. The caller may only be interested in the count of answers in the set and not the specific answers, so it may not be necessary to retrieve the actual answers from the database. If `winning_answers` consistently returns a list, it would have to force the answers to be read from the database in order to put them in a list. Thus, it's probably more efficient to always return a `QuerySet` and let the caller's requirements dictate what ultimately needs to be read from the database. (Given the small number of items we'd expect to be in this set, there is probably little to no efficiency to be gained here, but it is still a good habit to get into in order to consider such things when designing interfaces.)

A way to fix `winning_answers` to always return a `QuerySet` is to use the `none()` method applied to the `answer_set`, which will return an empty `QuerySet`:

```
def winning_answers(self):
    max_votes = self.answer_set.aggregate(Max('votes')).values()[0]
    if max_votes and max_votes > 0:
        rv = self.answer_set.filter(votes=max_votes)
    else:
        rv = self.answer_set.none()
    return rv
```

After making this change, the complete `QuestionWinningAnswersTest TestCase` runs successfully.

Creating data during test set up

While test fixtures are very convenient, they are sometimes not the right tool for the job. Specifically, since the fixture files contain fixed, hard-coded values for all model data, fixtures are sometimes not flexible enough for all tests.

As an example, let's return to the `Survey` model and consider some methods we are likely to want it to support. Recall that a survey has both, an `opens` and a `closes` date, so at any point in time a particular `Survey` instance may be considered "completed", "active", or "upcoming", depending on where the current date falls in relation to the survey's `opens` and `closes` dates. It will be useful to have easy access to these different categories of surveys. The typical way to support this in Django is to create a special model `Manager` for `Survey` that implements methods to return appropriately-filtered query sets. Such a `Manager` might look like this:

```
import datetime
from django.db import models

class SurveyManager(models.Manager):
    def completed(self):
        return self.filter(closes__lt=datetime.date.today())
    def active(self):
        return self.filter(opens__lte=datetime.date.today()).\
                    filter(closes__gte=datetime.date.today())
    def upcoming(self):
        return self.filter(opens__gt=datetime.date.today())
```

This manager implements three methods:

- `completed`: This returns a `QuerySet` of `Survey` filtered down to only those with `closes` values earlier than today. These are surveys that are closed to any more responses.

- `active`: This returns a `QuerySet` of `Survey` filtered down to only those with `opens` values earlier or equal to today, and `closes` later than or equal to today. These are surveys that are open to receiving responses.

- `upcoming`: This returns a `QuerySet` of `Survey` filtered down to only those with `opens` values later than today. These are surveys that are not yet open to responses.

To make this custom manager the default for the `Survey` model, assign an instance of it to the value of the `Survey` `objects` attribute:

```
class Survey(models.Model):
    title = models.CharField(max_length=60)
    opens = models.DateField()
    closes = models.DateField(blank=True)

    objects = SurveyManager()
```

Why might we have difficulty testing these methods using fixture data? The problem arises due to the fact that the methods rely on the moving target of today's date. It's not actually a problem for testing `completed`, as we can set up test data for surveys with `closes` dates in the past, and those `closes` dates will continue to be in the past no matter how much further forward in time we travel.

It is, however, a problem for `active` and `upcoming`, since eventually, even if we choose `closes` (and, for `upcoming`, `opens`) dates far in the future, today's date will (barring universal catastrophe) at some point catch up with those far-future dates. When that happens, the tests will start to fail. Now, we may expect that there is no way our software will still be running in that far-future time. (Or we may simply hope that we are no longer responsible for maintaining it then.) But that's not really a good approach. It would be much better to use a technique that doesn't result in time-bombs in the tests.

If we don't want to use a test fixture file with hard-coded dates to test these routines, what is the alternative? What we can do instead is much like what we were doing earlier: create the data dynamically in the test case. As noted earlier, this might be somewhat tedious, but note we do not have to re-create the data for each test method. Unit tests provide a hook method, `setUp`, which we can use to implement any common pre-test initialization. The test machinery will ensure that our `setUp` routine is run prior to each of our test methods. Thus `setUp` is a good place to put code that dynamically creates fixture-like data for our tests.

In a test for the custom `Survey` manager, then, we might have a `setUp` routine that looks like this:

```
class SurveyManagerTest(TestCase):
    def setUp(self):
        today = datetime.date.today()
        oneday = datetime.timedelta(1)
        yesterday = today - oneday
        tomorrow = today + oneday
        Survey.objects.all().delete()
```

```
Survey.objects.create(title="Yesterday", opens=yesterday,
                      closes=yesterday)
Survey.objects.create(title="Today", opens=today,
                      closes=today)
Survey.objects.create(title="Tomorrow", opens=tomorrow,
                      closes=tomorrow)
```

This method creates three Surveys: one that opened and closed yesterday, one that opens and closes today, and one that opens and closes tomorrow. Before it creates these, it deletes all Survey objects that are in the database. Thus, each test method in the SurveyManagerTest can rely on there being exactly three Surveys in the database, one in each of the three states.

Why does the test first delete all Survey objects? There should not be any Surveys in the database yet, right? That call is there just in case at some future point, the survey application acquires an initial data fixture that includes one or more Surveys. If such a fixture existed, it would be loaded during test initialization, and would break these tests that rely on there being exactly three Surveys in the database. Thus, it is safest for setUp here to ensure that the only Surveys in the database are the ones it creates.

A test for the Survey manager completed function might then be:

```
def testCompleted(self):
    self.assertEqual(Survey.objects.completed().count(), 1)
    completed_survey = Survey.objects.get(title="Yesterday")
    self.assertEqual(Survey.objects.completed()[0],
                     completed_survey)

    today = datetime.date.today()
    completed_survey.closes = today
    completed_survey.save()
    self.assertEqual(Survey.objects.completed().count(), 0)
```

The test first asserts that on entry there is one completed Survey in the database. It then verifies that the one Survey returned by the completed function is in fact that actual survey it expects to be completed, that is the one with title set to "Yesterday". The test then goes a step further and modifies that completed Survey so that its closes date no longer qualifies it as completed, and saves that change to the database. When that has been done, the test asserts that there are now zero completed Surveys in the database.

Testing with that routine verifies that the test works, so a similar test for active surveys might be written as:

```
def testActive(self):
    self.assertEqual(Survey.objects.active().count(), 1)
    active_survey = Survey.objects.get(title="Today")
    self.assertEqual(Survey.objects.active()[0], active_survey)
    yesterday = datetime.date.today() - datetime.timedelta(1)
    active_survey.opens = active_survey.closes = yesterday
    active_survey.save()
    self.assertEqual(Survey.objects.active().count(), 0)
```

This is very much like the test for `completed`. It asserts that there is one active `Survey` on entry, retrieves the active `Survey` and verifies that it is the one expected to be active, modifies it so that it no longer qualifies as active (by making it qualify as closed), saves the modification, and finally verifies that `active` then returns that there are no active `Survey`s.

Similarly, a test for upcoming surveys might be:

```
def testUpcoming(self):
    self.assertEqual(Survey.objects.upcoming().count(), 1)
    upcoming_survey = Survey.objects.get(title="Tomorrow")
    self.assertEqual(Survey.objects.upcoming()[0],
                     upcoming_survey)
    yesterday = datetime.date.today() - datetime.timedelta(1)
    upcoming_survey.opens = yesterday
    upcoming_survey.save()
    self.assertEqual(Survey.objects.upcoming().count(), 0)
```

But won't all those tests interfere with each other? For example, the test for `completed` makes the `"Yesterday"` survey appear to be active, and the test for `active` makes the `"Today"` survey appear to be closed. It seems that whichever one runs first is going to make a change that will interfere with the correct operation of the other test.

In fact, though, the tests don't interfere with each other, because the database is reset and the test case `setUp` method is re-run before each test method is run. So `setUp` is not run once per `TestCase`, but rather once per test method within the `TestCase`. Running the tests shows that all of these tests pass, even though each updates the database in a way that would interfere with the others, if the changes it made were seen by the others:

```
testActive (survey.tests.SurveyManagerTest) ... ok
testCompleted (survey.tests.SurveyManagerTest) ... ok
testUpcoming (survey.tests.SurveyManagerTest) ... ok
```

There is a companion method to setUp, called tearDown that can be used to perform any cleaning up after test methods. In this case it isn't necessary, since the default Django operation of resetting the database between test method executions takes care of un-doing the database changes made by the test methods. The tearDown routine is useful for cleaning up any non-database changes (such as temporary file creation, for example) that may be done by the tests.

Summary

We have now covered the basics of unit testing Django applications. In this chapter, we:

- Converted the previously-written doctests for the Survey model to unit tests, which allowed us to directly compare the pros and cons of each test approach
- Revisited the doctest caveats from the previous chapter and examined to what extent (if any) unit tests are susceptible to the same issues
- Began to learn some of the additional features available with unit tests; in particular, features related to loading test data

In the next chapter, we will start investigating even more advanced features that are available to Django unit tests.

4
Getting Fancier: Django Unit Test Extensions

In the last chapter, we started learning how to use unit tests to test Django applications. This included learning about some Django-specific support, such as how to get test data loaded from fixture files into the database for a particular test. So far, though, our testing focus has been on small building blocks that make up the application. We have not yet begun to write code to serve up web pages for our application, nor considered how we will test whether the pages are served properly and contain the correct content. The Django `TestCase` class provides support that is useful for this broader kind of testing, which will be the focus of this chapter. In this chapter, we will:

- First learn how to use a tests directory for our Django application tests instead of a single `tests.py` file. This will allow us to organize the tests logically instead of having all sorts of different tests mixed up in a single huge file.

- Develop some web pages for the survey application. For each, we will write unit tests to verify their correct operation, learning the specifics of the `TestCase` support for testing Django applications along the way.

- Experiment with adding custom validation to the `Survey` model in the admin application, and see how to test such customization.

- Briefly discuss some aspects of Django's test support that we don't run across in our example tests.

- Finally, we will learn under what conditions it may be necessary to use an alternate unit test class, `TransactionTestCase`. This class does not perform as well as `TestCase`, but it supports testing some database transaction behavior that is not possible with `TestCase`.

Organizing tests

Before we set out to write code (and tests) for serving web pages from the survey application, let's consider the tests we have so far. If we run `manage.py test survey -v2` and examine the tail end of the output, we can see that we've already accumulated over a dozen individual tests:

```
No fixtures found.
testClearWinner (survey.tests.QuestionWinningAnswersTest) ... ok
testNoAnswers (survey.tests.QuestionWinningAnswersTest) ... ok
testNoResponses (survey.tests.QuestionWinningAnswersTest) ... ok
testTwoWayTie (survey.tests.QuestionWinningAnswersTest) ... ok
testActive (survey.tests.SurveyManagerTest) ... ok
testCompleted (survey.tests.SurveyManagerTest) ... ok
testUpcoming (survey.tests.SurveyManagerTest) ... ok
Verify closes is autoset correctly ... ok
Verify closes is honored if specified ... ok
Verify closes is only autoset during initial create ... ok
Verify correct exception is raised in error case ... ok
testUnicode (survey.tests.SurveyUnicodeTest) ... ok
Doctest: survey.models.Survey.__unicode__ ... ok
Doctest: survey.models.Survey.save ... ok
Doctest: survey.tests.__test__.survey_save ... ok


----------------------------------------------------------------------
Ran 15 tests in 0.810s


OK
Destroying test database...
```

Two of those, namely the two doctests with labels that start with `survey.models.Survey`, are from the `survey/models.py` file. The remaining 13 tests are all in the `survey/tests.py` file, which has grown to around 150 lines. Those numbers are not that big, but if you consider that we have barely started writing this application, it is clear that continuing to simply add to `tests.py` will soon result in an unwieldy test file. Since we are about to start moving on from building and testing the survey models to building and testing the code that serves web pages, now would be a good time to come up with a better organization for tests than a single file.

Fortunately, this is not hard to do. Nothing in Django requires that the tests all reside in a single file; they simply need to be in a Python module named `tests`. So, we can create a subdirectory within `survey` named `tests`, and move our existing `tests.py` file into it. Since the tests in this file focus on testing the application's models, let's also rename it `model_tests.py`. We should also delete the `tests.pyc` file from `marketr/survey` since leaving stray `.pyc` files around after Python code reorganization can often cause confusion. Finally we need to create an `__init__.py` file inside the `tests` directory, so that Python will recognize it as a module.

Is that all? Not quite. Django uses `unittest.TestLoader.LoadTestsFromModule` to find and automatically load all of the `TestCase` classes in the `tests` module. However, we have now moved all of the `TestCase` classes into a submodule of tests, named `model_tests`. In order for `LoadTestsFromModule` to find them, we need to make them visible in the parent `tests` module, which we can do by adding an import for `model_tests` to the `__init__.py` file in `survey/tests`:

```
from model_tests import *
```

Now are we set? Almost. If we run `manage.py test survey -v2` now, we will see that the output reports 14 tests run, whereas the run prior to the reorganization reported 15 tests run:

```
No fixtures found.
testClearWinner (survey.tests.model_tests.QuestionWinningAnswersTest) ...
ok
testNoAnswers (survey.tests.model_tests.QuestionWinningAnswersTest) ... ok
testNoResponses (survey.tests.model_tests.QuestionWinningAnswersTest) ...
ok
testTwoWayTie (survey.tests.model_tests.QuestionWinningAnswersTest) ... ok
testActive (survey.tests.model_tests.SurveyManagerTest) ... ok
testCompleted (survey.tests.model_tests.SurveyManagerTest) ... ok
testUpcoming (survey.tests.model_tests.SurveyManagerTest) ... ok
Verify closes is autoset correctly ... ok
Verify closes is honored if specified ... ok
Verify closes is only autoset during initial create ... ok
Verify correct exception is raised in error case ... ok
testUnicode (survey.tests.model_tests.SurveyUnicodeTest) ... ok
Doctest: survey.models.Survey.__unicode__ ... ok
Doctest: survey.models.Survey.save ... ok
----------------------------------------------------------------
Ran 14 tests in 0.760s

OK
Destroying test database...
```

Which test is missing? The very last test from the earlier run, that is the doctest in the __test__ dictionary that had been in tests.py. Because __test__ starts with an underscore (signaling it is a private attribute), it is not imported by from model_tests import *. The privacy implied by the naming is not enforced by Python, so we could add an explicit import for __test__ as well to survey/tests/__init__.py:

```
from model_tests import __test__
from model_tests import *
```

If we did that and ran the tests again, we would see that we were back to having 15 tests. However that is a poor solution, since it is not extensible to multiple files in the tests directory. If we add another file to our tests directory, say view_tests.py, and simply replicate the imports used for model_tests.py, we will have:

```
from model_tests import __test__
from model_tests import *
from view_tests import __test__
from view_tests import *
```

This will not cause any errors, but it also does not quite work. The second import of __test__ completely replaces the first, so the doctests contained in model_tests.py are lost if we do this.

It would be easy enough to devise an approach that would be extensible to multiple files, perhaps by creating our own naming convention for doctests defined within individual test files. Then, code in __init__.py could create the __test__ dictionary for the overall tests module by combining dictionaries from the individual test files that defined doctests. But for the purposes of the examples we are going to be studying here, that is unnecessarily complicated, since the additional tests we will be adding are all unit tests, not doctests.

In fact the doctests now in model_tests.py have also been re-implemented as unit tests, so they are redundant as tests and could safely be dropped. However, they do serve to point out an issue with doctests that will arise if you decide to move away from the single-file tests.py approach in your own projects. We can keep the doctests we already have by simply moving the __test__ dictionary definition from the model_tests.py file to the survey/tests/__init__.py file. Then, if we decide additional doctests (beyond ones in models.py) would be useful, we can either simply add to this dictionary in survey/tests/__init__.py or come up with a more sophisticated approach to allow splitting out doctests as well as unit tests into different files.

Note that it is not necessary to limit the `tests` directory tree to a single level. We could create a subdirectory for model tests, and one for views, and further subdivide these tests into individual files. Using the approach we have started with here, all that needs to be done is to include the proper imports in the various `__init__.py` files so that the test cases are visible at the top level of the `tests` package. How deep to make the tree and how small to make the individual test files are matters of personal preference. We will stick to a single level for now.

Finally, note that you can take full control of what tests make up your application's test suite by defining a `suite()` function in the `models` and/or `tests` module for the application. The Django test runner looks for such a function in each of these modules, and if `suite()` exists, it is called to create the test suite. If provided, the `suite()` function must return an object suitable for passing as an argument to `unittest.TestSuite.addTest` (for example, a `unittest.TestSuite`).

Creating the survey application home page

It is now time to turn our attention to building some web pages for the survey application. The first page to consider is the home page, which will be the starting point for general users doing anything with surveys. Ultimately, we would likely plan for this page to have many different elements, such as a standard header and footer, also maybe a sidebar or two for news and feedback. We'd plan to develop comprehensive stylesheets to give the application a pretty and consistent appearance. But all of that is beside the point of what we want to focus on right now, which is the main content of the home page.

The primary function of the home page will be to provide a snapshot overview of the current state of surveys, and to provide links, where appropriate, to allow users to see details on individual surveys. The home page will show surveys grouped into three categories:

- First, there will be a list of currently open surveys. Each survey in this list will have a link for users to follow if they want to participate in the survey.

- Second, there will be a list of recently completed surveys. Each of these will also have a link to follow, but this link will bring up a page that allows users to see the survey results.

- Third, there will be a list of surveys that will be opening soon. Surveys in this list will not have links since users cannot participate yet, nor are there results to be seen.

In order to build and test this home page we need to do four things:

1. First, we need to define the URLs that will be used to access the home page and any pages it links to, and define in the urls.py file how these URLs should map to the view code that will serve the pages.

2. Second, we need to implement the view code for serving the pages identified in step 1.

3. Third, we need to define the Django templates that will be used to render the responses generated in step 2.

4. Finally, we need to write tests for each page.

The following sections will focus on each of these steps in turn.

Defining the survey application URLs

From the description of the survey home page, it sounds like we may have two or three different URLs to define. Certainly there is the home page itself, which is most naturally placed at the root of the survey application's URL tree. We can define this by creating a urls.py file within the survey directory:

```
from django.conf.urls.defaults import *

urlpatterns = patterns('survey.views',
    url(r'^$', 'home', name='survey_home'),
)
```

Here we have specified that a request for the empty (root) URL should be handled by the home function in the survey.views module. Further we have given this URL the name survey_home, which we can use to refer to this URL from other code. Always using named URLs is good practice, as it allows for changing the actual URLs by simply changing the urls.py file and no other code.

Besides the home page, there are also the pages linked from the home page to consider. First there are the pages linked from the list of active surveys, which allow users to participate in a survey. Second are the pages linked from the list of recently completed surveys, which allow users to see the results. You might ask, should these be covered by one or two URLs?

While it sounds like these may need different URLs, since the pages will show very different content, in a sense that they are both showing the same thing—the details for a particular survey. It is just that the current state of the survey will influence what its details page displays. Thus, we can choose to put the logic for deciding what exactly to display, based on survey state, into the view that handles displaying details for a survey. Then we can cover both of these types of pages with a single URL pattern. Taking this approach, the `survey/urls.py` file becomes:

```
from django.conf.urls.defaults import *

urlpatterns = patterns('survey.views',
    url(r'^$', 'home', name='survey_home'),
    url(r'^(?P<pk>\d+)/$', 'survey_detail', name='survey_detail'),
)
```

Here we have taken the approach of placing the primary key of the survey in the URL. Any URL which consists of a single path component containing one or more digits (the primary key) will be mapped to the `survey_detail` function in the `survey.views` module. This function will receive the primary key path component as an argument, `pk`, in addition to the standard request argument. Finally, this URL has been given the name `survey_detail`.

Those two URL patterns are enough to define the survey application pages we have considered so far. However, we still need to hook them into our project's overall URL configuration. To do this, edit the project's root `urls.py` file and add a line for the survey URLs. The `urlpatterns` variable in `urls.py` will then be defined like so:

```
urlpatterns = patterns('',
    # Example:
    # (r'^marketr/', include('marketr.foo.urls')),

    # Uncomment the admin/doc line below and add
    # 'django.contrib.admindocs'
    # to INSTALLED_APPS to enable admin documentation:
    # (r'^admin/doc/', include('django.contrib.admindocs.urls')),

    # Uncomment the next line to enable the admin:
    (r'^admin/', include(admin.site.urls)),
    (r'', include('survey.urls')),
)
```

The last line we have added here specifies an empty URL pattern, `r''`. All matching URLs will be tested against the patterns found in the `urls.py` file contained in the survey module. The pattern `r''` will match every URL, and no part of the URL will be removed as already matched when it is tested against the URL patterns in `survey/urls.py`, so this essentially mounts the survey `urls.py` file at the root of the project's URL tree.

Developing views to serve pages

Now that we have defined our URLs and specified the view functions that should be called to serve them, it is time to start writing these functions. Or, perhaps we should start with the templates for these pages? Both need to be done and they are dependent on each other. The data returned by views is dependent on what the templates need, while the specifics of how the templates are written are dependent on the naming and structure of the data provided by the views. Thus, it can be hard to know which to start with, and it is sometimes necessary to alternate between them.

However, we have to start somewhere, and we will start with the views. In fact, whenever you add a reference to a view in a `urls.py` file, it is a good idea to immediately write at least a minimal implementation of that view. For example, for the two views we just added to `survey/urls.py`, we might immediately place the following in `survey/views.py`:

```
from django.http import HttpResponse


def home(request):
    return HttpResponse("This is the home page.")


def survey_detail(request, pk):
    return HttpResponse("This is the survey detail page for survey, "
                        "with pk=%s" % pk)
```

These views both simply return an `HttpResponse` describing what the page is supposed to display. Creating placeholder views like this ensures that the overall URL pattern configuration for the project remains valid. Keeping this configuration valid is important because any attempt to perform a reverse URL mapping (from the name back to the actual URL) will result in an exception if there is any error (such as reference to a non-existent function) in any part of the URL pattern configuration. Thus, an invalid URL configuration can easily seem to break other perfectly innocent code.

The admin application, for example, needs to use reverse URL mapping to generate links on its pages. Thus an invalid URL pattern configuration can result in an exception being raised when a user attempts to access an admin page, even though there is no error in the admin code itself. This kind of exception can be very hard to debug since at first glance it seems that the problem is caused by code that is entirely separate from where the actual error is. Thus, even if you prefer to work on writing templates before view functions, it is best to always immediately provide at least a bare minimum implementation for any view you add to your URL pattern configuration.

We can go a step beyond the bare minimum, though, at least for the home page view. As previously described, the home page will display three different lists of surveys: active, recently completed, and opening soon. It is unlikely that the template will need that data to be structured in any way more complicated than a simple list (or QuerySet), so the view for the home page is straightforward to write:

```
import datetime
from django.shortcuts import render_to_response
from survey.models import Survey


def home(request):
    today = datetime.date.today()
    active = Survey.objects.active()
    completed = Survey.objects.completed().filter(closes__gte=today-
                    datetime.timedelta(14))
    upcoming = Survey.objects.upcoming().filter(
                    opens__lte=today+datetime.timedelta(7))
    return render_to_response('survey/home.html',
        {'active_surveys': active,
         'completed_surveys': completed,
         'upcoming_surveys': upcoming,
        })
```

This view sets three variables to be QuerySets containing the appropriate subsets of the Surveys in the database. The recently completed set is limited to surveys that have closed in the last two weeks, and the opening soon set is limited to those that will open in the next week. The view then calls the render_to_response shortcut to render the survey/home.html template passing along a context dictionary containing the three Survey subsets in the active_surveys, completed_surveys, and upcoming_surveys context variables.

At this point, we can either proceed to replace the placeholder `survey_detail` view implementation with some real code, or we could get started on some templates. Writing the second view does not get us any closer to testing out the first one we've written, though, so moving on to the templates is better. The placeholder content for the second view will do fine for now.

Creating templates for pages

To get started with writing templates for the survey application, first create a `templates` directory under `survey`, and then a `survey` directory under `templates`. Placing the templates under a `templates` directory in the application directory allows them to be automatically found by the `app_directories` template loader, which is enabled by default. Further, placing the templates in a `survey` directory under `templates` minimizes the chance of name conflicts with templates used by other applications.

Now, what templates do we need to create? The one named in the home view is `survey/home.html`. We could create just that one file and make it a full standalone HTTP document. But that would be unrealistic. Django provides a convenient template inheritance mechanism to allow for re-use of common page elements and selective override of defined blocks. At a minimum, we probably want to use a common base template that defines the overall document structure and block components, and then implements the individual page templates as child templates that extend the base template.

Here's a minimal `base.html` template we can use to start with:

```
<!DOCTYPE html PUBLIC "-//W3C//DTD XHTML 1.0 Strict//EN"
"http://www.w3.org/TR/xhtml1/DTD/xhtml1-strict.dtd">
<html xmlns="http://www.w3.org/1999/xhtml">
<head>
<title>{% block title %}Survey Central{% endblock %}</title>
</head>
<body>
{% block content %}{% endblock %}
</body>
</html>
```

This document provides the overall HTML structure tags and defines just two blocks: `title` and `content`. The `title` block has default content of `Survey Central` that may be overridden by child templates, or left as is. The `content` block is initially empty, so child templates are expected to always provide something to fill in the body of the page.

Given that base template, we can write our `home.html` template as a child template that extends `base.html` and provides the content for the block `content`. We know that the `home` view is supplying three context variables (`active_surveys`, `completed_surveys`, and `upcoming_surveys`) containing the data that should be displayed. An initial implementation of the `home.html` template might look like this:

```
{% extends "survey/base.html" %}
{% block content %}
<h1>Welcome to Survey Central</h1>

{% if active_surveys %}
<p>Take a survey now!</p>
<ul>
{% for survey in active_surveys %}
<li><a href="{{ survey.get_absolute_url }}">{{ survey.title }}</a>
</li>
{% endfor %}
</ul>
{% endif %}

{% if completed_surveys %}
<p>See how your opinions compared to those of others!</p>
<ul>
{% for survey in completed_surveys %}
<li><a href="{{ survey.get_absolute_url }}">{{ survey.title }}</a>
</li>
{% endfor %}
</ul>
{% endif %}

{% if upcoming_surveys %}
<p>Come back soon to share your opinion!</p>
<ul>
{% for survey in upcoming_surveys %}
<li>{{ survey.title }} opens {{ survey.opens }}</li>
{% endfor %}
</ul>
{% endif %}
{% endblock content %}
```

That may look a little intimidating, but it is straightforward. The template starts by specifying that it extends the `survey/base.html` template. It then proceeds to define what should be placed in the block `content` defined in `base.html`. The first element is a first-level heading `Welcome to Survey Central`. Then, if the `active_surveys` context variable is not empty, the heading is followed by a paragraph inviting people to take a survey, followed by a list of the active surveys. Each item in the list is specified as a link where the link target value is obtained by calling the Survey's `get_absolute_url` method (which we have not implemented yet). The visible text for each link is set to the `title` value of `Survey`.

A nearly identical paragraph and list is displayed for the `completed_surveys`, if there are any. Finally, the `upcoming_surveys` are handled similarly, except in their case no links are generated. Rather, the survey titles are listed along with the date when each survey will open.

Now, what is the `get_absolute_url` method used to generate the links to the active and completed surveys? This is a standard model method we can implement to provide the URL for a model instance on our site. In addition to using it in our own code, the admin application uses it, if it is implemented by a model, to provide a **View on site** link on the change page for model instances.

Recall that in our `urls.py` file we named the URL for survey details `survey_detail` and that this view takes one argument, `pk`, which is the primary key of the `Survey` instance to display details about. Knowing that, we can implement this `get_absolute_url` method in the `Survey` model:

```
def get_absolute_url(self):
    from django.core.urlresolvers import reverse
    return reverse('survey_detail', args=(self.pk,))
```

This method uses the `reverse` function provided by `django.core.urlresolvers` to construct the actual URL that will map to the URL named `survey_detail` with an argument value of the model instance's primary key value.

Alternatively, we could use the convenient `models.permalink` decorator and avoid having to remember where the `reverse` function needs to be imported from:

```
@models.permalink
def get_absolute_url(self):
    return ('survey_detail', (self.pk,))
```

This is equivalent to the first way of implementing `get_absolute_url`. This way simply hides the details of calling the reverse function, as that is done by the `models.permalink` code.

Now that we have created the home page view and the templates it uses, and implemented all of the model methods called from those templates, we can actually test the view. Ensure that the development server is running (or start it again with `manage.py runserver`), and then from a browser on the same machine, go to `http://localhost:8000/`. This should (assuming it has been less than a week since the `Winning Answers Test` from the last chapter was created) bring up a page that lists that survey as one that can be taken:

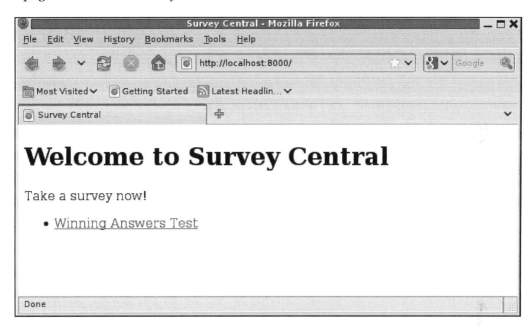

If it has been longer than a week since that survey was created, it should show up under a paragraph that invites you to **See how your opinions compared to those of others!** instead. If it has been more than three weeks, the survey should not show up at all, in which case you may want to go back to the admin application and change its `closes` date so that it appears on the home page.

That **Winning Answers Test** text is a link, which can be followed to verify that the get_absolute_url method for Survey is working, and further that the URL configuration we have set up is valid. Since we still have only the placeholder view implementation of the survey detail view, clicking the **Winning Answers Test** link will bring up a page that looks like this:

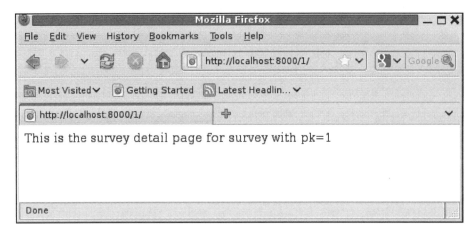

Not overly impressive, perhaps, but it does verify that the various pieces we have in place so far are working.

Of course, since we've only got one Survey in the database, we've only verified one part of the view and template. For a full test, we should also verify that the surveys in all three categories appear properly. In addition, we should verify that surveys in the database that should not appear either because they are too old or too far in the future do not in fact appear on the home page.

We might do all that now by manually adding surveys in the admin application and manually checking the contents of the home page as we make changes. However, what we really want to learn is how to write a test to verify that what we have now is correct and, more importantly, to allow us to verify that it remains correct as we continue to develop the application. Therefore, writing such a test is what we will focus on next.

Testing the survey home page

Before we think about how to write the test itself, let's consider the data the test will need and the best way to get that data into the database for the test. This test is going to be much like the SurveyManagerTest from the previous chapter, since determining correct behavior will depend on the relationship of the current date to dates contained in the test data. Therefore, using a fixture file for this data is not a good idea; it will be better to dynamically add the data in the test's setUp method.

We will begin, then, by writing a setUp method to create an appropriate set of data for testing the home page. Since we have moved on to testing the application's views, let's put it in a new file, survey/tests/view_tests.py. When we create that file, we need to also remember to add an import line for the new file (from view_tests import *) to the __init__.py file in survey/tests, so that the tests in it will be found by the test runner.

Here is a setUp method for our home page test:

```python
import datetime
from django.test import TestCase
from survey.models import Survey

class SurveyHomeTest(TestCase):
    def setUp(self):
        today = datetime.date.today()
        Survey.objects.all().delete()
        d = today - datetime.timedelta(15)
        Survey.objects.create(title="Too Old", opens=d, closes=d)
        d += datetime.timedelta(1)
        Survey.objects.create(title="Completed 1", opens=d, closes=d)
        d = today - datetime.timedelta(1)
        Survey.objects.create(title="Completed 2", opens=d, closes=d)
        Survey.objects.create(title="Active 1", opens=d)
        Survey.objects.create(title="Active 2", opens=today)
        d = today + datetime.timedelta(1)
        Survey.objects.create(title="Upcoming 1", opens=d)
        d += datetime.timedelta(6)
        Survey.objects.create(title="Upcoming 2", opens=d)
        d += datetime.timedelta(1)
        Survey.objects.create(title="Too Far Out", opens=d)
```

This method starts by stashing today's date in a local variable today. It then deletes all existing Surveys in the database, just in case there are any loaded by initial data fixtures that could interfere with the proper execution of the test methods in this test case. It then creates eight Surveys: three completed, two active, and three upcoming.

The closing dates for the completed surveys are specifically set so as to test the boundaries of the window for what should appear on the home page. The oldest closing date is set just one day too far in the past (15 days) to be listed on the home page. The other two are set to the extreme edges of the window for what should appear as completed on the home page. The opens date for upcoming surveys is set similarly to test the limits of that window. One upcoming survey opens just one day too far in the future to appear on the home page while the other two open at the limits of the window for what should be shown as upcoming on the home page. Finally, there are two active surveys, one that opened yesterday and one that opened today, each with a default closing date seven days later, so both still open.

Now that we have a `setUp` routine to create test data, how do we write a test to check the contents of the home page? Django provides a class, `django.test.Client`, to help out here. An instance of this `Client` class acts like a web browser and can be used to request pages and examine the responses returned. Each `django.test.TestCase` class is automatically assigned a `Client` class instance that can be accessed using `self.client`.

To see how to use the test `Client`, let's examine the beginnings of a test for the survey application home page:

```
def testHome(self):
    from django.core.urlresolvers import reverse
    response = self.client.get(reverse('survey_home'))
    self.assertEqual(response.status_code, 200)
```

Here we have defined a `testHome` method within the `SurveyHomeTest`. This method uses the `get` method of the test's `client` class instance to retrieve the survey home page (again using `reverse` to determine the correct URL so as to ensure all URL configuration information is isolated in `urls.py`). The return value of `get` is the `django.http.HttpResponse` object returned by the view called to serve the requested page, annotated with some additional information to facilitate testing. The last line of the test verifies that the request was served successfully by ensuring that the `status_code` attribute of the returned response is `200` (HTTP OK).

Note that the `get` method supplied by the test `Client` supports more than the single URL parameter we are passing here. In addition, it supports two keyword arguments, `data` and `follow`, which default to an empty dictionary and `False` respectively. Finally, any number of `extra` keyword arguments may also be supplied.

The `data` dictionary, if non-empty, is used to construct a query string for the request. For example, consider a `get` method such as this:

```
response = self.client.get('/survey/',
                           data={'pk': 4, 'type': 'results'})
```

The URL created for processing this request would be `/survey/?pk=4&type=results`.

Note you can also include a query string in the URL path passed to `get`. So an equivalent call would be:

```
response = self.client.get('/survey/?pk=4&type=results')
```

If both a `data` dictionary and a query string in the URL path are provided, the `data` dictionary is used for processing the request and the query string in the URL path is ignored.

The `follow` argument to `get` can be set to `True` in order to instruct the test client to follow redirects in the response. If it does so, a `redirect_chain` attribute will be set on the returned response. This attribute will be a list describing the intermediate URLs visited before the end of the redirect chain. Each element in the list will be a tuple containing the intermediate URL path and the status code that prompted it to be retrieved.

Finally, any `extra` keyword arguments can be used to set arbitrary HTTP header values in the request. For example:

```
response = self.client.get('/', HTTP_USER_AGENT='Tester')
```

This call will set the `HTTP_USER_AGENT` header in the request to `Tester`.

Returning to our own test, which supplies only the URL path argument, we can run it now with `manage.py test survey.SurveyHomeTest` and verify that so far everything looks good. We can retrieve the home page and the response comes back with a successful status code. But what about testing the contents of the page? We'd like to make sure that the various surveys that should appear are appearing, and further that the two surveys in the database that should not appear on the page are not listed.

The actual page content returned is stored in the `content` attribute of the response. We can examine this directly, but the Django `TestCase` class also provides two methods to check whether or not certain text appears in the response. These methods are named `assertContains` and `assertNotContains`.

To use the `assertContains` method we pass in the `response` and the text we are looking for. We can also optionally specify a `count` of the number of times that text should appear. If we specify `count`, the text must appear exactly that many times in the response. If we do not specify `count`, `assertContains` simply checks that the text appears at least once. Finally, we may specify the `status_code` that the response should have. If we do not specify this, then `assertContains` verifies that the status code is 200.

The `assertNotContains` method takes the same arguments as `assertContains` with the exception of `count`. It verifies that the passed text does not appear in the response content.

We can use these two methods to verify that the home page contains two instances each of `Completed`, `Active`, and `Upcoming`, and that it does not contain either `Too Old` or `Too Far Out`. Furthermore, since these methods check the status code, we can remove that check from our own test code. Thus the test method becomes:

```
def testHome(self):
    from django.core.urlresolvers import reverse
    response = self.client.get(reverse('survey_home'))
    self.assertContains(response, "Completed", count=2)
    self.assertContains(response, "Active", count=2)
    self.assertContains(response, "Upcoming", count=2)
    self.assertNotContains(response, "Too Old")
    self.assertNotContains(response, "Too Far Out")
```

If we try running this version, we will see that it works. However, it is not as specific as we might like it to be. Namely, it does not verify that the listed surveys are appearing in the right places on the page. This test as it is right now would pass with all of the listed surveys appearing under the paragraph **Take a survey now!**, for example. How can we verify that each is appearing in the appropriate list?

One approach would be to manually examine `response.content`, find where each of the expected strings is located, and ensure that they all appear in the expected order. However, that would make the test very dependent on the exact layout of the page. We might in the future decide to reorder the presentation of the lists and this test could then break, even though each survey was still being listed in the correct category.

What we really want to do is verify that the surveys are contained in the appropriate context variables passed to the template. We can in fact test this, since the response returned by `client.get` is annotated with the context used to render the template. Thus, we can check the completed survey list, for example, like so:

```
completed = response.context['completed_surveys']
self.assertEqual(len(completed), 2)
for survey in completed:
    self.failUnless(survey.title.startswith("Completed"))
```

This code retrieves the `completed_surveys` context variable from the response context, verifies it has 2 items in it, and further verifies that each of the items has a `title` that starts with the string `Completed`. If we run that code, we'll see it works for checking the completed surveys. We can then either duplicate that block two more times and tweak it appropriately to check the active and upcoming surveys, or we can get a little fancier and write something more like this:

```
context_vars = ['completed_surveys', 'active_surveys',
                'upcoming_surveys']
title_starts = ['Completed', 'Active', 'Upcoming']
for context_var, title_start in zip(context_vars,
                                    title_starts):
    surveys = response.context[context_var]
    self.assertEqual(len(surveys), 2)
    for survey in surveys:
        self.failUnless(survey.title.startswith(title_start))
```

Here we have avoided duplicating, essentially, the same block of code three times with just minor differences by constructing a list of things to check and then iterating through that list. Thus, we only have the code block appearing once, but it is looped through three times, once for each of the context variables we want to check. This is a common technique used to avoid duplicating code that is almost identical multiple times.

Note that when this sort of technique is used in tests, though, it is a good idea to take the effort to include specific messages in the assertion checks. In the original version of the code, which tested the completed list directly, if there was an error such as too many surveys in that list, a test failure would produce a reasonably descriptive error report:

```
FAIL: testHome (survey.tests.view_tests.SurveyHomeTest)
-----------------------------------------------------------------
Traceback (most recent call last):
  File "/dj_projects/marketr/survey/tests/view_tests.py", line 29, in
testHome
```

```
    self.assertEqual(len(completed), 2)
AssertionError: 3 != 2
```

There the code that is failing includes the string **completed** so it is clear which list is having a problem. With a more generalized version of the code, this report becomes much less helpful:

```
FAIL: testHome (survey.tests.view_tests.SurveyHomeTest)
```

```
Traceback (most recent call last):
  File "/dj_projects/marketr/survey/tests/view_tests.py", line 35, in
testHome
    self.assertEqual(len(surveys), 2)
AssertionError: 3 != 2
```

The poor programmer encountering that failure report would have no way of knowing which of the three lists had too many items. By providing a specific error message with the assertion, however, this can be made clear. So a better version of the full test method with descriptive errors would be:

```
def testHome(self):
    from django.core.urlresolvers import reverse
    response = self.client.get(reverse('survey_home'))
    self.assertNotContains(response, "Too Old")
    self.assertNotContains(response, "Too Far Out")
    context_vars = ['completed_surveys', 'active_surveys',
                    'upcoming_surveys']
    title_starts = ['Completed', 'Active', 'Upcoming']
    for context_var, title_start in zip(context_vars,
                                        title_starts):
        surveys = response.context[context_var]
        self.assertEqual(len(surveys), 2,
            "Expected 2 %s, found %d instead" %
            (context_var, len(surveys)))
        for survey in surveys:
            self.failUnless(survey.title.startswith(title_start),
                "%s title %s does not start with %s" %
                (context_var, survey.title, title_start))
```

Now if there is a failure during the checks in the generalized code, the error message is specific enough to indicate where the problem is:

```
FAIL: testHome (survey.tests.view_tests.SurveyHomeTest)

----------------------------------------------------------------------

Traceback (most recent call last):
  File "/dj_projects/marketr/survey/tests/view_tests.py", line 36, in
testHome
    (context_var, len(surveys)))
AssertionError: Expected 2 completed_surveys, found 3 instead


----------------------------------------------------------------------
```

We now have a reasonably complete test for our survey home page, or at least as much of it as we have implemented so far. It is time to turn our attention to the survey detail pages, which we will cover next.

Creating the survey detail pages

The second URL mapping we added to our project's URL configuration was for the survey detail pages. Implementing this view is a little more complicated than the home page view since quite different data will need to be presented depending on the state of the requested survey. If the survey is completed, we need to display the results. If the survey is active, we need to display a form allowing the user to participate in the survey. If the survey is upcoming, we don't want the survey to be visible at all.

To do all of that at once, without testing along the way to verify we are headed in the right direction, would be asking for trouble. It's best to break the task down into smaller pieces and test as we go. We'll take the first step in that direction in the following sections.

Refining the survey detail view

The first thing to do is to replace the simple placeholder view for the survey detail page with a view that determines the requested survey's state and routes the request appropriately. For example:

```
import datetime
from django.shortcuts import render_to_response, get_object_or_404
from django.http import Http404
from survey.models import Survey
```

```
def survey_detail(request, pk):
    survey = get_object_or_404(Survey, pk=pk)
    today = datetime.date.today()
    if survey.closes < today:
        return display_completed_survey(request, survey)
    elif survey.opens > today:
        raise Http404
    else:
        return display_active_survey(request, survey)
```

This `survey_detail` view uses the `get_object_or_404` shortcut to retrieve the requested `Survey` from the database. The shortcut will automatically raise an `Http404` exception if the requested survey does not exist, so the following code does not have to account for that case. The view then checks the `closes` date on the returned `Survey` instance. If it closed before today, the request is sent on to a function named `display_completed_survey`. Otherwise, if the survey has not yet opened, an `Http404` exception is raised. Finally, if neither of those conditions hold, the survey must be active so the request is routed to a function named `display_active_survey`.

To start out with, we will implement the two new functions very simply. They will not do any of the real work required for their case, but they will each use a different template when rendering their response:

```
def display_completed_survey(request, survey):
    return render_to_response('survey/completed_survey.html',
                              {'survey': survey})

def display_active_survey(request, survey):
    return render_to_response('survey/active_survey.html',
                              {'survey': survey})
```

With just that much code, we can proceed to test whether surveys in different states are being routed correctly. First though, we need to create the two new templates that the view code has introduced.

Templates for the survey detail pages

The two new templates are named survey/completed_survey.html and survey/active_survey.html. Create them under the survey/templates directory. To start out with, they can be very simple. For example, completed_survey.html may be:

```
{% extends "survey/base.html" %}
{% block content %}
<h1>Survey results for {{ survey.title }}</h1>
{% endblock content %}
```

Similarly, `active_survey.html` could be:

```
{% extends "survey/base.html" %}
{% block content %}
<h1>Survey questions for {{ survey.title }}</h1>
{% endblock content %}
```

Each of these extends the `survey/base.html` template and provides minimal but descriptive content for the `content` block. In each case, all that will be displayed is a first-level header identifying the survey by title and whether the page is showing results or questions.

Basic testing of the survey detail pages

Now consider how we can test whether the routing code in `survey_detail` is working correctly. Again, we are going to need test data containing at least one survey in each of the three states. We have that with the test data we created in the `setUp` method of `SurveyHomeTest`. However, adding methods to the home page test case that actually tests survey detail page views would be confusing. Duplicating very similar `setUp` code is also not very attractive.

Fortunately, we do not need to do either. What we can do is move the existing `setUp` code into a more general test case, say `SurveyTest`, and then base both `SurveyHomeTest` and our new `SurveyDetailTest` on this new `SurveyTest`. In this way, both the home page test and the detail page test will have the same data created in the database by the base `SurveyTest` `setUp` method. Furthermore, any additional tests that need similar data could also inherit from `SurveyTest`.

Given we have the test data in place, what can we do to test what we have implemented so far of the detail view? The case of an upcoming survey is easy enough, since it should simply return an HTTP 404 (NOT FOUND) page. Thus, we can start by creating a method for that case in our `SurveyDetailTest`:

```
from django.core.urlresolvers import reverse
class SurveyDetailTest(SurveyTest):
    def testUpcoming(self):
        survey = Survey.objects.get(title='Upcoming 1')
        response = self.client.get(reverse('survey_detail',
                                            args=(survey.pk,)))
        self.assertEqual(response.status_code, 404)
```

The testUpcoming method retrieves one of the upcoming surveys from the database, and uses the test client to request the page containing details on that survey. Again we use reverse to construct the appropriate URL for the details page, passing in the primary key of the survey we are requesting as the single argument in the args tuple. Correct handling of this request is tested by ensuring that the status_code of the response is 404. If we run this test now, we will see:

```
ERROR: testUpcoming (survey.tests.view_tests.SurveyDetailTest)
----------------------------------------------------------------------
Traceback (most recent call last):
  File "/dj_projects/marketr/survey/tests/view_tests.py", line 45, in
testUpcoming
    response = self.client.get(reverse('survey_detail', args=(survey.
pk,)))
  File "/usr/lib/python2.5/site-packages/django/test/client.py", line
281, in get
    response = self.request(**r)
  File "/usr/lib/python2.5/site-packages/django/core/handlers/base.py",
line 119, in get_response
    return callback(request, **param_dict)
  File "/usr/lib/python2.5/site-packages/django/views/defaults.py", line
13, in page_not_found
    t = loader.get_template(template_name) # You need to create a 404.
html template.
  File "/usr/lib/python2.5/site-packages/django/template/loader.py", line
81, in get_template
    source, origin = find_template_source(template_name)
  File "/usr/lib/python2.5/site-packages/django/template/loader.py", line
74, in find_template_source
    raise TemplateDoesNotExist, name
TemplateDoesNotExist: 404.html
```

Oops. In order for the survey_detail view to successfully raise an Http404 and have that result in a "page not found" response, a 404.html template must exist in the project. We have not yet created one, so this test generates an error. To fix this, we can create a simple survey/templates/404.html file containing:

```
{% extends "survey/base.html" %}
{% block content %}
<h1>Page Not Found</h1>
<p>The requested page was not found on this site.</p>
{% endblock content %}
```

At the same time, we should also create a survey/templates/500.html file in order to avoid any similar unhelpful errors in cases where a server error is encountered. A simple 500.html file to use for now would be much like this 404.html file, with the text changed to indicate the problem is a server error, and not a page not found situation.

With the `404.html` template in place, we can attempt to run this test again and this time, it will pass.

What about testing the pages for completed and active surveys? We could write tests that check `response.content` for the header text we have placed in each of their respective templates. However, that text may not remain the same as we continue development—at this point that is just placeholder text. It would be better to verify that the correct templates were used to render each of these responses. The `TestCase` class has a method for that: `assertTemplateUsed`. Thus, we can write tests for these cases that are likely to continue to work properly in the long-run, like so:

```python
def testCompleted(self):
    survey = Survey.objects.get(title='Too Old')
    response = self.client.get(reverse('survey_detail',
                                       args=(survey.pk,)))
    self.assertTemplateUsed(response,
                            'survey/completed_survey.html')


def testActive(self):
    survey = Survey.objects.get(title='Active 1')
    response = self.client.get(reverse('survey_detail',
                                       args=(survey.pk,)))
    self.assertTemplateUsed(response,
                            'survey/active_survey.html')
```

Each of these test methods retrieves a survey from the appropriate category and requests the detail page for that survey. So far, the only test done on the responses is to check that the expected template was used to render the response. Again, we can run these tests now and verify that they pass.

In addition to `assertTemplateUsed`, there is an `assertTemplateNotUsed` method provided by `TestCase`. It takes the same arguments as `assertTempalteUsed`. As you might expect, it verifies that the specified template was not used to render the response.

At this point, we are going to take a break from implementing `survey` application pages. The next unit test topic to cover is how to test pages that accept user input. We don't have any of those in the survey application yet, but the Django admin application does. Thus, the task of testing an admin customization provides a quicker route to learning how to test such pages, since we'll need to write less custom code before developing the test. In addition to this, learning how to test admin customizations is useful in its own right.

Customizing the admin add and change survey pages

We've already seen how the Django admin application provides a convenient way to examine and manipulate data in our database. In the previous chapter, we set up the admin with some simple customizations to allow editing Questions inline with Surveys and Answers inline with Questions. Besides those inline customizations, however, we made no changes to the admin defaults.

One additional change that would be good to make to the admin is to ensure that Survey opens and closes dates are valid. Clearly for this application, it makes no sense to have an opens date that is later than closes, but there is no way for the admin to know that. In this section, we will customize the admin to enforce our application requirement on the relationship between opens and closes. We will also develop a test for this customization.

Developing a custom survey form

The first step in implementing this admin customization is to implement a form for Survey that includes custom validation. For example:

```python
from django import forms
class SurveyForm(forms.ModelForm):
    class Meta:
        model = Survey
    def clean(self):
        opens = self.cleaned_data.get('opens')
        closes = self.cleaned_data.get('closes')
        if opens and closes and opens > closes:
            raise forms.ValidationError("Opens date cannot come, "
                                        "after closes date.")
        return self.cleaned_data
```

This is a standard ModelForm for the Survey model. Since the validation we want to perform involves multiple fields on the form, the best place to put it is in the overall form clean method. The method here retrieves the opens and closes values from the form's cleaned_data dictionary. Then, if they have both been provided, it checks to see if opens is later than closes. If so, a ValidationError is raised, otherwise everything is OK, so the existing cleaned_data dictionary is returned unmodified from clean.

As we are going to be using this form for the admin and do not presently anticipate the need to use it anywhere else, we can put this form definition in the existing survey/admin.py file.

Configuring admin to use the custom form

The next step is to tell the admin to use this form instead of a default `ModelForm` for the `Survey` model. To do this, change the `SurveyAdmin` definition in `survey/admin.py` to be:

```
class SurveyAdmin(admin.ModelAdmin):
    form = SurveyForm
    inlines = [QuestionsInline]
```

By specifying the `form` attribute, we tell the admin to use our custom form for both adding and editing `Survey` instances. We can quickly verify that this works by using the admin to edit our existing `Winning Answers Test` survey and attempting to change its `closes` date to something earlier than `opens`. If we do so, we will see the error reported like this:

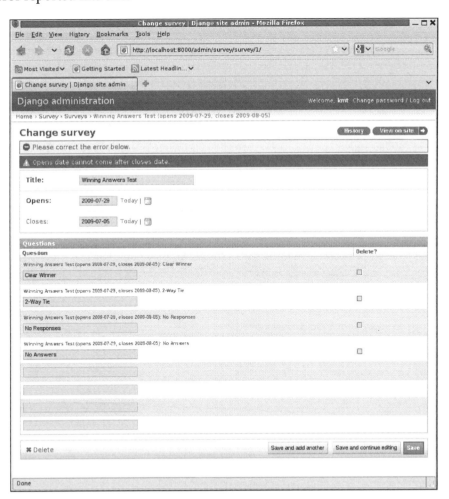

It's good that we have been able to manually validate that our customization is working, but what we really want is an automated test. That will be covered next.

Testing the admin customization

How do we write a test for this admin customization? There are at least a couple of things different about testing the behavior of pressing one of the **Save** buttons on an admin page than what we've tested so far. First, we need to issue an HTTP POST method, not a GET, to make the request. The test `Client` provides a `post` method for this, similar to `get`. For `post`, though, we will need to specify the form data values to be included with the request. We provide these as a dictionary of key / value pairs where the keys are the names of the form fields. Since we know the `ModelForm` the admin is using, we know that the key values here are the names of the model's fields.

We'll start with writing a test for the admin add survey page, since for that case we do not need to have any pre-existing data in the database. Let's create a new file for testing admin views, named `admin_tests.py`, in the tests directory. Also, remember to add `from admin_tests import *` to the `tests/__init__.py` file so that these tests are found when we run `tests`.

An initial attempt to implement a test of the admin application's use of our customized `Survey` form might look like this:

```python
import datetime
from django.test import TestCase
from django.core.urlresolvers import import reverse

class AdminSurveyTest(TestCase):
    def testAddSurveyError(self):
        post_data = {
            'title': u'Time Traveling',
            'opens': datetime.date.today(),
            'closes': datetime.date.today() - datetime.timedelta(1),
        }
        response = self.client.post(
            reverse('admin:survey_survey_add'), post_data)
        self.assertContains(response,
            "Opens date cannot come after closes date.")
```

Here we have a test method, testAddSurveyError, which creates a post_data dictionary with title, opens, and closes values for the Survey ModelForm. We use the test client to post that dictionary to the admin Survey add page for the survey application (using reverse on the documented name for that admin view). We expect that the returned response should contain the error message from our custom ModelForm, since we have specified an opens date that is later than the closes date. We use assertContains to check that the expected error message is found in the response.

Note that as was the case with get, our first test that is using post is only using a subset of the arguments that could be supplied to that method. In addition to the URL path and the data dictionary, post accepts a content_type keyword argument. This argument defaults to a value that results in the client sending mutlipart/form-data. In addition to content_type, post also supports the same follow and extra keyword arguments, with the same defaults and processing behavior, as get.

Does our first attempt at an admin customization test work? Unfortunately, no. If we run it with manage.py test survey.AdminSurveyTest, we will see this failure:

```
FAIL: testAddSurveyError (survey.tests.admin_tests.AdminSurveyTest)
--------------------------------------------------------------------
Traceback (most recent call last):
  File "/dj_projects/marketr/survey/tests/admin_tests.py", line 13, in
testAddSurveyError
    self.assertContains(response, "Opens date cannot come after closes
date.")
  File "/usr/lib/python2.5/site-packages/django/test/testcases.py", line
345, in assertContains
    "Couldn't find '%s' in response" % text)
AssertionError: Couldn't find 'Opens date cannot come after closes date.'
in response


--------------------------------------------------------------------
```

What might be wrong? It's hard to say without seeing what is actually contained in the returned response. Realizing that, we may be tempted to include the text of the response in the error message. However, responses tend to be quite long (as they are generally complete web pages) and including them in test failure output usually adds more noise than anything else. Thus it is usually better to make a temporary change to the test case to print the response, for example, in order to figure out what might be going on.

If we do that in this case, we will see that the returned response begins (after some standard HTML boilerplate):

```
<title>Log in | Django site admin</title>
```

Oh, right, we forgot that the admin requires a logged-in user for access. We did not do anything in our test case to set up and log in a user, so when the test attempts to access an admin page, the admin code simply returns a login page.

Our test, then, will first need to create a user, as the test database is initially empty. That user will need appropriate permissions to access the admin, and must be logged in before attempting to do anything with the admin application. This sort of thing is appropriate for a test setUp routine:

```
import datetime
from django.test import TestCase
from django.contrib.auth.models import User
from django.core.urlresolvers import reverse

class AdminSurveyTest(TestCase):
    def setUp(self):
        self.username = 'survey_admin'
        self.pw = 'pwpwpw'
        self.user = User.objects.create_user(self.username, '',
                                              self.pw)
        self.user.is_staff= True
        self.user.is_superuser = True
        self.user.save()
        self.assertTrue(self.client.login(username=self.username,
                                          password=self.pw),
            "Logging in user %s, pw %s failed." %
                (self.username, self.pw))
```

Here the setUp routine uses the create_user method provided by the standard django.contrib.auth User model to create a user named survey_admin. After creating the user, setUp sets its is_staff and is_superuser attributes to True and saves the user again to the database. This will allow the newly created user to access all pages in the admin application.

Finally, setUp attempts to log the new user in using the test Client login method. This method will return True if it is successful. Here, setUp asserts that login does return True. If it does not, the assertion will provide a specific indication of where things went wrong. This should be more helpful than simply continuing the test if the login call fails.

The `Client` `login` method has a companion method, `logout`. We should use it in a `tearDown` method after we have used `login` in `setUp`:

```
def tearDown(self):
    self.client.logout()
```

Now does our test work? No, but it does get farther. This time the error report is:

```
ERROR: testAddSurveyError (survey.tests.admin_tests.AdminSurveyTest)
--------------------------------------------------------------------
Traceback (most recent call last):
  File "/dj_projects/marketr/survey/tests/admin_tests.py", line 26, in
testAddSurveyError
    response = self.client.post(reverse('admin:survey_survey_add'), post_
data)
  File "/usr/lib/python2.5/site-packages/django/test/client.py", line
313, in post
    response = self.request(**r)
  File "/usr/lib/python2.5/site-packages/django/core/handlers/base.py",
line 92, in get_response
    response = callback(request, *callback_args, **callback_kwargs)
  File "/usr/lib/python2.5/site-packages/django/contrib/admin/options.
py", line 226, in wrapper
    return self.admin_site.admin_view(view)(*args, **kwargs)
  File "/usr/lib/python2.5/site-packages/django/views/decorators/cache.
py", line 44, in _wrapped_view_func
    response = view_func(request, *args, **kwargs)
  File "/usr/lib/python2.5/site-packages/django/contrib/admin/sites.py",
line 186, in inner
    return view(request, *args, **kwargs)
  File "/usr/lib/python2.5/site-packages/django/db/transaction.py", line
240, in _commit_on_success
    res = func(*args, **kw)
  File "/usr/lib/python2.5/site-packages/django/contrib/admin/options.
py", line 731, in add_view
    prefix=prefix)
  File "/usr/lib/python2.5/site-packages/django/forms/models.py", line
724, in __init__
    queryset=qs)
  File "/usr/lib/python2.5/site-packages/django/forms/models.py", line
459, in __init__
    super(BaseModelFormSet, self).__init__(**defaults)
  File "/usr/lib/python2.5/site-packages/django/forms/formsets.py", line
44, in __init__
```

```
    self._construct_forms()
  File "/usr/lib/python2.5/site-packages/django/forms/formsets.py", line
87, in _construct_forms
    for i in xrange(self.total_form_count()):
  File "/usr/lib/python2.5/site-packages/django/forms/models.py", line
734, in total_form_count
    return super(BaseInlineFormSet, self).total_form_count()
  File "/usr/lib/python2.5/site-packages/django/forms/formsets.py", line
66, in total_form_count
    return self.management_form.cleaned_data[TOTAL_FORM_COUNT]
  File "/usr/lib/python2.5/site-packages/django/forms/formsets.py", line
54, in _management_form
    raise ValidationError('ManagementForm data is missing or has been
tampered with')
ValidationError: [u'ManagementForm data is missing or has been tampered
with']
```

That may be a little confusing at first, but searching the Django documentation for **ManagementForm** quickly shows that it is something required when formsets are being used. Since, as part of our admin customization, we specified that Questions appear inline on a Survey page, the admin page for Survey contains a formset for Questions. However, we did not provide the required ManagementForm values in our post_data dictionary. The two values required are TOTAL_FORMS and INITIAL_FORMS for the question_set. Since we do not want to test any of the admin handling of the inlines here, we can just set these values to 0 in our data dictionary:

```
def testAddSurveyError(self):
    post_data = {
        'title': u'Time Traveling',
        'opens': datetime.date.today(),
        'closes': datetime.date.today() - datetime.timedelta(1),
        'question_set-TOTAL_FORMS': u'0',
        'question_set-INITIAL_FORMS': u'0',
    }
    response = self.client.post(
        reverse('admin:survey_survey_add'), post_data)
    self.assertContains(response,
        "Opens date cannot come after closes date.")
```

Now does this test work? Yes, if we run manage.py test survey.
AdminSurveyTest.testAddSurveyError we will see that the test runs successfully.

Note that `TestCase` provides a more specific assertion than `assertContains` to check for form errors, named `assertFormError`. The parameters to `assertFormError` are the response, the name of the form in the template context, the name of the field to check for errors (or `None` if the error is a non-field error), and the error string (or a list of error strings) to check for. However, it is not possible to use `assertFormError` when testing admin pages because the admin does not provide the form directly in the context. Instead, the context contains a wrapper object that contains the actual form. Thus, we cannot change this particular test to use the more specific `assertFormError` method.

Are we done testing our admin customization? Almost. Since the same form is used for both add and change actions in admin, it is not necessary to test the change page as well. However, it would be good to add a test that includes valid data and ensure that nothing has been broken for that case.

It is easy enough to add a test method that builds a data dictionary containing valid data and posts that to the admin add view. But what should it test for in response? The admin code does not return a simple `200 OK` response after successfully completing some action requested by the POST. Rather, it redirects to a different page, so that an attempt to reload the page resulting from the POST request does not result in another attempt to POST the same data. In the case of adding an object, the admin will redirect to the change list page for the added model. `TestCase` provides an `assertRedirects` method to test this sort of behavior. We can use this method like so:

```
def testAddSurveyOK(self):
    post_data = {
        'title': u'Time Traveling',
        'opens': datetime.date.today(),
        'closes': datetime.date.today(),
        'question_set-TOTAL_FORMS': u'0',
        'question_set-INITIAL_FORMS': u'0',
    }
    response = self.client.post(
        reverse('admin:survey_survey_add'), post_data)
    self.assertRedirects(response,
        reverse('admin:survey_survey_changelist'))
```

This `testAddSurveyOK` method sets up a valid data dictionary for a `Survey`, specifying `opens` and `closes` dates that are the same. It then posts that data to the admin add survey page, and saves the response. Finally, it asserts that the response should redirect to the admin survey application change list page for the `Survey` model. Two additional, optional parameters to `assertRedirects` are `status_code` and `target_status_code`. These default to `302` and `200` respectively, so we did not need to specify them here since those are the codes we expect in this case.

Additional test support

The tests that we have developed in this chapter provide a reasonably broad overview of how to use the test support provided by Django's TestCase and test Client class. However, the examples neither cover every detail of what these classes provide, nor every detail of the additional data available in the annotated response objects returned by the Client. In this section, we briefly mention some additional features of TestCase, Client, and the additional data available with response objects. We will not develop examples that use all of these features; they are mentioned here so that if you encounter a need for this type of support, you will know that it exists. The Django documentation provides full details on all of these topics.

Supporting additional HTTP methods

Our example tests only needed to use the HTTP GET and POST methods. The test Client class also provides methods to issue HTTP HEAD, OPTIONS, PUT, and DELETE requests. These methods are named head, options, put, and delete respectively. Each supports the same follow and extra arguments as get and post. In addition, put supports the same content_type argument as post.

Maintaining persistent state

The test Client maintains two attributes that maintain persistent state across request / response cycles: cookies and session. The cookies attribute is a Python SimpleCookie object containing any cookies that have been received with responses. The session attribute is a dictionary-like object containing session data.

E-mail services

Some views in a web application may create and send mail. When testing, we do not want such mail to actually be sent, but it is good to be able to verify that the code being tested generated and attempted to send the mail. The TestCase class supports this by replacing the standard Python SMTPConnection class (in the context of the running tests only) with a custom class that does not send the mail, but rather stores it in django.core.mail.outbox. Thus, test code can check the contents of this outbox in order to verify whether the code being tested attempted to send the expected mail.

Providing test-specific URL configuration

In the examples developed in this chapter, we were careful to make the tests independent of the specifics of the URL configuration in use by always using named URLs and using `reverse` to map these symbolic names back to URL path values. This is a good technique, but it may not be sufficient in all circumstances.

Consider that you are developing a reusable application with optional views that a particular installation of the application may or may not choose to deploy. For testing such an application, you cannot rely on the optional views actually being contained in the project's URL configuration, but you would still like to be able to include tests for them. To support this, the `TestCase` class allows an instance to set a `urls` attribute. If this attribute is set, the `TestCase` will use the URL configuration contained in the specified module instead of the project's URL configuration.

Response context and template information

In testing the survey home page, we examined values in the response `context` attribute using simple dictionary-style access. For example:

```
completed = response.context['completed_surveys']
```

While this works, it glosses over some complexity involved in considering the context used to render a response. Recall that we set up our project to have a two-level hierarchy of templates. The `base.html` template is extended by each of the individual page templates. Each template used to render a response has its own associated context, so the `context` attribute of a response is not a simple dictionary, but rather a list of the contexts used for rendering each of the templates. In fact, it is something called `django.test.utils.ContextList`, which contains a number of `django.template.context.Context` objects.

This `ContextList` object supports dictionary-style access for simplicity, and searches for the specified key in each of the contexts it contains. We made use of that simple style of access in the examples earlier in this chapter. However, if you ever have the need to get more specific about which template context you want to check something in, the response `context` attribute supports that as well, as you can also index by number into a `ContextList` and retrieve the full context associated with a particular template.

In addition, the responses returned by the test `Client` have a `template` attribute that is a list of the templates used to render the response. We did not need to use this attribute directly because we used the `assertTemplateUsed` method provided by `TestCase`.

Testing transactional behavior

The final topic to discuss in this chapter involves testing transactional behavior. If it is ever necessary to do this, there is an alternative test case class, `TransactionTestCase`, that should be used instead of `TestCase`.

What does **testing transactional behavior** mean? Suppose you have a view that makes a series of database updates, all within a single database transaction. Further, suppose you need to test a case where at least one of the updates works, but is followed by a failure that should result in the entire set of updates being rolled back instead of committed. To test this sort of behavior, you might try to verify in the test code that one of the updates that initially worked is not visible in the database when the response is received. To successfully run this sort of test code, you will need to use `TransactionTestCase` instead of `TestCase`.

The reason for this is that `TestCase` internally uses transaction rollback to reset the database to a clean state in between calling test methods. In order for this rollback approach of cleaning up between test methods to work, the code under test must not be allowed to issue any database commit or rollback operations itself. Thus, `TestCase` intercepts any such calls and simply returns without actually forwarding them on to the database. Your test code, then, will be unable to verify that updates which should have been rolled back were rolled back, since they will not have been when running under `TestCase`.

`TransactionTestCase` does not use rollback between test methods to reset the database. Rather it truncates and re-creates all the tables. This is much slower than the rollback method, but it does allow test code to verify that any database transaction behavior expected from the code under test was performed successfully.

Summary

We have now come to the end of discussing Django's unit test extensions to support testing web applications. In this chapter, we:

- Learned how to organize unit tests into separate files instead of placing everything into a single tests.py file

- Began to develop views for the survey application, and learned how to use Django's unit test extensions to test these views

- Saw how to customize the admin interface by providing custom validation for one of our models, and learned how to test that admin customization

- Briefly discussed some unit test extensions provided by Django that we did not encounter in any of our example tests

- Learned when it might be necessary to use `TransactionTestCase` instead of `TestCase` for a test

While we have covered a lot of ground in learning how to test a Django application, there are many aspects to testing a web application that we have not even touched on yet. Some of these are more appropriately tested using tools other than Django itself. The next chapter will explore some of these additional web application testing requirements and show how external tools can be integrated with Django's testing support in order to meet these requirements.

5
Filling in the Blanks: Integrating Django and Other Test Tools

Previous chapters have discussed the built-in application test support that comes with Django 1.1. We first learned how to use doctests to test the building blocks of our application, and then covered the basics of unit tests. In addition, we saw how functions provided by `django.test.TestCase` and `django.test.Client` aid in testing Django applications. Through examples, we learned how to use these functions to test more complete pieces of our application, such as the contents of pages it serves and its form handling behavior.

Django alone, however, does not provide everything one might want for test support. Django is, after all, a web application framework, not a test framework. It doesn't, for example, provide any test coverage information, which is essential for developing comprehensive test suites, nor does it provide any support for testing client-side behavior, since Django is purely a server-side framework. Other tools exist that fill in these gaps, but often it is desirable to integrate these other tools with Django rather than using several entirely different tool sets to build a full application test suite.

In some cases even when Django does support a function, some other tool may be preferred. For example, if you already have experience with a Python test framework such as `nose`, which provides a very flexible test discovery mechanism and a powerful test plugin architecture, you may find Django's test runner rather limiting. Similarly, if you are familiar with the `twill` web testing tool, you may find using Django's test `Client` cumbersome for testing form behavior in comparison with `twill`.

In this chapter, we will investigate integration of Django with other testing tools. Integration can sometimes be accomplished through the use of standard Python unit test extension mechanisms, but sometimes more is required. Both situations will be covered in this chapter. Specifically, we will:

- Discuss the issues involved in integration, and learn about the hooks Django provides for integrating other tools into its test structure.

- Look into answering the question: How much of our code is being executed by our tests? We will see how we can answer this question both without making any changes to our Django test setup and by utilizing the hooks discussed earlier.

- Explore the `twill` tool, and see how to use it instead of the Django test `Client` in our Django application tests. For this integration, we do not need to use any Django hooks for integration, we simply need to use Python's unit test hooks for test set up and tear down.

Problems of integration

Why is integration of Django testing with other tools even an issue? Consider the case of wanting to use the `nose` test framework. It provides its own command, `nosetests`, to find and run tests in a project tree. However, attempting to run `nosetests`, instead of `manage.py test`, in a Django project tree quickly reveals a problem:

```
kmt@lbox:/dj_projects/marketr$ nosetests
E
======================================================================
ERROR: Failure: ImportError (Settings cannot be imported, because
environment variable DJANGO_SETTINGS_MODULE is undefined.)
----------------------------------------------------------------------
Traceback (most recent call last):
  File "/usr/lib/python2.5/site-packages/nose-0.11.1-py2.5.egg/nose/
loader.py", line 379, in loadTestsFromName
    addr.filename, addr.module)
  File "/usr/lib/python2.5/site-packages/nose-0.11.1-py2.5.egg/nose/
importer.py", line 39, in importFromPath
    return self.importFromDir(dir_path, fqname)
  File "/usr/lib/python2.5/site-packages/nose-0.11.1-py2.5.egg/nose/
importer.py", line 86, in importFromDir
    mod = load_module(part_fqname, fh, filename, desc)
```

```
    File "/dj_projects/marketr/survey/tests/__init__.py", line 1, in
<module>
    from model_tests import *
    File "/dj_projects/marketr/survey/tests/model_tests.py", line 2, in
<module>
    from django.test import TestCase
    File "/usr/lib/python2.5/site-packages/django/test/__init__.py", line
5, in <module>
    from django.test.client import Client
    File "/usr/lib/python2.5/site-packages/django/test/client.py", line 24,
in <module>
    from django.db import transaction, close_connection
    File "/usr/lib/python2.5/site-packages/django/db/__init__.py", line 10,
in <module>
    if not settings.DATABASE_ENGINE:
    File "/usr/lib/python2.5/site-packages/django/utils/functional.py",
line 269, in __getattr__
    self._setup()
    File "/usr/lib/python2.5/site-packages/django/conf/__init__.py", line
38, in _setup
    raise ImportError("Settings cannot be imported, because environment
variable %s is undefined." % ENVIRONMENT_VARIABLE)
ImportError: Settings cannot be imported, because environment variable
DJANGO_SETTINGS_MODULE is undefined.


----------------------------------------------------------------------

Ran 1 test in 0.007s


FAILED (errors=1)
```

The problem here is that some environmental setup done by manage.py test is missing. Specifically, setting up the environment so that the appropriate settings are found when Django code is called, hasn't been done. This particular error could be fixed by setting the DJANGO_SETTINGS_MODULE environment variable before running nosetests, but nosetests would not get much farther, since there is more that is missing.

The next problem that would be encountered would result from tests that need to use the database. Creating the test database is done by support code called by `manage.py test` before any of the tests are run. The `nosetests` command knows nothing about the need for a test database, so when run under `nosetests`, Django test cases that require a database will fail since the database won't exist. This problem cannot be solved by simply setting an environment variable before running `nosetests`.

There are two approaches that can be taken to address integration issues like these. First, if the other tool provides hooks for adding functionality, they can be used to do things such as setting up the environment and creating the test database before the tests are run. This approach integrates Django tests into the other tool. Alternatively, hooks provided by Django can be used to integrate the other tool into Django testing.

The first option is outside the scope of this book, so it won't be discussed in any detail. However, for the particular case of `nose`, its plugin architecture certainly supports adding the necessary function to get Django tests running under `nose`. There are existing nose plugins that can be used to allow Django application tests to run successfully when called from `nosetests`. If this is an approach you want to take for your own testing, you probably want to search the web for existing solutions before building your own `nose` plugin to accomplish this.

The second option is what we will focus on in this section: the hooks that Django provides to allow for pulling other functions in to the normal path of Django testing. There are two hooks that may be used here. First, Django allows specification of an alternative test runner. Details of specifying this, the responsibilities of the test runner, and the interface it must support will be described first. Second, Django allows applications to provide entirely new management commands. Thus, it is possible to augment `manage.py test` with another command, which might support different options, and does whatever is necessary to integrate another tool into the testing path. Details on doing this will also be discussed.

Specifying an alternative test runner

Django uses the `TEST_RUNNER` setting to decide what code to call in order to run tests. By default, the value of `TEST_RUNNER` is `'django.test.simple.run_tests'`. We can look at the declaration and docstring for that routine to see what interface it must support:

```
def run_tests(test_labels, verbosity=1, interactive=True,
              extra_tests=[]):
    """
    Run the unit tests for all the test labels in the provided list.
    Labels must be of the form:
```

```
        - app.TestClass.test_method
            Run a single specific test method
        - app.TestClass
            Run all the test methods in a given class
        - app
            Search for doctests and unittests in the named application.


    When looking for tests, the test runner will look in the models
    and tests modules for the application.


    A list of 'extra' tests may also be provided; these tests
    will be added to the test suite.


    Returns the number of tests that failed.
    """
```

The test_labels, verbosity, and interactive arguments are clearly going to come straight from the manage.py test command line. The extra_tests argument is a bit mysterious, as there is no supported manage.py test argument that might correspond to that. In fact, when called from manage.py test, extra_tests will never be specified. This argument is used by the runtests.py program that Django uses to run its own test suite. Unless you are going to write a test runner that will be used to run Django's own tests, you probably don't need to worry about extra_tests. However, a custom runner should implement the defined behavior of including extra_tests among those run.

What exactly does a test runner need to do? This question is most easily answered by looking at the existing django.test.simple.run_tests code and seeing what it does. Briefly, without going through the routine line by line, it:

- Sets up the test environment by calling django.test.utils.setup_test_environment. This is a documented method that a custom test runner should call as well. It does things to ensure, for example, that the responses generated by the test client have the context and templates attributes mentioned in the previous chapter.

- Sets DEBUG to False.

- Builds a unittest.TestSuite containing all of the tests discovered under the specified test_labels. Django's simple test runner searches only in the models and tests modules for tests.

- Creates the test database by calling connection.creation.create_test_db. This is another routine that is documented in the Django test documentation for use by alternative test runners.

- Runs the tests.
- Destroys the test database by calling `connection.creation.destroy_test_db`.
- Cleans up the test environment by calling `django.test.utils.teardown_test_environment`.
- Returns the sum of the test failures and errors.

> Note that Django 1.2 adds support for a class-based approach to specifying an alternative test runner. While Django 1.2 continues to support the function-based approach used earlier and described here, using function-based alternative test runners will be deprecated in the future. The class-based approach simplifies the task of making a small change to the test running behavior. Instead of needing to re-implement (and often largely duplicate) the existing `django.tests.simple.run_tests` function, you can implement an alternative test runner class that inherits from the default class and simply overrides whatever specific methods are necessary to accomplish the desired alternative behavior.

It is reasonably straightforward, then, to write a test runner. However, in replacing just the test runner, we are limited by the arguments and options supported by the `manage.py test` command. If our runner supports some option that isn't supported by `manage.py test`, there is no obvious way to get that option passed through from the command line to our test runner. Instead, `manage.py test` will reject any option it doesn't know about.

There is a way to get around this. Django uses the Python `optparse` module to parse options from command lines. Placing a bare - or -- on the command line causes `optparse` to halt processing the command line, so options specified after a bare - or --won't be seen by the regular Django code doing the parsing. They will still be accessible to our test runner in `sys.argv`, though, so they could be retrieved and passed on to whatever tool we are integrating with.

This method works, but the existence of such options will be well-hidden from users, since the standard Django help for the `test` command knows nothing of them. By using this technique, we extend the interface supported by `manage.py test` without having any way to obviously publish the extensions we have made, as part of the built-in help for the `test` command.

Thus, a better alternative to specifying a custom test runner may be to supply an entirely new management command. When creating a new command, we can define it to take whatever options we like, and supply the help text that should be displayed for each new option when the user requests help for the command. This approach is discussed next.

Creating a new management command

Providing a new management command is simple. Django looks for management commands in a `management.commands` package in each installed application's directory. Any Python module found in an installed application's `management.commands` package is automatically available to specify as a command to `manage.py`.

So, to create a custom test command, say `survey_test`, for our survey application, we create a `management` subdirectory under survey, and a `commands` directory under `management`. We put `__init__.py` files in both of those directories so that Python will recognize them as modules. Then, we put the implementation for the `survey_test` command in a file named `survey_test.py`.

What would need to go in `survey_test.py`? Documentation on implementing management commands is scant as of Django 1.1. All it states is that the file must define a class named `Command` that extends `django.core.management.base.BaseCommand`. Beyond that, it recommends consulting some of the existing management commands to see what to do. Since we are looking to provide an enhanced test command, the easiest thing to do is probably copy the implementation of the `test` command (found in `django/core/management/commands/test.py`) to our `survey_test.py` file.

Looking at that file, we see that a management command implementation contains two main parts. First, after the necessary imports and class declaration, some attributes are defined for the class. These control things such as what options it supports and what help should be displayed for the command:

```python
from django.core.management.base import BaseCommand
from optparse import make_option
import sys

class Command(BaseCommand):
    option_list = BaseCommand.option_list + (
        make_option('--noinput', action='store_false',
            dest='interactive', default=True,
            help='Tells Django to NOT prompt the user for '
                'input of any kind.'),
    )
    help = 'Runs the test suite for the specified applications, or '\
        'the entire site if no apps are specified.'
    args = '[appname ...]'

    requires_model_validation = False
```

Note that while `BaseCommand` is not documented in the official Django 1.1 documentation, it does have an extensive docstring, so the exact purpose of each of these attributes (`option_list`, `help`, `args`, `requires_model_validation`) can be found by consulting the source or using the Python shell's help function. Even without checking the docstring, we can see that Python's standard `optparse` module is used to build the option string, so extending `option_list` to include additional arguments is straightforward. For example, if we wanted to add a `--cover` option to turn on generation of test coverage data, we could change the `option_list` specification to be:

```
option_list = BaseCommand.option_list + (
    make_option('--noinput', action='store_false',
        dest='interactive', default=True,
        help='Tells Django to NOT prompt the user for '
            'input of any kind.'),
    make_option('--cover', action='store_true',
        dest='coverage', default=False,
        help='Tells Django to generate test coverage data.'),
)
```

Here we have added support for specifying `--cover` on the command line. If specified, it will cause the value of the `coverage` option to be `True`. If not specified, this new option will default to `False`. Along with adding support for the option, we have the ability to add help text for it.

The declaration section of the `Command` implementation is followed by a `handle` function definition. This is the code that will be called to implement our `survey_test` command. The existing code from the `test` command is:

```
def handle(self, *test_labels, **options):
    from django.conf import settings
    from django.test.utils import get_runner

    verbosity = int(options.get('verbosity', 1))
    interactive = options.get('interactive', True)
    test_runner = get_runner(settings)

    failures = test_runner(test_labels, verbosity=verbosity,
                            interactive=interactive)
    if failures:
        sys.exit(failures)
```

As you can see, this performs a very straightforward retrieval of passed options, uses a utility function to find the correct test runner to call, and simply calls the runner with the passed options. When the runner returns, if there were any failures, the program exits with a system exit code set to the number of failures.

We can replace the last four lines with code that retrieves our new option and prints out whether it has been specified:

```
coverage = options.get('coverage', False)
print 'Here we do our own thing instead of calling the test '\
    'runner.'
if coverage:
    print 'Our new cover option HAS been specified.'
else:
    print 'Our new cover option HAS NOT been specified.'
```

Now, we can try running our `survey_test` command to verify that it is found and can accept our new option:

```
kmt@lbox:/dj_projects/marketr$ python manage.py survey_test --cover
Here we do our own thing instead of calling the test runner.
Our new cover option HAS been specified.
```

We can also verify that if we do not pass `--cover` on the command line, it defaults to `False`:

```
kmt@lbox:/dj_projects/marketr$ python manage.py survey_test
Here we do our own thing instead of calling the test runner.
Our new cover option HAS NOT been specified.
```

Finally, we can see that help for our option is included in the help response for the new command:

```
kmt@lbox:/dj_projects/marketr$ python manage.py survey_test --help
Usage: manage.py survey_test [options] [appname ...]


Runs the test suite for the specified applications, or the entire site if
no apps are specified.


Options:
  -v VERBOSITY, --verbosity=VERBOSITY
                        Verbosity level; 0=minimal output, 1=normal output,
                        2=all output
  --settings=SETTINGS   The Python path to a settings module, e.g.
                        "myproject.settings.main". If this isn't
                        provided, the
                        DJANGO_SETTINGS_MODULE environment variable will
                        be used.
```

```
--pythonpath=PYTHONPATH
                        A directory to add to the Python path, e.g.
                        "/home/djangoprojects/myproject".
--traceback             Print traceback on exception
--noinput               Tells Django to NOT prompt the user for input of
                        any kind.
--cover                 Tells Django to generate test coverage data.
--version               show program's version number and exit
-h, --help              show this help message and exit
```

Note that all of the other options displayed in the help message that were not specified in our `option_list` are inherited from `BaseCommand`. In some cases, (for example, the `settings` and `pythonpath` arguments) appropriate handling of the argument is done for us before they are called; in others (`verbosity`, for example) we are expected to honor the documented behavior of the option in our implementation.

Adding a new management command was easy! Of course, we didn't actually implement running tests and generating coverage data, since we do not know any way to do that yet. There are existing packages that provide this support, and we will see in the next section how they can be used to do exactly this.

For now, we might as well delete the `survey/management` tree created here. It was a useful exercise to experiment with seeing how to add management commands. However in reality, if we were to provide a customized test command to add function such as recording coverage data, it would be a bad approach to tie that function directly to our survey application. A test command that records coverage data would be better implemented in an independent application.

How much of the code are we testing?

When writing tests, the goal is to test everything. Although we can try to be vigilant and manually ensure that we have a test for every line of our code, that's a very hard goal to meet without some automated analysis to verify what lines of code are executed by our tests. For Python code, Ned Batchelder's `coverage` module is an excellent tool for determining what lines of code are being executed. In this section, we see how to use `coverage`, first as a standalone utility and then integrated into our Django project.

Using coverage standalone

Before using `coverage`, it must first be installed, since it's neither included with Python nor Django 1.1. If you are using Linux, your distribution package manager may have `coverage` available to be installed on your system. Alternatively, the latest version of `coverage` can always be found at its web page on the Python Package Index (PyPI), `http://pypi.python.org/pypi/coverage`. The version of `coverage` used here is 3.2.

Once installed, we can use the `coverage` command with the `run` subcommand to run our tests and record coverage data:

```
kmt@lbox:/dj_projects/marketr$ coverage run manage.py test survey
Creating test database...
Creating table auth_permission
Creating table auth_group
Creating table auth_user
Creating table auth_message
Creating table django_content_type
Creating table django_session
Creating table django_site
Creating table django_admin_log
Creating table survey_survey
Creating table survey_question
Creating table survey_answer
Installing index for auth.Permission model
Installing index for auth.Message model
Installing index for admin.LogEntry model
Installing index for survey.Question model
Installing index for survey.Answer model
....................
----------------------------------------------------------------------
Ran 21 tests in 11.361s

OK
Destroying test database...
```

As you see, the output from the test runner looks completely normal. The coverage module does not affect the program's output; it simply stores the coverage data in a file named `.coverage`.

The data stored in `.coverage` can be formatted as a report using the `report` subcommand of `coverage`:

```
kmt@lbox:/dj_projects/marketr$ coverage report
```

Name	Stmts	Exec	Cover
/usr/share/pyshared/mod_python/__init__	2	2	100%
/usr/share/pyshared/mod_python/util	330	1	0%
/usr/share/pyshared/mx/TextTools/Constants/Sets	42	42	100%
/usr/share/pyshared/mx/TextTools/Constants/TagTables	12	12	100%
/usr/share/pyshared/mx/TextTools/Constants/__init__	1	1	100%
/usr/share/pyshared/mx/TextTools/TextTools	259	47	18%
/usr/share/pyshared/mx/TextTools/__init__	27	18	66%
/usr/share/pyshared/mx/TextTools/mxTextTools/__init__	12	9	75%
/usr/share/pyshared/mx/__init__	2	2	100%
/usr/share/pyshared/pysqlite2/__init__	1	1	100%
/usr/share/pyshared/pysqlite2/dbapi2	41	26	63%
/usr/share/python-support/python-simplejson/simplejson/__init__	75	20	26%
/usr/share/python-support/python-simplejson/simplejson/decoder	208	116	55%
/usr/share/python-support/python-simplejson/simplejson/encoder	215	40	18%
/usr/share/python-support/python-simplejson/simplejson/scanner	51	46	90%
__init__	1	1	100%
manage	9	5	55%
settings	23	23	100%
survey/__init__	1	1	100%
survey/admin	24	24	100%
survey/models	38	37	97%
survey/tests/__init__	4	4	100%
survey/tests/admin_tests	23	23	100%
survey/tests/model_tests	98	86	87%
survey/tests/view_tests	47	47	100%
survey/urls	2	2	100%
survey/views	22	22	100%
urls	4	4	100%
TOTAL	1575	663	42%

That's a bit more than we actually want. We only care about coverage of our own code, so for a start, everything reported for modules located under /usr is not interesting. The --omit option to coverage report can be used to omit modules that start with particular paths. Additionally, the -m option can be used to get coverage to report on the lines that were not executed (missing) during the run:

```
kmt@1box:/dj_projects/marketr$ coverage report --omit /usr -m
Name                            Stmts   Exec  Cover   Missing
-----------------------------------------------------------------
__init__                            1      1   100%
manage                              9      5    55%   5-8
settings                           23     23   100%
survey/__init__                     1      1   100%
survey/admin                       24     24   100%
survey/models                      38     37    97%   66
survey/tests/__init__               4      4   100%
survey/tests/admin_tests           23     23   100%
survey/tests/model_tests           98     86    87%   35-42, 47-51
survey/tests/view_tests            47     47   100%
survey/urls                         2      2   100%
survey/views                       23     23   100%
urls                                4      4   100%
-----------------------------------------------------------------
TOTAL                             297    280    94%
```

That's much more manageable. Not surprisingly, since we have been developing tests for each bit of code discussed, just about everything is showing as covered. What's missing? If you look at lines 5 to 8 of manage.py, they handle the case where the import of settings.py raises an ImportError. Since that leg of code is not taken for a successful run, they were not executed and come up missing in the coverage report.

Similarly, the lines mentioned in model_tests (35 to 42, 47 to 51) are from alternative execution paths of the testClosesReset method, which contains this code starting at line 34:

```
if settings.DATABASE_ENGINE == 'mysql':
    from django.db import connection
    c = connection.cursor()
    c.execute('SELECT @@SESSION.sql_mode')
    mode = c.fetchone()[0]
    if 'STRICT' not in mode:
```

```
                        strict = False;
                        from django.utils import importlib
                        debug = importlib.import_module(
                            settings.SETTINGS_MODULE).DEBUG

            if strict:
                self.assertRaises(IntegrityError, s.save)
            elif debug:
                self.assertRaises(Exception, s.save)
            else:
                s.save()
                self.assertEqual(s.closes, None)
```

Lines 35 to 42 were not executed because the database used for this run was SQLite, not MySQL. Then, in any single test run, only one leg of the if strict/elif debug/ else block will execute, so the other legs will show up as not covered. (In this particular case, the if strict leg was the one taken.)

The remaining line noted as missing is line 66 in survey/models.py. This is the __unicode__ method implementation for the Question model, which we neglected to write a test for. We can put doing that on our to-do list.

Although this last one is a valid indication of a missing test, neither the missing lines in manage.py nor the missing lines in our test code are really things we care about, as they are not reporting missing coverage for our application code. (Actually, if we are thorough, we would probably want to ensure that several runs of our test code with different settings did result in full test code execution, but let's assume we are only interested in coverage of our application code for now.) The coverage module supports a couple of different ways of excluding code from reports. One possibility is to annotate source lines with a # pgrama no cover directive to tell coverage to exclude them from coverage consideration.

Alternatively, coverage provides a Python API that supports specifying regular expressions for code constructs that should be automatically excluded, and also for limiting the modules included in reports. This Python API is more powerful than what is available through the command line, and more convenient than manually annotating source with # pragma directives. We might, then, start looking into how to write some coverage utility scripts to easily generate coverage reports for the tests of our application code.

Before embarking on that task, though, we might wonder if anyone has already done the same and provided a ready-to-use utility that integrates coverage with the Django test support. Some searching on the Web shows that the answer is yes—there are several blog postings discussing the subject, and at least one project packaged as a Django application. Use of this package is discussed next.

Integrating coverage into a Django project

George Song and Mikhail Korobov provide a Django application named `django_coverage` that supports integrating `coverage` into testing for a Django project. Like the base `coverage` package, `django_coverage` can be found on PyPI: `http://pypi.python.org/pypi/django-coverage`. The version used here is 1.0.1.

The `django_coverage` package offers integration of `coverage` with Django using both of the methods previously discussed. First, it provides a test runner that can be specified in `settings.py`:

```
TEST_RUNNER = 'django_coverage.coverage_runner.run_tests'
```

Using this option, every time you run `manage.py test`, coverage information will be generated.

Alternatively, `django_coverage` can be included in `INSTALLED_APPS`. When this approach is used, the `django_coverage` application provides a new management command, named `test_coverage`. The `test_coverage` command can be used instead of `test` to run tests and generate coverage information. Since generating coverage information does make the tests run a bit more slowly, the second option is what we will use here. That way, we can choose to run tests without coverage data when we are interested in fast execution and not concerned with checking on coverage.

Beyond listing `django_coverage` in `INSTALLED_APPS`, nothing needs to be done to set up `django_coverage` to run with our project. It comes with a sample `settings.py` file that shows the settings it supports, all with default options and comments describing what they do. We can override any of the default settings provided in `django_coverage/settings.py` by specifying our preferred value in our own settings file.

We will start, though, by using all the default settings values provided. When we run `python manage.py test_coverage survey`, we will get coverage information displayed at the end of the test output:

```
----------------------------------------------------------------------
Ran 21 tests in 10.040s


OK
Destroying test database...
Name             Stmts    Exec    Cover    Missing
-------------------------------------------------
survey.admin       21      21     100%
```

```
survey.models      30    30    100%
survey.views       18    18    100%
-------------------------------------------------
TOTAL              69    69    100%
```

```
The following packages or modules were excluded: survey.__init__ survey.
tests survey.urls
```

```
There were problems with the following packages or modules: survey.
templates survey.fixtures
```

That is a bit curious. Recall that the coverage package reported in the previous section that one line of code in survey.models was not exercised by tests—the __unicode__ method of the Question model. This report, though, shows 100% coverage for survey.models. Looking closely at the two reports, we can see that the statements that count for the listed modules are all lower in the django_coverage report than they were in the coverage report.

This difference is due to the default value of the COVERAGE_CODE_EXCLUDES setting used by django_coverage. The default value of this setting causes all import lines, all __unicode__ method definitions, and all get_absolute_url method definitions to be excluded from consideration. These default exclusions account for the differences seen here between the two reports. If we don't like this default behavior, we can supply our own alternate setting, but for now, we will leave it as it is.

Furthermore, some modules listed by coverage are completely missing from the django_coverage report. These too are the result of a default setting value (in this case, COVERAGE_MODULE_EXCLUDES) and there is a message in the output noting which modules have been excluded due to this setting. As you can see, the __init__, tests, and urls modules inside survey were all automatically excluded from coverage consideration.

However, templates and fixtures are not excluded by default, and that caused a problem as they are not actually Python modules, so they cannot be imported. To get rid of the message about problems loading these, we can specify a value for COVERAGE_MODULE_EXCLUDES in our own settings.py file and include these two. Adding them to the default list, we have:

```
COVERAGE_MODULE_EXCLUDES = ['tests$', 'settings$', 'urls$',
                            'common.views.test', '__init__', 'django',
                            'migrations', 'fixtures$', 'templates$']
```

If we run the test_coverage command again after making this change, we will see that the message about problems loading some modules is gone.

The summary information displayed with the test output is useful, but even better are the HTML reports django_coverage can generate. To get these, we must specify a value for the COVERAGE_REPORT_HTML_OUTPUT_DIR setting, which is None by default. So, we can create a coverage_html directory in /dj_projects/marketr and specify it in settings.py:

```
COVERAGE_REPORT_HTML_OUTPUT_DIR = '/dj_projects/marketr/coverage_html'
```

The HTML reports are not particularly interesting when code coverage comes in at 100 percent. Hence, to see the full usefulness of the reports, let's run just a single test, say the admin test for trying to add a Survey with a closes date that is earlier than its opens date:

python manage.py test_coverage survey.AdminSurveyTest.testAddSurveyError

This time, since we have specified a directory for HTML coverage reports, instead of getting the summary coverage information at the end of the test run, we see:

Ran 1 test in 0.337s

OK

Destroying test database...

HTML reports were output to '/dj_projects/marketr/coverage_html'

Then, we can use a web browser to load the index.html file that has been placed in the coverage_html directory. It will look something like this:

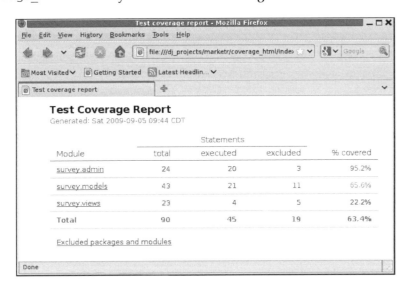

Since we ran just a single test, we only got partial coverage of our code. The **% covered** values in the HTML report are color-coded to reflect how well covered each module is. Green is good, yellow is fair, and red is poor. In this case, since we ran one of the admin tests, only **survey.admin** is colored green, and it is not 100 percent. To see what was missed in that module, we can click on the **survey.admin** link:

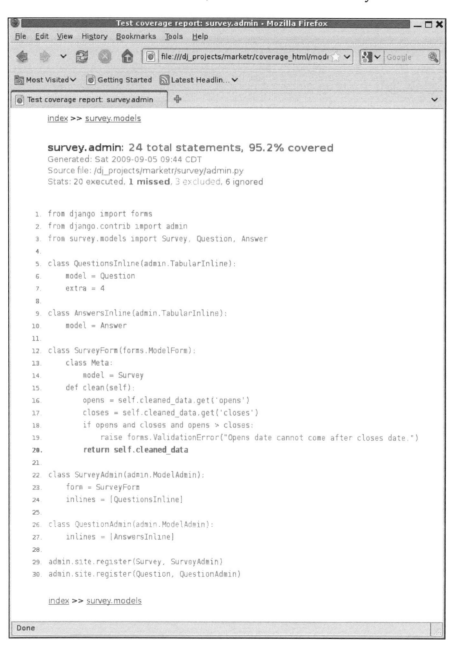

Reports like this provide a very convenient way to determine the parts of our application code that are covered by testing and the parts that are not. Lines not executed are highlighted in red. Here, we only ran the test that exercises the error path through the SurveyFrom clean method, so the successful code path through that method comes up in red. In addition, the color coding of the import lines indicates that they were excluded. This is due to the default COVERAGE_CODE_EXCLUDES setting. Finally, the six empty lines in the file were ignored (lines with comments would also be ignored).

Using a tool like coverage is essential for ensuring that a test suite is doing its job. It is likely that in the future, Django will provide some integrated code coverage support. But in the meantime, as we have seen, it is not difficult to integrate coverage as an add-on to our projects. In the case of django_coverage, it provides options for using either of the ways of extending Django discussed earlier. The next integration task we will discuss requires neither, but rather needs only the standard Python hooks into unit test set up and tear down.

The twill web browsing and testing tool

twill is a Python package that supports command-line interaction with web sites, primarily for testing purposes. Like the coverage and django_coverage packages, twill can be found on PyPI: http://pypi.python.org/pypi/twill. While twill offers a command-line tool for interactive use, the commands it provides are also available from a Python API, meaning it is possible to use twill from within a Django TestCase. When we do this, we essentially replace use of the Django test Client with an alternative twill implementation.

Note that the latest official release of twill available on PyPI (0.9 at the time of this writing) is quite old. The latest development release is available at http://darcs.idyll.org/~t/projects/twill-latest.tar.gz. Output from the latest development release as of January 2010 is what is shown in this section. The code included here was also tested with the official 0.9 release. Everything works using the older twill code, but the error output from twill is slightly less helpful and there is some twill output that cannot be suppressed when running as part of a Django TestCase. Thus, I'd recommend the latest development release over the 0.9 release.

Why would we want to use `twill` instead of the Django test `Client`? To understand the motivation for using `twill` instead of the Django test `Client`, let's revisit the admin customization test from the last chapter. Recall that we provided a custom form for adding and editing `Survey` objects. This form has a `clean` method that raises a `ValidationError` on any attempt to save a `Survey` with an `opens` date later than its `closes` date. The test to ensure that `ValidationError` is raised when it should be looks like this:

```
def testAddSurveyError(self):
    post_data = {
        'title': u'Time Traveling',
        'opens': datetime.date.today(),
        'closes': datetime.date.today() - datetime.timedelta(1),
        'question_set-TOTAL_FORMS': u'0',
        'question_set-INITIAL_FORMS': u'0',
    }
    response = self.client.post(
        reverse('admin:survey_survey_add'), post_data)
    self.assertContains(response,
        "Opens date cannot come after closes date.")
```

Notice that this test sends a POST to the server containing a dictionary of POST data without ever having issued a GET for the page. This caused a problem at first: recall that we did not initially include the `question_set-TOTAL_FORMS` and `question_set-INITIAL_FORMS` values in the POST dictionary. We were focused on testing the `Survey` part of the form on the page and did not realize the formset used by admin to display `Questions` in line with `Surveys` required these other values. When we found they were needed, we somewhat cavalierly set their values to `0` and hoped that would be acceptable for what we wanted to test.

A better approach would have been to first `get` the survey add page. The response would include a form with a set of initial values that could be used as the basis for the dictionary to `post` back. Before issuing the `post` request, we would change only the values necessary for our test (`title`, `opens`, and `closes`). Thus, when we did issue the `post` call, any other form values that the server had provided initially in the form would be sent back unchanged. We would not have to make up additional values for parts of the form that our test did not intend to change.

Besides being a more realistic server interaction scenario, this approach also ensures that the server is responding correctly to the GET request. Testing the GET path isn't necessary in this particular case since the additional validation we added to admin doesn't affect how it responds to a GET of the page. However, for one of our own views that provides a form in the response, we would want to test the response to `get` as well as `post`.

So why didn't we write the test that way? The test `Client` supports `get` as well as `post`; we certainly could start off by retrieving the page containing the form. The problem is that the returned response is HTML, and the Django test `Client` doesn't provide any utility functions to parse the HTML form and turn it into something we can easily manipulate. There is no straightforward way for Django to just take the response, change a few values in the form, and `post` it back to the server. The `twill` package, on the other hand, makes this easy.

In the following sections, we will re-implement the `AdminSurveyTest` using `twill`. First, we'll see how to use its command line tool and then transfer what we learn into a Django `TestCase`.

Using the twill command line program

The `twill` package includes a shell script, named `twill-sh`, to allow command-line testing. This is a convenient way to do some initial testing and figure out what the test case code will need to do. From the shell program, we can use the `go` command to visit a page. Once we've visited a page, we can use the `showforms` command to see what forms are on the page, and what fields and initial values the forms contain. Since we are going to use `twill` to re-implement the `AdminSurveyTest`, let's see what visiting the `Survey` add page for our test server produces:

```
kmt@lbox:~$ twill-sh

 -= Welcome to twill! =-

current page:  *empty page*
>> go http://localhost:8000/admin/survey/survey/add/
==> at http://localhost:8000/admin/survey/survey/add/
current page: http://localhost:8000/admin/survey/survey/add/
>> showforms


Form #1
## ##   __Name_____   __Type____  __ID_____  __Value_____
1       username                 text        id_username
2       password                 password    id_password
3       this_is_the_login_form   hidden      (None)         1
4  1     None                     submit      (None)         Log in


current page: http://localhost:8000/admin/survey/survey/add/
>>
```

Clearly, we didn't actually get to the survey add page. Since we aren't logged in, the server responded with a login page. We can fill the login form using the `formvalue` command:

```
>> formvalue 1 username kmt
current page: http://localhost:8000/admin/survey/survey/add/
>> formvalue 1 password secret
current page: http://localhost:8000/admin/survey/survey/add/
>>
```

The arguments to `formvalue` are first the form number, then the field name, and then the value we want to set for that field. Once we have filled the username and password in the form, we can `submit` the form:

```
>> submit
Note: submit is using submit button: name="None", value="Log in"


current page: http://localhost:8000/admin/survey/survey/add/
```

Note the `submit` command optionally also accepts the name of the submit button to use. In the case where there is only one (as here), or if using the first submit button on the form is acceptable, we can simply use `submit` with no argument. Now that we have logged in, we can use `showforms` again to see if we have now really retrieved a `Survey` add page:

```
>> showforms
```

```
Form #1
```

## ##	Name	Type	ID	Value
1	title	text	id_title	
2	opens	text	id_opens	
3	closes	text	id_closes	
4	question_set-TOTAL_FORMS	hidden	id_quest ...	4
5	question_set-INITIAL ...	hidden	id_quest ...	0
6	question_set-0-id	hidden	id_quest ...	
7	question_set-0-survey	hidden	id_quest ...	
8	question_set-0-question	text	id_quest ...	
9	question_set-1-id	hidden	id_quest ...	
10	question_set-1-survey	hidden	id_quest ...	
11	question_set-1-question	text	id_quest ...	

```
12      question_set-2-id           hidden      id_quest ...

13      question_set-2-survey       hidden      id_quest ...

14      question_set-2-question     text        id_quest ...

15      question_set-3-id           hidden      id_quest ...

16      question_set-3-survey       hidden      id_quest ...

17      question_set-3-question     text        id_quest ...

18 1    _save                       submit      (None)      Save

19 2    _addanother                 submit      (None)      Save and add
another

20 3    _continue                   submit      (None)      Save and continue
editing


current page: http://localhost:8000/admin/survey/survey/add/

>>
```

That looks more like a `Survey` add page. And indeed, our setting of `question_set-TOTAL_FORMS` to `0` in our first test case is unrealistic, since the server actually serves up a form with that set to `4`. But it worked. This means that we did not have to manufacture values for the four inline questions, so it is not a fatal flaw. However, with `twill` we can take the more realistic path of leaving all those values as-is and just changing the fields we are interested in, again using the `formvalue` command:

```
>> formvalue 1 title 'Time Traveling'
current page: http://localhost:8000/admin/survey/survey/add/
>> formvalue 1 opens 2009-08-15
current page: http://localhost:8000/admin/survey/survey/add/
>> formvalue 1 closes 2009-08-01
current page: http://localhost:8000/admin/survey/survey/add/
```

When we submit that form, we expect the server to respond with the same form re-displayed and the `ValidationError` message text from our custom `clean` method. We can verify that the text is on the returned page using the `find` command:

```
>> submit
Note: submit is using submit button: name="_save", value="Save"


current page: http://localhost:8000/admin/survey/survey/add/
>> find "Opens date cannot come after closes date."
current page: http://localhost:8000/admin/survey/survey/add/
>>
```

That response to `find` may not make it immediately obvious whether it worked or not. Let's see what it does with something that is most likely not on the page:

```
>> find "lalalala I don't hear you"

ERROR: no match to 'lalalala I don't hear you'

current page: http://localhost:8000/admin/survey/survey/add/
>>
```

OK, since `twill` clearly complains when the text is not found, the first `find` must have succeeded in locating the expected validation error text on the page. Now, we can use `showforms` again to see that indeed the server has sent back the form we submitted. Note that the initial values are what we submitted, not empty as they were when we first retrieved the page:

```
>> showforms
```

```
Form #1
## ##   Name                      Type     ID           Value
1       title                     text     id_title     Time Traveling
2       opens                     text     id_opens     2009-08-15
3       closes                    text     id_closes    2009-08-01
4       question_set-TOTAL_FORMS  hidden   id_quest ... 4
5       question_set-INITIAL ...  hidden   id_quest ... 0
6       question_set-0-id         hidden   id_quest ...
7       question_set-0-survey     hidden   id_quest ...
8       question_set-0-question   text     id_quest ...
9       question_set-1-id         hidden   id_quest ...
10      question_set-1-survey     hidden   id_quest ...
11      question_set-1-question   text     id_quest ...
12      question_set-2-id         hidden   id_quest ...
13      question_set-2-survey     hidden   id_quest ...
14      question_set-2-question   text     id_quest ...
15      question_set-3-id         hidden   id_quest ...
16      question_set-3-survey     hidden   id_quest ...
17      question_set-3-question   text     id_quest ...
18 1    _save                     submit   (None)       Save
```

```
19 2  _addanother          submit    (None)    Save and add another
20 3  _continue            submit    (None)    Save and continue editing
```

current page: http://localhost:8000/admin/survey/survey/add/

>>

At this point, we can simply adjust one of the dates in order to make the form valid and try submitting it again:

```
>> formvalue 1 opens 2009-07-15
current page: http://localhost:8000/admin/survey/survey/add/
>> submit
Note: submit is using submit button: name="_save", value="Save"


current page: http://localhost:8000/admin/survey/survey/
>>
```

Notice the **current page** has changed to be the survey changelist page (there is no longer an add at the end of the URL path). This is a clue that the Survey add worked this time, as the server redirects to the changelist page on a successful save. There is a twill command to display the HTML contents of a page, named show. It can be useful to see which page has been returned when you've got a display window you can scroll back through. However, HTML pages aren't very useful when reproduced on paper, so it's not shown here.

There are also many more useful commands that twill provides that are beyond the scope of what we are covering now. The discussion here is intended to simply give a taste of what twill provides and show how to use it in a Django test case. This second task will be covered next.

Using twill in a TestCase

What do we need to do to take what we've done in the twill-sh program and turn it into a TestCase? First, we will need to use twill's Python API in the test code. The twill commands we used from within twill-sh are available in the twill. commands module. Additionally, twill provides a browser object (accessible via twill.get_browser()) that may be more appropriate to call from Python. The browser object version of a command may return a value, for example, instead of printing something on the screen. However, the browser object does not support all of the commands in twill.commands directly, thus it is common to use a mixture of `twill.commands` methods and browser methods. Mixing the usage is fine since the code in `twill.commands` internally operates on the same browser instance returned from `twill.get_browser()`.

Second, for test code purposes, we'd like to instruct `twill` to interact with our Django server application code directly, instead of sending requests to an actual server. It's fine when using the `twill-sh` code to test against our running development server, but we don't want to have a server running in order for our tests to pass. The Django test `Client` does this automatically since it was written specifically to be used from test code.

With `twill`, we must call its `add_wsgi_intercept` method to tell it to route requests for a particular host and port directly to a WSGI application instead of sending the requests out on the network. Django provides a class that supports the WSGI application interface (named `WSGIHandler`) in `django.core.handlers.wsgi`. Thus, in our setup code for using `twill` in tests, we can include code like this:

```
from django.core.handlers.wsgi import WSGIHandler
import twill
TWILL_TEST_HOST = 'twilltest'
twill.add_wsgi_intercept(TWILL_TEST_HOST, 80, WSGIHandler)
```

This tells `twill` that a `WSGIHandler` instance should be used for the handling of any requests that are bound for the host named `twilltest` on the regular HTTP port, 80. The actual hostname and port used here are not important; they must simply match the host name and port that our test code tries to access.

This brings us to the third thing we must consider in our test code. The URLs we use with the Django test `Client` have no hostname or port components as the test `Client` does not perform any routing based on that information, but it rather just sends the request directly to our application code. The `twill` interface, on the other hand, does expect host (and optionally port) components in the URLs passed to it. Thus, we need to build URLs that are correct for `twill` and will be routed appropriately by it. Since we are generally using Django's `reverse` to create our URLs during testing, a utility function that takes a named URL and returns the result of reversing it into a form that will be handled properly by `twill` will come in handy:

```
def reverse_for_twill(named_url):
    return 'http://' + TWILL_TEST_HOST + reverse(named_url)
```

Note that since we used the default HTTP port in the `add_wsgi_intercept` call, we do not need to include the port number in the URLs.

One thing to note about using the WSGIHandler application interface for testing is that this interface, by default, suppresses any exceptions raised during processing of a request. This is the same interface that is used, for example, by the mod_wsgi module when running under Apache. It would be unacceptable in such an environment for WSGIHandler to expose exceptions to its caller, thus it catches all exceptions and turns them into server error (HTTP 500) responses.

Although suppressing exceptions is the correct behavior in a production environment, it is not very useful for testing. The server error response generated instead of the exception is completely unhelpful in determining where the problem originated. Thus, this behavior is likely to make it very hard to diagnose test failures in cases where the code under test raises an exception.

To fix this problem, Django has a setting, DEBUG_PROPAGATE_EXCEPTIONS, which can be set to True to tell the WSGIHandler interface to allow exceptions to propagate up. This setting is False by default and should never be set to True in a production environment. Our twill test setup code, however, should set it to True so that if an exception is raised during request processing, it will be seen when the test is run instead of being replaced by a generic server error response.

One final wrinkle involved with using Django's WSGIHandler interface for testing concerns maintaining a single database connection for multiple web page requests made by a single test. Ordinarily, each request (GET or POST of a page) uses its own newly-established database connection. At the end of the processing for a successful request, any open transaction on the database connection is committed and the database connection is closed.

However, as noted at the end of *Chapter 4, Getting Fancier: Django Unit Test Extensions*, the TestCase code prevents any database commits issued by the code under test from actually reaching the database. Thus, when testing the database will not see the commit normally present at the end of a request, but instead will just see the connection closed. Some databases, such as PostgreSQL and MySQL with the InnoDB storage engine, will automatically rollback the open transaction in this situation. This will cause problems for tests that need to issue multiple requests and have database updates made by earlier requests be accessible to later requests. For example, any test that requires a login will run into trouble since the login information is stored in the django_session database table.

One way to fix this would be to use a TransactionTestCase instead of a TestCase as the base class for all of our tests that use twill. With a TransactionTestCase, the commit that normally happens at the end of request processing will be sent to the database as usual. However, the process of resetting the database to a clean state between each test is much slower for a TransactionTestCase than TestCase, so this approach could considerably slow down our tests.

An alternative solution is to prevent the closing of the database connection at the end of request processing. That way there is nothing to trigger the database to rollback any updates in the middle of a test. We can accomplish this by disconnecting the `close_connection` signal handler from the `request_finished` signal as part of the test `setUp` method. This is not a very clean solution, but it is worth the performance gain (and it is also what the test `Client` does to overcome the same problem).

Let's start, then, by writing a `twill` version of the `setUp` method for the `AdminSurveyTest`. The test `Client` version from the previous chapter is:

```
class AdminSurveyTest(TestCase):
    def setUp(self):
        self.username = 'survey_admin'
        self.pw = 'pwpwpw'
        self.user = User.objects.create_user(self.username, '', "
                                             "self.pw)
        self.user.is_staff= True
        self.user.is_superuser = True
        self.user.save()
        self.assertTrue(self.client.login(username=self.username,
                                          password=self.pw),
            "Logging in user %s, pw %s failed." %
                (self.username, self.pw))
```

The `twill` version will need to do the same user creation steps, but something different for login. Instead of duplicating the user creation code, we will factor that out into a common base class (called `AdminTest`) for the `AdminSurveyTest` and the `twill` version `AdminSurveyTwillTest`. For logging into the `twill` version, we can fill in and submit the login form that will be returned if we attempt to go to any admin page before logging in. Thus, the `twill` version of `setUp` might look like this:

```
from django.db import close_connection
from django.core import signals
from django.core.handlers.wsgi import WSGIHandler
from django.conf import settings
import twill

class AdminSurveyTwillTest(AdminTest):
    def setUp(self):
        super(AdminSurveyTwillTest, self).setUp()
        self.old_propagate = settings.DEBUG_PROPAGATE_EXCEPTIONS
        settings.DEBUG_PROPAGATE_EXCEPTIONS = True
        signals.request_finished.disconnect(close_connection)
        twill.add_wsgi_intercept(TWILL_TEST_HOST, 80, WSGIHandler)
        self.browser = twill.get_browser()
```

```
        self.browser.go(reverse_for_twill('admin:index'))
        twill.commands.formvalue(1, 'username', self.username)
        twill.commands.formvalue(1, 'password', self.pw)
        self.browser.submit()
        twill.commands.find('Welcome')
```

This setUp first calls the superclass setUp to create the admin user, and then saves the existing DEBUG_PROPAGATE_EXCEPTIONS setting before setting that to True. It then disconnects the close_connection signal handler from the request_finished signal. Next, it calls twill.add_wsgi_intercept to set up twill to route requests for the twilltest host to Django's WSGIHandler. For convenient access, it stashes the twill browser object in self.browser. It then uses the previously mentioned reverse_for_twill utility function to create the appropriate URL for the admin index page, and calls the browser go method to retrieve that page.

The returned page should have a single form containing username and password fields. These are set to the values for the user created by the superclass setUp using the formvalue command, and the form is submitted using the browser submit method. The result should be the admin index page, if the login works. That page will have the string Welcome on it, so the last thing this setUp routine does is verify that text is found on the page, so that if the login failed an error is raised at the point the problem was encountered rather than later.

When we write setUp, we should also write the companion tearDown method to undo the effects of setUp:

```
    def tearDown(self):
        self.browser.go(reverse_for_twill('admin:logout'))
        twill.remove_wsgi_intercept(TWILL_TEST_HOST, 80)
        signals.request_finished.connect(close_connection)
        settings.DEBUG_PROPAGATE_EXCEPTIONS = self.old_propagate
```

Here, we go to the admin logout page to log out from the admin site, call remove_wsgi_intercept to remove the special routing for the host named twilltest, reconnect the normal close_connection signal handler to the request_finished signal, and lastly restore the old value of DEBUG_PROPAGATE_EXCEPTIONS.

A twill version of the test case routine that checks for the error case of closes being earlier than opens would then be:

```
    def testAddSurveyError(self):
        self.browser.go(reverse_for_twill('admin:survey_survey_add'))
        twill.commands.formvalue(1, 'title', 'Time Traveling')
        twill.commands.formvalue(1, 'opens',
            str(datetime.date.today()))
```

```
twill.commands.formvalue(1, 'closes',
    str(datetime.date.today()-datetime.timedelta(1)))
self.browser.submit()
twill.commands.url(reverse_for_twill(
    'admin:survey_survey_add'))
twill.commands.find("Opens date cannot come after closes "
    "date.")
```

Unlike the test `Client` version, here we start by visiting the admin `Survey` add page. We expect the response to contain a single form, and set the values in it for `title`, `opens`, and `closes`. We don't care about anything else that may be in the form and leave it unchanged. We then `submit` the form.

We expect that in the error case (which this should be, given that we made `closes` one day before `opens`) the admin will redisplay the same page with an error message. We test for this by first using the `twill url` command to test that the current URL is still the `Survey` add page URL. We then also use the `twill find` command to verify that the expected error message is found on the page. (It's probably only necessary to perform one of those checks, but it doesn't hurt to do both. Hence, both are included here for illustration purposes.)

If we now run this test with `python manage.py test survey.`
`AdminSurveyTwillTest`, we will see that it works, but `twill` is a bit chatty, even when using the Python API. At the end of the test output, we will see:

```
Installing index for survey.Answer model
==> at http://twilltest/admin/
Note: submit is using submit button: name="None", value="Log in"


==> at http://twilltest/admin/survey/survey/add/
Note: submit is using submit button: name="_save", value="Save"


==> at http://twilltest/admin/logout/
.
----------------------------------------------------------------------
Ran 1 test in 0.845s

OK
Destroying test database...
```

We'd rather not have output from `twill` cluttering up our test output, so we'd like to redirect this output elsewhere. Luckily, `twill` provides a routine for this, `set_output`. So, we can add the following to our `setUp` method:

```
twill.set_output(StringIO())
```

Place this prior to any `twill` commands that print output, and remember to include `from StringIO import StringIO` among the imports before referencing `StringIO`. We should also undo this in our `tearDown` routine by calling `twill.commands.reset_output()` there. That will restore the `twill` default behavior of sending output to the screen. After making those changes, if we run the test again, we will see that it passes, and the `twill` output is no longer present.

The last piece to write, then, is the test case for adding a `Survey` with dates that do not trigger the validation error. It might look like this:

```
def testAddSurveyOK(self):
    self.browser.go(reverse_for_twill('admin:survey_survey_add'))
    twill.commands.formvalue(1, 'title', 'Not Time Traveling')
    twill.commands.formvalue(1, 'opens',
        str(datetime.date.today()))
    twill.commands.formvalue(1, 'closes',
        str(datetime.date.today()))
    self.browser.submit()
    twill.commands.url(reverse_for_twill(
        'admin:survey_survey_changelist'))
```

This is much like the previous test except we attempt to verify that we are redirected to the admin changelist page on the expected successful submit. If we run this test, it will pass, but it is actually not correct. That is, it will not fail if in fact the admin re-displays the add page instead of redirecting to the changelist page. Thus, if we have broken something and caused submits that should be successful to fail, this test won't catch that.

To see this, change the `closes` date in this test case to be one day before `opens`. This will trigger an error as it does in the `testAddSurveyError` method. However, if we run the test with that change, it will still pass.

The reason for this is that the `twill url` command takes a regular expression as its argument. It isn't checking for an exact match of the passed argument with the actual URL, but rather that the actual URL matches the regular expression passed to the `url` command. The changelist URL that we are passing into the `url` method is:

```
http://twilltest/admin/survey/survey/
```

The URL for the add page that will be re-displayed in case of an error on submit will be:

```
http://twilltest/admin/survey/survey/add/
```

An attempt to match the add page URL with the changelist page URL will be successful, since the changelist URL is contained within the add page URL. Thus, the `twill url` command will not raise an error as we want it to. To fix this, we must indicate in the regular expression we pass into `url` that we require the actual URL to end as the value we are passing in ends, by including an end of string marker on the value we pass:

```
twill.commands.url(reverse_for_twill(
    'admin:survey_survey_changelist') + '$')
```

We could also include a string marker at the beginning, but that isn't actually required to fix this particular problem. If we make that change and leave in the incorrect `closes` date setting, we will see that this test case now does fail as it should when the server re-displays the add page, instead of successfully processing the submit:

```
======================================================================
ERROR: testAddSurveyOK (survey.tests.admin_tests.AdminSurveyTwillTest)
----------------------------------------------------------------------
Traceback (most recent call last):
  File "/dj_projects/marketr/survey/tests/admin_tests.py", line 91, in
testAddSurveyOK
    twill.commands.url(reverse_for_twill('admin:survey_survey_
changelist') + '$')
  File "/usr/lib/python2.5/site-packages/twill/commands.py", line 178, in
url
    """ % (current_url, should_be,))
TwillAssertionError: current url is 'http://twilltest/admin/survey/
survey/add/';

does not match 'http://twilltest/admin/survey/survey/$'



----------------------------------------------------------------------
Ran 2 tests in 1.349s


FAILED (errors=1)
Destroying test database...
```

Once we verify the test does fail in the case where the server does not respond as we expect, we can restore the `closes` date setting to be acceptable for saving and again the tests will pass. One lesson here is to be careful when using the `url` command that `twill` provides. A second lesson is to always attempt to verify that a test will report failure when appropriate. When focusing on writing tests that pass, we can often forget to verify that tests will properly fail when they should.

We've now got working `twill`-based versions of our admin customization tests. Achieving that was not exactly easy—the need for some of the `setUp` code, for example, is not necessarily immediately obvious. However, once in place it can be easily reused by tests that require more sophisticated form manipulation than we needed here. Form manipulation is a weak point of Django's test framework, and it is unlikely that it will be addressed in Django by the addition of functions that would duplicate functions already available in external tools. It is more likely that in the future, Django will offer more easy integration with `twill` or another tool like it. Therefore, investing in learning how to use a tool like `twill` is likely a good use of time.

Summary

This brings us to the end of discussing the testing of Django applications. In this chapter, we focused on how to fill in any gaps of testing functions within Django by integrating with other test tools. It is impossible to cover the specifics of integrating with every tool out there, but we learned the general mechanisms available and discussed a couple of examples in detail. This provides a solid foundation for understanding how to accomplish the task in general.

As Django continues to develop, such gaps may become fewer, but it is unlikely that Django will ever be able to provide everything that everyone wants in terms of testing support. In some cases, Python's class inheritance structure and unit test extension mechanisms allow for straightforward integration of other test tools into Django test cases. In other cases, this is not sufficient. Thus, it is helpful that Django also provides hooks for adding additional functionality. In this chapter, we:

- Learned what hooks Django provides for adding test functions
- Saw an example of how these hooks can be used, specifically in the case of adding code coverage reporting
- Also explored an example where using these hooks was not necessary— when integrating the use of the `twill` test tool into our Django test cases

In the next chapter, we will move from testing to debugging, and begin to learn what facilities Django provides to aid in debugging our Django applications.

Django Debugging Overview

6

The best test suite in the world won't save you from having to debug problems. Tests simply report whether code is working correctly. When there is a problem in the code, found either via a failing test or some other means, debugging is necessary to figure out what exactly has gone wrong. A good test suite, run regularly, can certainly help in debugging. The specifics of the error message from the failure, the aggregate information provided by what tests pass versus what tests fail, in addition to the knowledge of what code change introduced the problem, can all provide important clues for debugging. Sometimes those clues are enough to figure out what has gone wrong and how to fix it, but often it is necessary to perform additional debugging.

This chapter introduces Django's debugging support. It provides an overview of topics that will be covered in greater depth in subsequent chapters. Specifically, this chapter will:

- List the Django settings that control the collection and presentation of debugging information, and briefly describe the effects of enabling debug

- Illustrate the results of running with debug enabled in the case of serious code failure

- Describe the database query history that is collected with debug enabled, and show how to access it

- Discuss features of the development server that help in debugging

- Describe how errors are handled during production, when debug is off, and how to ensure that information about such errors is reported appropriately

Django debug settings

Django has a number of settings that control the collection and presentation of debug information. The primary one is named DEBUG; it broadly controls whether the server operates in development (if DEBUG is True) or production mode.

In development mode, the end-user is expected to be a site developer. Thus, if an error arises during processing of a request, it is useful to include specific technical information about the error in the response sent to the web browser. This is not useful in production mode, when the user is expected to be simply a general site user.

This section describes three Django settings that are useful for debugging during development. Additional settings are used during production to control what errors should be reported, and where error reports should be sent. These additional settings will be discussed in the section on handling problems in production.

The DEBUG and TEMPLATE_DEBUG settings

DEBUG is the main debug setting. One of the most obvious effects of setting this to True is that Django will generate fancy error page responses in the case of serious code problems, such as exceptions raised during processing of a request. If TEMPLATE_DEBUG is also True, and the exception raised is related to a template error, then the fancy error page will also include information about where in the template the error occurred.

The default value for both of these settings is False, but the settings.py file created by manage.py startproject turns both of them on by including these lines at the top of the file:

```
DEBUG = True
TEMPLATE_DEBUG = DEBUG
```

Note that setting TEMPLATE_DEBUG to True when DEBUG is False isn't useful. The additional information collected with TEMPLATE_DEBUG turned on will never be displayed if the fancy error pages, controlled by the DEBUG setting, are not displayed. Similarly, setting TEMPLATE_DEBUG to False when DEBUG is True isn't very useful. In this case, for template errors, the fancy debug page will be lacking helpful information. Thus, it makes sense to keep these settings tied to each other, as previously shown.

Details on the fancy error pages and when they are generated will be covered in the next section. Besides generating these special pages, turning DEBUG on has several other effects. Specifically, when DEBUG is on:

- A record is kept of all queries sent to the database. Details of what is recorded and how to access it will be covered in a subsequent section.

- For the MySQL database backend, warnings issued by the database will be turned into Python Exceptions. These MySQL warnings may indicate a serious problem, but a warning (which only results in a message printed to stderr) may pass unnoticed. Since most development is done with DEBUG turned on, raising exceptions for MySQL warnings then ensures that the developer is aware of the possible issue. We ran into this behavior back in *Chapter 3, Testing 1, 2, 3: Basic Unit Testing*, when we saw that the testClosesReset unit test produced different results depending on the DEBUG setting and the MySQL server configuration.

- The admin application performs extensive validation of the configuration of all registered models and raises an ImproperlyConfigured exception on the first attempt to access any admin page if an error is found in the configuration. This extensive validation is fairly expensive and not something you'd generally want done during production server start-up, when the admin configuration likely has not changed since the last start-up. When running with DEBUG on, though, it is possible that the admin configuration has changed, and thus it is useful and worth the cost to do the explicit validation and provide a specific error message about what is wrong if a problem is detected.

- Finally, there are several places in Django code where an error will occur while DEBUG is on, and the generated response will contain specific information about the cause of the error, whereas when DEBUG is off the generated response will be a generic error page.

The TEMPLATE_STRING_IF_INVALID setting

A third setting that can be useful for debugging during development is TEMPLATE_STRING_IF_INVALID. The default value for this setting is the empty string. This setting is used to control what gets inserted into a template in place of a reference to an invalid (for example, non-existent in the template context) variable. The default value of an empty string results in nothing visible taking the place of such invalid references, which can make them hard to notice. Setting TEMPLATE_STRING_IF_INVALID to some value can make tracking down such invalid references easier.

However, some code that ships with Django (the admin application, in particular), relies on the default behavior of invalid references being replaced with an empty string. Running code like this with a non-empty TEMPLATE_STRING_IF_INVALID setting can produce unexpected results, so this setting is only useful when you are specifically trying to track down something like a misspelled template variable in code that always ensures that variables, even empty ones, are set in the template context.

Debug error pages

With DEBUG on, Django generates fancy debug error pages in two circumstances:

- When a django.http.Http404 exception is raised
- When any other exception is raised and not handled by the regular view processing code

In the latter case, the debug page contains a tremendous amount of information about the error, the request that caused it, and the environment at the time it occurred. Deciphering this page and making best use of the information it presents will be covered in the next chapter. The debug pages for Http404 exceptions are considerably simpler and will be covered here.

To see examples of the Http404 debug pages, consider the survey_detail view from *Chapter 4*:

```
def survey_detail(request, pk):
    survey = get_object_or_404(Survey, pk=pk)
    today = datetime.date.today()
    if survey.closes < today:
        return display_completed_survey(request, survey)
    elif survey.opens > today:
        raise Http404
    else:
        return display_active_survey(request, survey)
```

There are two cases where this view may raise an `Http404` exception: when the requested survey is not found in the database, and when it is found but has not yet opened. Thus, we can see the debug 404 page by attempting to access the survey detail for a survey that does not exist, say survey number 24. The result will be as follows:

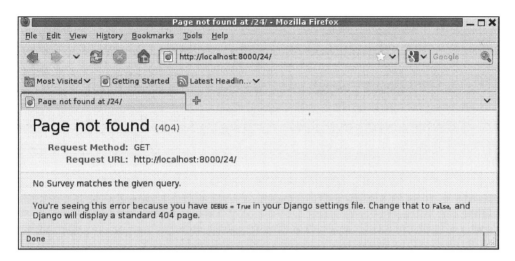

Notice there is a message in the middle of the page that describes the cause of the page not found response: **No Survey matches the given query**. This message was generated automatically by the `get_object_or_404` function. By contrast, the bare `raise Http404` in the case where the survey is found but not yet open does not look like it will have any descriptive message. To confirm this, add a survey that has an opens date in the future, and try to access its detail page. The result will be something like the following:

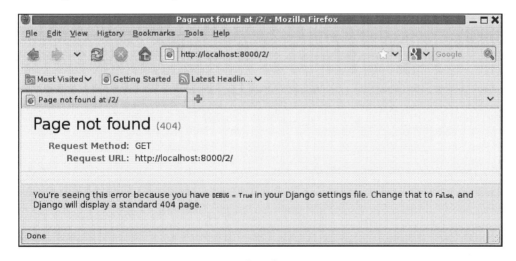

That is not a very helpful debug page, since it lacks any information about what was being searched for and why it could not be displayed. To make this page more useful, include a message when raising the `Http404` exception. For example:

```
raise Http404("%s does not open until %s; it is only %s" %
         (survey.title, survey.opens, today))
```

Then an attempt to access this page will be a little more helpful:

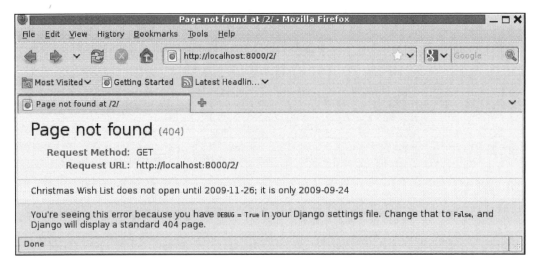

Note that the error message supplied with the `Http404` exception is only displayed on the debug 404 page; it would not appear on a standard 404 page. So you can make such messages as descriptive as you like and not worry that they will leak private or sensitive information to general users.

Another thing to note is that a debug 404 page is only generated when an `Http404` exception is raised. If you manually construct an `HttpResponse` with a 404 status code, it will be returned, not the debug 404 page. Consider this code:

```
return HttpResponse("%s does not open until %s; it is only %s" %
         (survey.title, survey.opens, today), status=404)
```

If that code were used in place of the `raise Http404` variant, then the browser will simply display the passed message:

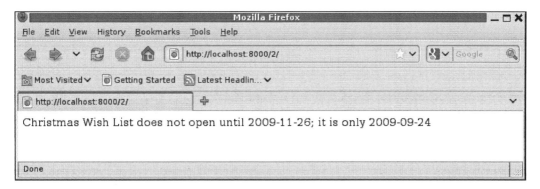

Without the prominent **Page not found** message and distinctive error page formatting, this page isn't even obviously an error report. Note also that some browsers by default will replace the server-provided content with a supposedly "friendly" error page that tends to be even less informative. Thus, it is both easier and more useful to use the `Http404` exception instead of manually building `HttpResponse` objects with status code 404.

A final example of the debug 404 page that is very useful is the one that is generated when URL resolution fails. For example, if we add an extra space before the survey number in the URL, the debug 404 page generated will be as follows:

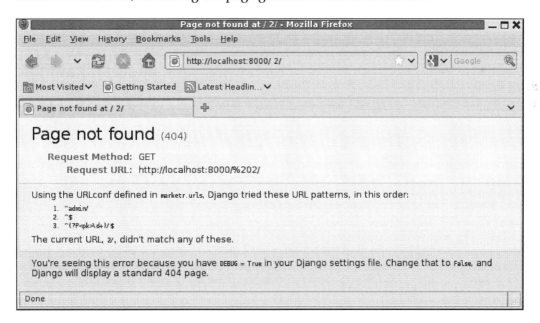

The message on this page includes all of the information necessary to figure out why URL resolution failed. It includes the current URL, the name of the base URLConf used for resolution, and all patterns that were tried, in order, for matching.

If you do any significant amount of Django application programming, it's highly likely that at some time this page will appear and you will be convinced that one of the listed patterns should match the given URL. You would be wrong. Do not waste energy trying to figure out how Django could be so broken. Rather, trust the error message, and focus your energies on figuring out why the pattern you think should match doesn't in fact match. Look carefully at each element of the pattern and compare it to the actual element in the current URL: there will be something that doesn't match.

In this case, you might think the third listed pattern should match the current URL. The first element in the pattern is the capture of the primary key value, and the actual URL value does contain a number that could be a primary key. However, the capture is done using the pattern **\d+**. An attempt to match this against the actual URL characters—a space followed by **2**—fails because **\d** only matches numeric digits and the space character is not a numeric digit. There will always be something like this to explain why the URL resolution failed.

The next chapter will include many more examples of common errors that result in debug pages, and will delve into all of the information available on these pages. For now, we will leave the subject of debug pages and learn about accessing the history of database queries that is maintained when DEBUG is on.

Database query history

When DEBUG is True, Django maintains a history of all SQL commands sent to the database. This history is kept in a list, named queries, located in the django. db.connection module. The easiest way to see what is kept in this list is to examine it from a shell session:

```
>>> from django.db import connection
>>> connection.queries
[]
>>> from survey.models import Survey
>>> Survey.objects.count()
2
>>> connection.queries
[{'time': '0.002', 'sql': u'SELECT COUNT(*) FROM "survey_survey"'}]
>>>
```

Here we see that `queries` is initially empty at the beginning of the shell session. We then retrieve a count of the number of `Survey` objects in the database, which comes back as **2**. When we again display the contents of `queries`, we see that there is now one query in the `queries` list. Each element in the list is a dictionary containing two keys: `time` and `sql`. The value of `time` is how long, in seconds, the query took to execute. The value of `sql` is the actual SQL query that was sent to the database.

One thing to note about the SQL contained in `connection.queries`: it does not include quoting of query parameters. For example, consider the SQL shown for a query on `Surveys` with titles that start with `Christmas`:

```
>>> Survey.objects.filter(title__startswith='Christmas')
[<Survey: Christmas Wish List (opens 2009-11-26, closes 2009-12-31)>]
>>> print connection.queries[-1]['sql']
SELECT "survey_survey"."id", "survey_survey"."title",
"survey_survey"."opens", "survey_survey"."closes"
FROM "survey_survey" WHERE "survey_survey"."title"
LIKE Christmas% ESCAPE '\'  LIMIT 21

>>>
```

In the displayed SQL, `Christmas%` would need to be quoted in order for the SQL to be valid. However, we see here it is not quoted when stored in `connection.queries`. The reason is because Django does not actually pass the query in this form to the database backend. Rather, Django passes parameterized queries. That is, the passed query string contains parameter placeholders, and parameter values are passed separately. It is up to the database backend, then, to perform parameter substitution and proper quoting.

For the debug information placed in `connection.queries`, Django does parameter substitution, but it does not attempt to do the quoting, as that varies from backend to backend. So do not be concerned by the lack of parameter quoting in `connection.queries`: it does not imply that parameters are not quoted correctly when they are actually sent to the database. It does mean, though, that the SQL from `connection.queries` cannot be successfully cut and pasted directly into a database shell program. If you want to use the SQL form `connection.queries` in a database shell, you will need to supply the missing parameter quoting.

You might have noticed and may be curious about the `LIMIT 21` included in the previous SQL. The `QuerySet` requested did not include a limit, so why did the SQL include a limit? This is a feature of the `QuerySet repr` method, which is what the Python shell calls to display the value returned by the `Survey.objects.filter` call.

A `QuerySet` may have many elements, and displaying the entire set, if it is quite large, is not particularly useful in Python shell sessions, for example. Therefore, `QuerySet` repr displays a maximum of 20 items. If there are more, `repr` will add an ellipsis to the end to indicate that the display is incomplete. Thus, the SQL resulting from a call to `repr` on a `QuerySet` will limit the result to 21 items, which is enough to determine if an ellipsis is needed to indicate that the printed result is incomplete.

Any time you see `LIMIT 21` included in a database query, that is a signal the query was likely the result of a call to `repr`. Since `repr` is not frequently called from application code, such queries are likely resulting from other code (such as the Python shell, here, or a graphical debugger variable display window) that may be automatically displaying the value of a `QuerySet` variable. Keeping this in mind can help reduce confusion when trying to figure out why some queries are appearing in `connection.queries`.

There is one final item to note about `connection.queries`: despite the name, it is not limited to just SQL queries. All SQL statements sent to the database, including updates and inserts, are stored in `connection.queries`. For example, if we create a new `Survey` from the shell session, we will see the resulting SQL INSERT stored in `connection.queries`:

```
>>> import datetime
>>> Survey.objects.create(title='Football Favorites',opens=datetime.date.
today())
<Survey: Football Favorites (opens 2009-09-24, closes 2009-10-01)>
>>> print connection.queries[-1]['sql']
INSERT INTO "survey_survey" ("title", "opens", "closes") VALUES (Football
Favorites, 2009-09-24, 2009-10-01)
>>>
```

Here we have been accessing `connection.queries` from a shell session. Often, however, it may be useful to see what it contains after a request has been processed. That is, we might want to know what database traffic was generated during the creation of a page. Recreating the calling of a view function from within a Python shell and then manually examining `connection.queries` is not particularly convenient, however. Therefore, Django provides a context processor, `django.core.contextprocessors.debug`, that provides convenient access to the data stored in `connection.queries` from a template. In *Chapter 8, When Problems Hide: Getting More Information*, we will see how we can use this context processor to include information from `connection.queries` in our generated pages.

Debug support in the development server

The development server, which we have been using since *Chapter 3*, has several characteristics which aid in debugging. First, it provides a console that allows for easy reporting, during development, of what is going on in Django application code. The development server itself reports general information about its operation to the console. For example, typical output from the development server looks like this:

```
kmt@lbox:/dj_projects/marketr$ python manage.py runserver
Validating models...
0 errors found

Django version 1.1, using settings 'marketr.settings'
Development server is running at http://127.0.0.1:8000/
Quit the server with CONTROL-C.
[25/Sep/2009 07:51:24] "GET / HTTP/1.1" 200 480
[25/Sep/2009 07:51:27] "GET /survey/1/ HTTP/1.1" 200 280
[25/Sep/2009 07:51:33] "GET /survey/888/ HTTP/1.1" 404 1704
```

As you can see, the development server starts out by explicitly validating models. If any errors are found they will be prominently reported during server start-up, and will prevent the server from entering its request processing loop. This helps to ensure that any erroneous model changes made during development are noticed quickly.

The server then reports the level of Django that is running, the settings file in use, and the host address and port it is listening on. The first of these, in particular, is very useful when you have multiple Django versions installed and are switching between them. For example, if you have the latest release installed in site-packages but also have an SVN checkout of current trunk that you use by explicitly setting PYTHONPATH, you can use the version reported by the development server to confirm (or not) that you are in fact using the version you intend to be using at the moment.

The final start-up message notes that you can terminate the server by pressing *Ctrl-C*. The server then enters its request processing loop and will proceed to report information on each request that it handles. The information printed for each request is:

- The date and time the request was processed, in square brackets
- The request itself, which includes the HTTP method (for example, GET or POST), the path, and the HTTP version specified by the client, all enclosed in quotes
- The HTTP status code returned
- The number of bytes in the returned response

In the previous example output, we can see that the server has responded to three GET requests, all specifying an HTTP version of 1.1. First for the root URL /, which resulted in an HTTP 200 (OK) status code with a 480 byte response. The request for /survey/1/ was similarly processed successfully and produced a 280 byte response, but /survey/888/ resulted in a 404 HTTP status with a 1704 byte response. The 404 status was returned because no survey with primary key 888 existed in the database. Simply being able to see what requests, exactly, are being received by the development server, and what is being returned in response, often comes in handy.

There are some requests handled by the development server that are not shown on the console. First, requests for admin media files (that is, CSS, JavaScript, and images) are not logged. If you look at the HTML source for an admin page, you will see it does include links to CSS files in its <head> section. For example:

```
<head>
<title>Site administration | Django site admin</title>
<link rel="stylesheet" type="text/css" href="/media/css/base.css" />
<link rel="stylesheet" type="text/css" href="/media/css/dashboard.css"
/>
```

A web browser receiving this document will proceed to retrieve /media/css/base.css and /media/css/dashboard.css from the same server that produced the original page. The development server will receive and automatically serve these files, but it does not log that activity. Specifically, it will serve but not log requests for URLs that begin with the ADMIN_MEDIA_PREFIX setting. (This setting's default value is /media/).

The second request that will not get logged by the development server is any request for /favicon.ico. This is a file automatically requested by many web browsers in order to associate an icon with a bookmarked page or to display an icon in the address bar. There is no point in cluttering up the output of the development server with requests for this file, so it is never logged.

Often when debugging a problem, the very basic information logged automatically by the development server will not be sufficient to figure out what is going on. When this happens, you may add logging to your application code. Assuming you route the log output you add to `stdout` or `stderr`, it will appear on the console of the development server along with the normal development server output.

Note that some production deployment environments do not allow sending output to `stdout`. In such environments, a mistakenly leftover debugging print statement in the application code could cause a server failure in production. To avoid this, always route debug print statements to `stderr` instead of `stdout`.

Also note that the request logging done by the development server happens at the very end of the request processing. The logged information includes the size of the response, so the response has been completely generated before this line appears. Thus, any logging added in application view functions, for example, will appear before the single line logged by the development server. Don't get confused and think that prints from a view function are referring to the work done to service the request logged above them. More specifics on adding logging to application code will be discussed in *Chapter 8*.

A second feature of the development server that is useful when developing and debugging code is that it automatically notices when source code changes on disk and re-starts itself, so that it is always running current code. You can tell when this happens because when it restarts, it will again print the start-up messages. For example, consider this output:

```
kmt@lbox:/dj_projects/marketr$ python manage.py runserver
Validating models...
0 errors found

Django version 1.1, using settings 'marketr.settings'
Development server is running at http://127.0.0.1:8000/
Quit the server with CONTROL-C.
[25/Sep/2009 07:51:24] "GET / HTTP/1.1" 200 480
[25/Sep/2009 07:51:27] "GET /survey/1/ HTTP/1.1" 200 280
[25/Sep/2009 07:51:33] "GET /survey/888/ HTTP/1.1" 404 1704
Validating models...
0 errors found

Django version 1.1, using settings 'marketr.settings'
Development server is running at http://127.0.0.1:8000/
Quit the server with CONTROL-C.
[25/Sep/2009 08:20:15] "GET /admin/ HTTP/1.1" 200 7256
```

Here some code change was made that resulted in the development server restarting itself between the handling of the **GET /survey/888/** and the **GET /admin/** request.

While this automatic restart behavior is convenient, it can sometimes run into trouble. This most frequently happens when code is edited and saved with an error. Sometimes, but not always, loading the erroneous file causes the development server to fail to notice subsequent changes in the file. Thus, the corrected version may not be automatically loaded even when the error is noticed and fixed. If it seems like the development server is not reloading when it should, it is a good idea to manually stop and restart it.

This automatic reloading feature of the development server can be turned off by passing the `--noreload` option to `runserver`. You likely will not often want to specify this when running the development server on its own, but if you are running it under a debugger, you may need to specify this option in order for debugger breakpoints to be properly recognized. This is a final feature of the development server that makes it useful for debugging: it is easy to run under a debugger. Details on this will be covered in *Chapter 9, When You Don't Even Know What to Log: Using Debuggers*.

Handling problems in production

In an ideal world, all code problems would be found during development, and nothing would ever go wrong when the code was in production. However, despite best efforts, this ideal is rarely achieved in reality. We must prepare for the case where something will go seriously wrong while the code is running in production mode, and arrange to do something sensible when it happens.

What's involved in doing something sensible? First some response must still be returned to the client that sent the request that resulted in the error. But the response should just be a general error indication, bare of the specific internal details found in the fancy debug error pages produced when DEBUG is active. At best, a Django debug error page might confuse a general web user, but at worst information gleaned from it might be used by some malicious user to attempt to break the site. Thus, the public response produced for a request that causes an error should be a generic error page.

The specific details of such errors, though, should still be made available to site administrators so that the problems can be analyzed and fixed. Django accomplishes this by e-mailing details of errors encountered when DEBUG is False to a list of e-mail addresses specified in `settings.py`. The information included in the e-mail is not as extensive as what would be found on a debug page, but it is often enough to get started on recreating and fixing the problem.

This section discusses the steps needed to handle errors encountered during production. First, what needs to be done to return generic error pages is described, and then the settings necessary to specify where to send more detailed error information are discussed.

Creating general error pages

As with the fancy error pages, there are two types of general error pages: one to report that a page does not exist on the site, and one to report that some internal server error occurred during processing of the request. Django provides default handlers for these error cases that automatically load and render templates named `404.html` and `500.html` respectively. A project that relies on the default handling of these errors must provide templates with these names to be loaded and rendered. No defaults for these files are created by `manage.py startproject`.

When the `404.html` template it rendered, it is passed a `RequestContext` in which a variable named `request_path` has been set to the value of the URL path that caused the `Http404` exception to be raised. The `404.html` template, then, can use the `request_path` value and the other variables set by context processors to tailor the specific response generated.

The `500.html` template, on the other hand, is rendered with an empty context. When a internal server error occurs, something has gone seriously wrong with the server code. Attempting to process a `RequestContext` through context processors might well cause yet another exception to be raised. To attempt to ensure that the response will be generated without any further errors, then, the `500.html` template is rendered with an empty context. This means that the `500.html` template cannot rely on any context variables that are ordinarily set by context processors.

It is possible to override the default error handling by providing custom error handlers for either one or both of these error situations. The Django documentation provides full details on how to do this; it is not covered here as the default handlers are fine for the vast majority of situations.

Reporting production error information

Though it is good to avoid presenting detailed technical error information to general users, it is not good to lose such information entirely. Django supports notifying site administrators when errors are encountered in production. Settings related to these notifications are discussed in this section. *Chapter 11, When it's Time to Go Live: Moving to Production*, provides more guidance on the task of moving to production and solving some common problems that are encountered along the way.

Internal server error notifications

When a server error occurs, Django sends an e-mail containing details of the request that generated the error and the traceback from the error to all of the e-mail addresses listed in the ADMINS setting. ADMINS is a list of tuples containing names and e-mail addresses. The value set by manage.py startproject is:

```
ADMINS = (
    # ('Your Name', 'your_email@domain.com'),
)
```

The commented line shows the format you should use for adding values to this setting.

There is no setting to control whether server error notifications should be sent: Django will always attempt to send these notifications. However, if you really do not want e-mail notifications generated for internal server errors, you can leave the ADMINS setting empty. This is not a recommended practice, though, as you will not have any idea, unless your users complain to you, that your site is experiencing difficulty.

Django uses Python's SMTP support to send e-mail. In order for this to work, Django must be configured properly to communicate with an SMTP server. There are several settings that control sending mail which you may need to customize for your installation:

- EMAIL_HOST is the name of the host running the SMTP server. The default value for this setting is localhost, so if there is no SMTP server running on the same machine as the Django server, this will need to be set to a host running an SMTP server that can be used to send mail.

- EMAIL_HOST_USER and EMAIL_HOST_PASSWORD together may be used to authenticate to the SMTP server. Both are set to an empty string by default. If either is set to the empty string, then Django does not attempt to authenticate to the SMTP server. If you are using a server that requires authentication, you will need to set these to valid values for the SMTP server in use.

- EMAIL_USE_TLS specifies whether to use a secure (Transport Layer Security) connection to the SMTP server. The default value is False. If you are using an SMTP server that requires a secure connection, you will need to set this to True.

- EMAIL_PORT specifies the port to connect to. The default value is the default SMTP port, 25. If your SMTP server is listening on a different port (typical when EMAIL_USE_TLS is True), you must specify it here.

- SERVER_EMAIL is the e-mail address that will be used as the From address on the sent mail. The default value is root@localhost. Some e-mail providers refuse to accept mail that uses this default From address, so it is a good idea to set this to a value that is a valid From address for the e-mail server you are using.

- EMAIL_SUBJECT_PREFIX is a string that will be placed at the start of the Subject for the e-mail. The default value is [Django]. You might want to customize this to be something that is site-specific, so administrators that support multiple sites will be able to tell from a glance at the e-mail subject which site encountered the error.

Once you have set all of the values you believe are correct for the SMTP server you are using, it is a good idea to verify that mail is successfully sent. To do this, set ADMINS to include your own e-mail address. Then set DEBUG=False and do something that will cause a server error. One easy way to accomplish this is to rename the 404.html template to something else and then attempt to access the server specifying a URL that will cause an Http404 exception to be raised.

For example, attempt to access the detail page for a survey that does not exist or has an opens date in the future. This attempt should result in an e-mail getting sent to you. The subject will start with your server's EMAIL_SUBJECT_PREFIX and will include the URL path of the request that generated the error. The text of the e-mail will contain the traceback from the error followed by the details of the request that caused it.

Page not found notifications

Page not found errors are considerably less serious than server errors. In fact, they may not indicate errors in the code at all, since they can result from users incorrectly typing addresses in the browser address bar. If, however, they are the result of users attempting to follow links, you might want to know about that. This second case is termed a broken link and can usually be distinguished from the first by the presence of an HTTP Referer [sic] header in the request. Django supports sending e-mail notifications when it detects a user attempting to access a nonexistent page via a broken link.

Unlike internal server error notifications, sending broken link notifications is optional. The setting that controls whether Django sends e-mail notifications for broken links is SEND_BROKEN_LINK_EMAILS. The default value for this setting is False; you will need to set it to True if you want Django to generate these e-mails. In addition, the common middleware (django.middleware.common. CommonMiddleware) must be enabled in order for broken link e-mails to be sent. This middleware is enabled by default.

The e-mails generated by this setting are sent to the e-mail addresses found in the MANAGERS setting. Thus, you can send these notifications to a different set of people than the server error e-mails. If, however, you want to send these to the same set of people who receive the server error e-mails, simply set MANAGERS = ADMINS in settings.py after ADMINS has been set.

Except for the e-mail recipients, all of the same e-mail settings will be used for sending broken link e-mails as are used for server error e-mails. So if you have verified that server error e-mails are successfully sent, broken link e-mails will also be successful.

Broken link e-mail notifications are only useful so long as reports of legitimate problems are not drowned in a sea of reports related to the activity of web crawlers, bots, and malicious people probing the site bent on mischief. To help ensure that the notifications sent are related to valid problems, there are a couple of additional settings that can be used to limit the URL paths reported as broken links. These are IGNORABLE_404_STARTS and IGNORABLE_404_ENDS. A broken link e-mail is only sent for request pages that do not start with IGNORABLE_404_STARTS and do not end with IGNORABLE_404_ENDS.

The default value for IGNORABLE_404_STARTS is:

```
('/cgi-bin/', '/_vti_bin', '/_vti_inf')
```

The default value for IGNORABLE_404_ENDS is:

```
('mail.pl', 'mailform.pl', 'mail.cgi', 'mailform.cgi', 'favicon.ico',
'.php')
```

You can add to these as necessary to ensure that the e-mails generated for broken links are reporting actual problems.

Summary

We have now completed the overview of debugging support in Django. In this chapter, many topics were introduced that will be covered in greater depth in subsequent chapters. Specifically, we have:

- Learned about the Django settings that control the collection and presentation of debug information
- Seen how when debug is turned on, special error pages are produced that help with the task of debugging problems
- Learned about the history of database queries that is maintained when debugging is turned on, and saw how to access it
- Discussed several features of the development server that are helpful when debugging
- Described how errors are handled in production, and the settings related to ensuring that helpful debug information is routed to the correct people

The next chapter will proceed to delve into the details of Django debug pages.

7
When the Wheels Fall Off: Understanding a Django Debug Page

Just about the last thing you want when your code is running in production is for it to encounter an error so severe that the only message that can be returned to the client is "We're sorry, the server has encountered an error, please try again later." During development, however, these server error situations are among the best of the bad outcomes. They generally indicate an exception has been raised, and when that happens there is a wealth of information available to figure out what has gone wrong. When DEBUG is on, this information is returned, in the form of a Django debug page, as the response to the request that caused the error. In this chapter, we will learn how to understand and make use of the information provided by a Django debug page.

Specifically, in this chapter we will:

- Continue development of the example survey application, making some typical mistakes along the way

- See how these mistakes manifest themselves in the form of Django debug pages

- Learn what information is provided on these debug pages

- For each mistake, dig into the information available on the resulting debug page to see how it can be used to understand the error and determine how to fix it

Starting the Survey voting implementation

In *Chapter 4, Getting Fancier: Django Unit Test Extensions,* we began developing code to serve pages for the `survey` application. We implemented the home page view. This view generates a page that lists both active and recently closed surveys and provides links, as appropriate, to either take an active survey or display results from a closed survey. Both of these kinds of links route to the same view function, `survey_detail`, which further routes the request based on the state of the `Survey` for which details have been requested:

```
def survey_detail(request, pk):
    survey = get_object_or_404(Survey, pk=pk)
    today = datetime.date.today()
    if survey.closes < today:
        return display_completed_survey(request, survey)
    elif survey.opens > today:
        raise Http404("%s does not open until %s; it is only %s" %
            (survey.title, survey.opens, today))
    else:
        return display_active_survey(request, survey)
```

We did not then, however, write the code to actually display an active `Survey` or display results from a `Survey`. Rather we created placeholder views and templates that simply state what the pages are eventually intended to show. For example, the `display_active_survey` function was left simply as:

```
def display_active_survey(request, survey):
    return render_to_response('survey/active_survey.html',
                              {'survey': survey})
```

The template it references, `active_survey.html`, contains:

```
{% extends "survey/base.html" %}
{% block content %}
<h1>Survey questions for {{ survey.title }}</h1>
{% endblock content %}
```

We will now pick up where we left off here and start replacing this placeholder view and template with real code that handles displaying an active `Survey`.

What's involved in doing this? First, when a request comes in to display an active survey, we want to return a page that displays the list of questions in the `Survey`, each with their associated possible answers. Furthermore, we want to present these in a manner so that the user can participate in the `Survey`, and submit their chosen answers for the questions. Thus, we will need to present the question and answer data in an HTML form, and also have code on the server that handles receiving, validating, recording, and responding to posted `Survey` responses.

All of that is a lot to tackle at once. What is the smallest piece we can implement first that will allow us to start experimenting and verifying that we are moving in the right direction? We'll start with the display of a form that allows users to see a single question and choose from among its associated answers. First, though, let's get our development database set up with some reasonable test data to work with.

Creating test data for voting

As it's been a while since we were working with these models, we may no longer have any active surveys. Let's start with a clean slate by running `manage.py reset survey`. Then, ensure the development server is running and use the admin application to create a new `Survey`, `Question`, and `Answers`. This is the `Survey` that will be used in the upcoming examples:

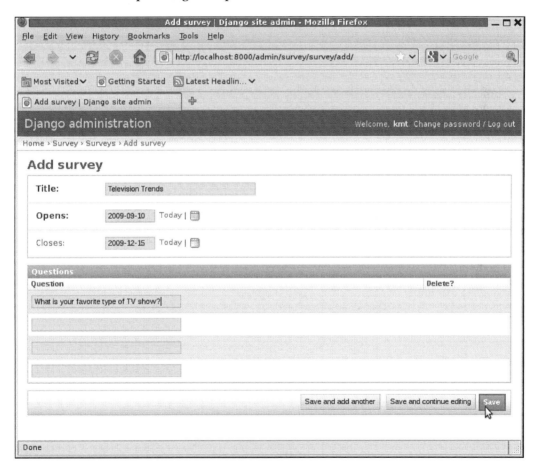

The `Answers` defined for the one `Question` in this `Survey` are:

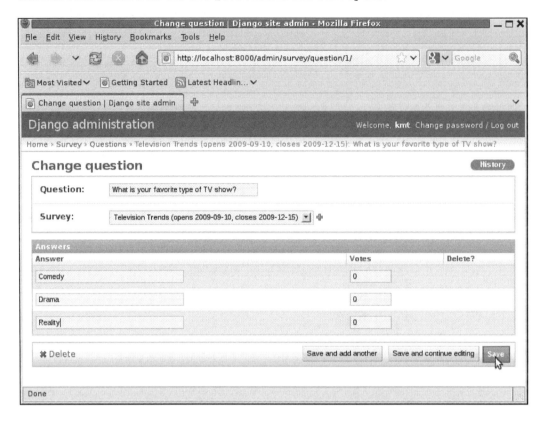

That's enough to get started with. We can come back later and add more data as necessary. Now, we will move on to developing the form used to display a `Question` and choose one of its answers.

Defining a question form for voting

The Django `forms` package provides a convenient framework for creating, displaying, validating, and processing HTML form data. Within the forms package, the `ModelForm` class is often useful for automatically building forms that represent models. We might initially think that using a `ModelForm` would come in handy for our task here, but a `ModelForm` would not provide what we need. Recall that the `survey` application `Question` model contains these fields:

```
class Question(models.Model):
    question = models.CharField(max_length=200)
    survey = models.ForeignKey(Survey)
```

Further, the `Answer` model is:

```
class Answer(models.Model):
    answer = models.CharField(max_length=200)
    question = models.ForeignKey(Question)
    votes = models.IntegerField(default=0)
```

A `ModelForm` contains HTML input fields for each field defined in the model. Thus, a `ModelForm` for the `Question` model would consist of a text input allowing the user to change the content of the `question` field, and a selection box allowing the user to select which `Survey` instance this `Question` is associated with. That's not at all what we want. Nor is a `ModelForm` built from the `Answer` model what we are looking for.

Rather, we want a form that will display the text of the `question` field (but not allow the user to change that text), along with all of the `Answer` instances associated with the `Question` instance, in a manner that allows the user to select exactly one of the listed answers. That sounds like an HTML radio input group where the individual radio button values are defined by the set of `Answers` associated with the `Question` instance.

We can create a custom form to represent this, using the basic form field and widget classes provided by Django. Let's create a new file, `survey/forms.py`, and put in it an initial attempt at implementing the form that will be used to display a `Question` and its associated answers:

```
from django import forms
class QuestionVoteForm(forms.Form):
    answer = forms.ModelChoiceField(widget=forms.RadioSelect)

    def __init__(self, question, *args, **kwargs):
        super(QuestionVoteForm, self).__init__(*args, **kwargs)
        self.fields['answer'].queryset = question.answer_set.all()
```

This form is named `QuestionVoteForm` and has only one field, `answer`, which is a `ModelChoiceField`. This type of field allows selection from a set of choices defined by a `QuerySet`, specified by its `queryset` attribute. Since the correct set of answers for this field will depend on the specific `Question` instance for which the form is built, we omit specifying a `queryset` on the field declaration and set it later, in the `__init__` routine. We do, however, specify in the field declaration that we want to use a `RadioSelect` widget for display, instead of the default `Select` widget (which presents the choices in an HTML select drop-down box).

Following the declaration for the single `answer` field, the form defines an override for the `__init__` method. This `__init__` requires that a `question` argument be passed in when creating an instance of the form. After first calling the `__init__` superclass with whatever other arguments may have been provided, the passed `question` is used to set the `queryset` attribute for the `answer` field to be the set of answers that are associated with this `Question` instance.

In order to see if this form displays as intended, we need to create one of these forms in the `display_active_survey` function and pass it to the template for display. For now, we do not want to worry about displaying a list of questions; we'll just pick one to pass to the template. So, we can change `display_active_survey` to be:

```
from survey.forms import QuestionVoteForm
def display_active_survey(request, survey):
    qvf = QuestionVoteForm(survey.question_set.all()[0])
    return render_to_response('survey/active_survey.html',
                              {'survey': survey, 'qvf': qvf})
```

Now this function creates an instance of a `QuestionVoteForm` for the first question in the set of questions for the specified survey, and passes that form along to the template for rendering as the context variable `qvf`.

We also need to modify the template to display the passed form. To do this, change the `active_survey.html` template to be:

```
{% extends "survey/base.html" %}
{% block content %}
<h1>{{ survey.title }}</h1>
<form method="post" action=".">
<div>
{{ qvf.as_p }}
<button type="submit">Submit</button>
</div>
</form>
{% endblock content %}
```

Here we have added the necessary HTML elements to surround the Django form and make it a valid HTML form. We've used the form `as_p` method for display, just because it is easy. Long-term, we will likely replace that with custom output, but displaying the form in an HTML paragraph element will do for the present.

Now, we are hopefully at a point where we can test and see whether our `QuestionVoteForm` displays what we want it to. We will try that next.

Debug page #1: TypeError at /

In order to see how the `QuestionVoteForm` is looking so far, we can first go to the survey home page and from there we should be able to click on the link for the one active survey we have, and see how the question and answer choices are displayed. How well does that work? Not so well. With the code changes we have made, we can no longer even display the home page. Instead, attempting to access it produces a debug page:

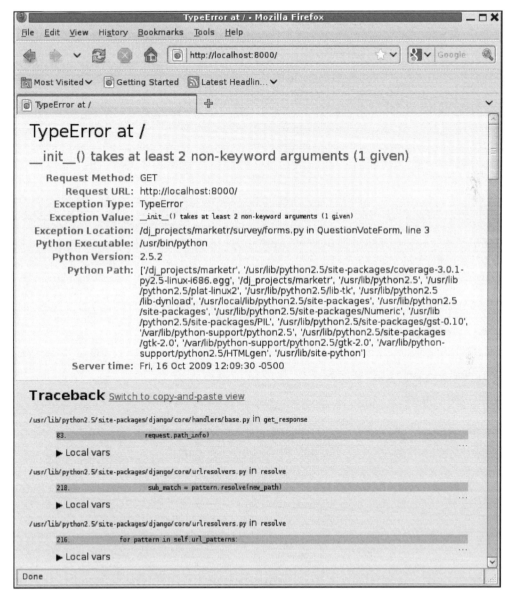

Yikes, that looks bad. Before we dig into the details of what the page is showing, let's try to understand what has happened here. We added a new form, and we changed the view used to display active surveys so that it creates one of the newly-defined forms. We also changed the template used by that view. But we did not change the home page view at all. So how could it now be broken?

The answer is that the home page view itself is not broken, but something else is. That broken something else is preventing the home page view from even being called. Note that in order to call the home page view, the module that contains it (`survey.views`) must be imported without error. Thus, `survey.views` itself and anything it references when it is imported must be error-free. Even if nothing in the home page view, or even all of `survey.views`, is broken, an error may be raised on an attempt to call the home page view if an error has been introduced into any module imported as a result of importing `survey.views`.

The point is that changes made in one place may cause initially surprising breakage in what seems to be an entirely unrelated area. In fact, the other area is not entirely unrelated, but is somehow (usually via a chain of imports) connected to the area where the change was made. It is important in cases like this to focus attention on the right place in order to find and fix the error.

In this case, for example, staring blankly at the home page view code, because that is the code we were attempting to run, and trying to figure out what is wrong with it, would be fruitless. That is not where the problem is. Rather, we need to put aside any preconceived ideas we have about what code might have been running at the time of the error, and use the debug information presented to figure out what code was actually running. It can also be instructive to figure out why one bit of code ends up running when we were trying to run something else entirely, although it is not always necessary to do that in order to fix the problem at hand.

Elements of the debug page

Now let's turn our attention to the debug page we've encountered. There is quite a lot of information on it, split into four parts (only the first and beginning of the second are visible in the screenshot). In this section, we focus on what information, in general, is included in each part of the debug page, noting the values we see on this page simply as examples. Later in the chapter, we will see how the specific information presented on this debug page can be used to fix the error we have made.

Basic error information

The very top part of the debug page contains basic error information. Both the page title and the first line of the page body state the type of exception encountered, and the URL path contained in the request that triggered the exception. In our case, the type of exception is a **TypeError**, and the URL path is **/**. So, we see **TypeError at /** as the first line on the page.

The second line contains the exception value. This is usually a specific description of what caused the error. In this case, we see **__init__() takes at least 2 non-keyword arguments (1 given)**.

Following the exception value is a list of nine items:

- **Request Method**: The HTTP method specified in the request. In this case, it is **GET**.

- **Request URL**: The full URL of the request. In this case it is **http://localhost:8000/**. The path part of this is a repeat of the path reported on the first line.

- **Exception Type**: This is a repeat of the exception type included on the first line.

- **Exception Value**: This is a repeat of the exception value included on the second line.

- **Exception Location**: The line of code where the exception occurred. In this case, it is **/dj_projects/marketr/survey/forms.py in QuestionVoteForm, line 3**.

- **Python Executable**: The Python executable running at the time of the error. In this case, it is **/usr/bin/python**. This information is usually only interesting if you are doing something like testing with different Python versions.

- **Python Version**: This identifies the version of Python that is running. Again, this will often be uninteresting unless you are testing with different Python versions. However, it can be a very useful bit of information when looking at problems reported by other people, if there is any suspicion that the problem may be dependent on the Python version.

- **Python Path**: The full Python path in effect. This is most often useful when the exception type relates to an error importing something. It can also come in handy when multiple versions of an add-on package have been installed in different places. This, plus an incorrect path specification, can cause an unexpected version to be used, which might lead to an error. Having the full Python path in use available helps in tracking down what is going on in this type of situation.

- **Server time**: This shows the date, time, and time zone at the server when the exception occurred. This can be useful for any views that return time-dependent results.

The exception type, exception value, and exception location are the first things to look at when presented with a debug page. These three items reveal what went wrong, why, and where it happened. Often, that is all you will need to know in order to fix the problem. Sometimes though, this basic information alone is not enough to understand and fix the error. In such situations, it may be helpful to know how the code got to where it ultimately ran into trouble. For that, the next part of the debug page is useful.

Traceback

The traceback portion of the debug page shows how the thread of control got to where it encountered the error. At the top, it starts with the outermost level of the code that was running to process the request, showing where it called the next level down, then where the next call was made, ultimately ending at the bottom with the line of code that caused the exception. Thus, it is often the very bottom of the traceback (not visible in the screenshot) that is most interesting, though at times the path taken by the code to get there is the key to understanding and fixing what went wrong.

For each call level shown in the traceback, there are three pieces of information displayed: first the line of code is identified, then it is shown, and then there is a line with a triangle and the text **Local vars**.

For example, the first bit of information for the top level in the traceback on this debug page identifies the line of code as **/usr/lib/python2.5/site-packages/ django/core/handlers/base.py in get_response**. This shows the file containing the code and the name of the function (or method or class) within that file where the code was executing.

Next is a line with a darker background that shows: **83.   request.path_info)**. That looks a little odd. The number on the left is the line number within the file, and on the right are the contents of that line. In this case the call statement spans multiple lines, and we're seeing only the last line of the call, which is not very informative. All we can tell is that **request.path_info** is being passed as the last argument to something. It might be nice to see the other lines of code around this line, which would make it clearer what was being called. In fact we can do that, just by clicking on the line:

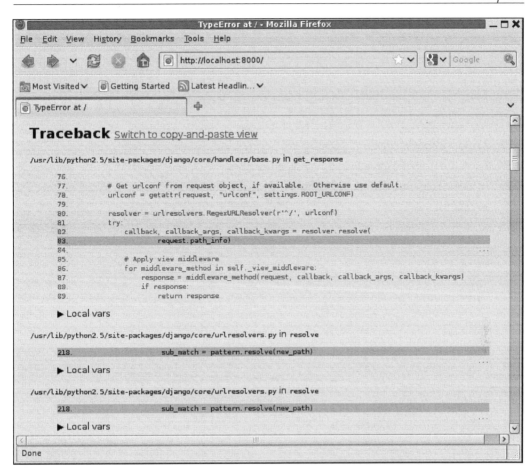

Aha! Now, we can see that something named **resolver.resolve** was being called and passed **request.path_info**. Clearly the code at this level is starting with the requested path and trying to determine what code should be called to handle the current request.

Clicking again anywhere within the displayed code will toggle the display of the surrounding code context back to the hidden state, so that only one line is displayed. Often, it's not necessary to see the surrounding code in the traceback, which is why it is hidden initially. But when it is helpful to see more, it is convenient that more context is just a click away.

Local variables are contained in the third block of information displayed for each level of the traceback. These too are initially hidden, since they can take up quite a lot of space and clutter the page if they are displayed, making it hard to see at a glance what the flow of control was. Clicking on any **Local vars** line expands the block to show the list of local variables at that level and the value for each. For example:

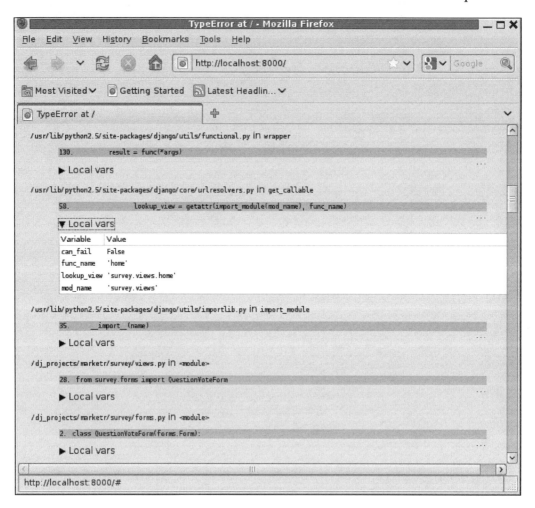

We do not need to fully understand the Django code running here in order to guess based on the names and values for the variables shown, that the code is trying to look up the view that handles displaying the home page. Clicking again on the **Local vars** line toggles the block back to being hidden.

There is one final very useful feature of the traceback section of the debug page. Right next to the **Traceback** heading is a link: **Switch to copy-and-paste view**. Clicking that link changes the traceback display into one that can be usefully copied and pasted elsewhere. For example on this page, clicking that link produces a text box that contains:

```
Environment:


Request Method: GET

Request URL: http://localhost:8000/

Django Version: 1.1

Python Version: 2.5.2

Installed Applications:

['django.contrib.auth',

 'django.contrib.contenttypes',

 'django.contrib.sessions',

 'django.contrib.sites',

 'django.contrib.admin',

 'survey',

 'django_coverage']

Installed Middleware:

('django.middleware.common.CommonMiddleware',

 'django.contrib.sessions.middleware.SessionMiddleware',

 'django.contrib.auth.middleware.AuthenticationMiddleware')



Traceback:

File "/usr/lib/python2.5/site-packages/django/core/handlers/base.py" in
get_response

  83.                        request.path_info)

File "/usr/lib/python2.5/site-packages/django/core/urlresolvers.py" in
resolve

  218.                    sub_match = pattern.resolve(new_path)

File "/usr/lib/python2.5/site-packages/django/core/urlresolvers.py" in
resolve

  218.                    sub_match = pattern.resolve(new_path)

File "/usr/lib/python2.5/site-packages/django/core/urlresolvers.py" in
resolve
```

```
  125.               return self.callback, args, kwargs
File "/usr/lib/python2.5/site-packages/django/core/urlresolvers.py" in
_get_callback
  131.               self._callback = get_callable(self._callback_str)
File "/usr/lib/python2.5/site-packages/django/utils/functional.py" in
wrapper
  130.               result = func(*args)
File "/usr/lib/python2.5/site-packages/django/core/urlresolvers.py" in
get_callable
  58.                lookup_view = getattr(import_module(mod_name),
func_name)
File "/usr/lib/python2.5/site-packages/django/utils/importlib.py" in
import_module
  35.         __import__(name)
File "/dj_projects/marketr/survey/views.py" in <module>
  24. from survey.forms import QuestionVoteForm
File "/dj_projects/marketr/survey/forms.py" in <module>
  2. class QuestionVoteForm(forms.Form):
File "/dj_projects/marketr/survey/forms.py" in QuestionVoteForm
  3.        answer = forms.ModelChoiceField(widget=forms.RadioSelect)


Exception Type: TypeError at /
Exception Value: __init__() takes at least 2 non-keyword arguments (1
given)
```

As you can see, this block of information contains both the basic traceback plus some other useful information pulled from other sections on the debug page. It is far less complete than what is available on the full debug page, but it is often enough to get help from others when solving a problem. If you find you cannot solve a problem yourself and want to ask others for help, it is this information that you want to provide to others, not a screenshot of the debug page.

In fact, the cut-and-paste view itself has a button at the bottom: **Share this traceback on a public Web site**. If you press that button, the cut-and-paste version of the traceback information will be posted to the dpaste.com site, and you will be taken to that site where you can either record the assigned URL for reference or delete the entry.

Clearly this button will only work if your computer is connected to the Internet and can reach dpaste.com. If you try it and don't have connectivity to that site, you'll get an error reported by your browser that it is unable to connect to dpaste.com. Pressing the back button will return you to the debug page. *Chapter 10, When All Else Fails: Getting Outside Help,* will go into more detail on techniques for getting additional help with intractable problems.

When clicked, the **Switch to copy-and-paste view** link is automatically replaced by another link: **Switch back to interactive view**. Thus, it is easy to toggle between the two forms of the traceback information.

Request information

Following the traceback information section on the debug page is detailed request information. Often you will not need to look at this section at all, but when an error is triggered by some odd characteristic of the request being processed, this section can be invaluable. It is split into five subsections, each described below.

GET

This section contains a list of all the keys and their values in the request.GET dictionary. Alternatively, if the request had no GET data, the string **No GET data** is displayed.

POST

This section contains a list of all the keys and their values in the request.POST dictionary. Alternatively, if the request had no POST data, the string **No POST data** is displayed.

FILES

This section contains a list of all the keys and their values in the request.FILES dictionary. Note that the displayed information here is just the file name uploaded, not the actual file data (which could be quite large). Alternatively, if no file data was uploaded with the request, the string **No FILES data** is displayed.

COOKIES

This section contains any cookies sent by the browser with the request. For example, if the contrib.sessions application is listed in INSTALLED_APPS, you will see the sessionid cookie that it uses listed here. Alternatively, if the browser did not include any cookies with the request, the string **No cookies data** is displayed.

META

This section contains a list of all the keys and their values in the `request.META` dictionary. This dictionary contains all of the HTTP request headers, in addition to other variables that have nothing to do with HTTP.

For example, if you look at the contents of this section as reported when you are running the development server, you will see it lists all of the environment variables that were exported in the environment of the command prompt where the development server is running. That is because this dictionary is initially set to the value of the Python `os.environ` dictionary, and then additional values are added. Thus, there can be a lot of extraneous information listed here, but if you ever need to check up on the value of an HTTP header, for example, you can find it in here.

Settings

The final part of the debug page is an exhaustive list of the settings in effect at the time of the error. This is another section that you may rarely need to look at, but when you do it, is very helpful to have it listed.

Two items from this section: the installed applications, and the installed middleware, are included in the cut-and-paste version of the debug information mentioned earlier, since they are often helpful to know when analyzing problems posted by others.

If you glance through this section of the debug page, you may notice that the values of some settings are not actually reported, but rather a string of asterisks is listed instead. This is a way of hiding information that should not be casually exposed to any users who may see a debug page. The hiding technique is applied to any setting that has the string PASSWORD or SECRET in its name.

Note that this hiding technique is applied only to the values as they are reported in the settings section of the debug page. It does not imply that it is safe to run with DEBUG enabled for a production site. It is still possible to retrieve sensitive information from a debug page. For example, this would be the case if the value of a password setting is stored in a local variable, as will be typical when it is being used to set up a connection to the database or mail server. If an exception is raised during the connection attempt, the password value can be retrieved from the local variable information in the traceback section of the page.

We've now finished with the general description of the information available on a debug page. Next, we will see how to use the specific information on the page we have encountered in order to track down and fix the error in the code.

Understanding and fixing the TypeError

What went wrong that led to the debug page we've encountered here? In this case, the basic error information is enough to identify and fix the problem. We have a **TypeError** reported, with an exception value of **__init__() takes at least 2 non-keyword arguments (1 given)**. Furthermore, the location of the code that caused the error is **/dj_projects/marketr/survey/forms.py in QuestionVoteForm, line 3**. Looking at that line we see:

```
answer = forms.ModelChoiceField(widget=forms.RadioSelect)
```

We have not specified all of the necessary arguments to create a `ModelChoiceField`. If you are new to Python, the specifics of the error message may be a bit confusing, as that line of code doesn't reference anything named `__init__` nor does it appear to pass any non-keyword arguments, yet the message says one was given. The explanation for that is that `__init__` is the method called by Python when an object is created, and it, like all object instance methods, automatically receives a reference to itself as its first positional argument.

Thus the one non-keyword argument that has been supplied is `self`. What is missing? Checking the documentation, we find that `queryset` is a required argument for a `ModelChoiceField`. We omitted it because the correct value is not known at the time the field is declared, but only when an instance of the form containing the field is created. We cannot just leave it out though, so we need to specify something as the `queryset` value when the field is declared. What should it be? As it is going to be reset as soon as any instance of the form is created, `None` will probably do. So let's try changing that line to:

```
answer = forms.ModelChoiceField(widget=forms.RadioSelect,
    queryset=None)
```

Does that work? Yes, if we click the browser reload page button we now get the survey home page:

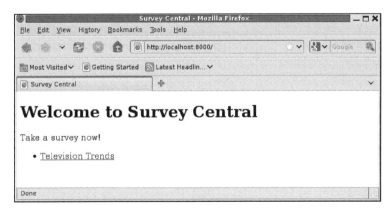

Again, if you are new to Python the fact that the fix worked might seem a bit confusing. The error message says that at least two non-keyword arguments are needed, but we did not add a non-keyword argument with the fix. The message makes it sounds like the only correct fix might be to supply the `queryset` value as a non-keyword argument:

```
answer = forms.ModelChoiceField(None, widget=forms.RadioSelect)
```

Clearly that's not the case, though, since the alternative fix shown above does work. The explanation for this is that the message is not referring to how many non-keyword arguments are specified by the caller, but rather how many are specified in the declaration of the target method (that is the `__init__` method of `ModelChoiceField` in this case). The caller is free to pass arguments using keyword syntax, even if they are not listed as keyword arguments in the method declaration, and the Python interpreter will match them up correctly. Thus, the first fix works fine.

Now that we have the home page working again, we can get back to seeing whether we are able to create and display our new `QuestionVoteForm`. To do that, click on the link to the **Television Trends** survey. The result will be:

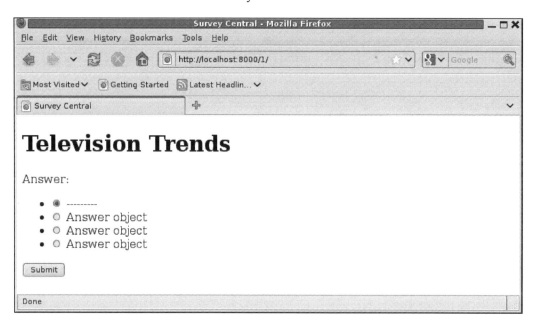

While it is nice not to get a debug page, that's not quite what we are looking for. There are a few problems here.

First, the heading for the list of answers is **Answer**, yet we want that to be the question text. The value displayed here is the label assigned to the `ModelChoiceField`. The default label for any form field is the name of the field, capitalized and with a colon following. We did not override that default when we declared the `ModelChoiceField` answer, so we see **Answer** displayed. The fix is to manually set the `label` attribute for the field. Like the `queryset` attribute, the correct value for a particular form instance is only known when the form is created, so we do this by adding this line to the form's `__init__` method:

```
self.fields['answer'].label = question.question
```

Second, the list of answers includes an empty first choice, shown as a list of dashes. This default behavior is helpful for select drop-down boxes to ensure that the user is forced to choose a valid value. However, it is unnecessary when using a radio input group since with radio inputs, we do not need to have any of the radio buttons initially selected when the form is displayed. Thus, we don't need the empty choice. We can get rid of it by specifying `empty_label=None` in our `ModelChoiceField` declaration.

Third, all the choices listed are displayed as **Answer object** instead of the actual answer text. By default, the value displayed here is whatever is returned by the model instance's `__unicode__` method. Since we have not yet implemented a `__unicode__` method for the `Answer` model, we simply get **Answer object** displayed. One fix is to implement a `__unicode__` method in `Answer` that returns the `answer` field value:

```
class Answer(models.Model):
    answer = models.CharField(max_length=200)
    question = models.ForeignKey(Question)
    votes = models.IntegerField(default=0)

    def __unicode__(self):
        return self.answer
```

Note that if we wanted the `Answer` model's `__unicode__` method to return something else, we could accommodate that also. The way to do that would be to subclass `ModelChoiceField` and provide an override for the `label_from_instance` method. This is the method called to display the value of the choice in the list, and the default implementation uses the textual representation of the instance. So, we could take that approach if we needed to display something other than the model's default textual representation in the choice list, but for our purposes simply having the `Answer` model's `__unicode__` method return the answer text will work fine.

Fourth, the answer choices are displayed as an unordered list, and that list is being displayed with bullets, which is a bit ugly. There are various ways of fixing this—by either adding a CSS style specification or by changing the way the choice list is rendered. However, the bullets are not a functional problem and getting rid of them doesn't further our task of learning about the Django debug page, so for now we will let them be.

The fixes previously made to the `QuestionVoteForm`, result in code that now looks like this:

```python
class QuestionVoteForm(forms.Form):
    answer = forms.ModelChoiceField(widget=forms.RadioSelect,
        queryset=None, empty_label=None)

    def __init__(self, question, *args, **kwargs):
        super(QuestionVoteForm, self).__init__(*args, **kwargs)
        self.fields['answer'].queryset = question.answer_set.all()
        self.fields['answer'].label = question.question
```

With that form, and the implementation of a `__unicode__` method in the `Answer` model, reloading our survey detail page produces a result that looks better:

We've now got a form that displays reasonably well and are ready to move on to the next step in implementing survey voting.

Handling multiple Survey questions

We have the display of a single question form working, what's left to do? First, we need to handle the display of however many questions that are associated with a survey, instead of just a single question. Second, we need to handle receiving, validating, and processing the results. We'll focus on the first task in this section.

Creating the data for multiple questions

Before writing the code to handle multiple questions, let's add another question to our test survey so that we'll be able to see the new code work. The upcoming examples will display this additional question:

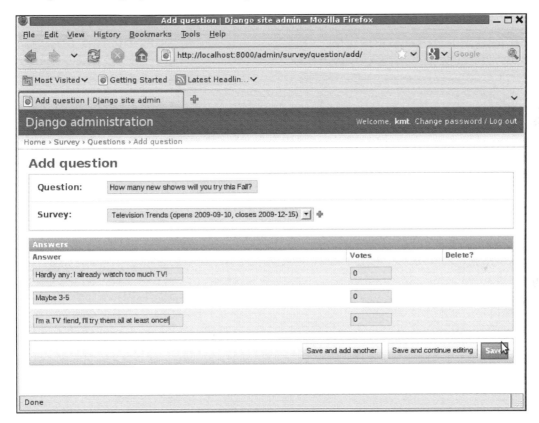

Coding support for multiple questions

Next, change the view to create a list of `QuestionVoteForms` and pass this list in the template context:

```
def display_active_survey(request, survey):
    qforms = []
    for i, q in enumerate(survey.question_set.all()):
        if q.answer_set.count() > 1:
            qforms.append(QuestionVoteForm(q, prefix=i))
    return render_to_response('survey/active_survey.html',
                              {'survey': survey, 'qforms': qforms})
```

Here we start with an empty list named `qforms`. Then, we loop through all questions in the set associated with the passed `survey` and create a form for each question that has more than one answer associated with it. (A `Question` that has fewer than two answers is probably a set-up error. Since it's best to avoid presenting a general user with a question for which they cannot actually choose an answer, we opt here to just leave such questions out of the display for an active `Survey`.)

Notice that we added passing a `prefix` argument on the form creation, and set the value to the position of the current question in the full set of questions for the survey. This gives each form instance a unique `prefix` value. The `prefix` value, if present in a form, is used when `id` and `name` attributes are generated for the HTML form elements. Specifying a unique `prefix` is necessary to ensure that the generated HTML is valid when there are multiple forms of the same type on a page, as there will be for the case we are implementing here.

Finally, each `QuestionVoteForm` created is appended to the `qforms` list, and at the end of the function the `qforms` list is passed in the context to be rendered in the template.

The last step, then, is to change the template to support displaying multiple questions instead of just one. To do this, we might change the `active_survey.html` template like so:

```
{% extends "survey/base.html" %}
{% block content %}
<h1>{{ survey.title }}</h1>
<form method="post" action=".">
<div>
{% for qform in qforms %}
    {{ qform.as_p }}
<button type="submit">Submit</button>
</div>
</form>
{% endblock content %}
```

The only change from the previous version is to replace {{ qvf.as_p }}, which displays a single form, with a {% for %} block that loops through the list of forms in the qforms context variable. Each form is displayed in turn, again still using the as_p convenience method.

Debug page #2: TemplateSyntaxError at /1/

How well does that work? Not so well. If we attempt to reload the page displaying the questions for this survey, we will see:

We've made a mistake, and triggered a slightly different debug page. Instead of the basic exception information being followed immediately by the traceback section, we see a **Template error** section. This section is included for exceptions of type `TemplateSyntaxError`, when `TEMPLATE_DEBUG` is `True`. It displays some context from the template that caused the exception, and highlights the line identified as causing the error. Usually for a `TemplateSyntaxError`, the problem is found in the template itself, not the code that is attempting to render the template (which will be what is shown in the traceback section), so it is helpful for the debug page to prominently display the template contents.

Understanding and fixing the TemplateSyntaxError

In this case, the line identified as causing the error may be somewhat puzzling. The `{% endblock content %}` line hasn't changed since the previous, working, version of the template; it is certainly not an invalid block tag. Why is the template engine now reporting that it is invalid? The answer is that template syntax errors, like many syntax errors reported in programming languages, are sometimes misleading when they attempt to point out where the error is. The point identified as in error is actually where an error was recognized, when in fact the error may have occurred somewhat earlier.

This misleading identification often happens when something required is left out. The parser continues on processing the input, but eventually reaches something not allowed given the current state. At that point, the place where the missing bit should have been may be several lines away. That is what has happened here. The `{% endblock content %}` is reported as being invalid because it is not allowed, given that the template has a still-open `{% for %}` tag.

In making the template changes for supporting multiple questions, we added a `{% for %}` tag, but neglected to close it. The Django template language is not Python, it does not consider indentation significant. Thus, it does not consider the `{% for %}` block terminated by a return to the previous indentation level. Rather, we must explicitly close the new `{% for %}` block with an `{% endfor %}`:

```
{% extends "survey/base.html" %}
{% block content %}
<h1>{{ survey.title }}</h1>
<form method="post" action=".">
<div>
{% for qform in qforms %}
    {{ qform.as_p }}
{% endfor %}
<button type="submit">Submit</button>
```

```
    </div>
    </form>
{% endblock content %}
```

Once we make that change, we can reload the page and see that we do now have multiple questions displayed on the page:

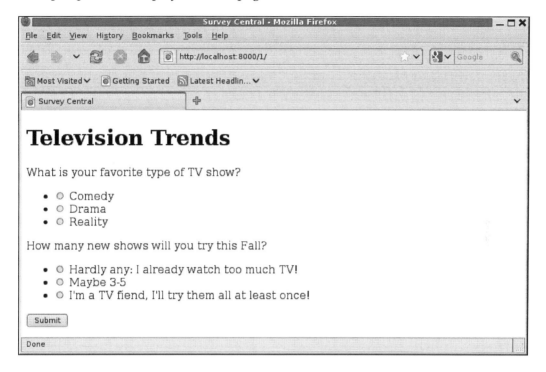

With the display of multiple questions working, we can move on to adding the code to process submitted responses.

Recording Survey responses

We've already got test data we can use to exercise processing survey responses, so we do not need to add any data to our development database for the next step. Furthermore, nothing needs to be changed in the template to support submitting responses. It already includes a submit button in the HTML form, and specifies that the form data should be submitted as an HTTP POST when the form is submitted. Right now the **Submit** button will work, in that it can be pressed and no error will occur, but the only result will be that the page is re-displayed. This is because the view code does not attempt to distinguish between a GET and a POST, and just treats all requests as though they were GET requests. Thus, it is the view code we need to change to add support for handling POST requests as well as GET requests.

Coding support for recording Survey responses

The view code, then, needs to change to check what method is specified in the request. The handling of a GET request should stay the same. If the request is a POST, however, then the QuestionVoteForms should be constructed using the submitted POST data. These can then be validated, and if all of the responses are valid (meaning, in this case, that the user selected a choice for each question), then the votes can be recorded and an appropriate response sent to the user. If there are any validation errors, the constructed forms should be re-displayed with error messages. An initial implementation of this is:

```python
def display_active_survey(request, survey):
    if request.method == 'POST':
        data = request.POST
    else:
        data = None

    qforms = []
    for i, q in enumerate(survey.question_set.all()):
        if q.answer_set.count() > 1:
            qforms.append(QuestionVoteForm(q, prefix=i, data=data))

    if request.method == 'POST':
        chosen_answers = []
        for qf in qforms:
            if not qf.is_valid():
                break;
            chosen_answers.append(qf.cleaned_data['answer'])
        else:
            from django.http import HttpResponse
            response = ""
            for answer in chosen_answers:
                answer.votes += 1
                response += "Votes for %s is now %d<br/>" % (
                    answer.answer, answer.votes)
                answer.save()
            return HttpResponse(response)

    return render_to_response('survey/active_survey.html',
                              {'survey': survey, 'qforms': qforms})
```

Here we start by setting the local variable `data` to either the `request.POST` dictionary, if the request method is `POST`, or `None`. We will use this during form construction, and it must be `None` (not an empty dictionary) in order to create unbound forms, which are what we need for the initial display when a user gets the page.

We then build the list of `qforms` as before. The only difference here is that we pass in the `data` argument so that the created forms will be bound to the posted data in the case where the request is a POST. Binding the data to the forms allows us to later check if the submitted data is valid.

We then have a new block of code to handle the case where the request is a POST. We create an empty list to hold the chosen answers and then loop through the forms checking if each is valid. If any are not, we immediately break out of the `for` loop. This will have the effect of skipping the `else` clause associated with the loop (since that is executed only if the list of items in the `for` loop is exhausted). Thus, as soon as an invalid form is encountered, this routine will skip down to the `return render_to_response` line, which will result in the page being re-displayed with error annotations on the invalid forms.

But wait—we break out of the `for` loop as soon as the first invalid form is found. If there is more than one invalid form, don't we want to display errors on all forms, not just the first? The answer is yes, we do, but we do not need to explicitly call `is_valid` in the view in order to accomplish that. When the form is rendered in the template, if it is bound and has not yet been validated, `is_valid` will be called before its values are rendered. Thus, errors in any of the forms will be displayed in the template, regardless of whether `is_valid` is explicitly called by the view code.

If all the forms are valid, the `for` loop will exhaust its list, and the `else` clause on the `for` loop will run. Here we want to record the votes and return an appropriate response to the user. We've done the first, by incrementing the vote count for each chosen answer instance. For the second, though, we've implemented a development version that builds a response indicating what the current vote values are for all of the questions. This is not what we want general users to see, but we can use it as a quick verification that the answer recording code is doing what we expect.

If we now choose **Drama** and **Hardly any: I already watch too much TV!** as answers and submit the form, we see:

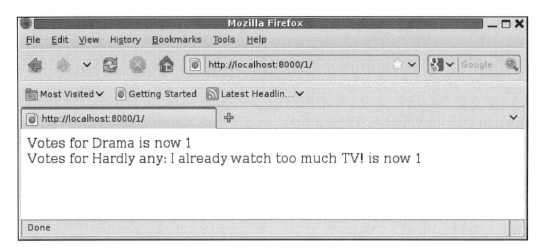

That looks good: there's no debug page and the vote values are correct for what was chosen, so the vote recording code is working. We can now replace the development version of the generated response with one appropriate for general users.

Best practice in responding to a successful POST request is to redirect to some other page, so that a user pressing the browser's reload button does not result in the posted data being re-submitted and re-processed. To do this, we can change the else block to be:

```
else:
    from django.http import HttpResponseRedirect
    from django.core.urlresolvers import reverse
    for answer in chosen_answers:
        answer.votes += 1
        answer.save()
    return HttpResponseRedirect(
        reverse('survey_thanks', args=(survey.pk,)))
```

Note the imports have been included here only to show what needs to be imported; ordinarily these would be placed at the top of the file rather than nested deep within a function like this. Instead of building a response noting all of the new answer vote values, this code now sends an HTTP redirect. As always, to avoid hard-coding URL configuration anywhere outside of the actual `urls.py` files, we have used reverse here to generate the URL path corresponding to a new named URL pattern, `survey_thanks`. We pass along the survey's primary key value as an argument so that the page generated in response can be tailored to reflect the survey that was submitted.

Before that `reverse` call can work, we need to add a new pattern named `survey_thanks` to our `survey/urls.py` file. We might add it like so, so that the full `urlpatterns` in `survey/urls.py` is:

```
urlpatterns = patterns('survey.views',
    url(r'^$', 'home', name='survey_home'),
    url(r'^(?P<pk>\d+)/$', 'survey_detail', name='survey_detail'),
    url(r'^thanks/(?P<pk>\d+/)$', 'survey_thanks',
        name='survey_thanks'),
)
```

The added `survey_thanks` pattern is much like the `survey_detail` pattern, except the associated URL path has the string `thanks` before the segment containing the survey's primary key value.

In addition, we will need to add a `survey_thanks` view function to `survey/views.py`:

```
def survey_thanks(request, pk):
    survey = get_object_or_404(Survey, pk=pk)
    return render_to_response('survey/thanks.html',
                                {'survey': survey})
```

This view looks up the specified survey using `get_object_or_404`. If a matching survey does not exist, then an `Http404` error will be raised and a page not found response will be returned. If the survey is found, then a new template, `survey/thanks.html` will be used to render a response. The survey is passed in the context to the template allowing a tailored response reflecting the survey that was submitted.

Debug page #3: NoReverseMatch at /1/

Before writing the new template, let's check to see if redirect works, as all it needs is the changes to `survey/urls.py` and the view implementation. What happens if we submit a response with the new redirect code in `views.py`? Not what we might have hoped:

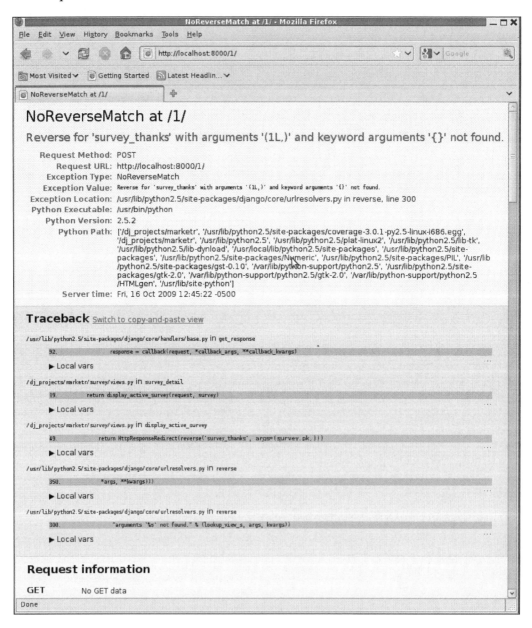

`NoReverseMatch` exceptions can be among the most frustrating ones to debug. Unlike when forward matching fails, the debug page does not provide a list of patterns tried and the order in which matching was attempted. This may sometimes lead us to think the proper pattern wasn't even considered. Rest assured, it was. The problem is not that the appropriate pattern wasn't considered, it was that it didn't match.

Understanding and fixing the NoReverseMatch exception

How do you figure out why a pattern expected to match is not matching? Guessing what might be wrong and making changes based on those guesses has a chance of working, but is also likely to make things worse. A better approach is to be methodical and check things one by one, which usually leads to discovery of the source of the problem. The following is a sequence of things to check. We'll go through this sequence and consider how it applies to our pattern where `reverse` is unexpectedly failing:

```
url(r'^thanks/(?P<pk>\d+/)$', 'survey_thanks',
    name='survey_thanks'),
```

First, verify that the name identified in the exception matches the name in the URL pattern specification. In this case, the exception cites `survey_thanks`, and the URL pattern we expect to match has `name='survey_thanks'` specified, so those match.

Note that if the URL pattern omits the `name` argument, and the `patterns` call it is an argument to specifies a view `prefix`, then the caller of `reverse` must also include the view `prefix` when specifying the name to reverse. In this case, for example, if we did not specify a name for the `survey_thanks` view, then a successful `reverse` call would need to specify `survey.views.survey_thanks` as the name to reverse, since `survey.views` is specified as the `patterns prefix` in `survey/urls.py`.

Second, make sure that the number of arguments listed in the exception message matches the number of regular expression groups in the URL pattern. In this case, there is one argument listed by the exception, `1L`, and one regular expression group, `(?P<pk>\d+/)`, so the numbers match.

Third, if the exception shows keyword arguments were specified, verify that the regular expression groups are named. Further, verify that the names of the groups match the names of the keyword arguments. In this case, keyword arguments were not specified on the `reverse` call, so there is nothing to check for this step.

Note that it is not necessary to ensure non-named groups are used in the URL pattern when positional arguments are shown in the exception, because it is possible for positional arguments to be matched to named groups in a URL pattern. Thus, there is no problem when, as in our case, the URL pattern uses named groups while the reverse caller specifies positional arguments.

Fourth, for each argument, verify that the string representation of the actual argument value listed in the exception matches the associated regular expression group from the URL pattern. Note that the values shown in the exception are the results of calling repr on the arguments, thus they may not exactly match the string representation of the argument. Here, for example, the exception reports the argument value as 1L, signifying a Python long integer value (the value is a long integer because that is what MySQL, the database in use for this example, always returns for integer values). The L suffix is used to make the type in the repr clear, but it does not appear in the string representation of the value, which is simply 1.

Thus for our example, the string representation of the argument shown in the exception message is 1. Does that match the associated regular expression group in the URL pattern? Recall that the group is (?P<pk>\d+/). The enclosing parentheses identify the fact that it is a group. The ?P<pk> assigns the group the name pk. The remainder, \d+/, is then the regular expression we are trying to match with 1. These don't match. The regular expression is specifying one of more digits followed by a slash, yet the actual value we have is a single numeric digit, without a trailing slash. We made a typo here and included the slash inside the group instead of following it. The correct specification for our new survey_thanks view is:

```
url(r'^thanks/(?P<pk>\d+)/$', 'survey_thanks',
    name='survey_thanks'),
```

It is very easy for typos like this to creep into URL pattern specifications, as the pattern specifications tend to be long and full of punctuation characters with special meaning. Breaking them down into component pieces and verifying that each piece is correct will save you a great deal of hassle. If, however, that does not work, and you get to a point where all of the bits look right but still you get a NoReverseMatch exception, it might be time to tackle the problem from the other direction.

Start with the simplest part of the overall pattern, and verify that reverse for that works. You might, for example, get rid of all arguments from the reverse call and all groups from the URL pattern specification, and verify that you can reverse the URL by name. Then add back one argument and its associated pattern group in the URL specification, and verify if that works. Continue until you hit an error. Then change back to trying the simplest version in addition to just the argument that caused the error. If that works, then there is some problem with combining that argument with the others in the overall pattern, which is a clue, so you can start investigating what might cause that.

This approach is a general debugging technique that can be applied whenever you encounter a mysterious problem in a complicated set of code. First, back off to something very simple that works. Then add things back, one by one, until things fail again. You've now identified one piece that is involved in the failure, and you can start investigating whether it is that piece alone that is a problem or if it works in isolation but only causes a problem when combined with other pieces.

Debug page #4: TemplateDoesNotExist at /thanks/1/

For now, let's return to our example. Now that we have fixed the `reverse` problem, does the redirect to our survey thanks page work? Not quite. If we again attempt to submit our survey results, we see:

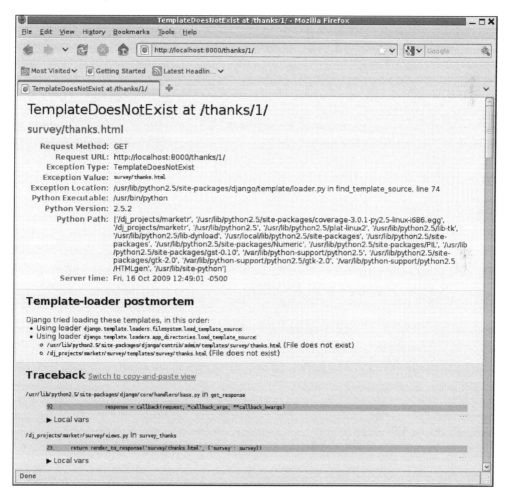

This one is self-explanatory; in tracking down the `NoReverseMatch` error we forgot we still had not gotten around to writing the template for the new view. The fix will be easy, but there is something to note about this debug page first: the section titled **Template-loader postmortem**. This is another optional section, like the **Template error** section included with `TemplateSyntaxError` debug pages, that provides additional information helpful for determining the exact cause of the error.

The **Template-loader postmortem** section, specifically, lists all of the template loaders that were tried in attempting to locate the template. For each loader, it then lists the full file names searched for by that loader, and the outcome.

On this page we can see that the `filesystem` template loader was called first. But no files are listed as tried by that loader. The `filesystem` loader is included in our `settings.py` file, since it is the first listed in `TEMPLATE_LOADERS` in the `settings.py` file generated by `django-admin.py startproject`, and we have not changed that setting. It looks in all the directories specified in the settings `TEMPLATE_DIRS` value. However, `TEMPLATE_DIRS` is empty by default, and we have not changed that setting either, so the `filesystem` loader had no place to look in order to try and find `survey/thanks.html`.

The second loader tried was the `app_directories` loader. This is the one we have been relying on so far to load the templates for our survey application. It loads templates from a `templates` directory under each application directory. The debug page shows that it attempted to find the `survey/thanks.html` file first under the `admin` application's `templates` directory and then under the `survey` application's `templates` directory. The result of searching for the specified file is placed in parentheses after the file name; in both cases here we see **File does not exist**, which is no surprise.

Sometimes this message will state **File exists**, which can be a little confusing. If the file exists, and the loader could see it exists, why didn't the loader load it? This often occurs when running under a web server such as Apache, and the problem is that the web server process does not have the necessary permissions to read the file. The fix in that case is to make the file readable by the web server process. Dealing with production-time issues such as this will be discussed in more detail in *Chapter 11, When it's Time to Go Live: Moving to Production.*

Understanding and fixing TemplateDoesNotExist

The fix in our case is simple, and we do not really even need to look closely at the error message to know what needs to be done, but note that this section gives everything needed in order to track down TemplateDoesNotExist errors. You will know what loader you are relying on to load the template. If that loader is not shown in the **Template-loader postmortem**, then the problem is likely an incorrect TEMPLATE_LOADERS setting in settings.py.

If the loader is listed, but does not list attempting to load the expected file, then the next step is to figure out why. This step is loader-dependent, since each loader has its own rules for where to look for template files. The app_directories loader, for example, looks under a templates directory for each application listed in INSTALLED_APPS. Thus ensuring the application is in INSTALLED_APPS and has a templates directory would be two things to check when it is the app_directories loader that isn't searching for the file as expected.

If the loader is listed and the expected file is listed as attempted, then the problem is hinted at by whatever is listed as the status for the file by the loader. **File does not exist** is a clear status with an easy fix. If **File does not exist** appears unexpectedly, double and triple check the filename. Cutting-and-pasting from the debug page into a command prompt and attempting to display the file may be useful here, as it may help clarify what is different about the name of the file the loader is trying to load compared to the name of the file that actually exists. Other status messages, such as **File exists**, may not be as direct but still hint at the nature of the problem and point towards a direction to look in order to fix the problem.

For our example case, the fix is simple: create the survey/thanks.html template file we forgot to create earlier. This template returns a basic page with a message thanking the user for participating in the survey:

```
{% extends "survey/base.html" %}
{% block content %}
<h1>Thanks</h1>
<p>Thanks for completing our {{ survey.title }} survey.  Come back
soon and check out the full results!</p>
{% endblock content %}
```

With this template in place under the `survey/templates` directory, we are now able to submit a survey without error. Instead we see:

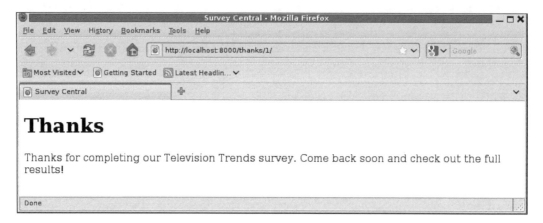

Good! Are we now done with displaying a survey and processing results? Not quite. We have not yet tested to see what happens if an invalid survey response is submitted. We will try that next.

Handling invalid Survey submissions

We've already coded the view that handles survey submission to re-display the page with errors instead of processing the results, if any errors are found in the submitted forms. On the display side, since we are using the `as_p` convenience method for displaying the form, it will take care of displaying any errors in the forms. So, we should have no code or template changes to make in order to see what happens when an invalid survey is submitted.

What would make a survey submission invalid? The only likely error case for our `QuestionVoteForm` is if no answer is chosen. What happens, then, if we attempt to submit a survey with missing answers? If we try it, we see that the result is not ideal:

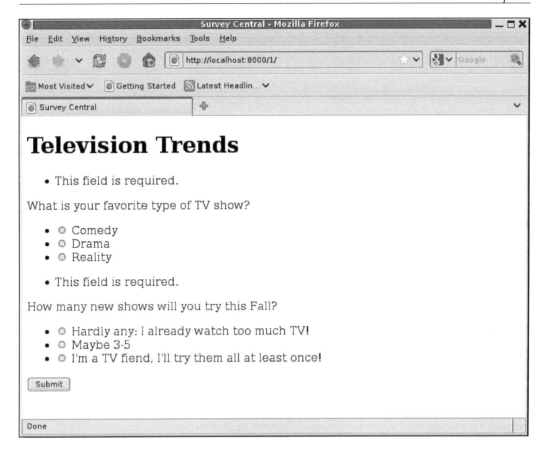

There are at least two problems here. First, the placement of the error messages, above the survey questions, is confusing. It is hard to know what the first error message on the page is referring to, and the second error looks like it is associated with the first question. It would be better to move the error messages closer to where the selection is actually made, such as between the question and answer choice list.

Second, the text of the error message is not very good for this particular form. Technically the list of answer choices is a single form field, but to a general user the word **field** in reference to a list of choices sounds odd. We will correct both of these errors next.

Coding custom error message and placement

Changing the error message is easy, since Django provides a hook for this. To override the value of the error message issued when a required field is not supplied, we can specify the message we would like as the value for the required key in an error_messages dictionary we pass as an argument in the field declaration. Thus, this new definition for the answer field in QuestionVoteForm will change the error message to Please select an answer below:

```
class QuestionVoteForm(forms.Form):
    answer = forms.ModelChoiceField(widget=forms.RadioSelect,
        queryset=None,
        empty_label=None,
        error_messages={'required':
                        'Please select an answer below:'})
```

Changing the placement of the error message requires changing the template. Instead of using the as_p convenience method, we will try displaying the label for the answer field, errors for the answer field, and then the answer field itself, which displays the choices. The {% for %} block that displays the survey forms in the survey/active_survey.html template then becomes:

```
{% for qform in qforms %}
    {{ qform.answer.label }}
    {{ qform.answer.errors }}
    {{ qform.answer }}
{% endfor %}
```

How does that work? Better than before. If we try submitting invalid forms now, we see:

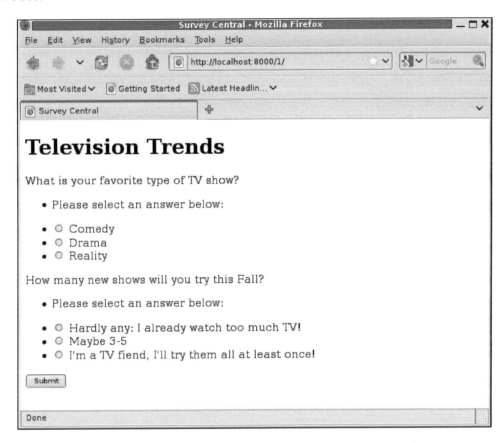

While the error message itself is improved, and the placement is better, the exact form of the display is not ideal. By default, the errors are shown as an HTML unordered list. We could use CSS styling to remove the bullet that is appearing (as we will eventually do for the list of choices), but Django also provides an easy way to implement custom error display, so we could try that instead.

To override the error message display, we can specify an alternate `error_class` attribute for `QuestionVoteForm`, and in that class, implement a `__unicode__` method that returns the error messages with our desired formatting. An initial implementation of this change to `QuestionVoteForm` and the new class might be:

```
class QuestionVoteForm(forms.Form):
    answer = forms.ModelChoiceField(widget=forms.RadioSelect,
        queryset=None,
        empty_label=None,
        error_messages={'required':
                        'Please select an answer below:'})

    def __init__(self, question, *args, **kwargs):
        super(QuestionVoteForm, self).__init__(*args, **kwargs)
        self.fields['answer'].queryset = question.answer_set.all()
        self.fields['answer'].label = question.question
        self.error_class = PlainErrorList

from django.forms.util import ErrorList
class PlainErrorList(ErrorList):
    def __unicode__(self):
        return u'%s' % ' '.join([e for e in sefl])
```

The only change to `QuestionVoteForm` is the addition of setting its `error_class` attribute to `PlainErrorList` in its `__init__` method. The `PlainErrorList` class is based on the `django.form.util.ErrorList` class and simply overrides the `__unicode__` method to return the errors as a string with no special HTML formatting. The implementation here makes use of the fact that the base `ErrorList` class inherits from `list`, so iterating over the instance itself returns the individual errors in turn. These are then joined together with spaces in between, and the whole string is returned.

Note that we're only expecting there to ever be one error here, but just in case we are wrong in that assumption, it is safest to code for multiple errors existing. Although our assumption may never be wrong in this case, it's possible we might decide to re-use this custom error class in other situations where the single possible error expectation doesn't hold. If we code to our assumption and simply return the first error in the list, this may result in confusing error displays in some situations where there are multiple errors, since we will have prevented reporting all but the first error. If and when we get to that point, we may also find that formatting a list of errors with just spaces intervening is not a good presentation, but we can deal with that later. First, we'd like to simply verify that our customization of the error list display is used.

Debug page #5: Another TemplateSyntaxError

What happens if we try submitting an invalid survey now that we have our custom error class specified? An attempt to submit an invalid survey now returns:

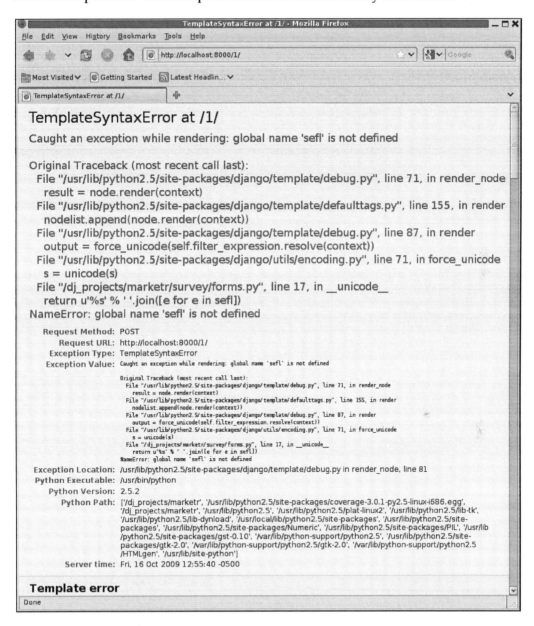

Oops, we have made another error. The exception value displayed on the second line makes it pretty clear that we've mistyped `self` as `sefl`, and since the code changes we just made only affected five lines in total, we don't have far to look in order to find the typo. But let's take a closer look at this page, since it looks a little different than the other `TemplateSyntaxError` we encountered.

What is different about this page compared to the other `TemplateSyntaxError`? Actually, there is nothing structurally different; it contains all the same sections with the same contents. The notable difference is that the exception value is not a single line, but is rather a multi-line message containing an **Original Traceback**. What is that? If we take a look at the traceback section of the debug page, we see it is rather long, repetitive, and uninformative. The end portion, which is usually the most interesting part of a traceback, is:

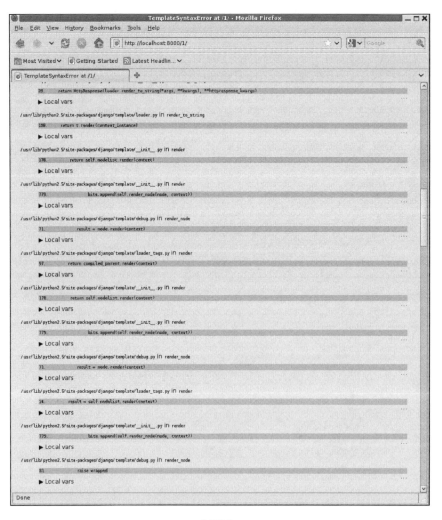

Every line of code cited in that traceback is Django code, not our application code. Yet, we can be pretty sure the problem here was not caused by the Django template processing code, but rather by the change we just made to `QuestionVoteForm`. What's going on?

What has happened here is that an exception was raised during the rendering of a template. Exceptions during rendering are caught and turned into `TemplateSyntaxErrors`. The bulk of the stack trace for the exception will likely not be interesting or helpful in terms of solving the problem. What will be more informative is the stack trace from the original exception, before it was caught and turned into a `TemplateSyntaxError`. This stack trace is made available as the **Original Traceback** portion of the exception value for the `TemplateSyntaxError` which is ultimately raised.

A nice aspect of this behavior is that the significant part of what is likely a very long traceback is highlighted at the top of the debug page. An unfortunate aspect is that the significant part of the traceback is no longer available in the traceback section itself, thus the special features of the traceback section of the debug page are not available for it. It is not possible to expand the context around the lines identified in the original traceback, nor to see the local variables at each level of the original traceback. These limitations will not cause any difficulty in solving this particular problem, but can be annoying for more obscure errors.

 Note that Python 2.6 introduced a change to the base `Exception` class that causes the **Original Traceback** information mentioned here to be omitted in the display of the `TemplateSyntaxError` exception value. Thus, if you are using Python 2.6 and Django 1.1.1, you will not see the **Original Traceback** included on the debug page. This will likely be corrected in newer versions of Django, since losing the information in the **Original Traceback** makes it quite hard to debug the error. The fix for this problem may also address some of the annoyances previously noted, related to `TemplateSyntaxErrors` wrapping other exceptions.

Fixing the second TemplateSyntaxError

Fixing this second `TemplateSyntaxError` is straightforward: simply correct the `sefl` typo on the line noted in the original traceback. When we do that and again try to submit an invalid survey, we see in response:

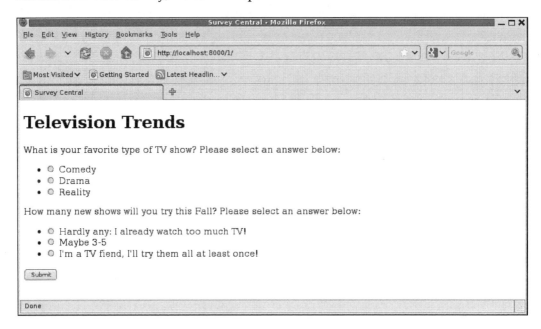

That is not a debug page, so that is good. Furthermore, the error messages are no longer appearing as HTML unordered lists, which was our goal for this change, so that is good. Their exact placement may not quite be exactly what we want, and we may want to add some CSS styling so that they stand out more prominently, but for now they will do.

Summary

We have now completed the implementation of survey voting, and the in-depth coverage of Django debug pages. In this chapter, we:

- Set out to replace the placeholder view and template for display of an active Survey with a real implementation
- Made some typical mistakes during implementation, which led to us being presented with five different Django debug pages
- On encountering the first debug page, learned about all of the different sections of debug pages and what information is included in each
- For each debug page encountered, used the information presented to locate and correct the coding error

In the next chapter, we will proceed to learn techniques for gathering debug information even when the code is not causing a debug page to be displayed.

8
When Problems Hide: Getting More Information

Sometimes code does not trigger a debug page to be displayed, but it also does not produce the correct results. In fact even when code does seem to be working correctly, at least in terms of the visible results shown in the browser, behind the scenes it may be doing unexpected things that could lead to trouble down the road. For example, if a page requires many (or very time-consuming) SQL queries, then it may seem to be working fine during development but then quickly cause server overload in a production environment.

It's good practice, then, to get into the habit of checking up on how code is behaving, even when external results are not showing any problems. First, this practice can reveal hidden problems that are best known about sooner rather than later. Second, knowing what the normal code path looks like is very valuable when tracking down where things have gone wrong when a problem does crop up.

This chapter focuses on ways to get more information about what Django application code is doing. Specifically, in this chapter we will:

- Develop template code that can be used to include information about all of the SQL queries needed to render a page in the page itself
- Learn how to use the Django Debug Toolbar for gathering similar information, and more
- Discuss techniques for adding logging to Django application code

Tracking SQL queries for a request

For a typical Django application, database interactions are of key importance. Ensuring that the database queries being made are correct helps to ensure that the application results are correct. Further, ensuring that the database queries produced for the application are efficient helps to make sure that the application will be able to support the desired number of concurrent users.

Django provides support in this area by making the database query history available for examination. *Chapter 6, Django Debugging Overview*, introduced this history and showed how it could be accessed from a Python shell session. This type of access is useful to see the SQL that is issued as a result of calling a particular model method. However, it is not helpful in learning about the bigger picture of what SQL queries are made during the processing of a particular request.

This section will show how to include information about the SQL queries needed for production of a page in the page itself. We will alter our existing survey application templates to include query information, and examine the query history for some of the existing survey application views. Though we are not aware of any problems with the existing views, we may learn something in the process of verifying that they issue the queries we expect.

Settings for accessing query history in templates

Before the query history can be accessed from a template, we need to ensure some required settings are configured properly. Three settings are needed in order for the SQL query information to be available in a template. First, the debug context processor, `django.core.context_processors.debug`, must be included in the `TEMPLATE_CONTEXT_PROCESSORS` setting. This context processor is included in the default value for `TEMPLATE_CONTEXT_PROCESSORS`. We have not changed that setting; therefore we do not need to do anything to enable this context processor in our project.

Second, the IP address of the machine sending the request must be listed in the `INTERNAL_IPS` setting. This is not a setting we have used before, and it is empty by default, so we will need to add it to the settings file. When testing using the same machine as where the development server runs, setting `INTERNAL_IPS` to include the loopback address is sufficient:

```
# Addresses for internal machines that can see potentially sensitive
# information such as the query history for a request.
INTERNAL_IPS = ('127.0.0.1', )
```

If you also test from other machines, you will need to include their IP addresses in this setting as well.

Third and finally, DEBUG must be True in order for the SQL query history to be available in templates.

When those three settings conditions are met, the SQL query history may be available in templates via a template variable named sql_queries. This variable contains a list of dictionaries. Each dictionary contains two keys: sql and time. The value for sql is the SQL query itself, and the value for time is the number of seconds the query took to execute.

Note that the sql_queries context variable is set by the debug context processor. Context processors are only called during template rendering when a RequestContext is used to render the template. Up until now, we have not used RequestContexts in our survey application views, since they were not necessary for the code so far. But in order to access the query history from the template, we will need to start using RequestContexts. Therefore, in addition to modifying the templates, we will need to change the view code slightly in order to include query history in the generated pages for the survey application.

SQL queries for the home page

Let's start by seeing what queries are issued in order to generate the survey application home page. Recall that the home page view code is:

```
def home(request):
    today = datetime.date.today()
    active = Survey.objects.active()
    completed = Survey.objects.completed().filter(closes__gte=today-
                    datetime.timedelta(14))
    upcoming = Survey.objects.upcoming().filter(
                    opens__lte=today+datetime.timedelta(7))
    return render_to_response('survey/home.html',
        {'active_surveys': active,
        'completed_surveys': completed,
        'upcoming_surveys': upcoming,
        })
```

There are three `QuerySet`s rendered in the template, so we would expect to see that this view generates three SQL queries. In order to check that, we must first change the view to use a `RequestContext`:

```python
from django.template import RequestContext
def home(request):
    today = datetime.date.today()
    active = Survey.objects.active()
    completed = Survey.objects.completed().filter(closes__gte=today-
                    datetime.timedelta(14))
    upcoming = Survey.objects.upcoming().filter(
                    opens__lte=today+datetime.timedelta(7))
    return render_to_response('survey/home.html',
        {'active_surveys': active,
         'completed_surveys': completed,
         'upcoming_surveys': upcoming,},
        RequestContext(request))
```

The only change here is to add the `RequestContext(request)` as a third parameter to `render_to_response`, after adding an `import` for it earlier in the file. When we make this change, we may as well also change the `render_to_response` lines for the other views to use `RequestContext`s as well. That way when we get to the point of examining the SQL queries for each, we will not get tripped up by having forgotten to make this small change.

Second, we'll need to display the information from `sql_queries` somewhere in our `survey/home.html` template. But where? We don't necessarily want this information displayed in the browser along with the genuine application data, since that could get confusing. One way to include it in the response but not have it be automatically visible on the browser page is to put it in an HTML comment. Then the browser will not display it on the page, but it can be seen by viewing the HTML source for the displayed page.

As a first attempt at implementing this, we might change the top of `survey/home.html` to look like this:

```html
{% extends "survey/base.html" %}
{% block content %}
<!--
{{ sql_queries|length }} queries
{% for qdict in sql_queries %}
{{ qdict.sql }} ({{ qdict.time }} seconds)
{% endfor %}
-->
```

This template code prints out the contents of `sql_queries` within an HTML comment at the very beginning of the `content` block supplied by `survey/home. html`. First, the number of queries is noted by filtering the list through the `length` filter. Then the code iterates through each dictionary in the `sql_queries` list and displays `sql`, followed by a note in parentheses about the `time` taken for each query.

How well does that work? If we try it out by retrieving the survey home page (after ensuring the development server is running), and use the browser's menu item for viewing the HTML source for the page, we might see that the comment block contains something like:

```
<!--

1 queries

SELECT `django_session`.`session_key`, `django_session`.`session_data`,
`django_session`.`expire_date` FROM `django_session` WHERE (`django_
session`.`session_key` = d538f13c423c2fe1e7f8d8147b0f6887  AND `django_
session`.`expire_date` &gt; 2009-10-24 17:24:49 ) (0.001 seconds)

-->
```

Note that the exact number of queries displayed here will depend on the version of Django you are running. This result is from Django 1.1.1; later versions of Django may not show any queries displayed here. Furthermore, the history of the browser's interaction with the site will affect the queries issued. This result is from a browser that had been used to access the admin application, and the last interaction with the admin application was to log out. You may see additional queries if the browser had been used to access the admin application but the user had not logged out. Finally, the database in use can also affect the specific queries issued and their exact formatting. This result is from a MySQL database.

That's not exactly what we expected. First, a minor annoyance, but `1 queries` is wrong, it should be `1 query`. Perhaps that wouldn't annoy you, particularly just in internal or debug information, but it would annoy me. I would change the template code that displays the query count to use correct pluralization:

```
{% with sql_queries|length as qcount %}
{{ qcount }} quer{{ qcount|pluralize:"y,ies" }}
{% endwith %}
```

Here, since the template needs to use the `length` result multiple times, it is first cached in the `qcount` variable by using a `{% with %}` block. Then it is displayed, and it is used as the variable input to the `pluralize` filter that will put the correct letters on the end of `quer` depending on the `qcount` value. Now the comment block will show `0` queries, `1` query, `2` queries, and so on.

With that minor annoyance out of the way, we can concentrate on the next, larger, issue, which is that the displayed query is not a query we were expecting. Furthermore, the three queries we were expecting, to retrieve the lists of completed, active, and upcoming surveys, are nowhere to be seen. What's going on? We'll take each of these in turn.

The query that is shown is accessing the `django_session` table. This table is used by the `django.contrib.sessions` application. Even though the survey application does not use this application, it is listed in our `INSTALLED_APPS`, since it is included in the `settings.py` file that `startproject` generates. Also, the middleware that the `sessions` application uses is listed in `MIDDLEWARE_CLASSES`.

The `sessions` application stores the session identifier in a cookie, named `sessionid` by default, that is sent to the browser as soon as any application uses a session. The browser will return the cookie in all requests to the same server. If the cookie is present in a request, the session middleware will use it to retrieve the session data. This is the query we see previously listed: the session middleware is retrieving the data for the session identified by the session cookie sent by the browser.

But the survey application does not use sessions, so how did the browser get a session cookie in the first place? The answer is that the admin application uses sessions, and this browser had previously been used to access the admin application. At that time, the `sessionid` cookie was set in a response, and the browser faithfully returns it on all subsequent requests. Thus, it seems likely that this `django_session` table query is due to a `sessionid` cookie set as a side-effect of using the admin application.

Can we confirm that? If we find and delete the cookie from the browser and reload the page, we should see that this SQL query is no longer listed. Without the cookie in the request, whatever code was triggering access to the session data won't have anything to look up. And since the survey application does not use sessions, none of its responses should include a new session cookie, which would cause subsequent requests to include a session lookup. Is this reasoning correct? If we try it, we will see that the comment block changes to:

```
<!--

0 queries

-->
```

Thus, we seem to have confirmed, to some extent, what happened to cause a `django_session` table query during processing of a survey application response. We did not track down what exact code accessed the session identified by the cookie—it could have been middleware or a context processor, but we probably don't need to know the details. It's enough to keep in mind that there are other applications running in our project besides the one we are working on, and they may cause database interactions independent of our own code. If we observe behavior which looks like it might cause a problem for our code, we can investigate further, but for this particular case we will just avoid using the admin application for now, as we would like to focus attention on the queries our own code is generating.

Now that we understand the query that was listed, what about the expected ones that were not listed? The missing queries are due to a combination of the lazy evaluation property of `QuerySets` and the exact placement of the `comment` block that lists the contents of `sql_queries`. We put the `comment` block at the top of the `content` block in the home page, to make it easy to find the SQL query information when looking at the page source. The template is rendered after the three `QuerySets` are created by the view, so it might seem that the comment placed at the top should show the SQL queries for the three `QuerySets`.

However, `QuerySets` are lazy; simply creating a `QuerySet` does not immediately cause interaction with the database. Rather, sending the SQL to the database is delayed until the `QuerySet` results are actually accessed. For the survey home page, that does not happen until the parts of the template that loop through each `QuerySet` are rendered. Those parts are all below where we placed the `sql_queries` information, so the corresponding SQL queries had not yet been issued. The fix for this is to move the placement of the `comment` block to the very bottom of the `content` block.

When we do that we should also fix two other issues with the query display. First, notice that the query displayed above has `&gt;` shown instead of the > symbol that would actually have been in the query sent to the database. Furthermore, if the database in use is one (such as PostgreSQL) that uses straight quotes instead of back quotes for quoting, all of the back quotes in the query would be shown as `&quot;`. This is due to Django's automatic escaping of HTML markup characters. This is unnecessary and hard to read in our HTML comment, so we can suppress it by sending the `sql` query value through the `safe` filter.

Second, the query is very long. In order to avoid needing to scroll to the right in order to see the entire query, we can also filter the `sql` value through `wordwrap` to introduce some line breaks and make the output more readable.

To make these changes, remove the added comment block from the top of the
content block in the survey/home.html template and instead change the bottom
of this template to be:

```
{% endif %}
<!--
{% with sql_queries|length as qcount %}
{{ qcount }} quer{{ qcount|pluralize:"y,ies" }}
{% endwith %}
{% for qdict in sql_queries %}
{{ qdict.sql|safe|wordwrap:60 }} ({{ qdict.time }} seconds)
{% endfor %}
-->
{% endblock content %}
```

Now, if we again reload the survey home page and view the source for the returned
page, we will see the queries listed in a comment at the bottom:

```
<!--

3 queries

SELECT `survey_survey`.`id`, `survey_survey`.`title`,
`survey_survey`.`opens`, `survey_survey`.`closes` FROM
`survey_survey` WHERE (`survey_survey`.`opens` <= 2009-10-25
 AND `survey_survey`.`closes` >= 2009-10-25 ) (0.000 seconds)

SELECT `survey_survey`.`id`, `survey_survey`.`title`,
`survey_survey`.`opens`, `survey_survey`.`closes` FROM
`survey_survey` WHERE (`survey_survey`.`closes` < 2009-10-25
 AND `survey_survey`.`closes` >= 2009-10-11 ) (0.000 seconds)

SELECT `survey_survey`.`id`, `survey_survey`.`title`,
`survey_survey`.`opens`, `survey_survey`.`closes` FROM
`survey_survey` WHERE (`survey_survey`.`opens` > 2009-10-25
AND `survey_survey`.`opens` <= 2009-11-01 ) (0.000 seconds)

-->
```

That is good, those look like exactly what we expect to see for queries for the home
page. Now that we seem to have some working template code to show queries, we
will consider packaging up this snippet so that it can easily be reused elsewhere.

Packaging the template query display for reuse

We've now got a small block of template code that we can put in any template to easily see what SQL queries were needed to produce a page. However, it is not so small that it can be easily re-typed whenever it might come in handy. Therefore, it would be good to package it up in a form where it can be conveniently included wherever and whenever it might be needed. The Django template {% include %} tag makes this easy to do.

Where should the snippet go? Note that this template snippet is completely general and not in any way tied to the survey application. While it would be easy to simply include it among the survey templates, putting it there will make it harder to reuse for future projects. A better approach is to put it in an independent application.

Creating an entirely new application just for this one snippet may seem a bit extreme. However, it is common during development to create small utility functions or template snippets that don't really belong in the main application. So it is likely during development of a real project that there would be other such things that should logically be placed somewhere besides the main application. It's helpful to have someplace else to put them.

Let's create a new Django application, then, to hold any general utility code that does not logically belong within the survey application:

```
kmt@lbox:/dj_projects/marketr$ python manage.py startapp gen_utils
```

Since its purpose is to hold general utility code, we've named the new application gen_utils. It can serve as a place to put any non-survey-specific code that seems like it might be potentially re-usable elsewhere. Note that as time goes on and more and more stuff accumulates in an application like this, it may become apparent that some subset of it would be useful to package into its own independent, self-contained application with a more descriptive name than gen_utils. But for now it is enough to start with one place to put utility code that is not really tied to the survey application.

Next, we can create a `templates` directory within `gen_utils`, and a `gen_utils` directory under `templates`, and create a file, `showqueries.html`, to hold the template snippet:

```
{% if sql_queries %}<!--
{% with sql_queries|length as qcount %}
{{ qcount }} quer{{ qcount|pluralize:"y,ies" }}
{% endwith %}
{% for qdict in sql_queries %}
{{ qdict.sql|safe|wordwrap:60 }} ({{ qdict.time }} seconds)
{% endfor %}
-->{% endif %}
```

We've made one change here from the previous code placed directly in the `survey/home.html` template, which is to place the entire HTML `comment` block inside an `{% if sql_qureies %}` block. If the `sql_queries` variable has not been included in the template context, then there is no reason to produce the comment at all.

As part of packaging code for reuse, it's also good practice to double-check and make sure that the code is truly reusable and not going to fail in odd ways if given unexpected or unusual input. Taking a look at that snippet, is there anything that might be found in an arbitrary `sql_queries` input that could cause a problem?

The answer is yes. If a SQL query value contains the HTML end-of-comment delimiter, then the comment block will be terminated early. This could result in the browser rendering what was intended to be a comment as part of the page content displayed to the user. To see this, we can try inserting a model `filter` call that includes the HTML end-of-comment delimiter into the home page view code, and see what the browser shows.

But what is the HTML end-of-comment delimiter? You might guess that it is `-->`, but in fact it is just the two dashes in a row. Technically, the `<!` and `>` are defined as the beginning and end of markup declaration, while the dashes mark the beginning and end of the comment. Thus, a query that contains two dashes in a row should trigger the behavior we are worried about here. To test this, add this line of code to the `home` view:

```
Survey.objects.filter(title__contains='--').count()
```

Note nothing has to be done with the results of the call; the added code must simply ensure that the query containing the two dashes is actually sent to the database. This added line does that by retrieving the count of results matching the pattern containing two dashes. With that added line in the `home` view, Firefox will display the survey home page like so:

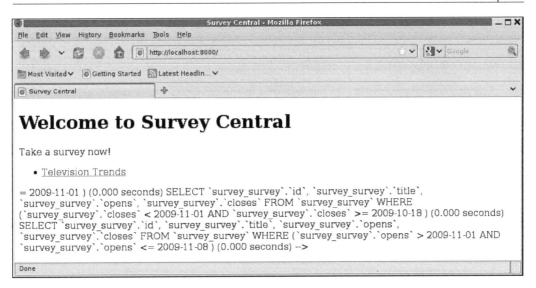

The two dashes in a row in a SQL query value caused Firefox to prematurely terminate the comment block, and data we had intended to be still inside the comment has appeared in the browser page. In order to avoid this, we need to ensure that two dashes in a row never appear in the SQL query values included in the comment block.

A quick glance through the built-in Django filters doesn't reveal any that could be used to replace a string of two dashes with something else. The `cut` filter could be used to remove them, but simply removing them would make the `sql` value misleading as there would be no indication that the characters had been removed from the string. Therefore, it seems we will need to develop a custom filter for this.

We will put the custom filter in the `gen_utils` application. Filters and template tags must be placed in a `templatetags` module in an application, so we must first create the `templatetags` directory. Then, we can put an implementation for a `replace_dashes` filter into a file named `gentags.py` within `gen_utils/templatetags`:

```
from django import template

register = template.Library()

@register.filter
def replace_dashes(value):
    return value.replace('--','~~double-dash~~')
replace_dashes.is_safe = True
```

The bulk of this code is the standard boilerplate `import`, `register` assignment, and `@register.filter` decoration needed to register the `replace_dashes` function so that it is available for use as a filter. The function itself simply replaces any occurrences of a pair of dashes in a string with `~~double-dash~~` instead. Since there is no way to escape the dashes so that they will not be interpreted as the end of the comment yet still appear as dashes, we replace them with a string describing what had been there. The last line marks the `replace_dashes` filter as safe, meaning it does not introduce any HTML markup characters that would need to be escaped in its output.

We also need to change the template snippet in `gen_utils/showqueries.html` to load and use this filter for display of the SQL query values:

```
{% if sql_queries %}<!--
{% with sql_queries|length as qcount %}
{{ qcount }} quer{{ qcount|pluralize:"y,ies" }}
{% endwith %}
{% load gentags %}
{% for qdict in sql_queries %}
{{ qdict.sql|safe|replace_dashes|wordwrap:60 }} ({{ qdict.time }}
seconds)
{% endfor %}
-->{% endif %}
```

The only changes here are the addition of the `{% load gentags %}` line and the addition of `replace_dashes` in the sequence of filters applied to `qdict.sql`.

Finally, we can remove the comment snippet from the `survey/home.html` template. Instead, we will put the new general snippet in the `survey/base.html` template, so this becomes:

```
<!DOCTYPE html PUBLIC "-//W3C//DTD XHTML 1.0 Strict//EN"
"http://www.w3.org/TR/xhtml1/DTD/xhtml1-strict.dtd">
<html xmlns="http://www.w3.org/1999/xhtml">
<head>
<title>{% block title %}Survey Central{% endblock %}</title>
</head>
<body>
{% block content %}{% endblock %}
</body>
{% include "gen_utils/showqueries.html" %}
</html>
```

Placing {% include %} in the base template will cause every template that inherits from base to automatically have the comment block added, assuming that the other conditions of DEBUG being turned on, the requesting IP address being listed in INTERNAL_IPS, and the response being rendered with a RequestContext, are met. We'd likely want to remove this before putting the application in a production environment, but during development it can come in handy to have easy automatic access to the SQL queries used to generate any page.

Testing the repackaged template code

How well does the repackaged version of the code work? If we try to reload our survey home page now, we will find that we have forgotten a couple of things. The first attempt brings up a Django debug page:

This is an instance of one of the special debug pages mentioned in the last chapter. It is a `TemplateSyntaxError` resulting from an exception being raised during rendering. The original exception was caught and turned into a `TemplateSyntaxError`, and the original traceback is shown as part of the exception value. Looking at that, we can see that the original exception was `TemplateDoesNotExist`. For some reason, the `gen_utils/showqueries.html` template file was not found by the template loader.

Paging further down on the debug page received here, we learn why the template engine behavior of wrapping original exceptions in a `TemplateSyntaxError` can sometimes be aggravating. Because the exception that was ultimately raised was a `TemplateSyntaxError`, not a `TemplateDoesNotExist`, this debug page does not have the template loader postmortem that would detail exactly what template loaders were tried, and what files they attempted to load while searching for `gen_utils/showqueries.html`. So, we've lost some helpful debug information due to the way `TemplateSyntaxError` exceptions are used to wrap others.

If we needed to, we could force production of the template loader postmortem for this template file by attempting to render it directly from a view, instead of by including it in another template. So we could, with a little work, get the information that has unfortunately not been included in this particular debug page.

But in this case it is not necessary, since the reason for the exception is not particularly obscure: we didn't do anything to ensure that the templates in the new `gen_utils` application would be found. We did not include `gen_utils` in `INSTALLED_APPS` so that its `templates` directory would be searched by the application template loader, nor did we put the path to the `gen_utils templates` directory into the `TEMPLATE_DIRS` setting. We need to do one of these things in order to have the new template file found. Since `gen_utils` also now has a filter, and in order for that to be loaded `gen_utils` will need to be in `INSTALLED_APPS`, we will fix the `TemplateDoesNotExist` exception by including `gen_utils` in `INSTALLED_APPS`.

Once we make that change, does the new code work? Not quite. Attempting to reload the page now brings up a different debug page:

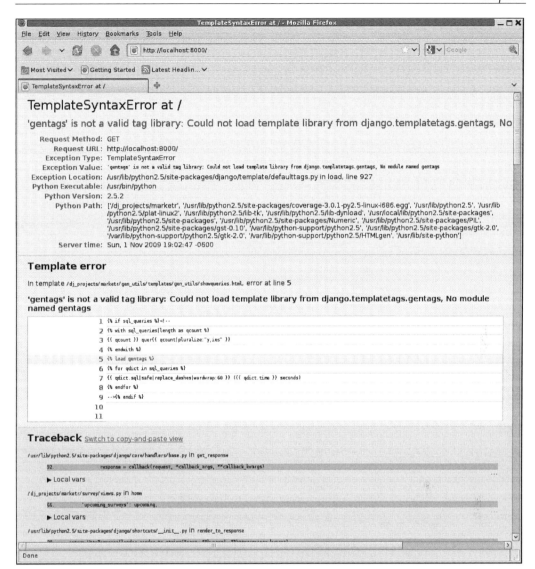

This one is a little more mysterious. The displayed template is `gen_utils/showqueries.html`, so we have gotten farther than in the previous case. But for some reason, the attempt to `{% load gentags %}` is failing. The error message states:

'gentags' is not a valid tag library: Could not load template library from django.templatetags.gentags, No module named gentags.

This is one of the rare cases where you do not want to entirely believe what the error message seems to be saying. It seems to be implying that the problem is that there is no `gentags.py` file in `django.templatetags`. A natural next thought may be that it is required to place custom template tag and filter libraries inside Django's own source tree. However, that would be a very odd requirement and the documentation clearly contradicts it, since it states that custom tags and filters should be placed in the application's `templatetags` directory. Are we supposed to use something other than a plain `{% load %}` tag to force Django to search beyond its own `templatetags` directory for a tag library?

No, in this case the error is just misleading. Although `django.templatetags` is the only module named in the error message, in fact the Django code attempted to load `gentags` from a `templatetags` directory under each application listed in INSTALLED_APPS. So the question is not why did Django fail to look for `gentags` under the `gen_utils/templatetags` directory, but why did an attempt to load `gentags` from `genutils.templatetags` fail?

We can attempt to answer that question by trying the same code that Django is running during `{% load %}` from a Python shell session:

```
kmt@lbox:/dj_projects/marketr$ python manage.py shell
Python 2.5.2 (r252:60911, Oct  5 2008, 19:24:49)
[GCC 4.3.2] on linux2
Type "help", "copyright", "credits" or "license" for more information.
(InteractiveConsole)
>>> from gen_utils.templatetags import gentags
Traceback (most recent call last):
  File "<console>", line 1, in <module>
ImportError: No module named templatetags
>>>
```

Sure enough, an attempt to import `gentags` from `gen_utils.templatetags` is failing. Python claims the `templatetags` module does not exist. But the directory certainly exists, and `gentags.py` exists, so what is missing? The answer is an `__init__.py` file in that directory to make Python recognize it as a module. Creating that file and re-trying the import from the shell shows that the import will now work.

However, attempting to simply reload the page in a browser causes the same debug page to be re-displayed. This is also one of the rare cases where the development server needs to be manually stopped and re-started in order for it to pick up on the changes made. That done, we can finally re-load the survey home page and see:

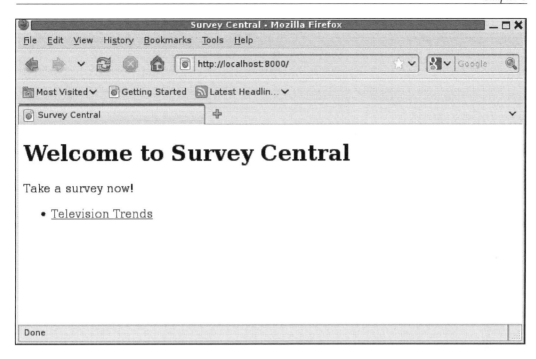

We're back to the page being served without an exception being raised, and there is no more stray debug information from the `sql_queries` being included in an HTML comment. If we look further, at the HTML source for the page, we will see something like the following at the bottom:

```
<!--

4 queries


SELECT COUNT(*) FROM `survey_survey` WHERE
`survey_survey`.`title` LIKE BINARY %~~double-dash~~%   (0.015 seconds)

SELECT `survey_survey`.`id`, `survey_survey`.`title`,
`survey_survey`.`opens`, `survey_survey`.`closes` FROM
`survey_survey` WHERE (`survey_survey`.`opens` <= 2009-11-01
 AND `survey_survey`.`closes` >= 2009-11-01 ) (0.001 seconds)

SELECT `survey_survey`.`id`, `survey_survey`.`title`,
`survey_survey`.`opens`, `survey_survey`.`closes` FROM
`survey_survey` WHERE (`survey_survey`.`closes` < 2009-11-01
 AND `survey_survey`.`closes` >= 2009-10-18 ) (0.000 seconds)
```

```
SELECT `survey_survey`.`id`, `survey_survey`.`title`,
`survey_survey`.`opens`, `survey_survey`.`closes` FROM
`survey_survey` WHERE (`survey_survey`.`opens` > 2009-11-01
AND `survey_survey`.`opens` <= 2009-11-08 ) (0.000 seconds)

-->
```

That looks good. The `replace_dashes` filter successfully got rid of the two dashes in a row, so the browser no longer thinks the comment block was terminated before it was intended to be. Now we can move on to checking the SQL queries needed to produce the other survey pages.

SQL queries for the active Survey form display page

Clicking on the link to the one active survey brings up the active survey page for that survey:

Looking at the source for this page, we see that six SQL queries were needed to produce it:

```
<!--

6 queries


SELECT `survey_survey`.`id`, `survey_survey`.`title`,
`survey_survey`.`opens`, `survey_survey`.`closes` FROM
`survey_survey` WHERE `survey_survey`.`id` = 1  (0.000 seconds)

SELECT `survey_question`.`id`, `survey_question`.`question`,
`survey_question`.`survey_id` FROM `survey_question` WHERE
`survey_question`.`survey_id` = 1  (0.000 seconds)

SELECT COUNT(*) FROM `survey_answer` WHERE
`survey_answer`.`question_id` = 1  (0.001 seconds)

SELECT COUNT(*) FROM `survey_answer` WHERE
`survey_answer`.`question_id` = 2  (0.001 seconds)

SELECT `survey_answer`.`id`, `survey_answer`.`answer`,
`survey_answer`.`question_id`, `survey_answer`.`votes` FROM
`survey_answer` WHERE `survey_answer`.`question_id` = 1  (0.024 seconds)

SELECT `survey_answer`.`id`, `survey_answer`.`answer`,
`survey_answer`.`question_id`, `survey_answer`.`votes` FROM
`survey_answer` WHERE `survey_answer`.`question_id` = 2  (0.001 seconds)

-->
```

Can we match up those queries to the code used to produce the page? Yes, in this case it is reasonably straightforward to see where each query comes from. The very first query is looking up a survey based on its primary key, and corresponds to the get_object_or_404 call in the very first line in the survey_detail view:

```
def survey_detail(request, pk):
    survey = get_object_or_404(Survey, pk=pk)
```

Since this is an active survey, the thread of control then proceeds to the display_active_survey function, which contains the following code to build the forms for the page:

```
        qforms = []
        for i, q in enumerate(survey.question_set.all()):
            if q.answer_set.count() > 1:
                qforms.append(QuestionVoteForm(q, prefix=i, data=data))
```

The call to `enumerate(survey.question_set.all())` is responsible for the second SQL query for this page, which retrieves all of the questions for the survey being displayed. The call to `q.answer_set.count()` within the `for` loop explains the third and fourth SQL queries, which retrieve the count of answers for each question in the survey.

The last two queries, then, retrieve the set of answers for each question in the survey. We might first think that these queries are issued when the `QuestionVoteForm` for each question in the survey is created. The `__init__` routine for a `QuestionVoteForm` contains this line, to initialize the set of answers for the question:

```
self.fields['answer'].queryset = question.answer_set.all()
```

However, that line of code does not result in a call to the database. It simply sets the `queryset` attribute for the form's `answer` field to a `QuerySet` value. Since `QuerySets` are lazy, this does not cause a database hit. This is confirmed by the fact that both queries that request `COUNT(*)` are issued before the queries that retrieve the actual answer information. If the creation of `QuestionVoteForm` caused the retrieval of the answer information, then the last two queries would not be last, but rather would be interleaved with the `COUNT(*)` queries. The trigger for issuing the queries that retrieve the answer information, then, is the rendering of the answer values in the `survey/active_survey.html` template.

If we were focused on optimization, at this point we might try to see if we could reduce the number of queries needed for this page. Retrieving the count of answers and then the answer information itself in two separate queries seems inefficient compared to simply retrieving the answer information and deriving the count based on the returned information. It seems like we could produce this page with four queries instead of six.

However, since we are focused on understanding the current behavior as an aid to debugging, we are not going to divert into an optimization discussion here. Even if we were developing a real project, at this point in development it would not be a good time to work on such optimizations. The inefficiency here is not so bad as to be termed a bug, so it is best just to note it as a possible thing to look at in the future, when a full picture of the overall performance of the application can be determined. At that point the inefficiencies that are the most expensive are the ones that will be worth taking the time to investigate improving.

SQL queries for posting survey answers

If we now choose some answers for the survey questions and press the **Submit** button, we get the **Thanks** page in response:

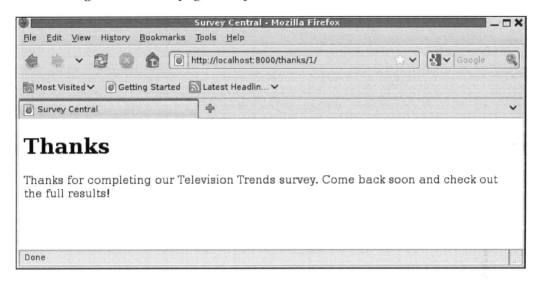

Looking at the source for this page, we find a single SQL query, to retrieve a survey given the primary key:

```
<!--

1 query


SELECT `survey_survey`.`id`, `survey_survey`.`title`,
`survey_survey`.`opens`, `survey_survey`.`closes` FROM
`survey_survey` WHERE `survey_survey`.`id` = 1   (0.001 seconds)

-->
```

The line of code associated with that query is obvious; it is the `get_object_or_404` in the `survey_thanks` view:

```
    def survey_thanks(request, pk):
        survey = get_object_or_404(Survey, pk=pk)
        return render_to_response('survey/thanks.html',
            {'survey': survey },
            RequestContext(request))
```

But what about all the SQL queries involved in processing the form data when it was submitted? Long before the `survey_thanks` view was called, `display_active_survey` must have run in order to receive the posted form data and update the database for the selected answers. Yet we don't see any of the SQL queries needed for that among the queries shown for the thanks page.

The reason for this is because the `display_active_survey` function, in the case where the form processing is successful and the database is updated, does not render a template directly but rather returns an `HttpResponseRedirect`. The web browser, on receiving the HTTP redirect response, automatically fetches the location identified in the redirect.

Thus, there are two full request/response cycles that take place in between pressing the **Submit** button on the browser and seeing the thanks page appear. The thanks page itself can show the SQL queries that were executed during its (the second) request/response cycle, but it cannot show any of the ones that happened in the first request/response cycle.

That's disappointing. At this point, we've gone to a fair amount of trouble developing what seemed at first like it was going to be a quite simple little bit of utility code. Now, we find that it is not going to work for some of the most interesting views in an application — the ones that actually update the database. What do we do?

We certainly don't want to just give up on seeing the SQL queries for pages that successfully process posted data. But nor do we want to spend much more development effort on this utility code. Although we have learned a few things along the way, we've started to stray a bit too much from our main application. Fortunately, we don't need to do either of these. Instead, we can simply install and start using an already-developed general debugging tool for Django applications, the Django Debug Toolbar. This tool is the focus of the next section.

The Django Debug Toolbar

Rob Hudson's Django Debug Toolbar is a very useful general purpose debugging tool for Django applications. As with the code we developed earlier in this chapter, it lets you see the SQL queries that were needed to produce a page. However, as we will see, it also goes far beyond that, providing easy access to much more information about the SQL queries and other aspects of request processing. Furthermore, the debug toolbar has a far more advanced way of displaying the information than simply embedding it in HTML comments. The capabilities are best shown by example, so we will immediately proceed with installing the toolbar.

Installing the Django Debug Toolbar

The toolbar can be found on the Python package index site: `http://pypi.python.org/pypi/django-debug-toolbar`. Once installed, activating the debug toolbar in a Django project is accomplished with the addition of just a couple of settings.

First, the debug toolbar middleware, `debug_toolbar.middleware.DebugToolbarMiddleware`, must be added to the `MIDDLEWARE_CLASSES` setting. The documentation for the toolbar notes that it should be placed after any other middleware that encodes the response content, so it is best to place it last in the middleware sequence.

Second, the `debug_toolbar` application needs to be added to `INSTALLED_APPS`. The `debug_toolbar` application uses Django templates to render its information, thus it needs to be listed in `INSTALLED_APPS` so that its templates will be found by the application template loader.

Third, the debug toolbar requires that the requesting IP address be listed in `INTERNAL_IPS`. Since we already made this settings change earlier in the chapter, nothing needs to be done now for this.

Finally, the debug toolbar is displayed only when `DEBUG` is `True`. We've been running with debug turned on, so again we don't have to make any changes here. Note also that the debug toolbar allows you to customize under what conditions the debug toolbar is displayed. It's possible, then, to set things up so that the toolbar will be displayed for requesting IP addresses not in `INTERNAL_IPS` or when debug is not turned on, but for our purposes the default configuration is fine so we will not change anything.

One thing that is not required is for the application itself to use a `RequestContext` in order for things such as the SQL query information to be available in the toolbar. The debug toolbar runs as middleware, and thus is not dependent on the application using a `RequestContext` in order for it to generate its information. Thus, the changes made to the survey views to specify `RequestContext`s on `render_to_response` calls would not have been needed if we started off first with the Django Debug Toolbar.

Debug toolbar appearance

Once the debug toolbar is added to the middleware and installed applications settings, we can see what it looks like by simply visiting any page in the survey application. Let's start with the home page. The returned page should now look something like this:

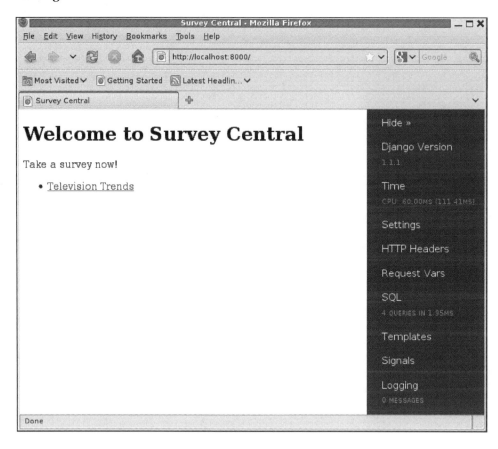

Note this screenshot shows the appearance of the 0.8.0 version of the debug toolbar. Earlier versions looked considerably different, so if your results do not look like this you may be using a different version than 0.8.0. The version that you have will most likely be newer than what was available when this was written, and there may be additional toolbar panels or functions that are not covered here.

As you can see, the debug toolbar appears on the right-hand side of the browser window. It consists of a series of panels that can be individually enabled or disabled by changing the toolbar configuration. The ones shown here are the ones that are enabled by default.

Before taking a closer look at some of the individual panels, notice that the toolbar contains an option to hide it at the top. If **Hide** is selected, the toolbar reduces itself to a small tab-like indication to show that it is present:

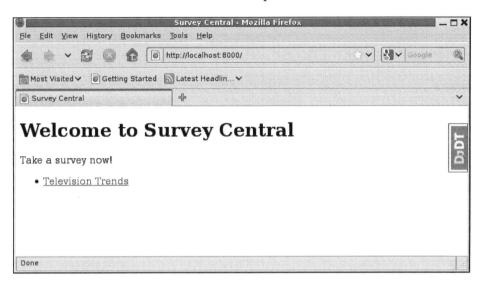

This can be very useful for cases where the expanded version of the toolbar obscures application content on the page. All of the information provided by the toolbar is still accessible, after clicking again on the **DjDT** tab; it is just out of the way for the moment.

Most of the panels will provide detailed information when they are clicked. A few also provide summary information in the main toolbar display. As of debug toolbar version 0.8.0, the first panel listed, **Django Version**, only provides summary information. There is no more detailed information available by clicking on it. As you can see in the screenshot, Django 1.1.1 is the version in use here.

Note that the current latest source version of the debug toolbar already provides more information for this panel than the 0.8.0 release. Since 0.8.0, this panel has been renamed to **Versions**, and can be clicked to provide more details. These additional details include version information for the toolbar itself and for any other installed Django applications that provide version information.

The other three panels that show summary information are the **Time**, **SQL**, and **Logging** panels. Thus, we can see at a glance from the first appearance of the page that 60 milliseconds of CPU time were used to produce this page (111 milliseconds total elapsed time), that the page required four queries, which took 1.95 milliseconds, and that zero messages were logged during the request.

In the following sections, we will dig into exactly what information is provided by each of the panels when clicked. We'll start first with the SQL panel, since it is one of the most interesting and provides the same information (in addition to a lot more) that we worked earlier in this chapter to access on our own.

The SQL panel

If we click on the **SQL** section of the debug toolbar, the page will change to:

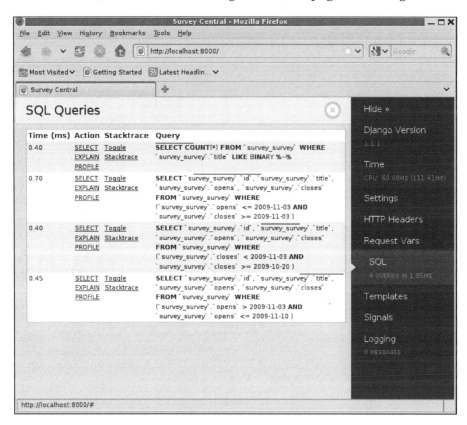

At a glance, this is a much nicer display of the SQL queries for the page than what we came up with earlier. The queries themselves are highlighted so that SQL keywords stand out, making them easier to read. Also, since they are not embedded inside an HTML comment, their content does not need to be altered in any way—there was no need to change the content of the query containing the double dash in order to avoid it causing display problems. (Now would probably be a good time to remove that added query, before we forget why we added it.)

Notice also that the times listed for each query are more specific than what was available in Django's default query history. The debug toolbar replaces Django's query recording with its own, and provides timings in units of milliseconds instead of seconds.

The display also includes a graphical representation of how long each query took, in the form of horizontal bars that appear above each query. This representation makes it easy to see when there are one or more queries that are much more expensive than the others. In fact, if a query takes an excessive amount of time, its bar will be colored red. In this case, there is not a great deal of difference in the query times, and none took particularly long, so all the bars are of similar length, and are colored gray.

Digging deeper, some of the information we had to manually figure out earlier in this chapter is just a click away on this SQL query display. Specifically, the answer to the question of what line of our code triggered a particular SQL query to be issued. Each of the displayed queries has a **Toggle Stacktrace** option, which when clicked will show the stack trace associated with the query:

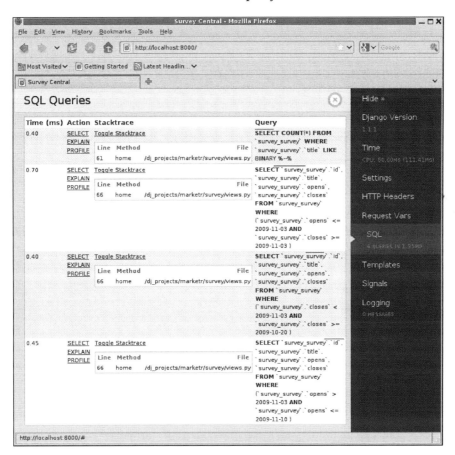

Here we can see that all queries are made by the `home` method in the survey `views.py` file. Note that the toolbar filters out levels in the stack trace that are within Django itself, which explains why each of these has only one level shown. The first query is triggered by **Line 61**, which contains the `filter` call added to test what will happen if a query containing two dashes in a row was logged. The remaining queries are all attributed to **Line 66**, which is the last line of the `render_to_response` call in the `home` view. These queries, as we figured out earlier, are all made during the rendering of the template. (Your line numbers may vary from those shown here, depending on where in the file various functions were placed.)

Finally, this SQL query display makes available information that we had not even gotten around to wanting yet. Under the **Action** column are links to **SELECT**, **EXPLAIN**, and **PROFILE** each query. Clicking on the **SELECT** link shows what the database returns when the query is actually executed. For example:

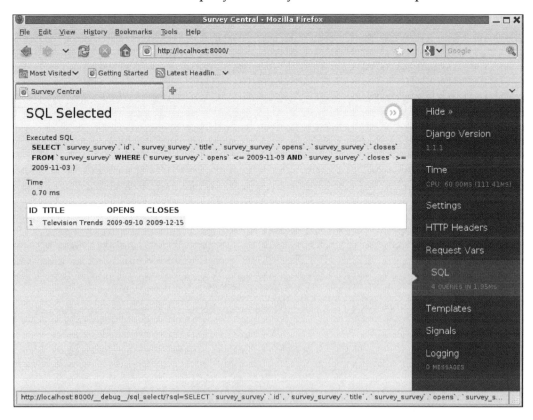

Similarly, clicking on **EXPLAIN** and **PROFILE** displays what the database reports when asked to explain or profile the selected query, respectively. The exact display, and how to interpret the results, will differ from database to database. (In fact, the **PROFILE** option is not available with all databases—it happens to be supported by the database in use here, MySQL.) Interpreting the results from **EXPLAIN** and **PROFILE** is beyond the scope of what's covered here, but it is useful to know that if you ever need to dig deep into the performance characteristics of a query, the debug toolbar makes it easy to do so.

We've now gotten a couple of pages deep into the SQL query display. How do we get back to the actual application page? Clicking on the circled **>>** at the upper-right of the main page display will return to the previous SQL query page, and the circled **>>** will turn into a circled **X**. Clicking the circled **X** on any panel detail page closes the details and returns to displaying the application data. Alternatively, clicking again on the panel area on the toolbar for the currently displayed panel will have the same effect as clicking on the circled symbol in the display area. Finally, if you prefer using the keyboard to the mouse, pressing *Esc* has the same effect as clicking the circled symbol.

Now that we have completely explored the SQL panel, let's take a brief look at each of the other panels provided by the debug toolbar.

The Time panel

Clicking on the **Time** panel brings up more detailed information on where time was spent during production of the page:

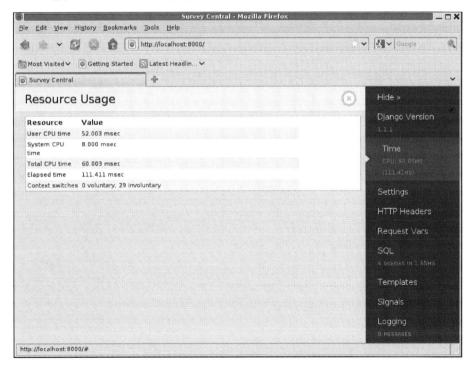

The total CPU time is split between user and system time, the total elapsed (wall clock) time is listed, and the number of voluntary and involuntary context switches are displayed. For a page that is taking too long to generate, these additional details about where the time is being spent can help point towards a cause.

Note that the detailed information provided by this panel comes from the Python `resource` module. This is a Unix-specific Python module that is not available on non-Unix-type systems. Thus on Windows, for example, the debug toolbar time panel will only show summary information, and no further details will be available.

The Settings panel

Clicking on **Settings** brings up a scrollable display of all the settings in effect. The code used to create this display is identical to the code used to display the settings on a Django debug page, so the display here will be identical to what you would see on a debug page.

The HTTP Headers panel

Clicking on **HTTP Headers** brings up a display of all the HTTP headers for the request:

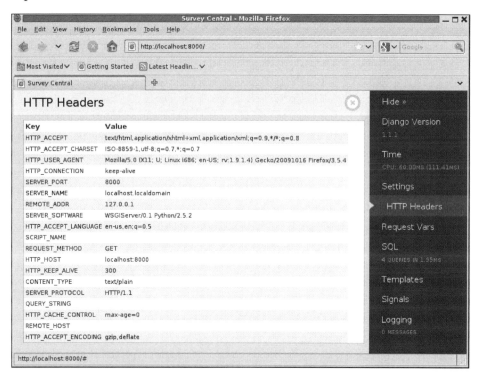

This is a subset of the information available in the **META** section of a debug page. As mentioned in the previous chapter, the `request.META` dictionary contains all of the HTTP headers for a request in addition to other information that has nothing to do with the request, since `request.META` is initially copied from the `os.environ` dictionary. The debug toolbar has chosen to filter the displayed information to include only information pertinent to the HTTP request, as shown in the screenshot.

The Request Vars panel

Clicking on **Request Vars** brings up a display of cookies, session variables, GET variables, and POST data for the request. Since the survey application home page doesn't have any information to display for any of those, the **Request Vars** display for it is not very interesting. Instead, here is an example from the admin application, which does use a session, and so it actually has something to display:

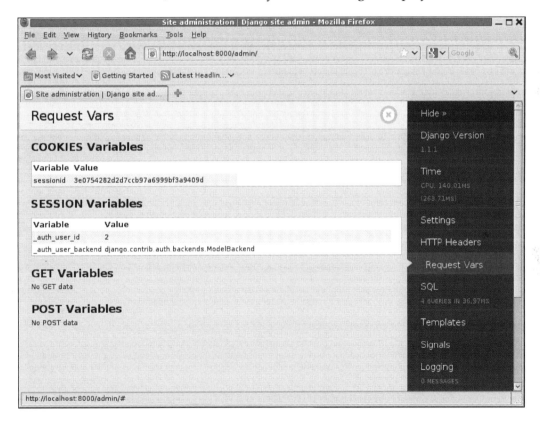

Here you can see the `sessionid` cookie that was set as a result of the admin application using the `django.contrib.sessions` application, and you can also see the individual session variables that have been set in the session.

The Templates panel

Clicking on **Templates** brings up a display of information about template processing for the request. Returning to the survey home page as an example:

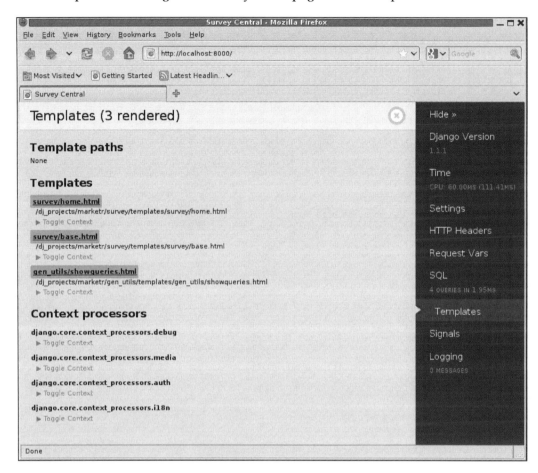

The **Template paths** section lists the paths specified in the TEMPLATE_DIRS setting; since we have not added anything to that setting, it is empty.

The **Templates** section shows all of the templates rendered for the response. Each template is listed, showing the name specified by the application for rendering first. Clicking on this name will bring up a display of the actual template file contents. Under the application-specified name is the full file path for the template. Finally, each template also has a **Toggle Context** link that can be used to see the details of the context used by each of the rendered templates.

The **Context processors** section shows all of the installed context processors. Under each is a **Toggle Context** link that when clicked will show the context variables that the associated context processor adds to the context.

Note that the context processors are listed regardless of whether the application used a `RequestContext` to render the response. Thus, their being listed on this page does not imply that the variables they set were added to the context for this particular response.

The Signals panel

Clicking on **Signals** brings up a display of the signal configuration:

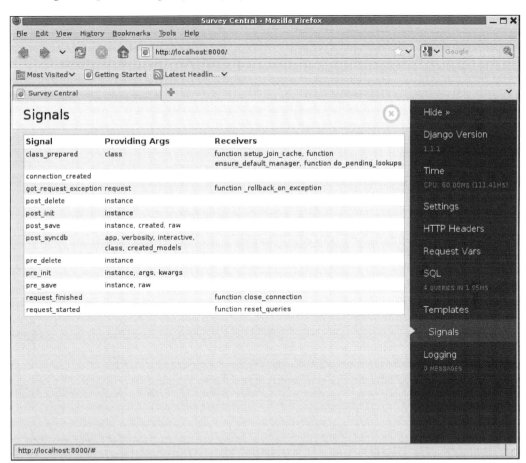

All of the defined Django signals are listed. For each, the arguments provided are shown along with the receivers that have been connected to the signal.

Note that this display does not indicate anything about what signals were actually triggered during the production of the current page. It simply shows how the signals are configured.

The Logging panel

Finally, the **Logging** panel shows any messages sent via Python's `logging` module during the course of the request processing. Since we have not yet investigated using logging in the survey application, and since as of Django 1.1, Django itself does not use the Python logging module, there is nothing for us to see on this panel yet.

Redirect handling by the debug toolbar

Now recall the reason we started investigating the debug toolbar: we found that our original approach to tracking SQL queries for a page did not work for pages that returned an HTTP redirect instead of rendering a template. How does the debug toolbar handle this better? To see this, click on the **Television Trends** link on the home page, select answers for the two questions, and press **Submit**. The result will be:

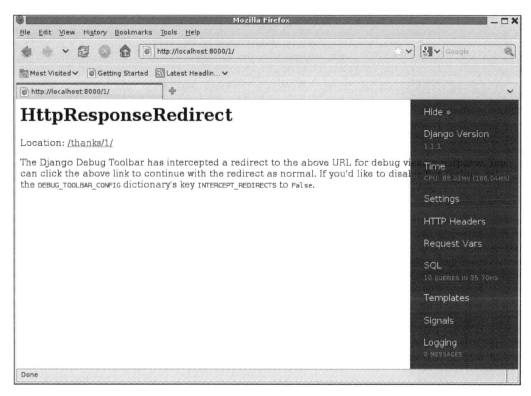

This page shows an example of why it is sometimes necessary to use the **Hide** option on the toolbar, since the toolbar itself obscures part of the message on the page. Hiding the toolbar shows that the full message is:

The Django Debug Toolbar has intercepted a redirect to the above URL for debug viewing purposes. You can click the above link to continue with the redirect as normal. If you'd like to disable this feature, set the DEBUG_TOOLBAR_CONFIG dictionary's key INTERCEPT_REDIRECTS to False.

What the debug toolbar has done here is intercepted the redirect request and replaced it with a rendered response containing a link to the location specified in the original redirect. The toolbar itself is still in place and available to investigate whatever information we might like to see about the processing of the request that generated the redirect. For example, we can click on the **SQL** section and see:

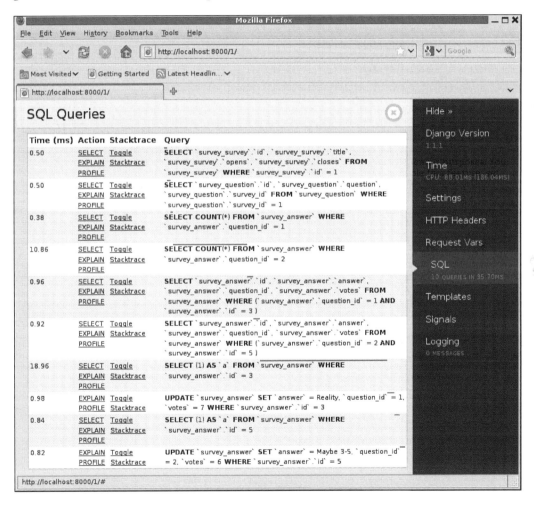

These are the SQL queries that were needed to process the inbound posted form. Not surprisingly, the first four are exactly the same as what we saw for generating the form in the first place, since the same code path is initially followed for both GET and POST requests.

It is only after those queries are issued that the `display_active_survey` view has different code paths for GET and POST. Specifically, in the case of a POST, the code is:

```
if request.method == 'POST':
    chosen_answers = []
    for qf in qforms:
        if not qf.is_valid():
            break;
        chosen_answers.append(qf.cleaned_data['answer'])
    else:
        for answer in chosen_answers:
            answer.votes += 1
            answer.save()
        return HttpResponseRedirect(
            reverse('survey_thanks', args=(survey.pk,)))
```

The fifth and sixth queries listed on this page are retrieving the specific answer instances that were selected on the submitted form. Unlike the GET case, where all answers for a given question were being retrieved in the fifth and sixth queries, these queries specify an answer `id` in the SQL WHERE clause as well as a question `id`. In the POST case, it is not necessary to retrieve all answers for a question; it is sufficient to retrieve only the one that was chosen.

Toggling the stack trace for these queries shows that they are resulting from the `if not qf.is_valid()` line of code. This makes sense, since in addition to validating the input, the `is_valid` method normalizes the posted data before placing it in the form's `cleaned_data` attribute. In the case of a `ModelChoiceField`, the normalized value is the chosen model object instance, so it is necessary for the validation code to retrieve the chosen object from the database.

After both submitted forms are found to be valid, the `else` leg of this code runs. Here, the vote count for each chosen answer is incremented, and the updated `answer` instance is saved to the database. This code, then, must be responsible for the final four queries previously shown. This can be confirmed by checking the stack trace for those four queries: all point to the `answer.save()` line of code.

But why are four SQL statements, two SELECT and two UPDATE, needed to save two answers to the database? The UPDATE statements are self-explanatory, but the SELECT statements that precede them are a bit curious. In each case, the constant 1 is selected from the `survey_answer` table with a WHERE clause specifying a primary key value that matches the `survey` that is in the process of being saved. What is the intent of this query?

What the Django code is doing here is attempting to determine if the `answer` being saved already exists in the database or if it is new. Django can tell by whether any results are returned from the SELECT if it needs to use an UPDATE or an INSERT when saving the model instance to the database. Selecting the constant value is more efficient than actually retrieving the result when the only information needed is whether the result exists.

You might think the Django code should know, just based on the fact that the primary key value is already set for the model instance, that the instance reflects data that is already in the database. However, Django models can use manually-assigned primary key values, so the fact that the primary key value has been assigned does not guarantee the model has already been saved to the database. Therefore, there is an extra SELECT to determine the model status before saving the data.

The survey application code, though, certainly knows that all of the `answer` instances it is saving when processing a survey response are already saved in the database. When saving, the survey code can indicate that the instance must be saved via an UPDATE and not an INSERT by specifying `force_update` on the save call:

```
answer.save(force_update=True)
```

If we make that change and try submitting another survey, we see that the SELECT queries have been eliminated from processing for this case, reducing the total number of queries needed from 10 to 8:

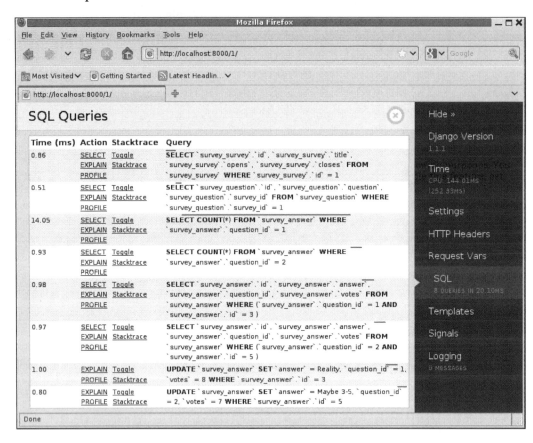

(Yes, I realize that earlier I said now was not the time for making optimizations, yet here I went ahead and made one. This one was just too easy to pass up.)

We have now covered all of the panels displayed by default by the Django Debug Toolbar, and seen how its default handling of returned redirects allows investigation of the processing that led up to the redirect. It is a very flexible tool: it supports adding panels, changing what panels are displayed, changing when the toolbar is displayed, and configuration of various other options. Discussing all of this is beyond the scope of what is covered here. Hopefully what has been covered gives you a taste for the power of this tool. If you are interested in learning more details on how to configure it, the README linked from its home page is a good place to start.

For now we will leave the Django Debug Toolbar and continue with a discussion of how to track the internal state of our application code through logging. For this we will want to first see how the logging appears without the toolbar, so at this point we should comment out the toolbar middleware in `settings.py`. (Note that it is not necessary to remove the `debug_toolbar` listing from INSTALLED_APPS, since this is only necessary for the application template loader to find templates specified by the middleware.)

Tracking internal code state

Sometimes even all of the information available from a tool like the Django Debug Toolbar is not enough to figure out what is going wrong to produce incorrect results during processing of a request. The problem probably lies somewhere in the application code, but from visual inspection we just cannot figure out what is wrong. To solve the problem we need to get more information about the internal state of the application code. Perhaps we need to see what the flow of control is through the functions in the application, or see what values are calculated for some intermediate results that ultimately cause the code to go down a wrong path.

How do we get this kind of information? One way is to run the code under a debugger, and actually step through it line by line to see what it is doing. This approach will be covered in detail in the next chapter. It is very powerful, but can be time-consuming and is not practical in all situations. For example, it is difficult to use for problems that crop up only during production.

Another way is to get the code to report, or log, what it is doing. This is the approach that will be covered in this section. This approach does not provide access to the full range of information that would be available under a debugger, but with good choices of what to log, it can provide enough clues to solve many problems. It can also be used more easily for production-only problems than the approach of running under a debugger.

Resist the urge to sprinkle prints

When running under the development server, the output from `print` appears on the console, so it is easily accessible. Thus, when faced with some Django application code that is misbehaving during development, it is tempting to simply start adding ad-hoc `print` statements at key points in an attempt to figure out what is going on inside the code. While very tempting, it is usually a bad idea.

Why is it a bad idea? First, the problem rarely becomes obvious with just one or two `print` statements. It may seem at first that if we just know if the code gets to here or there, all will be clear. But it isn't, and we wind up adding more and more `print` statements, perhaps printing out values of variables, and both the code itself and the development server console become a mess of ad-hoc debug information.

Then, once the problem is solved, all of those `print` statements need to be removed. We generally don't want them cluttering up either the code or the console with their output. Removing them all is a nuisance, but necessary, since some production environments disallow access to `sys.stdout`. Thus, a stray `print` left over from development debugging can cause a server error during production.

Then, when the same or a similar problem comes up again, and it was solved in the past by the "sprinkle `print`" method, virtually all of the work done before may need to be re-done again in order to figure out what is wrong this time. The previous experience might give us a better idea of what `print` statements to put where, but if we've already deleted them after solving the first problem, a fair amount of work may be involved in re-doing essentially the same thing for the next variant of the problem that arises. This is a waste of effort.

This sequence highlights a few main problems with the "sprinkle `print`" method of development debugging. First, the developer needs to decide, right at the point where the `print` is added, under what conditions it should be produced and where the output should go. It's possible to bracket added `print` statements with conditionals such as `if settings.DEBUG`, which might allow the added debugging support to remain in the code long-term, but this is a nuisance and adds clutter to the code, so it tends not to be done. It's also possible to specify in the `print` that the output should be routed someplace other than the default of `sys.stdout`, but again that is more work and tends not to be done.

These problems lead to sprinkled `print` statements that are immediately removed when a problem is solved, leaving the code in a state where by default it reports nothing about its operation. Then when the next problem occurs, the developer has to start all over again with adding reporting of debug information.

A far better approach is to use some disciplined logging throughout development, so that by default, at least when DEBUG is turned on, the code reports something about what it is doing. If it does so, then it is quite possible that no additional debug information needs to be collected in order to solve problems that crop up. Furthermore, use of a logging facility allows for the configuration of under what conditions messages should be output, and where they should go, to be separated from the actual logging statements.

Simple logging configuring for development

A preferred alternative to `print` statements for debugging, then, is to use the python `logging` module. The actual logging calls are as easy to make as they are with `print`. For example, a `print` to track calls into `display_active_survey` might look like this:

```
def display_active_survey(request, survey):
    print 'display_active_survey called for a %s of survey '\
            'with pk %s' % (request.method, survey.pk)
```

Here the print reports the function that has been called; along with the `request.method` and the primary key of the survey it has been passed. On the development server console, the output for getting an active survey page would be:

```
Django version 1.1.1, using settings 'marketr.settings'
Development server is running at http://0.0.0.0:8000/
Quit the server with CONTROL-C.
display_active_survey called for a GET of survey with pk 1
[04/Nov/2009 19:14:10] "GET /1/ HTTP/1.1" 200 2197
```

The equivalent call, only using Python `logging`, might be:

```
import logging
def display_active_survey(request, survey):
    logging.debug('display_active_survey called for a %s of '
                    'survey with pk %s', request.method, survey.pk)
```

Here the `logging.debug` call is used to specify that the passed string is a debug-level message. The concept of levels allows the calling code to assign a measure of importance to the message without actually making any decisions about whether the message should be output in the current circumstances. Rather, that decision is made by the logging facility, based on the currently set threshold level for logging.

The Python `logging` module provides a set of convenience methods for logging messages with the default defined levels. These are, in increasing order of level: `debug`, `info`, `warning`, `error`, and `critical`. Thus, this `logging.debug` message will only be output if the `logging` module's level threshold has been set to include debug-level messages.

The only problem with using this `logging.debug` statement in place of a `print` is that by default the logging module level threshold is set to `warning`. Thus, only `warning`, `error`, and `critical` messages are output by default. We need to configure the `logging` module to output debug-level statements in order for this message to appear on the console. An easy way to do this is to add a call to `logging.basicConfig` in the `settings.py` file. We can make the call contingent on DEBUG being turned on:

```
import logging
if DEBUG:
    logging.basicConfig(level=logging.DEBUG)
```

With that code added to `settings.py`, and the `logging.debug` call in the `display_active_survey` function, the development console will now show the message when the `display_active_survey` function is entered:

```
Django version 1.1.1, using settings 'marketr.settings'
Development server is running at http://0.0.0.0:8000/
Quit the server with CONTROL-C.
DEBUG:root:display_active_survey called for a GET of survey with pk 1
[04/Nov/2009 19:24:14] "GET /1/ HTTP/1.1" 200 2197
```

Note that the DEBUG:root: prefix on the message is a result of the default formatting applied to logged messages. DEBUG indicates the level associated with the message and root identifies the logger that was used to log the message. Since the `logging.debug` call does not specify any particular logger, the default of root was used.

Other parameters to `logging.basicConfig` could be used to change the formatting of the message, but full coverage of all the features of Python logging is beyond the scope of what we need to cover here. For our purposes, the default formatting will be fine.

Another thing that can be specified in the logging configuration is where the messages should be routed. We did not do so here, since the default of `sys.stderr` is sufficient for development debugging purposes.

Deciding what to log

By switching from `print` to `logging`, we've removed the need for the developer adding the logging to decide under exactly what conditions the logged information should be produced, and where exactly it should go. The developer simply needs to identify the level of importance associated with the message, and then the logging facility itself will decide what to do with the logged information. The next question, then, is what should be logged?

In general, it is hard to know what information will be most useful to log when writing code. As developers we might make some guesses, but until we get some experience with the code as it actually runs, it is hard to be sure. Yet, as previously mentioned, it can be very helpful for code to have some built-in reporting of basic information about what it is doing. Thus, it is good to have some guidelines to follow for logging that should be included by default when initially writing code.

One such guideline might be to log entry and exit to all "significant" functions. The entry log message should include the values for any key parameters, and the exit log message should give some indication of what the function returned. With just this type of entry and exit logging (assuming a reasonably good split of code into manageable functions), we'll be able to get a pretty clear picture of the flow of control through the code.

Manually adding entry and exit logging, however, is a nuisance. It can also add clutter to the code. In reality, it is unlikely that a guideline to log all significant function entries and exits will be happily followed, unless it is much easier to do than adding the type of logging message previously noted for entry to `display_active_survey`.

Fortunately, Python provides facilities to make it easy to do exactly what we are looking for here. Functions can be wrapped in other functions, allowing the wrapping function to do things such as log entry and exit, with parameter and return information. Furthermore, the Python decorator syntax allows such wrapping to be accomplished with minimal added code clutter. In the next section, we will develop some simple logging wrappers for use with our existing survey application code.

Decorators to log function entry and exit

One disadvantage of using general-purpose wrappers instead of embedding entry/exit logging in the functions themselves is that it makes it more difficult to accomplish fine-grained control over what parameter and return information is logged. It is easy to write a general wrapper that logs all parameters, or no parameters, but it is difficult to impossible to write one that logs some subset of the parameters, for example.

Why not just log all parameters? The problem with this is that some often-used parameters in Django applications, such as request objects, have a very verbose representation. Logging their full values would produce too much output. It's better to start with a general-purpose wrapping logger that does not log any parameter values, in addition to maybe one or more special-purpose ones that can be used for functions with predictable parameters to log key information in those parameters.

For example, a special-purpose wrapper for logging entry and exit to view functions is likely worthwhile. A view always gets an HttpRequest object as its first parameter. While logging the full object is not helpful, logging the request method is both short and useful. Furthermore, since additional parameters to the view function come from the requested URL, they are probably not too verbose to log as well.

What about return values—should they be logged? Probably not in general for a Django application, which will often have functions that return HttpResponse objects. These are generally too large to be helpful when logged. However, it is typically useful to log at least some information about return values, such as their type.

We've come up with two wrappers, then, to start with. The first, which will be named log_call, will log the entry to and exit from a function. No entry parameter information will be logged by log_call, but it will log the type of result it returns. The second wrapper will be more specialized, and will be used for wrapping view functions. This one will be named log_view. It will log the request method and any additional parameters passed to the wrapped view, as well as the type of its return value.

Where should this code go? Again, it is not tied in any way to the survey application, so it makes sense to put it in gen_utils. We'll create a file in gen_utils then, named logutils.py, that can hold any general logging utility code. We'll start with an implementation of the log_call wrapper previously described:

```python
import logging

class LoggingDecorator(object):
    def __init__(self, f):
        self.f = f

class log_call(LoggingDecorator):
    def __call__(self, *args, **kwargs):
        f = self.f
        logging.debug("%s called", f.__name__)
        rv = f(*args, **kwargs)
        logging.debug("%s returned type %s", f.__name__, type(rv))
        return rv
```

This implementation uses the class-based style of writing wrapping functions. Using this style, the wrapper is defined as a class that implements __init__ and __call__ methods. The __init__ method is called at the time the wrapper is created, and is passed the function it is wrapping. The __call__ method is called when the wrapped function is actually called. The __call__ implementation is responsible for doing whatever the wrapping function requires, calling the wrapped function, and returning its result.

Here the implementation is split into two classes: the base LoggingDecorator that implements __init__, and then log_call, which inherits __init__ from LoggingDecorator and implements __call__. The reason for this split is so that we can share the common __init__ for multiple logging wrappers. All the __init__ does is save a reference to the wrapped function to be used later when __call__ is called.

The log_call __call__ implementation, then, first logs a message that the function was called. The name of the wrapped function can be found in its __name__ attribute. The wrapped function is then called, and its return value is saved in rv. A second message is logged noting the type returned by the called function. Finally, the value returned by the wrapped function is returned.

The log_view wrapper is very similar to log_call, differing only in the details of what it logs:

```
class log_view(LoggingDecorator):
    def __call__(self, *args, **kwargs):
        f = self.f
        logging.debug("%s called with method %s, kwargs %s",
            f.__name__, args[0].method, kwargs)
        rv = f(*args, **kwargs)
        logging.debug("%s returned type %s", f.__name__, type(rv))
        return rv
```

Here the first logged message includes, in addition to the name of the wrapped function, the method attribute of the first positional argument and the keyword arguments passed to the wrapped function. This wrapper, since it is intended to be used for wrapping view functions, assumes the first positional argument is an HttpRequest object, which has a method attribute.

Further, this code assumes all other arguments will be passed as keyword arguments. We know that this will be the case for the survey application code, since all of the survey URL patterns specify named groups. A more general view wrapper would need to log `args` (except the first one, an `HttpRequest` object) as well, if it wanted to support non-named groups used in the URL pattern configuration. For the survey application, this would just result in logging information that is always the same, so it has been omitted here.

Applying the decorators to the Survey code

Now let's add these decorators to the survey view functions and see what some typical output from browsing looks like. Adding the decorators is easy. First, in `views.py`, add an import for the decorators near the top of the file:

```
from gen_utils.logutils import log_view, log_call
```

Then, for all functions that are actually views, add `@log_view` above the function definition. (This syntax assumes the Python version in use is 2.4 or higher.) For example, for the home page, view definition becomes:

```
@log_view
def home(request):
```

Do the same for `survey_detail` and `survey_thanks`. For the utility functions `display_active_survey` and `display_completed_survey`, use `@log_call` instead. For example:

```
@log_call
def display_active_survey(request, survey):
```

Now when we browse around the survey site, we will have messages logged on the console that track basic information about what code is being called. For example, we might see:

```
DEBUG:root:home called with method GET, kwargs {}

DEBUG:root:home returned type <class 'django.http.HttpResponse'>

[05/Nov/2009 10:46:48] "GET / HTTP/1.1" 200 1184
```

This shows that the home page view was called, and returned an `HttpResponse`. Following the survey application's logged messages, we see the normal printout from the development server noting that a GET for / returned a response with code 200 (HTTP OK) and containing 1184 bytes. Next, we might see:

```
DEBUG:root:survey_detail called with method GET, kwargs {'pk': u'1'}

DEBUG:root:display_active_survey called

DEBUG:root:display_active_survey returned type <class 'django.http.
```

```
HttpResponse'>
DEBUG:root:survey_detail returned type <class 'django.http.HttpResponse'>
[05/Nov/2009 10:46:49] "GET /1/ HTTP/1.1" 200 2197
```

This shows the `survey_detail` view being called with a `GET`, likely from a link on the home page returned by the previous response. Further, we can see that the particular survey requested has a primary key of `1`. The next log message reveals that this must be an active survey, since `display_active_survey` is called. It returns an `HttpResponse`, as does the `survey_detail` view, and again the last survey log message is followed by Django's own printout summarizing the request and its outcome.

Next, we might see:

```
DEBUG:root:survey_detail called with method POST, kwargs {'pk': u'1'}
DEBUG:root:display_active_survey called
DEBUG:root:display_active_survey returned type <class 'django.http.
HttpResponse'>
DEBUG:root:survey_detail returned type <class 'django.http.HttpResponse'>
[05/Nov/2009 10:46:52] "POST /1/ HTTP/1.1" 200 2466
```

Again this looks like a natural progression from the previous response: a `POST` for the same survey that was retrieved by the previous request. The `POST` indicates that the user is submitting a survey response. However, the return type of `HttpResponse` that is logged indicates that there is some problem with the submission. (We know an `HttpResponse` to a POST only occurs when a form is found to be invalid in `display_active_survey`.)

This might be a place where we would want to add additional logging beyond the entry/exit information, to track the specific reasons why a posted form was deemed invalid. In its current form, all we can know is that the returned response, since it was slightly larger than the original (`2466` versus `2197` bytes), likely included an error annotation noting what needed to be fixed on the form in order for it to be valid.

Next, we might see:

```
DEBUG:root:survey_detail called with method POST, kwargs {'pk': u'1'}
DEBUG:root:display_active_survey called
DEBUG:root:display_active_survey returned type <class 'django.http.
HttpResponseRedirect'>
DEBUG:root:survey_detail returned type <class 'django.http.
HttpResponseRedirect'>
[05/Nov/2009 10:46:56] "POST /1/ HTTP/1.1" 302 0
```

This starts out as a repeat of the previous request, a POST to the survey_detail view for the survey with primary key 1. However, this time an HttpResponseRedirect is returned, indicating that the user must have corrected whatever problem existed in the first submission.

Following this, we would likely see:

```
DEBUG:root:survey_thanks called with method GET, kwargs {'pk': u'1'}
DEBUG:root:survey_thanks returned type <class 'django.http.HttpResponse'>
[05/Nov/2009 10:46:56] "GET /thanks/1/ HTTP/1.1" 200 544
```

This shows the request that the browser will automatically make on receiving the redirect returned by the previous request. We see the survey_thanks view logging a GET for the same survey as all the previous requests, and an HttpResponse being returned.

Thus, we can see how with very little effort we can add some basic logging that provides a general overview of the flow of control through our Django application code. Note that the logging decorators defined here are not perfect. For example, they don't support decoration of methods instead of functions, they impose some overhead even when no logging is desired, and they have some side-effects resulting from turning functions into classes.

All of these drawbacks can be overcome with some care in the development of the wrappers. However, the details of that are beyond the scope of what we can cover here. The ones presented here have the advantage of being reasonably simple to understand, and functional enough to hopefully demonstrate the usefulness of having an easy built-in logging mechanism to see the flow of control, along with perhaps some key parameters, through the code.

Logging in the debug toolbar

Recall that we skipped over any examination of the debug toolbar's logging panel since we had no logging in the survey application code. Let's return now to the debug toolbar and see how the added logging appears there.

First, though, let's add an additional log message to note what causes a POST request for an active survey to fail. As mentioned in this previous section, this could be useful to know. So, in the display_active_survey function add a logging call after a form is found to be invalid:

```
for qf in qforms:
    if not qf.is_valid():
        logging.debug("form failed validation: %r", qf.errors)
        break;
```

(Note it will also be necessary to add an `import logging` before use of `logging`.) With that additional log message, we should be able to get specific information about why a particular survey submission was considered invalid.

Now re-activate the debug toolbar by un-commenting its middleware in `settings.py`, browse to an active survey page, and attempt to force production of that log message by submitting an incomplete survey. When the response is returned, clicking on the toolbar's **Logging** panel will bring up a page that looks like this:

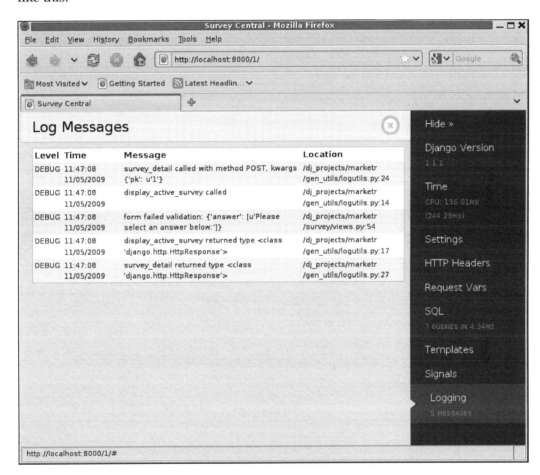

On this page, we can see that in addition to the messages themselves and their assigned levels, the toolbar also reports the date and time they were logged in addition to the location in the code where they were generated. Since most of these log messages are coming from the wrapping functions, the location information here is not particularly useful. However, the newly added log message is correctly matched to where it appears in the code. Indeed the logged message makes it clear that the problem with the form was a missing choice for an answer.

Summary

We have now reached the end of discussing techniques for getting more information about how Django application code is running. In this chapter, we:

- Developed some template utility code to track what SQL requests are made during production of a page
- Learned that creating re-usable general utility code can turn into more work than it might first seem to require
- Learned how the Django Debug Toolbar can be used to get the same information as in our home-grown code in addition to more information, with much less effort
- Discussed the usefulness of applying a general logging framework during code development, as opposed to relying on the ad-hoc "sprinkle `print`" method of debugging problems

With the use of these tools and techniques, we are able to glean a great deal of information about the working of our code. Having a good understanding of how the code behaves when it is working properly makes it much easier to debug problems when they occur. Furthermore, checking on exactly what the code is doing even when it seems, from all outward appearances, to be working correctly, may reveal hidden issues that could become big problems as the code moves from development to production.

Sometimes, however, even all of the information available by using these techniques is insufficient to solve a problem at hand. In those cases, the next step may be to run the code under a debugger. This is the topic of the next chapter.

9
When You Don't Even Know What to Log: Using Debuggers

For many problems encountered during development, a debugger is the most efficient tool to use to help figure out what is going on. A debugger lets you see exactly what the code is doing, step by step if necessary. It lets you see, and change, the values of variables along the way. With a debugger, you can even test out potential code fixes before making changes to the source code.

This chapter focuses on using debuggers to help debug during development of Django applications. Specifically, in this chapter we will:

- Continue development of the survey application, seeing how the Python debugger, pdb, can be used to help figure out any problems that arise

- Learn how to use the debugger to verify correct operation of code that is subject to multi-process race conditions

- Briefly discuss the use of graphical debuggers for debugging Django applications

Implementing the Survey results display

The survey application has one major piece that still remains to be implemented: display of the results for a completed survey. What form should this display take? A text-only tally of votes received for each answer for each question in the survey would be easy enough to write, but not very good at communicating results. A graphical representation of the results, such as a pie chart, would be far more effecting in conveying the breakdown of votes.

In this chapter, we will explore a couple of different approaches to implementing a survey results view that incorporates pie charts to display vote distributions. Along the way we'll encounter some difficulties, and see how the Python debugger can be used to help figure out what is going wrong.

Before starting on the implementation of code to display survey results, let's set up some test data to use in testing out the results as we go along. We can use the existing **Television Trends** survey and simply adjust its data to reflect what we want to test. First, we need to change its `closes` date to be in the last two weeks, so that it will display as a completed survey instead of an active one.

Second, we need to set the `votes` counts for the question answers to ensure we test any special cases we want to cover. This `Survey` has two questions, thus we can use it to test both the case where there is a single clear winner among the answers and the case where there is a tie.

We can use the admin application to set up a tie for the winner on the first question:

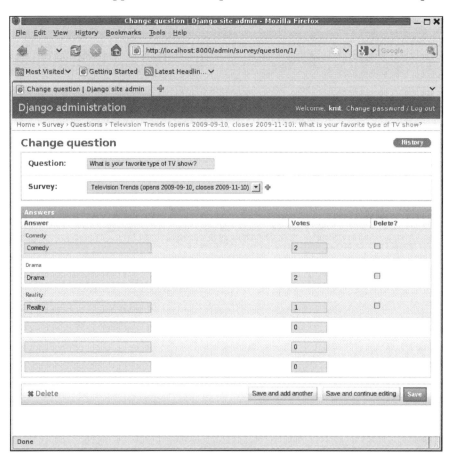

Here we have set **Comedy** and **Drama** to be in a two-way tie for the winning answer. The total number of votes (5) has been kept low for simplicity. It will be easy to verify that the pie charts look correct when the wedges are supposed to contain amounts such as one and two fifths of the total.

For the second question, we can set up the data so that there is a single clear winner:

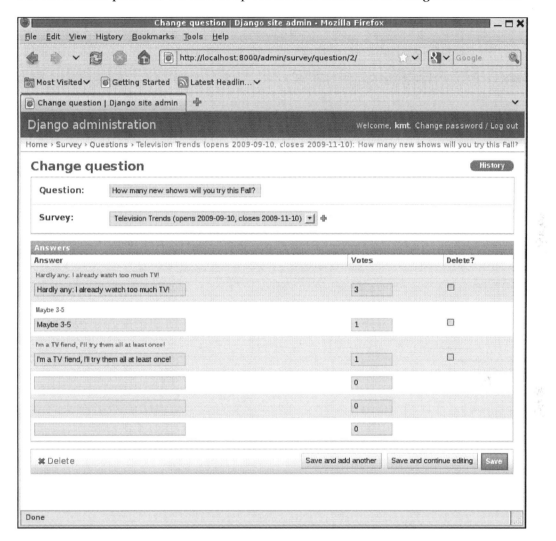

For this question, our results display should list only **Hardly any: I already watch too much TV!** as the single winning answer.

Results display using pygooglechart

Once we've decided we want to create pie charts, the next question is: how do we do that? Chart creation is not built into the Python language. There are, however, several add-on libraries that provide this function. We'll start by experimenting with one of the simplest alternatives, `pygooglechart`, which is a Python wrapper around the Google chart API.

The `pygooglechart` package is available on the Python Package Index site, `http://pypi.python.org/pypi/pygooglechart`. Information on the underlying Google chart API can be found at `http://code.google.com/apis/chart/`. The version of `pygooglechart` used in this chapter is 0.2.0.

One reason using `pygooglechart` is very simple, for a web application, is that the result of constructing a chart is simply a URL that can be used to fetch the chart image. There is no need to generate or serve an image file from our application. Rather, all of the work can be pushed off to the Google chart API, and our application simply includes HTML `img` tags that refer to images served by Google.

Let's start, then, with the template for displaying results of a survey. The current implementation of this template, `survey/completed_survey.html`, does nothing more than print a header noting the title of the survey:

```
{% extends "survey/base.html" %}
{% block content %}
<h1>Survey results for {{ survey.title }}</h1>
{% endblock content %}
```

We want to change this now, and add template code that loops through the questions in the survey and prints out the results for each. Recall that the `Question` model has a method (implemented in *Chapter 3, Testing 1, 2, 3: Basic Unit Testing*) that returns the winning answers:

```
class Question(models.Model):
    question = models.CharField(max_length=200)
    survey = models.ForeignKey(Survey)

    def winning_answers(self):
        max_votes = self.answer_set.aggregate(Max('votes')).values()[0]
        if max_votes and max_votes > 0:
            rv = self.answer_set.filter(votes=max_votes)
        else:
            rv = self.answer_set.none()
        return rv
```

In the template, then, we can use this method to access the winning answer (or answers, in the case of a tie). For each `Question` in the `Survey`, we will print out the question text, a list of the winning answers, and a pie chart showing a breakdown of the votes for each `Answer`. Template code that does this is:

```
{% extends "survey/base.html" %}
{% block content %}
<h1>Survey results for {{ survey.title }}</h1>
{% for q in survey.question_set.all %}
{% with q.winning_answers as winners %}
{% if winners %}
<h2>{{ q.question }}</h2>
<p>Winner{{ winners|length|pluralize }}:</p>
<ul>
{% for answer in winners %}
<li>{{ answer.answer }}</li>
{% endfor %}
</ul>
<p><img src="{{ q.get_piechart_url }}" alt="Pie Chart"/></p>
{% endif %}
{% endwith %}
{% endfor %}
{% endblock content %}
```

Here we have added a `{% for %}` block which loops through the questions in the passed survey. For each, the list of winning answers is retrieved using the `winning_answers` method and cached in the `winners` template variable. Then, if there is anything in `winners`, the following items are displayed:

- The question text, as a level two heading.
- A heading paragraph for the winners list that is properly pluralized depending on the length of `winners`.
- A text list of the winning answers formatted as an unordered list.
- An embedded image that will be the pie chart breakdown of answer votes. The URL for this image is retrieved using a routine that needs to be implemented on the `Question` model: `get_piechart_url`.

Note that the display of this entire list of items is protected by an `{% if winners %}` block to guard against the edge case of attempting to display results for a `Question` that received no answers. That may be unlikely but it's best to never display likely odd-looking output for edge cases to users, so at the template level here we simply avoid showing anything at all in this case.

Next, we need to implement the `get_piechart_url` method for the `Question` model. After some reading up on the `pygooglechart` API, an initial implementation might be:

```
def get_piechart_url(self):
    from pygooglechart import PieChart3D
    answer_set = self.answer_set.all()
    chart = PieChart3D(500, 230)
    chart.set_data([a.votes for a in answer_set])
    chart.set_pie_labels([a.answer for a in answer_set])
    return chart.get_url()
```

This code retrieves the set of answers associated with the `Question` and caches it in the local variable `answer_set`. (This is done because the set is iterated through multiple times in the following code and caching it in a local variable ensures the data is fetched from the database only once.) Then, the `pygooglechart` API is called to create a three-dimensional pie chart, `chart`, which will be 500 pixels wide and 230 pixels high. Then, data values are set for the pie chart wedges: these data values are the `votes` count for each answer in the set. Next, labels are set for each of the wedges to be the `answer` values. Finally, the method returns the URL for the constructed chart, using the `get_url` method.

How well does that work? When we navigate to the survey application home page, the **Television Trends** survey should now (since its `closes` date has been set to have already passed) be listed under the heading that indicates we can see its results:

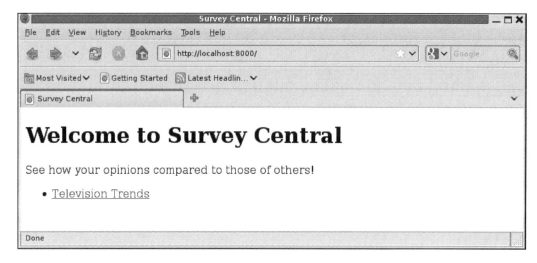

Clicking on the **Television Trends** link now brings up a completed survey results page:

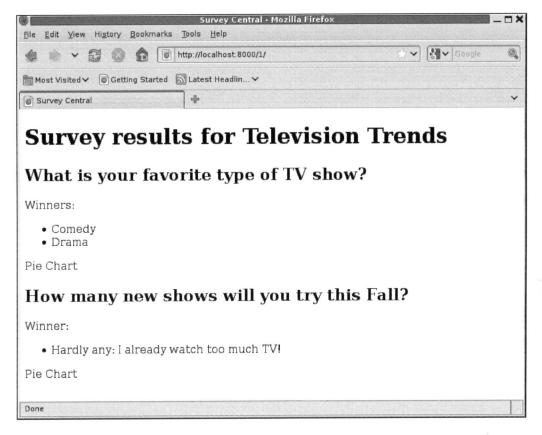

That's not quite right. While the text displays of winning answer lists look fine, the pie charts are not appearing. Rather, the browser is displaying the alternate text defined for the image, **Pie Chart**, which means something went wrong in retrieving the specified image.

Looking at the HTML source for the page, we see that both paragraphs containing the image tags look like this:

```
<p><img src="" alt="Pie Chart"/></p>
```

Somehow, the `get_piechart_url` method returned an empty string instead of a value. We might first add some logging to `get_piechart_url` to try to figure out why:

```
def get_piechart_url(self):
    from pygooglechart import PieChart3D
    import logging
    logging.debug('get_piechart_url called for pk=%d', self.pk)
    answer_set = self.answer_set.all()
    chart = PieChart3D(500, 230)
    chart.set_data([a.votes for a in answer_set])
    chart.set_pie_labels([a.answer for a in answer_set])
    logging.debug('get_piechart_url returning: %s',
                  chart.get_url())
    return chart.get_url()
```

We've added a log statement on entry noting the primary key of the `Question` instance, and a log statement prior to exit logging what the method is about to return. However, reloading the page with the logging included produces confusing output on the server console:

```
DEBUG:root:survey_detail called with method GET, kwargs {'pk': u'1'}
DEBUG:root:display_completed_survey called
DEBUG:root:get_piechart_url called for pk=1
DEBUG:root:get_piechart_url called for pk=2
DEBUG:root:display_completed_survey returned type <class 'django.http.
HttpResponse'>
DEBUG:root:survey_detail returned type <class 'django.http.HttpResponse'>
[14/Nov/2009 11:29:08] "GET /1/ HTTP/1.1" 200 2573
```

We can see that `survey_detail` called `display_completed_survey` and `get_piechart_url` was called twice, but there are no messages showing what it was returning either time. What happened? There's no branching in the code between the two `logging.debug` calls, so how could one get executed and the other skipped?

We could try adding more logging calls, interspersed between each line of code. However, while that may reveal how far execution proceeds in the method before unexpectedly leaving, it won't provide any clue as to why execution stops proceeding to the next line. It is also a nuisance to add logging after every line of code, even for methods as small as this one. For problems like this, a debugger is a much more efficient way to figure out what is going on.

Getting started with the debugger

A debugger is a powerful development tool that allows us to see what code is doing as it runs. When a program is run under the control of a debugger, the user is able to pause execution, examine and change the value of variables, flexibly continue execution to the next line or other explicitly set "breakpoints", and more. Python has a built-in debugger named pdb which provides a user interface that is essentially an augmented Python shell. In addition to normal shell commands, pdb supports various debugger-specific commands, many of which we will experiment with in this chapter as we debug the survey results display code.

How, then, do we use pdb to help figure out what is going on here? We'd like to enter the debugger and step through the code to see what is happening. The first task, breaking into the debugger, can be accomplished by adding `import pdb; pdb.set_trace()` wherever we'd like the debugger to get control. The `set_trace()` call sets an explicit breakpoint in our program where execution will pause under debugger control so we can investigate what the current state is and control how the code proceeds. Thus, we can change the `get_piechart_url` method like so to invoke the debugger on entry:

```
def get_piechart_url(self):
    from pygooglechart import PieChart3D
    import logging
    import pdb; pdb.set_trace()
    logging.debug('get_piechart_url called for pk=%d', self.pk)
    answer_set = self.answer_set.all()
    chart = PieChart3D(500, 230)
    chart.set_data([a.votes for a in answer_set])
    chart.set_pie_labels([a.answer for a in answer_set])
    logging.debug('get_piechart_url returning: %s',
                  chart.get_url())
    return chart.get_url()
```

Now, when we reload the survey results page, the browser will appear to hang while it tries to load the page:

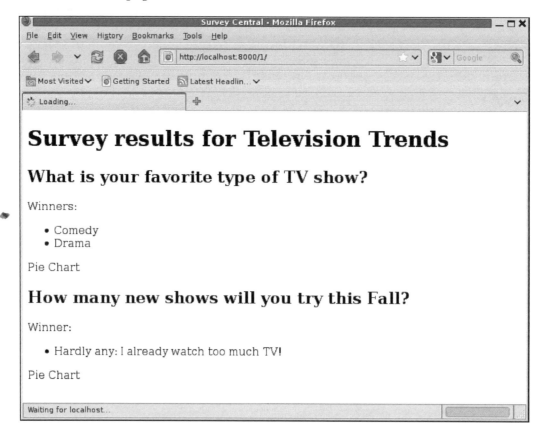

When we switch to the window containing the `runserver` console, we see:

```
DEBUG:root:survey_detail called with method GET, kwargs {'pk': u'1'}
DEBUG:root:display_completed_survey called
> /dj_projects/marketr/survey/models.py(71)get_piechart_url()
-> logging.debug('get_piechart_url called for pk=%d', self.pk)
(Pdb)
```

Here we see that another call to the `survey_detail` view has been made, which forwarded the request to the `display_completed_survey` function. Then, the debugger was entered, due to the `pdb.set_trace()` call placed in `get_piechart_url`. On entry, the debugger prints out two lines identifying the location of the next line of code that is to be executed, and the contents of that line. So we can see that we are on line 71 of the `survey/models.py` file, in the `get_piechart_url` method, about to issue the call to log entry to the method. After the two lines noting where execution stopped, the debugger prints its prompt, `(Pdb)`, and waits for user input.

Before proceeding to step through the code and see what's happening as the code runs, let's see what we can learn about where we are and the present state of things. Pdb supports many commands and not all will be covered here, rather just the ones that are most commonly useful will be demonstrated. We'll start with a few that are helpful in getting context for where the code is, how it got there, and what arguments were passed to the current function.

The list command

For example, if the single line of context provided on entry to the debugger is not sufficient, more of the surrounding code can be seen by using the `list` command. This command, like most pdb commands, can be abbreviated to its initial letter. Using it here we see:

```
(Pdb) l
 66
 67            def get_piechart_url(self):
 68                    from pygooglechart import PieChart3D
 69                    import logging
 70                    import pdb; pdb.set_trace()
 71   ->             logging.debug('get_piechart_url called for pk=%d',
                      self.pk)
 72                    answer_set = self.answer_set.all()
 73                    chart = PieChart3D(500, 230)
 74                    chart.set_data([a.votes for a in answer_set])
 75                    chart.set_pie_labels([a.answer for a in answer_set])
 76                    logging.debug('get_piechart_url returning: %s',
(Pdb)
 77                        chart.get_url())
 78                    return chart.get_url()
 79
```

```
80      class Answer(models.Model):
81          answer = models.CharField(max_length=200)
82          question = models.ForeignKey(Question)
83          votes = models.IntegerField(default=0)
84
85          def __unicode__(self):
86              return self.answer
87
(Pdb)
```

Here we see that the response to the list command first displayed five lines above the current line of execution, then the current line of execution (noted by a -> prefix), then five lines following the current line. At the (Pdb) prompt, an empty line was then entered, which causes the last entered command to be repeated. In the case of list, repeating the command results in the display of 11 additional lines following the last ones that were displayed.

Arguments can be passed to list to specify exactly what lines to display, for example l 1,5 will display the first five lines in the current file:

```
(Pdb) l 1,5
1      # -*- encoding: utf-8 -*-
2
3      import datetime
4      from django.db import models
5      from django.db.models import Max
(Pdb)
```

The list command is most useful, though, for seeing the lines of code right around where execution is currently stopped. If more context is needed, I find it easier to have the file open in an editor in a separate window than to try to get a more complete picture of the file using list with arguments.

The where command

The where command, which can be shorted to w, prints the current stack trace. In this case, there is no particular mystery about how the code got to where it is, but it can still be instructive to examine the details.

The `get_piechart_url` method is called during template rendering, which means it will have a long stack trace due to the recursive way in which template nodes are rendered. The length of the response and the density of what gets printed out may seem overwhelming at first, but by ignoring a lot of the details and just focusing on the names of the files and functions you can get a good idea of the overall code flow. For example, at the start of the response, the `where` command here is:

```
(Pdb) w
  /usr/lib/python2.5/site-packages/django/core/management/commands/
runserver.py(60)inner_run()
-> run(addr, int(port), handler)
  /usr/lib/python2.5/site-packages/django/core/servers/basehttp.
py(698)run()
-> httpd.serve_forever()
  /usr/lib/python2.5/SocketServer.py(201)serve_forever()
-> self.handle_request()
  /usr/lib/python2.5/SocketServer.py(222)handle_request()
-> self.process_request(request, client_address)
  /usr/lib/python2.5/SocketServer.py(241)process_request()
-> self.finish_request(request, client_address)
  /usr/lib/python2.5/SocketServer.py(254)finish_request()
-> self.RequestHandlerClass(request, client_address, self)
  /usr/lib/python2.5/site-packages/django/core/servers/basehttp.py(560)__
init__()
-> BaseHTTPRequestHandler.__init__(self, *args, **kwargs)
  /usr/lib/python2.5/SocketServer.py(522)__init__()
-> self.handle()
  /usr/lib/python2.5/site-packages/django/core/servers/basehttp.
py(605)handle()
-> handler.run(self.server.get_app())
  /usr/lib/python2.5/site-packages/django/core/servers/basehttp.
py(279)run()
-> self.result = application(self.environ, self.start_response)
  /usr/lib/python2.5/site-packages/django/core/servers/basehttp.py(651)__
call__()
-> return self.application(environ, start_response)
  /usr/lib/python2.5/site-packages/django/core/handlers/wsgi.py(241)__
call__()
```

```
-> response = self.get_response(request)
  /usr/lib/python2.5/site-packages/django/core/handlers/base.py(92)get_
response()
-> response = callback(request, *callback_args, **callback_kwargs)
```

We may not be entirely sure what all of this code is doing, but with names like
serve_forever(), handle_request(), process_request(), finish_request(),
and get_response(), it seems likely that this is all part of a standard server
request-processing loop. In particular, get_response() sounds like the code is
getting close to the point where the real work of producing a response for the
request will be done. Next, we see:

```
  /dj_projects/marketr/gen_utils/logutils.py(21)__call__()
-> rv = f(*args, **kwargs)
  /dj_projects/marketr/survey/views.py(30)survey_detail()
-> return display_completed_survey(request, survey)
  /dj_projects/marketr/gen_utils/logutils.py(11)__call__()
-> rv = f(*args, **kwargs)
  /dj_projects/marketr/survey/views.py(40)display_completed_survey()
-> RequestContext(request))
```

Indeed, in the get_response function, at the point where it invokes callback(), the
code transitions from Django code (files in /usr/lib/python2.5/site-packages/
django) to our own code in /dj_projects. We then see that we have introduced our
own noise into the tracebacks with the logging wrapper functions—the references to
__call__ in logutils.py.

These don't convey much information other than that the function calls being made
are being logged. But ignoring the noise, we can still see that survey_detail was
called, which in turned called display_completed_survey, which ran to the point
where it is about to return (the last displayed line is the end of the multi-line call
to render_to_response in display_completed_survey). The call to render_to_
response transitions back into Django code:

```
  /usr/lib/python2.5/site-packages/django/shortcuts/__init__
.py(20)render_to_response()
-> return HttpResponse(loader.render_to_string(*args, **kwargs),
**httpresponse_kwargs)
  /usr/lib/python2.5/site-packages/django/template/loader.py(108)render_
to_string()
-> return t.render(context_instance)
  /usr/lib/python2.5/site-packages/django/template/__init__
.py(178)render()
```

```
-> return self.nodelist.render(context)
   /usr/lib/python2.5/site-packages/django/template/__init__
.py(779)render()
-> bits.append(self.render_node(node, context))
   /usr/lib/python2.5/site-packages/django/template/debug.py(71)render_
node()
-> result = node.render(context)
   /usr/lib/python2.5/site-packages/django/template/loader_tags.
py(97)render()
-> return compiled_parent.render(context)
```

What we can glean from this, and from the following `render()` and `render_node()` calls, is that the Django code is processing through rendering the template. Eventually, a few calls that are a bit different start appearing:

```
   /usr/lib/python2.5/site-packages/django/template/debug.py(87)render()
-> output = force_unicode(self.filter_expression.resolve(context))
   /usr/lib/python2.5/site-packages/django/template/__init__
.py(546)resolve()
-> obj = self.var.resolve(context)
   /usr/lib/python2.5/site-packages/django/template/__init__
.py(687)resolve()
-> value = self._resolve_lookup(context)
   /usr/lib/python2.5/site-packages/django/template/__init__.py(722)_
resolve_lookup()
-> current = current()
> /dj_projects/marketr/survey/models.py(71)get_piechart_url()
-> logging.debug('get_piechart_url called for pk=%d', self.pk)
(Pdb)
```

During rendering, the code finally got to the point where it needed to render the value of the {{ q.get_piechart_url }} in the template. Ultimately that got routed to a call to the `Question` model's `get_piechart_url` method, where we had placed the call to enter the debugger, and that is where we are now.

The args command

The `args` command, abbreviated as `a`, can be used to see the values of the arguments passed to the currently executing function:

```
(Pdb) a
self = Television Trends (opens 2009-09-10, closes 2009-11-10): What is
your favorite type of TV show?
(Pdb)
```

The whatis command

The `whatis` command displays the type of its argument. For example:

```
(Pdb) whatis self
<class 'survey.models.Question'>
(Pdb)
```

Recall pdb also behaves like a Python shell session, so the same result can be obtained by taking the `type` of `self`:

```
(Pdb) type(self)
<class 'survey.models.Question'>
(Pdb)
```

We can also interrogate individual attributes of variables, which can be helpful. Here the value of `self` displayed for the `args` command includes all of the individual attributes for this model, excepting its primary key value. We can find out what it is:

```
(Pdb) self.pk
1L
(Pdb)
```

The print and pp commands

The `print` command, abbreviated as `p`, prints the representation of a variable:

```
(Pdb) p self
<Question: Television Trends (opens 2009-09-10, closes 2009-11-10): What
is your favorite type of TV show?>
(Pdb)
```

For large data structures, the output of `print` may be hard to read if it ends up spilling across line boundaries. The alternative `pp` command pretty-prints the output using the Python `pprint` module. This can result in output that is more easily read. For example:

```
(Pdb) p locals()
{'PieChart3D': <class 'pygooglechart.PieChart3D'>, 'self': <Question:
Television Trends (opens 2009-09-10, closes 2009-11-10): What is your
favorite type of TV show?>, 'logging': <module 'logging' from '/usr/lib/
python2.5/logging/__init__.pyc'>, 'pdb': <module 'pdb' from '/usr/lib/
python2.5/pdb.pyc'>}
```

Contrast that `print` output to the `pp` output:

```
(Pdb) pp locals()
{'PieChart3D': <class 'pygooglechart.PieChart3D'>,
 'logging': <module 'logging' from '/usr/lib/python2.5/logging/__init__
.pyc'>,
 'pdb': <module 'pdb' from '/usr/lib/python2.5/pdb.pyc'>,
 'self': <Question: Television Trends (opens 2009-09-10, closes 2009-11-
10): What is your favorite type of TV show?>}
(Pdb)
```

Debugging the pygooglechart results display

At this point we know the code is at the beginning of processing in the `get_piechart_url` method, and the current value of `self` indicates that the `Question` instance we have been called for is the question that asks **What is your favorite type of TV show?** That's good to know, but what we'd really like to understand is what happens as execution continues.

The step and next commands

What we'd like to do now is instruct the debugger to continue execution, but keep the debugger active. There are two commands typically used here: `step` (abbreviated as `s`) and `next` (abbreviated as `n`).

The `step` command begins execution of the current line and returns to the debugger at the first available opportunity. The `next` command also begins execution of the current line, but it does not return to the debugger until the next line in the current function is about to be executed. Thus, if the current line contains a function or method call, `step` is used to step into that function and trace through it, while `next` is used to execute the called function in its entirety and only return to the debugger when it is complete.

For where we are now, `next` is the command we'd want to use, since we do not particularly want to step into the logging code and trace through what it does:

```
(Pdb) n
DEBUG:root:get_piechart_url called for pk=1
> /dj_projects/marketr/survey/models.py(72)get_piechart_url()
-> answer_set = self.answer_set.all()
(Pdb)
```

Here, `next` caused execution of the `logging.debug` call, resulting in the logged message getting printed to the console. Then the debugger stopped again, right before execution of the next line in the current function. Entering nothing causes the `next` command to be executed again, causing answer_set to be assigned the value of `self.answer_set.all()`. We can see the result using the `print` command:

```
(Pdb)
> /dj_projects/marketr/survey/models.py(73)get_piechart_url()
-> chart = PieChart3D(500, 230)
(Pdb) p answer_set
[<Answer: Comedy>, <Answer: Drama>, <Answer: Reality>]
(Pdb)
```

So far everything looks fine, so we continue on:

```
(Pdb) n
> /dj_projects/marketr/survey/models.py(74)get_piechart_url()
-> chart.set_data([a.votes for a in answer_set])
(Pdb)
AttributeError: "'PieChart3D' object has no attribute 'set_data'"
> /dj_projects/marketr/survey/models.py(74)get_piechart_url()
-> chart.set_data([a.votes for a in answer_set])
(Pdb)
```

There's a problem: the call to set_data on chart raised an attribute error with a message indicating that the chart has no such attribute. We made a mistake in implementing this routine. While many of the pygooglechart methods start with set_, the call to set the data for the chart is actually named add_data. So the attempt to specify the data for the chart has failed. But why didn't we see that error reflected as a debug page returned instead of just an empty string returned from get_piechart_url? We can get the answer to that question by continuing on tracing through the code as it runs:

```
(Pdb)
--Return--
> /dj_projects/marketr/survey/models.py(74)get_piechart_url()->None
-> chart.set_data([a.votes for a in answer_set])
```

This shows that the get_piechart_url method is returning None at the point in the code where the AttributeError was raised. Since we did not enclose the code in get_piechart_url in a try/except block, the error is being propagated up the call stack.

```
(Pdb)
AttributeError: "'PieChart3D' object has no attribute 'set_data'"
> /usr/lib/python2.5/site-packages/django/template/__init__.py(722)_
resolve_lookup()
-> current = current()
(Pdb)
> /usr/lib/python2.5/site-packages/django/template/__init__.py(723)_
resolve_lookup()
-> except TypeError: # arguments *were* required
(Pdb)
> /usr/lib/python2.5/site-packages/django/template/__init__.py(727)_
resolve_lookup()
-> except Exception, e:
```

Here we see that the code which called `get_piechart_url` was enclosed in a `try/except` block, and the `except` clauses are being tested for a match against the actual exception raised. The first clause, `except TypeError`, did not match `AttributeError`. The second one, `except Exception`, does match, since `AttributeError` is derived from the base `Exception` class. Thus, the code should proceed to run whatever code is in this except clause. Remember we can use the `list` command to see what that is:

```
(Pdb) l
722                              current = current()
723                         except TypeError: # arguments *were* required
724                             # GOTCHA: This will also catch any TypeError
725                             # raised in the function itself.
726                             current = settings.TEMPLATE_STRING_IF_INVALID
# invalid method call
727  ->                     except Exception, e:
728                             if getattr(e, 'silent_variable_failure', Fal
se):
729                                 current = settings.TEMPLATE_STRING_IF_
INVALID
730                             else:
731                                 raise
732                         except (TypeError, AttributeError):
```

These `except` clauses appear to be testing for special cases where the raised exception will be suppressed and the result produced will be set to the value of `settings.TEMPLATE_STRING_IF_INVALID`. That gives a hint of how this exception is ultimately not reflected in a debug page, though it may not happen immediately in the `except` clause that is about to be executed:

```
(Pdb) n
> /usr/lib/python2.5/site-packages/django/template/__init__.py(728)_
resolve_lookup()
-> if getattr(e, 'silent_variable_failure', False):
(Pdb)
> /usr/lib/python2.5/site-packages/django/template/__init__.py(731)_
resolve_lookup()
-> raise
```

Indeed, at this point the code is proceeding to re-raise the exception, only to have it be immediately caught again:

```
(Pdb) n
> /usr/lib/python2.5/site-packages/django/template/__init__.py(732)_
resolve_lookup()
-> except (TypeError, AttributeError):
```

The `list` command at this point shows what this `except` clause will do:

```
(Pdb) l
727                             except Exception, e:
728                                 if getattr(e, 'silent_variable_fa
ilure', False):
729                                     current = settings.TEMPLATE_S
TRING_IF_INVALID
730                                 else:
731                                     raise
732  ->                    except (TypeError, AttributeError):
733                         try: # list-index lookup
734                             current = current[int(bit)]
735                         except (IndexError, # list index out of range
736                                 ValueError, # invalid literal for int
()
737                                 KeyError,   # current is a dict witho
ut `int(bit)` key
(Pdb)
738                                 TypeError,  # unsubscriptable object
739                                 ):
740                             raise VariableDoesNotExist("Failed lookup
for key [%s] in %r", (bit, current)) # missing attribute
741                         except Exception, e:
742                             if getattr(e, 'silent_variable_failure', Fals
e):
743                                 current = settings.TEMPLATE_STRING_IF_INV
ALID
744                             else:
745                                 raise
746
747             return current
748
(Pdb)
```

Here it helps to recall exactly how constructs such as {{ q.get_piechart_url }} are handled during template rendering. Django template processing attempts to resolve the value on the right-hand side of the dot using these four methods, in order:

- Dictionary lookup
- Attribute lookup
- Method call
- List-index lookup

We entered the debugger right in the middle of the method call attempt, after the first two options failed. The code that attempted the method call does not distinguish between an AttributeError resulting from the method not existing and an AttributeError raised by a called method, so the next step is going to be to attempt a list-index lookup. This too is going to fail:

```
(Pdb) n
> /usr/lib/python2.5/site-packages/django/template/__init__.py(733)_
resolve_lookup()
-> try: # list-index lookup
(Pdb)
> /usr/lib/python2.5/site-packages/django/template/__init__.py(734)_
resolve_lookup()
-> current = current[int(bit)]
(Pdb)
ValueError: "invalid literal for int() with base 10: 'get_piechart_url'"
> /usr/lib/python2.5/site-packages/django/template/__init__.py(734)_
resolve_lookup()
-> current = current[int(bit)]
```

Specifically, the list-index lookup attempt raises a ValueError, which we can see from the previous code is going to be treated specially and turned into a VariableDoesNotExist exception. We could continue tracing through the code, but at this point it is pretty clear what is going to happen. Invalid variables are turned into whatever is assigned to the TEMPLATE_STRING_IF_INVALID setting. Since the survey project has this setting set to the default of the empty string, an empty string is the ultimate result of the rendering of {{ q.get_piechart_url }}.

The continue command

At this point, we know what the problem is, how the problem resulted in an empty string in the template instead of a debug page, and we are ready to go fix the code. We can use the `continue` command, abbreviated as `c`, to tell the debugger to exit and let program execution continue normally. When we do that here we see:

```
(Pdb) c
> /dj_projects/marketr/survey/models.py(71)get_piechart_url()
-> logging.debug('get_piechart_url called for pk=%d', self.pk)
(Pdb)
```

What happened? We are right back where we started. The reason is because there are two questions in the survey, and the template loops over them. The `get_piechart_url` method is called once for each question. When we exited the debugger after figuring out what happened with the first question, template processing continued and soon enough it again called `get_piechart_url`, where again the `pdb.set_trace()` call resulted in entry to the debugger. We can confirm this by seeing that `self` now refers to the second question in the survey:

```
(Pdb) self
<Question: Television Trends (opens 2009-09-10, closes 2009-11-10): How
many new shows will you try this Fall?>
(Pdb)
```

We could just `continue` again and proceed to fix our Python source file, but this actually presents an opportunity to play with some additional debugger commands, so we will do that.

The jump command

First, use `next` to proceed to the line of code where the wrong method is about to be called on `chart`:

```
(Pdb) n
DEBUG:root:get_piechart_url called for pk=2
> /dj_projects/marketr/survey/models.py(72)get_piechart_url()
-> answer_set = self.answer_set.all()
(Pdb) n
> /dj_projects/marketr/survey/models.py(73)get_piechart_url()
-> chart = PieChart3D(700, 230)
(Pdb) n
```

```
> /dj_projects/marketr/survey/models.py(74)get_piechart_url()
-> chart.set_data([a.votes for a in answer_set])
(Pdb)
```

Now, manually issue the call that should be there instead, `chart.add_data`:

```
(Pdb) chart.add_data([a.votes for a in answer_set])
0
(Pdb)
```

That call returned 0, which is much better than raising an attribute error. Now we want to jump over the erroneous line of code. We can see that `set_data` call is on line 74 of `models.py`; we want to skip line 74 and instead go straight to line 75. We do this with the `jump` command, which can be shortened to `j`:

```
(Pdb) j 75
> /dj_projects/marketr/survey/models.py(75)get_piechart_url()
-> chart.set_pie_labels([a.answer for a in answer_set])
(Pdb)
```

That seems to have worked. We can proceed through with `next` to confirm we're moving along without error in the code:

```
(Pdb) n
> /dj_projects/marketr/survey/models.py(75)get_piechart_url()
-> chart.set_pie_labels([a.answer for a in answer_set])
(Pdb) n
> /dj_projects/marketr/survey/models.py(75)get_piechart_url()
-> chart.set_pie_labels([a.answer for a in answer_set])
(Pdb)
```

Except we don't seem to be moving along, we seem to be stuck on one line. We're not though. Notice that line includes a list comprehension: `[a.answer for a in answer_set]`. The `next` command will avoid tracing through called functions, but it does not do the same for list comprehensions. The line containing the comprehension is going to appear to be executed once for every item added to the list by the comprehension. This can get tedious, especially for long lists. In this case, the list is only three elements long, since there are only three answers in the set, so we could easily just keep hitting enter to get past it. However, there is also a way to get around this, which we may as well learn next.

The break command

The `break` command, which can be shortened to `b`, sets a breakpoint on the specified line. Since `next` isn't getting us past line 75 as quickly as we would like, we can set a breakpoint on line 76 and use `continue` to get through the list comprehension on line 75 in one step:

```
(Pdb) b 76
Breakpoint 1 at /dj_projects/marketr/survey/models.py:76
(Pdb) c
> /dj_projects/marketr/survey/models.py(76)get_piechart_url()
-> logging.debug('get_piechart_url returning: %s', chart.get_url())
(Pdb)
```

This can come in handy for getting past other looping constructs besides list comprehensions, or for quickly moving forward in code when you get to a point where you don't need to trace through each line, but you do want to stop a bit further on and see the state of things.

The `break` command issued without arguments prints out a list of the currently set breakpoints, and how many times they have been hit:

```
(Pdb) b
Num Type         Disp Enb   Where
1   breakpoint    keep yes   at /dj_projects/marketr/survey/models.py:76
    breakpoint already hit 1 time
(Pdb)
```

Notice the breakpoint resulting from `pdb.set_trace()` isn't included here, this display just shows breakpoints set via the `break` command.

The `break` command also supports other arguments besides a simple line number. You can specify a function name or a line in another file. In addition, you can also specify a condition that must be met for the breakpoint to be triggered. None of these more advanced options are covered in detail here. The Python documentation, however, provides full details.

The clear command

After setting a breakpoint, there may come a time when you want to clear it. This is done by the `clear` command, which can be shorted to `cl` (not `c`, since that is `continue`):

```
(Pdb) cl 1
Deleted breakpoint 1
(Pdb)
```

Now the debugger will no longer stop on line 76 of `models.py`. At this point, we've probably seen enough of the various debugger commands, and can just enter `c` to let the code continue on:

```
(Pdb) c
DEBUG:root:get_piechart_url returning: http://chart.apis.google.com/chart
?cht=p3&chs=700x230&chd=s:9UU&chl=Hardly%20any%3A%20I%20already%20watch%2
0too%20much%20TV%21|Maybe%203-5|I%27m%20a%20TV%20fiend%2C%20I%27ll%20try%
20them%20all%20at%20least%20once%21
DEBUG:root:display_completed_survey returned type <class 'django.http.
HttpResponse'>
DEBUG:root:survey_detail returned type <class 'django.http.HttpResponse'>
[14/Nov/2009 18:03:38] "GET /1/ HTTP/1.1" 200 2989
```

There we see the code continued processing, logging the return value from `get_piechart_url`, and exit from `display_completed_survey` and `survey_detail`. Ultimately, a `2989` byte response was returned for this request. Switching back to the web browser window, we see the browser waited all that time for a response. Furthermore, our manual calling of the correct method and jumping over the wrong one did work. The browser shows it was able to successfully retrieve the pie chart for the second question:

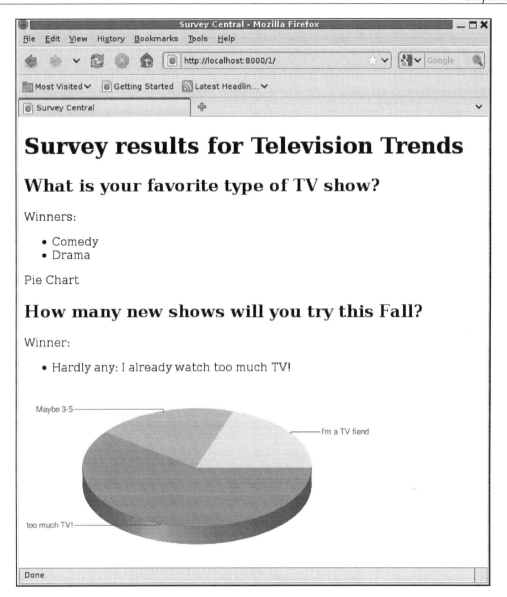

Unfortunately, although the figure was produced without error, there is a bit of a problem with the labels being too long to fit properly. To fix this, we can try using a legend instead of labels. We'll do that, and make the change of replacing `set_data` with `add_data`, next.

Fixing the pygooglechart results display

We seem close to having a working implementation of pie charts for our results display. We can update the get_piechart_url method to look like this:

```
def get_piechart_url(self):
    import pdb; pdb.set_trace()
    answer_set = self.answer_set.all()
    chart = PieChart3D(500, 230)
    chart.add_data([a.votes for a in answer_set])
    chart.set_legend([a.answer for a in answer_set])
    return chart.get_url()
```

The changes from the previous version are first removal of the logging calls (since they weren't particularly helpful) and also removal of the import of logging. The import for PieChart3D has been moved to the top of the file, with the other imports. The erroneous call to chart.set_data has been replaced with the correct chart. add_data. Finally, the call to chart.set_pie_labels had been replaced by chart. set_legend, in hopes that when the answers are arranged as a legend, they will be able to fit on the chart without spilling off the edges.

How well does that work? If we reload the browser page, the browser again appears to hang, because the get_piechart_url method still has the pdb.set_trace() call that breaks into the debugger. We might have removed that along with the other changes, in hopeful belief that the new version of the code is surely going to work, but often such hopes are dashed and we find ourselves having to re-add the call to figure out what is going wrong next. In this case, there are also a few more debugger commands to experiment with, which we'll do next.

The up and down commands

When we switch to the runserver console window, we again find the code sitting at the beginning of get_piechart_url:

```
DEBUG:root:survey_detail called with method GET, kwargs {'pk': u'1'}
DEBUG:root:display_completed_survey called
> /dj_projects/marketr/survey/models.py(71)get_piechart_url()
-> answer_set = self.answer_set.all()
(Pdb)
```

We could just continue and see how the new code behaves, but there are a few debugger commands we have not experimented with, so let's do that first. One is the step command, which was mentioned previously, but never used since we have exclusively used next for stepping through the code. If we try step a few times here, we see:

```
(Pdb) s
--Call--
> /usr/lib/python2.5/site-packages/django/db/models/fields/related.
py(319)__get__()
-> def __get__(self, instance, instance_type=None):
(Pdb)
> /usr/lib/python2.5/site-packages/django/db/models/fields/related.
py(320)__get__()
-> if instance is None:
(Pdb)
> /usr/lib/python2.5/site-packages/django/db/models/fields/related.
py(323)__get__()
-> return self.create_manager(instance,
(Pdb)
> /usr/lib/python2.5/site-packages/django/db/models/fields/related.
py(324)__get__()
-> self.related.model._default_manager.__class__)
(Pdb)
--Call--
> /usr/lib/python2.5/site-packages/django/db/models/fields/related.
py(346)create_manager()
-> def create_manager(self, instance, superclass):
(Pdb)
> /usr/lib/python2.5/site-packages/django/db/models/fields/related.
py(350)create_manager()
-> rel_field = self.related.field
(Pdb)
```

Here we have single-stepped six times and as a result are now nested a couple of call levels deep into the Django code. We did it intentionally, and it's often a useful way of learning more about how Django (or other support library) code works. But it is also quite common when debugging to mistakenly start single-stepping through support library code when we really only wanted to be single-stepping through our own code. We then find ourselves suddenly nested possibly a few levels deep in completely unfamiliar code, and we want to get back to stepping through the code we are developing.

One way to accomplish this is with the up command, which can be shortened to u. The up command moves the current stack frame up one level in the call chain:

```
(Pdb) u
> /usr/lib/python2.5/site-packages/django/db/models/fields/related.
py(324)__get__()
-> self.related.model._default_manager.__class__)
(Pdb) u
> /dj_projects/marketr/survey/models.py(71)get_piechart_url()
-> answer_set = self.answer_set.all()
(Pdb) u
> /usr/lib/python2.5/site-packages/django/template/__init__.py(722)_
resolve_lookup()
-> current = current()
(Pdb)
```

Here we have moved up three levels. The original current stack frame was the one for the call to create_manager. The first up command switched the current stack frame to the one for __get__, the next switched to get_piechart_url, and the third went all the way back to the caller of get_piechart_url, _resolve_lookup. Switching the current stack frame does not execute any code, it just changes the context for commands. For example, now with the current stack frame for _resolve_lookup being current, we can examine variables that exist in that frame:

```
(Pdb) whatis current
Function get_piechart_url
(Pdb)
```

Also, list now will show us the code associated with the current stack frame:

```
(Pdb) l
717                         if callable(current):
718                             if getattr(current, 'alters_data', False):
719                                 current = settings.TEMPLATE_STRING_IF
_INVALID
720                             else:
721                                 try: # method call (assuming no args
required)
722  ->                              current = current()
```

```
723                           except TypeError: # arguments *were*
required
724                               # GOTCHA: This will also catch
any TypeError
725                               # raised in the function itself.
726                               current = settings.TEMPLATE_STRIN
G_IF_INVALID # invalid method call
727                           except Exception, e:
(Pdb)
```

If we have switched stack frames and wonder where the current stack frame is relative to where the current execution point is, the where command shows that. In this case, the end of the where command output looks like this:

```
  /usr/lib/python2.5/site-packages/django/template/__init__
.py(687)resolve()
-> value = self._resolve_lookup(context)
> /usr/lib/python2.5/site-packages/django/template/__init__.py(722)_
resolve_lookup()
-> current = current()
  /dj_projects/marketr/survey/models.py(71)get_piechart_url()
-> answer_set = self.answer_set.all()
  /usr/lib/python2.5/site-packages/django/db/models/fields/related.
py(324)__get__()
-> self.related.model._default_manager.__class__)
  /usr/lib/python2.5/site-packages/django/db/models/fields/related.
py(350)create_manager()
-> rel_field = self.related.field
(Pdb)
```

The last line listed is always the current execution point, while the current stack frame is indicated by the > in the first column. Here, it indicates that the current stack frame is the one for _resolve_lookup.

In this case we moved up one stack frame further than we really wanted to. To get back to our own code, we need to move back down one level. This is done by using the down command (which can be shortened to d):

```
(Pdb) d
> /dj_projects/marketr/survey/models.py(71)get_piechart_url()
-> answer_set = self.answer_set.all()
(Pdb)
```

Now, if we want to continue running up to the next line from here, we can use the next command:

```
(Pdb) n
> /dj_projects/marketr/survey/models.py(72)get_piechart_url()
-> chart = PieChart3D(500, 230)
(Pdb)
```

Now we are back in familiar territory, and can continue with debugging our own code.

The return command

A second way to accomplish the same thing is to use the return command, which can be shortened to r. This command continues execution until the current function returns, and then the debugger is entered again. To see it in action, let's step into the PieChart3D call:

```
(Pdb) s
--Call--
> /var/lib/python-support/python2.5/pygooglechart.py(820)__init__()
-> def __init__(self, *args, **kwargs):
(Pdb)
> /var/lib/python-support/python2.5/pygooglechart.py(821)__init__()
-> assert(type(self) != PieChart)  # This is an abstract class
(Pdb)
> /var/lib/python-support/python2.5/pygooglechart.py(822)__init__()
-> Chart.__init__(self, *args, **kwargs)
(Pdb)
```

We've taken a couple of steps into the method, but have made only one call, so a single return should get us back to our survey code:

```
(Pdb) r
--Return--
> /var/lib/python-support/python2.5/pygooglechart.py(823)__init__()->None
-> self.pie_labels = []
(Pdb)
```

This method apparently does not have an explicit return line, so the line of code displayed is the last line in the method. The ->None in the output shows what the method is returning. If we step from here:

```
(Pdb) s
> /dj_projects/marketr/survey/models.py(73)get_piechart_url()
-> chart.add_data([a.votes for a in answer_set])
(Pdb)
```

We are now back to the next line of code after the call to create the pie chart. From here, we can use return to see what the get_piechart_url method is going to return:

```
(Pdb) r
--Return--
> /dj_projects/marketr/survey/models.py(75)get_piechart_url()->'http://
chart...Drama|Reality'
-> return chart.get_url()
(Pdb)
```

That looks good; the function ran to completion and is returning a value. Also, it seems that pdb shortens the displayed return values if they are long, since the displayed value doesn't look quite right. We can confirm this with either of the print commands, which show that the actual value is a good bit longer:

```
(Pdb) pp chart.get_url()
'http://chart.apis.google.com/chart?cht=p3&chs=500x230&chd=s:99f&chdl=Com
edy|Drama|Reality'
(Pdb)
```

At this point, it looks like all is working fine, so we may as well use continue to let the program keep running, then continue again when the debugger is entered for the second pie chart:

```
(Pdb) c
> /dj_projects/marketr/survey/models.py(71)get_piechart_url()
-> answer_set = self.answer_set.all()
(Pdb) c
DEBUG:root:display_completed_survey returned type <class 'django.http.
HttpResponse'>
DEBUG:root:survey_detail returned type <class 'django.http.HttpResponse'>
[15/Nov/2009 11:48:07] "GET /1/ HTTP/1.1" 200 3280
```

That all looks good. What does the browser show? Switching to its window, we see the following:

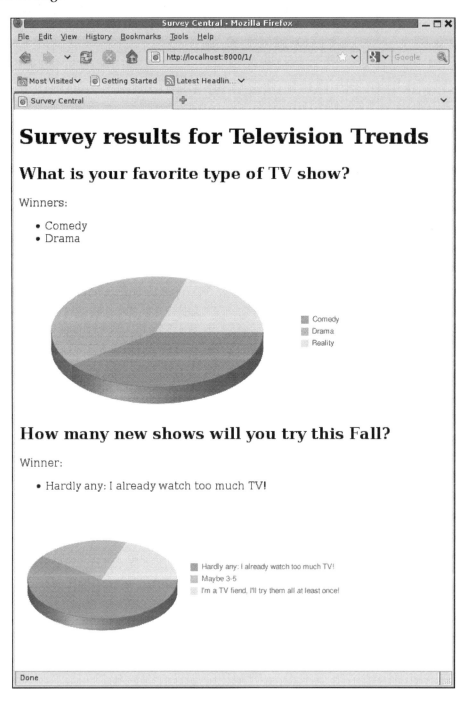

That's better than before. Switching from labels to a legend has solved the problem of the answer text spilling off the figure. However, it's a little disconcerting for the pie charts themselves to be so different in size, depending on the length of the answers. Also, it might be nice if the pie chart wedges could be labeled with the percentage of the total that each represents.

Researching more on the Google chart API doesn't reveal any way to control the legend placement to perhaps keep the pie sizes the same, nor how to annotate the wedges with information like the percentage of total. While reasonably simple and straightforward to use, this API does not offer a lot in terms of customizing the charts that are generated. Thus, we might want to investigate other alternatives for generating charts, which we'll do next.

We'll keep the current implementation of `get_piechart_url`, though, since at this point we don't know that we are going to really switch to an alternative. Before moving on to the next thing, it makes sense to remove the import `pdb; pdb.set_trace()` in that function. The routine is working now, and if we do return to using it at a later point, it will be better if it runs to completion without user intervention instead of breaking into the debugger.

Results display using matplotlib

The `matplotlib` library provides another alternative for generating charts from Python. It can be found on the Python Package Index site, `http://pypi.python.org/pypi/matplotlib`. The version of `matplotlib` used in this chapter is 0.98.3.

With `matplotlib`, our application cannot simply construct a URL and push the task of generating and serving the image data off to another host. Instead, we need to write a view that will generate and serve the image data. After some investigation of the `matplotlib` APIs, an initial implementation (in `survey/views.py`) might be:

```
from django.http import HttpResponse
from survey.models import Question
from matplotlib.figure import Figure
from matplotlib.backends.backend_agg import FigureCanvasAgg as \
    FigureCanvas

@log_view
def answer_piechart(request, pk):
    q = get_object_or_404(Question, pk=pk)
    answer_set = q.answer_set.all()
    x = [a.votes for a in answer_set]
    labels = [a.answer for a in answer_set]
```

```
fig = Figure()
axes = fig.add_subplot(1, 1, 1)
patches, texts, autotexts = axes.pie(x, autopct="%.0f%%")
legend = fig.legend(patches, labels, 'lower left')

canvas = FigureCanvas(fig)
response = HttpResponse(content_type='image/png')
canvas.print_png(response)
return response
```

That is a bit more complicated than the `pygooglechart` version. First, we need two imports from `matplotlib`: the basic `Figure` class, and an appropriate backend that can be used to render figures. Here, we have chosen the `agg` (Anti-Grain Geometry) backend, since it supports rendering to PNG format.

Within the `answer_piechart` view, the first four lines are straightforward. The `Question` instance is retrieved from the primary key value passed to the view. The answer set for that question is cached in the local variable `answer_set`. Then two arrays of data are created from the answer set: x contains the vote count values for each answer and `labels` contains the answer text values.

Next, a basic `matplotlib` `Figure` is created. A `matplotlib` `Figure` supports having multiple subplots contained in it. For the simple case where the `Figure` holds a single plot, `add_sublot` still needs to be called to create the subplot and return an `Axes` instance that can be used to draw on the plot. The arguments to `add_subplot` are the number of rows and columns in the subplot grid, then the number of the plot being added to the `Figure`. The arguments 1, 1, 1 here indicate the single subplot in a 1 x 1 grid.

The `pie` method is then invoked on the returned subplot `axes` to generate a pie chart figure. The first argument x is the array of data values for the pie wedges. The `autopct` keyword argument is used to specify a format string for annotating each pie wedge with its percentage of the total. The value `%.0f%%` specifies that the float percentage values should be formatted with zero digits after the decimal point, followed by a percent sign.

The `pie` method returns three data sequences. The first of these, `patches`, describes the pie wedges and needs to be passed to the figure's `legend` method for creating a legend to match the wedges to their associated answer values. Here we have specified that the legend should be placed in the lower left corner of the figure.

The other two sequences returned by `pie` describe the text labels (which will be blank here since `labels` were not specified when `pie` was called) and `autopct` annotations for the wedges. The code here does not need to use these sequences for anything.

With the legend in place, the figure is complete. A `canvas` for it is created using the previously imported `agg` backend `FigureCanvas`. An `HttpResponse` with content type `image/png` is created, and the image is written in PNG format to the response using the `print_png` method. Finally, the `answer_piechart` view returns this response.

With the view code done, we need to update the `survey/urls.py` file to include a mapping that will route requests to that view:

```
urlpatterns = patterns('survey.views',
    url(r'^$', 'home', name='survey_home'),
    url(r'^(?P<pk>\d+)/$', 'survey_detail', name='survey_detail'),
    url(r'^thanks/(?P<pk>\d+)/$', 'survey_thanks',
        name='survey_thanks'),
    url(r'^piechart/(?P<pk>\d+)\.png/$', 'answer_piechart',
        name='survey_answer_piechart'),
)
```

Here we have added the last pattern. This pattern matches URL paths that start with `piechart/`, followed by one or more digits (the primary key), ending with `.png`. These URLs are routed to the `survey.views.answer_piechart` view, passing the captured primary key value as a parameter. The pattern is named `survey_answer_piechart`.

The final piece needed to switch to using `matplotlib` instead of `pygooglechart` is to update the `survey/completed_survey.html` template to generate URLs using this pattern. The only change needed is to update the line containing the `img` tag:

```
<p><img src="{% url survey_answer_piechart q.pk %}" alt="Pie
Chart"/></p>
```

Here we have replaced the call to the question's `get_piechart_url` method with a `url` template tag referencing the new pattern just added.

How does that work? Reasonably well. We did not specify a size for the figures, and the default size from `matplotlib` is a bit larger than what we had specified for `pygooglechart`, so we cannot see the whole page without scrolling. However, each individual figure looks pretty good. For example, the first one appears like so:

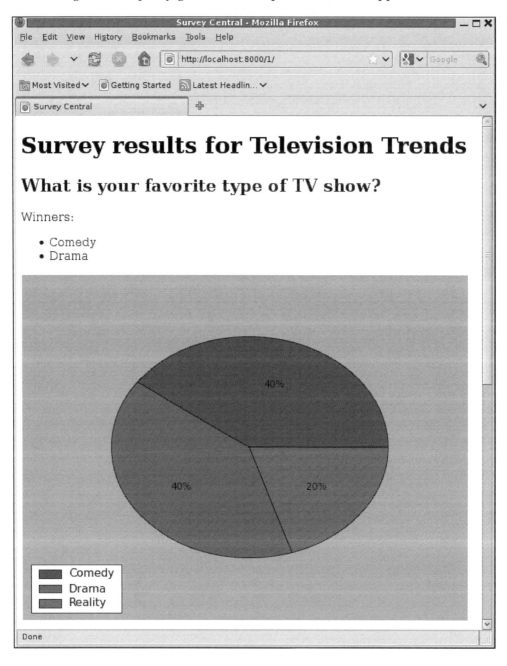

And the second looks like this:

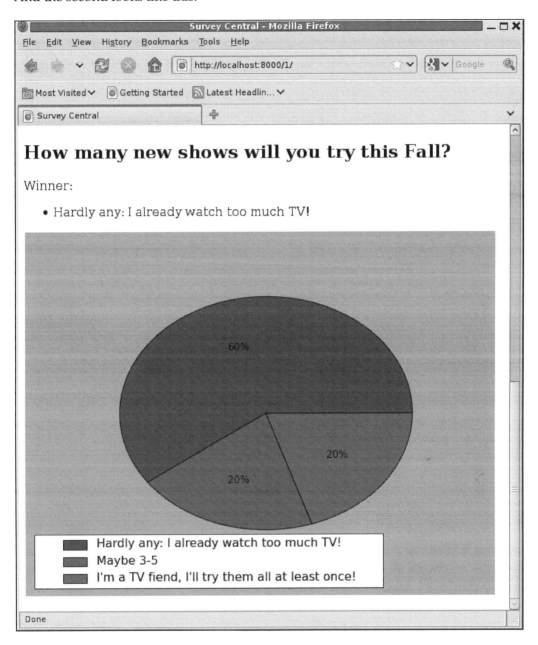

The `matplotlib` API supports much more customization than we have used here. The size of the figure could be changed, as could placement of the pie, colors of the wedge pieces, and font's properties for the text. The pie wedge for the winning answer could be emphasized by exploding it out from the rest of the pie. However, all of those items are cosmetic and beyond the scope of what we will cover here. To get back to the subject of debugging, we will turn our attention in the next section to removing some wasteful duplicate processing that was just introduced as a result of switching to `matplotlib`.

Improving the matplotlib approach

Consider what happens now when the page for a completed survey is requested by a browser. For each question in the survey, the returned completed survey page has an embedded image that, when fetched, will trigger a call to the `answer_piechart` view. That view dynamically generates an image and is computationally expensive. In fact, depending on your hardware, if you try stepping through that view you may be able to observe appreciable pauses when stepping over some of the `matplotlib` calls.

Now consider what happens when many different users request the same completed survey page. That will trigger many calls into the computationally expensive `answer_piechart` view. Ultimately, all of the users will be served the exact same data, since results are not displayed until the survey is closed, so the underlying vote counts used to create the pie chart will not be changing. Yet `answer_piechart` will be called over and over to re-do the same considerable amount of work to produce the exact same result. This is a wasteful use of our server capacity.

How can we eliminate this waste? There are (at least) three possible approaches:

- Introduce caching, and cache the results of the `answer_piechart` view.

- Set up some external process that pre-computes all of the pie charts for a survey when it closes and saves them on disk somewhere. Change the `img` tags in the completed survey response template to refer to these static files instead of a view that dynamically generates the images.

- Dynamically generate the pie charts for a completed survey when the first request for it comes in, and save them to disk somewhere. This is essentially the same as the second approach, in that the `img` tags in the completed survey response will now refer to static files, but the computation of the charts is moved from some external process into the web server.

Each of these approaches has pros and cons. The one we are going to pursue is the last, simply because it offers the most opportunity to learn a couple of new things. Specifically, in implementing this third approach we will see how to set up the development server to serve static files, and we will see how pdb can be used to ensure that code operates properly in the face of multi-process race conditions.

Setting up static file serving

So far in the development of the survey application we have concentrated entirely on serving dynamic content. While dynamic content is certainly the focus of Django applications, in reality even the most dynamic of applications will have some data that needs to be served from files. Here with the survey application we have run into a case where we want to serve image files from disk. Most applications will also have CSS and possibly JavaScript files that are better served directly from disk rather than through Django view code.

Django is a framework for serving dynamic content. Although it does not directly support serving data from files, there are a couple of settings that facilitate incorporating some static files into a project. These are MEDIA_ROOT and MEDIA_URL.

MEDIA_ROOT is a file system path—the path to the directory that holds the static files for the project. It is used by Django internally as the base path for saving files uploaded to a model containing a FileField. For the survey application, we will use it as the base path for saving dynamically-generated pie chart image files.

The default value for this setting is an empty string, so we need to set it to something else now that we want to use it:

```
MEDIA_ROOT = '/dj_projects/marketr/site_media/'
```

Here we have set MEDIA_ROOT to point to a site_media directory (which we must create) under our main marketr project directory.

MEDIA_URL, which also defaults to an empty string, is the base URL path for referring to static files. It is used by Django internally to general the url attribute of a file referenced by a FileField model.

In addition, the django.core.context_processors.media context processor makes the value of this setting available in templates by setting MEDIA_URL in the template context. This context processor is enabled by default, so any templates rendered with a RequestContext have access to MEDIA_URL.

Let's set MEDIA_URL in settings.py as follows:

```
MEDIA_URL = '/site_media/'
```

Note that one value that should not be used for MEDIA_URL is '/media/'. This is the default setting for ADMIN_MEDIA_PREFIX, which defines the root URL for static files used by the admin. Trying to place two different trees of static files in the same place in the URL hierarchy does not work, and is most easily avoided by setting MEDIA_URL to something other than '/media/'.

Note that though these settings are defined in terms that establish a mapping from URL paths to files on disk, nothing in Django will automatically serve files based on that mapping. During URL resolution, Django does not test to see if the requested URL starts with MEDIA_URL and if so, serve up the corresponding file found under MEDIA_ROOT. Rather, Django assumes that URLs referring to static files on disk will be served by the web server directly and not routed through Django code at all.

However, so far during development we have not been using any web server other than Django's own development server. If we want to continue using the development server, we need to somehow get it to serve the image files created by the survey application. How do we do that?

Django does provide a static file serving capability, specifically for use during development. To use it, we need to update the project's urls.py file to route requests for URLs that start with 'site_media/' to Django's static file serving view. Thus, we need to change the urls.py file to contain:

```
from django.conf.urls.defaults import *

# Uncomment the next two lines to enable the admin:
from django.contrib import admin
admin.autodiscover()

from django.conf import settings

urlpatterns = patterns('',
    # Example:
    # (r'^marketr/', include('marketr.foo.urls')),

    # Uncomment the admin/doc line below and add
    # 'django.contrib.admindocs'
    # to INSTALLED_APPS to enable admin documentation:
    # (r'^admin/doc/', include('django.contrib.admindocs.urls')),

    # Uncomment the next line to enable the admin:
    (r'^admin/', include(admin.site.urls)),
    (r'^site_media/(.*)$', 'django.views.static.serve',
        {'document_root': settings.MEDIA_ROOT, 'show_indexes': True}),
    (r'', include('survey.urls')),
)
```

The first change here from the previous version is the addition of the `import` of `settings` from `django.conf`. Second is the addition of the pattern referring to URLs that start with `site_media/`. These URLs are routed to `django.views.static.serve`. Two parameters are passed to this view: `document_root` and `show_indexes`. For `document_root`, the `MEDIA_ROOT` setting is specified, which means that the static server will look for the requested files under `MEDIA_ROOT`. `True` is specified for `show_indexes`, which means that the static server will return a list of files when the requested URL refers to a directory instead of a file.

Dynamically generating image files

Now that we have set everything up for serving image files from disk, we can start to make the code changes necessary for this approach. First, we should remove the `piechart` pattern from the `survey/urls.py` file, as it is no longer needed.

Second, we can update the `display_completed_survey` function in `views.py` to include code that ensures the pie chart image files for each question in the survey have been generated before returning the completed survey response:

```
@log_call
def display_completed_survey(request, survey):
    for q in survey.question_set.all():
        q.check_piechart()
    return render_to_response('survey/completed_survey.html',
        {'survey': survey},
        RequestContext(request))
```

Here we have added the `for` loop that loops through all of the questions in the survey. For each, it calls a new method on the question, `check_piechart`. This routine will be responsible for ensuring that the pie chart file exists, creating it if necessary.

Next, we can move on to the `survey/models.py` file and update the `Question` model to include an implementation of `check_piechart` and anything else that might be needed to support the new approach. What else might be needed? For referencing the pie chart URL from a template, it would be convenient if the `Question` model supported returning the path to the pie chart file relative to `MEDIA_URL`. Thus, we need two new methods in the `Question` model:

```
from survey import pie_utils
class Question(models.Model):
    [... other code unchanged ...]

    @property
    def piechart_path(self):
```

```
        if self.pk and self.survey.closes < datetime.date.today():
            return pie_utils.PIE_PATH + '%d.png' % self.pk
        else:
            raise AttributeError

    def check_piechart(self):
        pie_utils.make_pie_if_necessary(self.piechart_path,
                                        self.answer_set.all())
```

Here we have opted not to include a lot of file checking and creation code directly in `survey/models.py`, but rather to factor that work out into a new independent module in `survey/pie_utils.py`. The two routines implemented here, then, can be kept very simple.

`piechart_path`, which is implemented as a read-only property, returns the path for the pie chart. This value can be combined with the `MEDIA_URL` setting to create a URL path, or with the `MEDIA_ROOT` setting to create a file system path. Since in the long-term we would expect to have more files than just pie chart images in the tree, it's not appropriate to put the pie charts in the root of this tree. Thus, the `pie_utils.PIE_PATH` value is used to carve out a subtree within the static file tree to hold the pie charts.

Note that this routine is implemented to raise an `AttributeError` if the model instance has not yet been saved to the database, or if it references a survey that has not yet closed. In these situations, the pie chart file should not exist, so any attempt to reference it should trigger an error.

The `check_piechart` method is implemented to forward the call to the `pie_utils` `make_pie_if_necessary` function. This function takes two parameters: the path for the pie chart, and the set of answers for the question.

Before we move on to the implementation of the `pie_utils` module, we can make a simple update to the `survey/completed_survey.html` template. The line containing the `img` tag needs to be changed to use the `Question` model's `piechart_path` when creating the URL that references the pie chart image:

```
<p><img src="{{ MEDIA_URL }}{{ q.piechart_path }}"
alt="Pie Chart"/></p>
```

Here, `piechart_path` is combined with `MEDIA_URL` (available in the template since `display_completed_survey` specifies a `RequestContext` when calling `render_to_response`) to build the full URL for the image.

Finally, we need to implement the `survey/pie_utils.py` code. This module must define a value for `PIE_PATH`, and implement the `make_pie_if_necessary` function. The first task is trivial and accomplished with something like the following:

```
import os
from django.conf import settings
PIE_PATH = 'piecharts/'
if not os.path.exists(settings.MEDIA_ROOT + PIE_PATH):
    os.mkdir(settings.MEDIA_ROOT + PIE_PATH)
```

This code defines a value for `PIE_PATH` and ensures that the resulting subdirectory under the project's `MEDIA_ROOT` exists, creating it if necessary. With this code and the previously noted setting for `MEDIA_ROOT`, the pie chart image files for the survey application will be placed in `/dj_projects/marketr/site-media/piecharts/`.

The second piece needed to complete the `pie_utils` module, an implementation of the `make_pie_if_necessary` function, may also seem quite simple at first glance. If the file already exists, `make_pie_if_necessary` does not need to do anything, otherwise it needs to create the file. However, things get more complicated when you consider that the deployment environment for this code will eventually be a potentially multi-process multi-threaded web server. This introduces the opportunity for race conditions, which we'll discuss next.

Dealing with race conditions

A naïve implementation of the `make_pie_if_necessary` module might be:

```
def make_pie_if_necessary(rel_path, answer_set):
    fname = settings.MEDIA_ROOT + rel_path
    if not os.path.exists(fname):
        create_piechart(fname, answer_set)
```

Here `make_pie_if_necessary` creates the full file path by combining the passed relative path with the settings `MEDIA_ROOT` value. Then, if that file does not exist, it calls `create_piechart`, passing along the filename and the answer set, to create the pie chart file. This routine could be implemented like so:

```
from matplotlib.figure import Figure
from matplotlib.backends.backend_agg import FigureCanvasAgg as \
    FigureCanvas

def create_piechart(f, answer_set):
    x = [a.votes for a in answer_set]
    labels = [a.answer for a in answer_set]
```

```
fig = Figure()
axes = fig.add_subplot(1, 1, 1)
patches, texts, autotexts = axes.pie(x, autopct="%.0f%%")
legend = fig.legend(patches, labels, 'lower left')

canvas = FigureCanvas(fig)
canvas.print_png(f)
```

This code is essentially what was in the original `matplotlib` implementation in the `answer_piechart` view, modified to account for the fact that the answer set has been passed directly, as has the file to which the image data should be written.

This implementation of `make_pie_if_necessary`, when tested with the development server, would work fine. It might even seem to work fine in a lightly loaded production environment. However, if you consider a heavily loaded production environment, with a multi-process web server where requests for the same page may be arriving nearly simultaneously, a potential problem emerges. There is nothing to prevent multiple nearly-simultaneous calls to `make_pie_if_necessary` from resulting in multiple nearly-simultaneous calls to `canvas.print_png` to create the same file.

It's clear how this could happen on a multi-processor machine, since it's easy to see how two simultaneous requests might get dispatched to different processors and result in the same code running simultaneously on each. Both processes check to see if the file exists, both find it does not, and both embark on creating it.

The same situation can also occur even on a single-processor machine, with preemptive scheduling by the operating system. One process may check to see if the file exists, find it does not, and start down the path of creating it. However, before this code actually gets to the point of creating the file, the operating system's preemptive scheduler suspends it and lets the process handling the second nearly-simultaneous request run. This process also fails to find the file when it checks, and also starts down the path of creating it.

What would be the end result if this were to happen? Would it be that bad? Perhaps not. Possibly one process would do its job of creating and writing the file, and then the second one would do its work, overwriting the results from the first. There would have been some duplicate work done, but the end result might be fine: a file on disk containing the PNG image of the pie chart.

However, is there any guarantee that the work of the two nearly simultaneous calls would be serialized like that? No. The `matplotlib` API doesn't provide any such guarantee. Without digging into the implementation it's hard to be sure, but it seems likely that the task of writing out an image file may be split into several different individual write calls. This affords ample opportunity for random interleaving of calls from different processes that reference the same file to result in a corrupt image file ultimately written out to disk.

To prevent this, we need to change the `make_pie_if_necessary` function to use an atomic method of checking for the file's existence and create it if necessary:

```
import errno
def make_pie_if_necessary(rel_path, answer_set):
    fname = settings.MEDIA_ROOT + rel_path
    try:
        fd = os.open(fname, os.O_WRONLY | os.O_CREAT | os.O_EXCL)
        try:
            f = os.fdopen(fd, 'wb')
            create_piechart(f, answer_set)
        finally:
            f.close()
    except OSError, e:
        if e.errno == errno.EEXIST:
            pass
        else:
            raise
```

This code uses a combination of flags passed to the `os.open` routine to atomically create the file. `os.O_WRONLY` specifies that the file is open for writing only, `os.O_CREAT` specifies that the file should be created if it does not exist, and `os.O_EXCL`, in combination with `os.O_CREAT`, specifies that an error should be raised if the file exists. Even if multiple processes simultaneously issue this `os.open` call, the underlying implementation guarantees that only one will be successful, and an error will be raised for the others. Thus, only one process will proceed with the code that creates the pie chart.

Note that when running on Windows, `os.O_BINARY` also needs to be included in the set of flags passed into `os.open`. Without that flag, Python will treat the file data as text and automatically insert carriage return characters whenever a linefeed is encountered in the data written to the file. This behavior will result in corrupt PNG image files that cannot be displayed.

One wrinkle introduced by this change is that the file descriptor returned by os.open cannot be passed to matplotlib as a target file for the PNG data. The matplotlib library accepts filenames, or Python file-like objects, but it does not support a file descriptor as returned by os.open. Thus, the code here converts the file descriptor to a Python file object using os.fdopen, and passes the returned file to the create_piechart routine.

In the case where the os.open call raises an OSError, the exception's errno attribute is tested against errno.EEXIST. This is the specific error that will be raised when the file already exists, and should not be reflected up as an error but rather should be ignored. Any other errors are reflected to the caller of make_pie_if_necessary.

These changes ensure that the image file will be created only once, which is good. However, there's another potential problem. Consider what happens now with multiple simultaneous requests. Only one will proceed down the path of creating the file. All the others will see that the file already exists and simply proceed to send a response referencing it.

But note that the file existence does not guarantee that the image data has been written to it: there is a fair amount of processing to be done first to create the image, before it is written to the file. Is there any guarantee that this processing will complete before any requests for the file are received and processed? No. Depending on how fast clients are and how slow the image generation is, it's possible for a request for the file to arrive and be processed before the image data is actually written to the file.

Is this likely to happen? Probably not. What would be the effect if it did? Probably nothing terrible. Likely the browser would display a partial image or the **Pie Chart** alternate text for the image. The user might try re-loading the page to see if it worked better the second time, and by then the image file would probably be served correctly.

Given the seemingly slim chances of this situation arising, and its fairly minor effect, we might choose not to fix this particular problem. However, in some situations it may be necessary to ensure that the file not only exists but also contains data. It might be worthwhile to investigate fixing this potential problem. One approach is to modify make_pie_if_necessary as follows:

```
import fcntl
def make_pie_if_necessary(rel_path, answer_set):
    fname = settings.MEDIA_ROOT + rel_path
    try:
        fd = os.open(fname, os.O_WRONLY | os.O_CREAT | os.O_EXCL)
        try:
            f = os.fdopen(fd, 'wb')
```

```
        fcntl.flock(f, fcntl.LOCK_EX)
        create_piechart(f, answer_set)
    finally:
        fcntl.flock(f, fcntl.LOCK_UN)
        f.close()
except OSError, e:
    if e.errno == errno.EEXIST:
        wait_for_data(fname)
    else:
        raise
```

Here the first change is to obtain an exclusive lock on the file, using `fcntl.flock`, before calling `create_piechart`. (Note that `fcntl` is a Unix-only Python module. Thus, this code will not work on Windows. There are add-on packages to get file locking capabilities in Windows, but specifics of using any of them are beyond the scope of what will be covered here.) Second, this file lock is released before the file is closed after `create_piechart` returns. Third, in the case where the file is found to already exist, instead of immediately returning, a new `wait_for_data` function is called. The implementation of `wait_for_data` is:

```
import time
def wait_for_data(fname):
    try:
        fd = os.open(fname, os.O_RDONLY)
        empty = True
        while empty:
            fcntl.flock(fd, fcntl.LOCK_SH)
            st = os.fstat(fd)
            if st.st_size > 0:
                empty = False
            fcntl.flock(fd, fcntl.LOCK_UN)
            if empty:
                time.sleep(.5)
    finally:
        if fd:
            os.close(fd)
```

This code, given a filename, first opens the file for reading. It then assumes the file is empty and enters a loop that will continue as long as the file remains empty. In the loop, the code obtains a shared lock on the file, and then calls os.fstat to determine the file's size. If the returned size is non-zero, then emtpy is set to False, which will terminate the loop at the end of this iteration. Before that, though, the file lock is released, and if the file is in fact empty, the code sleeps for half a second before proceeding with the next iteration of the loop. The sleep is intended to give the other process, presumably busy trying to create and write the data, time to finish its work. Before returning, the file is closed (if it was ever successfully opened).

That all looks OK, and seems to work well enough when we try it out, testing it in a browser. However, it is hard to be sure, just based on visual inspection of code like this, that it is completely correct. Using a debugger here to artificially create the kind of race conditions we are trying to guard against, can be helpful. We'll do this next.

Using the debugger to force race situations

It is not possible to force race conditions using the development server alone: it is single-threaded and single-process. However, we can use the development server in combination with a manage.py shell session, with debugger breakpoints and single-stepping, to force any combination of multi-process interleaved execution that we want to test out.

For example, we can insert a breakpoint near the top of the make_pie_if_necessary function:

```
def make_pie_if_necessary(rel_path, answer_set):
    fname = settings.MEDIA_ROOT + rel_path
    try:
        import pdb; pdb.set_trace()
        fd = os.open(fname, os.O_WRONLY | os.O_CREAT | os.O_EXCL)
```

Now, we need to delete any already-generated image files from disk, so that when this function is first entered it will go down the path of trying to create a file:

rm /dj_projects/marketr/site_media/piecharts/*

Next, we ensure the development server is running, and from a browser, re-load the results page for the **Television Trends** survey. The browser will appear to hang, and in the development server console we will see the debugger entered:

> /dj_projects/marketr/survey/pie_utils.py(13)make_pie_if_necessary()

-> fd = os.open(fname, os.O_WRONLY | os.O_CREAT | os.O_EXCL)

(Pdb)

If we use `next` to step over this call, we will see:

```
(Pdb) n
> /dj_projects/marketr/survey/pie_utils.py(14)make_pie_if_necessary()
-> try:
(Pdb)
```

Execution proceeded to the next line of code, so the `os.open` call was successful. This thread is now frozen at the point where the file has been created, but no data has been written to it. We want to verify that another process calling the same function will correctly proceed to wait for the file data to be written before continuing. To test this, we can start a `manage.py shell` in a separate window, manually retrieve the appropriate question, and call its `check_piechart` method:

```
kmt@lbox:/dj_projects/marketr$ python manage.py shell
Python 2.5.2 (r252:60911, Oct  5 2008, 19:24:49)
[GCC 4.3.2] on linux2
Type "help", "copyright", "credits" or "license" for more information.
(InteractiveConsole)
>>> from survey.models import Question
>>> q = Question.objects.get(pk=1)
>>> q.check_piechart()
> /dj_projects/marketr/survey/pie_utils.py(13)make_pie_if_necessary()
-> fd = os.open(fname, os.O_WRONLY | os.O_CREAT | os.O_EXCL)
(Pdb)
```

The breakpoint in `make_pie_if_necessary` has again stopped execution right before the call to open the file. In this case when we use next to step over the call, we should see the code take a different path, since the file already exists:

```
(Pdb) n
OSError: (17, 'File exists', '/dj_projects/marketr/site_media/
piecharts/1.png')
> /dj_projects/marketr/survey/pie_utils.py(13)make_pie_if_necessary()
-> fd = os.open(fname, os.O_WRONLY | os.O_CREAT | os.O_EXCL)
(Pdb) n
> /dj_projects/marketr/survey/pie_utils.py(21)make_pie_if_necessary()
-> except OSError, e:
(Pdb) n
```

```
> /dj_projects/marketr/survey/pie_utils.py(22)make_pie_if_necessary()
-> if e.errno == errno.EEXIST:
(Pdb) n
> /dj_projects/marketr/survey/pie_utils.py(23)make_pie_if_necessary()
-> wait_for_data(fname)
(Pdb)
```

That looks good. Stepping through the code we see that `os.open` raised an `OSError` with `errno` attribute `errno.EEXIST`, as expected. The shell thread, then, will proceed to wait for the file to have data. If we step into that routine, we can see if it runs as we expect:

```
(Pdb) s
--Call--
> /dj_projects/marketr/survey/pie_utils.py(43)wait_for_data()
-> def wait_for_data(fname):
(Pdb) n
> /dj_projects/marketr/survey/pie_utils.py(44)wait_for_data()
-> try:
(Pdb) n
> /dj_projects/marketr/survey/pie_utils.py(45)wait_for_data()
-> fd = os.open(fname, os.O_RDONLY)
(Pdb) n
> /dj_projects/marketr/survey/pie_utils.py(46)wait_for_data()
-> empty = True
(Pdb)
```

At this point, we've done the preliminary processing in this routine. The file is now open and `empty` has been initialized to `True`. We're ready to enter the first iteration of the loop. What should happen? Since the other thread of control is still blocked before it has even obtained the exclusive lock on the file, this thread should be able to obtain a shared lock on the file, test the file size, and end up sleeping for half a second since the file is empty. Stepping through, we see that is indeed what happens:

```
(Pdb) n
> /dj_projects/marketr/survey/pie_utils.py(47)wait_for_data()
-> while empty:
(Pdb) n
> /dj_projects/marketr/survey/pie_utils.py(48)wait_for_data()
-> fcntl.flock(fd, fcntl.LOCK_SH)
```

```
(Pdb) n
> /dj_projects/marketr/survey/pie_utils.py(49)wait_for_data()
-> st = os.fstat(fd)
(Pdb) n
> /dj_projects/marketr/survey/pie_utils.py(50)wait_for_data()
-> if st.st_size > 0:
(Pdb) n
> /dj_projects/marketr/survey/pie_utils.py(52)wait_for_data()
-> fcntl.flock(fd, fcntl.LOCK_UN)
(Pdb) n
> /dj_projects/marketr/survey/pie_utils.py(53)wait_for_data()
-> if empty:
(Pdb) n
> /dj_projects/marketr/survey/pie_utils.py(54)wait_for_data()
-> time.sleep(.5)
(Pdb) n
> /dj_projects/marketr/survey/pie_utils.py(47)wait_for_data()
-> while empty:
(Pdb)
```

The `fcntl.flock` to lock the file returned immediately since the file is not yet locked
by the other thread. This code found the file size to be zero, proceeded to sleep for
half a second, and is now beginning a second iteration of the loop. Let's step
it forward to a point where it has again obtained a shared lock on the file:

```
> /dj_projects/marketr/survey/pie_utils.py(48)wait_for_data()
-> fcntl.flock(fd, fcntl.LOCK_SH)
(Pdb) n
> /dj_projects/marketr/survey/pie_utils.py(49)wait_for_data()
-> st = os.fstat(fd)
(Pdb)
```

We will now leave this thread frozen here, return to the development server thread,
and attempt to move forward in it:

```
(Pdb) n
> /dj_projects/marketr/survey/pie_utils.py(15)make_pie_if_necessary()
-> f = os.fdopen(fd, 'wb')
(Pdb) n
> /dj_projects/marketr/survey/pie_utils.py(16)make_pie_if_necessary()
-> fcntl.flock(f, fcntl.LOCK_EX)
(Pdb) n
```

This code was not able to proceed very far. It did convert the file descriptor into a Python file object, but the next call is to get an exclusive lock on the file, and that call has been blocked—there is no (Pdb) prompt in response to the final n command, so execution has stopped somewhere inside the call. That's good, since a call to obtain an exclusive lock should not return until the other thread releases its lock.

We can switch back to that thread and move it forward to the point where it releases the lock:

```
(Pdb) n
> /dj_projects/marketr/survey/pie_utils.py(50)wait_for_data()
-> if st.st_size > 0:
(Pdb) n
> /dj_projects/marketr/survey/pie_utils.py(52)wait_for_data()
-> fcntl.flock(fd, fcntl.LOCK_UN)
(Pdb) n
> /dj_projects/marketr/survey/pie_utils.py(53)wait_for_data()
-> if empty:
(Pdb)
```

Immediately when we stepped over the call to release the lock, the development server console returned to the (Pdb) prompt:

```
> /dj_projects/marketr/survey/pie_utils.py(17)make_pie_if_necessary()
-> create_piechart(f, answer_set)
(Pdb)
```

This thread now has an exclusive lock on the file, and if we keep it frozen at this point, we should see that the other thread will be blocked on its next attempt to obtain a shared lock:

```
(Pdb) n
> /dj_projects/marketr/survey/pie_utils.py(54)wait_for_data()
-> time.sleep(.5)
(Pdb) n
> /dj_projects/marketr/survey/pie_utils.py(47)wait_for_data()
-> while empty:
(Pdb) n
> /dj_projects/marketr/survey/pie_utils.py(48)wait_for_data()
-> fcntl.flock(fd, fcntl.LOCK_SH)
(Pdb) n
```

That looks good, this thread has been blocked. It should now not be able to obtain the lock until the development server thread releases it, at which point the file will have data. Let's move the development server thread forward:

```
(Pdb) n
> /dj_projects/marketr/survey/pie_utils.py(19)make_pie_if_necessary()
-> fcntl.flock(f, fcntl.LOCK_UN)
(Pdb) n
> /dj_projects/marketr/survey/pie_utils.py(20)make_pie_if_necessary()
-> f.close()
(Pdb)
```

Here we stepped over the call to create the pie chart, and the call to unlock the file. At that point, the shell thread stopped blocking:

```
> /dj_projects/marketr/survey/pie_utils.py(49)wait_for_data()
-> st = os.fstat(fd)
(Pdb)
```

This thread should now see that the file has data:

```
(Pdb) n
> /dj_projects/marketr/survey/pie_utils.py(50)wait_for_data()
-> if st.st_size > 0:
(Pdb) n
> /dj_projects/marketr/survey/pie_utils.py(51)wait_for_data()
-> empty = False
(Pdb)
```

That looks good; the code is setting `empty` to `False`, which should trigger the end of the loop once the task of releasing the shared lock is finished:

```
(Pdb) n
> /dj_projects/marketr/survey/pie_utils.py(52)wait_for_data()
-> fcntl.flock(fd, fcntl.LOCK_UN)
(Pdb) n
> /dj_projects/marketr/survey/pie_utils.py(53)wait_for_data()
-> if empty:
(Pdb) n
> /dj_projects/marketr/survey/pie_utils.py(47)wait_for_data()
-> while empty:
(Pdb) n
> /dj_projects/marketr/survey/pie_utils.py(56)wait_for_data()
-> if fd:
```

```
(Pdb) n
> /dj_projects/marketr/survey/pie_utils.py(57)wait_for_data()
-> os.close(fd)
(Pdb) n
--Return--
> /dj_projects/marketr/survey/pie_utils.py(57)wait_for_data()->None
-> os.close(fd)
(Pdb)
```

Indeed, the code proceeded to exit the loop, close the file, and return. We can enter c to continue here, and get back the regular shell prompt. At this point we can also let the development server continue, and it will re-enter the debugger for processing of the second pie chart:

```
(Pdb) c
> /dj_projects/marketr/survey/pie_utils.py(13)make_pie_if_necessary()
-> fd = os.open(fname, os.O_WRONLY | os.O_CREAT | os.O_EXCL)
(Pdb)
```

Are we done or is there anything else we might want to test at this point? All seemed to look good, but one thing you might have noticed tracing through the code was that the second thread that was waiting on the file data was allowed to proceed before the first thread actually closed the file. Might that be a problem? In the absence of explicit calls to flush data to disk, it's possible that data is buffered in memory, and won't actually get written until the file is closed. Depending on how long that takes, the other thread that proceeded under the assumption that the file was now all set for reading might run into trouble, because in fact not all of the data is available on disk for reading by a separate thread.

Can we test that situation? Yes, we can use this second request by the development server to see if there might be a problem. In this case, we leave the development server blocked before the call to create the file, and from the shell session we proceed to retrieve the second question and call its check_piechart method:

```
>>> q = Question.objects.get(pk=2)
>>> q.check_piechart()
> /dj_projects/marketr/survey/pie_utils.py(13)make_pie_if_necessary()
-> fd = os.open(fname, os.O_WRONLY | os.O_CREAT | os.O_EXCL)
(Pdb) n
> /dj_projects/marketr/survey/pie_utils.py(14)make_pie_if_necessary()
-> try:
(Pdb) n
```

```
> /dj_projects/marketr/survey/pie_utils.py(15)make_pie_if_necessary()
-> f = os.fdopen(fd, 'wb')
(Pdb) n
> /dj_projects/marketr/survey/pie_utils.py(16)make_pie_if_necessary()
-> fcntl.flock(f, fcntl.LOCK_EX)
(Pdb) n
> /dj_projects/marketr/survey/pie_utils.py(17)make_pie_if_necessary()
-> create_piechart(f, answer_set)
(Pdb) n
> /dj_projects/marketr/survey/pie_utils.py(19)make_pie_if_necessary()
-> fcntl.flock(f, fcntl.LOCK_UN)
(Pdb) n
> /dj_projects/marketr/survey/pie_utils.py(20)make_pie_if_necessary()
-> f.close()
(Pdb)
```

Here we've moved along in the shell session all the way through locking the file, creating the pie chart, and unlocking the file. We've not yet closed the file. Now if we move forward in the development server, it will see that the file exists and has data:

```
(Pdb) n
OSError: (17, 'File exists', '/dj_projects/marketr/site_media/
piecharts/2.png')
> /dj_projects/marketr/survey/pie_utils.py(13)make_pie_if_necessary()
-> fd = os.open(fname, os.O_WRONLY | os.O_CREAT | os.O_EXCL)
(Pdb) n
> /dj_projects/marketr/survey/pie_utils.py(21)make_pie_if_necessary()
-> except OSError, e:
(Pdb) n
> /dj_projects/marketr/survey/pie_utils.py(22)make_pie_if_necessary()
-> if e.errno == errno.EEXIST:
(Pdb) n
> /dj_projects/marketr/survey/pie_utils.py(23)make_pie_if_necessary()
-> wait_for_data(fname)
(Pdb) n
--Return--
> /dj_projects/marketr/survey/pie_utils.py(23)make_pie_if_necessary()-
>None
-> wait_for_data(fname)
(Pdb) n
--Return--
(Pdb)
```

That looks good; the code in this case took the right path. But if we continue from here, still without giving the shell thread a chance to close the file, will the browser's subsequent request for this image file be served successfully? We can test it out by entering c here, and checking what the browser shows for the second pie chart. It seems we do have a problem:

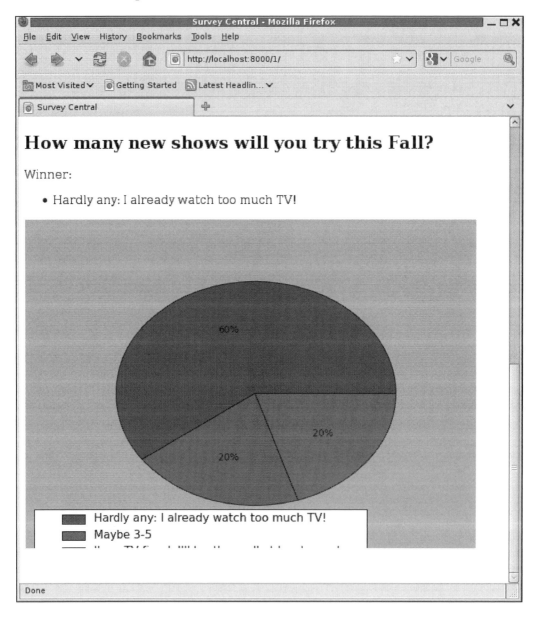

Either we've broken the code that generates the pie chart, or that's the result of serving an image file that has not yet been completely written to the disk. The latter seems more likely. How do we fix this? We can change the make_pie_if_necessary function to flush the data to disk before releasing the exclusive lock:

```
def make_pie_if_necessary(rel_path, answer_set):
    fname = settings.MEDIA_ROOT + rel_path
    try:
        import pdb; pdb.set_trace()
        fd = os.open(fname, os.O_WRONLY | os.O_CREAT | os.O_EXCL)
        try:
            f = os.fdopen(fd, 'wb')
            fcntl.flock(f, fcntl.LOCK_EX)
            create_piechart(f, answer_set)
        finally:
            f.flush()
            os.fsync(f.fileno())
            fcntl.flock(f, fcntl.LOCK_UN)
            f.close()
    except OSError, e:
        if e.errno == errno.EEXIST:
            wait_for_data(fname)
        else:
            raise
```

Consulting the Python documentation shows both a flush of the file and a call to os.fsync, for it is needed to ensure that all the file data is actually written to disk, so we have added both of those before the call to unlock the file.

Does that work? Testing it means again deleting the image files and again forcing the race condition we are looking to exercise. The detailed output isn't included here, but indeed if we force a new shell session to be the thread that creates the second image file, halt it before it closes the file, and let the development server thread proceed to send the completed survey response page and then serve the image files, we see a complete second image in the browser. So adding the calls to flush and os.fsync does appear to fix the problem.

This exercise has demonstrated how hard it can be to write code that correctly handles race conditions. Unfortunately, such race conditions often cannot be avoided in web applications, which will generally be deployed in multi-threaded, multi-process web servers. The debugger is a valuable tool for ensuring that code written to deal with these conditions works as intended.

Notes on using graphical debuggers

In this chapter, we have focused exclusively on use of the Python command-line debugger, pdb. Graphical integrated development environments such as Eclipse, NetBeans, and Komodo also provide debuggers that can be used for Django application code (though some require installation of particular plugins to support development of Python code). The details of setting up and using any of these environments is beyond the scope of what is covered here, but some general notes on using graphical debuggers for Django applications will be included next.

First, there are some definite advantages to using a graphical debugger. Usually, a graphical debugger will provide individual window panes that show the currently executing source code, the program stack trace, local variables, and program output. This can make it easy to quickly get an overall sense of the state of the program. It tends to be harder to do this in pdb, where you must run individual commands to get the same information, and be able to keep the results in mind after they scroll off the screen.

A second advantage to graphical debuggers is that you can generally set breakpoints simply by selecting the line of code in the debugger and choosing a menu item. Thus, you can easily debug without changing the source to include explicit breaks into the debugger.

One requirement for breakpoints in graphical debuggers to work, though, is that the `runserver` command used to start the development server in the debugger must specify the `--noreload` option. Without this option, the development server reloads itself automatically when it detects that running code has changed on disk. This reload mechanism interferes with the method used by graphical debuggers to trigger breakpoints activating the debugger, so it must be disabled by specifying `--noreload` when running the server.

A downside of this of course, is that the development server running in the integrated development environment will not automatically reload when code changes are made. If you have gotten used to the automatic reload feature when running from a simple command line, it can be hard to remember the need to manually restart the server after making code changes.

Another thing to watch out for when using a graphical debugger is the debugger itself triggering unexpected behavior. In order to produce the display of local variables, for example, the debugger must interrogate their values. For local variables that are `QuerySets`, this may mean that the debugger causes database interactions that the application itself would never initiate. Thus the debugger, in attempting to display the value of local variables, can trigger evaluation of `QuerySets` at points where the application itself does not.

`QuerySets` are just one example of how the debugger can inject unexpected behavior. Essentially the debugger may need to run a lot of code behind the scenes in order to do its work, and that behind the scenes work may have side-effects. These side-effects may or may not interfere with the task of debugging the application code. If they do (generally signaled by unexpected results that occur only when run under the debugger), it may be more productive to switch to a different debugging technique rather than trying to figure out what exactly is going on behind the scenes with the debugger.

Summary

This brings us to the end of discussing the use of debuggers when developing Django application code. In this chapter, we:

- Implemented the display of survey results using `pygooglechart` to create pie charts. When we ran into some trouble along the way, we saw how the Python debugger, pdb, could be used to help figure out what was going wrong. We experimented with many of the most useful pdb commands. We learned the commands used to see the context of the code that is running, examine and change the values of variables, and flexibly control the execution of the code as it proceeds in the debugger.

- Re-implemented the display of survey results using the `matplotlib` library. For this alternative implementation, we ended up needing to write code that was vulnerable to multi-process race conditions. Here we saw how pdb can be used to help verify correct behavior of this type of code, since it allows us to force problematic race conditions to occur, and then verify that the code behaves properly for such cases.

- Finally, some pros and cons of using graphical debuggers for Django application code were discussed.

In the next chapter, we will learn what to do when we encounter problems during development that none of the debugging techniques discussed so far seem to help in fixing.

10
When All Else Fails: Getting Outside Help

Sometimes we run into problems that do not seem to be caused by our own code. Though following the documentation to the best of our understanding, the results we are getting don't match what we expect. One of the benefits of building on open source code such as Django is that we can delve into its code and figure out exactly where things are going wrong. However, that may not be the best use of our time.

Most often a better first step in tracking down such problems is to consult community resources. Perhaps someone else has already encountered the problem we are facing and found a fix or workaround. If so, we can likely save a lot of time by taking advantage of their experience rather than finding our own solution to the problem.

This chapter describes the Django community resources and illustrates how to use them. Specifically, in this chapter we will:

- Walk through the discovery of a bug that existed in the Django 1.1 release and caused a problem for some of the survey application code

- See how the resources available on the Django website can be used to research the problem

- Discuss the best way to proceed based on the results of the research, for both this problem specifically and problems in general

- Learn what other avenues for getting help exist, and how best to make use of them

Tracking down a problem in Django

This book has been written using the latest available Django release at the time of writing. Early on that was Django 1.1. Then, during the course of writing, Django 1.1.1 was released and everything written after that release date used Django 1.1.1. The three 1s in that release number are the major, minor, and micro release numbers. (A missing micro number, as in Django 1.1, is an implied 0.) Django 1.1.1, since it has an explicit micro number, is called a micro release. The only changes made in micro releases are bug fixes, thus micro releases are 100 percent backwards compatible with the previous release. While a change in a major or minor version number may involve some backwards-incompatible changes that require code adjustments, the only difference you will see in updating to a new micro release is fewer bugs. Therefore, it is always recommended to run the latest micro release for the major. minor version you are using.

Despite this advice and compatibility guarantee, it's sometimes tempting to not upgrade to the latest available release. Upgrading requires some (likely small, but non-zero) amount of work. In addition, there's always the common-sense axiom: if it isn't broken, don't fix it. If you're not actually experiencing any problems, why upgrade?

I had exactly these thoughts when Django 1.1.1 was released. That release happened to occur right during the middle of writing *Chapter 7, When the Wheels Fall Off: Understanding a Django Debug Page,* a chapter full of screenshots and console displays showing tracebacks that included Django code. If I changed the Django code base right in the middle of writing that chapter, even by just a micro release, who knew what subtle differences might be introduced in early compared to late-chapter tracebacks? Such differences could cause confusion for eagle-eyed readers.

If I did upgrade mid-chapter, it would be safest to re-do all the examples from the beginning to ensure they were consistent. That was an unattractive option since it was both a fair amount of work and error-prone. Thus my initial inclination when Django 1.1.1 was released was to delay upgrading until at least the next chapter break.

However, in the end I found I did have to upgrade in the middle of the chapter, because I ran into a Django bug that was fixed by the 1.1.1 release. The following sections describe encountering the bug and show how it can be tracked down to a problem that had been fixed in Django 1.1.1.

Revisiting the Chapter 7 voting form

Recall in *Chapter 7* we implemented the code to display an active survey. This includes a form to allow a user to choose answers for each question in the survey. One of the final changes made to the form code involved customizing the error format. The final code for the `QuestionVoteForm` looks like this:

```
class QuestionVoteForm(forms.Form):
    answer = forms.ModelChoiceField(widget=forms.RadioSelect,
        queryset=None,
        empty_label=None,
        error_messages={'required': 'Please select an answer below:'})

    def __init__(self, question, *args, **kwargs):
        super(QuestionVoteForm, self).__init__(*args, **kwargs)
        self.fields['answer'].queryset = question.answer_set.all()
        self.fields['answer'].label = question.question
        self.error_class = PlainErrorList

from django.forms.util import ErrorList
class PlainErrorList(ErrorList):
    def __unicode__(self):
        return u'%s' % ' '.join([e for e in self])
```

The inclusion of the `PlainErrorList` class, and setting the form instance's `error_class` attribute to it during `__init__`, is intended to change the display of an error for a question from an HTML unordered list (the default behavior) to a simple string. However, when running this code under Django 1.1, and forcing an error situation by attempting to submit a survey with both questions unanswered, the result displayed is:

The inclusion of the bullets to the left of the two error messages shows that the error lists are still being formatted as HTML unordered lists. This can also be confirmed by checking the HTML source for the page, which includes the following snippet for each error message:

```
<ul class="errorlist"><li>Please select an answer below:</li></ul>
```

It seems that setting the `error_class` attribute is not having any effect. How can we best track down a problem like this?

Is the right code actually running?

First, we need to make sure the code that is running is actually the code we think is running. In this case, when I encountered the problem I could see that the development server had restarted after the code changes to add the `PlainErrorList` class and the setting of the `error_class` attribute, so I was pretty sure the right code was running. Still, inserting an `import pdb; pdb.set_trace()` right before the `error_class` assignment allowed me to confirm the code was there and doing what I expected:

```
> /dj_projects/marketr/survey/forms.py(14)__init__()
-> self.error_class = PlainErrorList
(Pdb) self.error_class
<class 'django.forms.util.ErrorList'>
(Pdb) s
--Return--
> /dj_projects/marketr/survey/forms.py(14)__init__()->None
-> self.error_class = PlainErrorList
(Pdb) self.error_class
<class 'survey.forms.PlainErrorList'>
(Pdb) c
```

Here we can see that on entry to the debugger, before our assignment of `PlainErrorList` to `error_class`, this attribute had the value `django.forms.util.ErrorList`. Stepping through the assignment shows that the `__init__` method is then about to return, and checking the value of the `error_class` attribute again shows that indeed the value has been changed to our customized `PlainErrorList`. That all looks good. At the very end of the form creation code, the `error_class` attribute has been set to the customized class. Why isn't it being used?

Is the code correct as per the documentation?

The next step (after removing the added breakpoint) is to double-check the documentation. Though it seems unlikely, perhaps there is something else required to use a custom error class? After rechecking the documentation, there doesn't seem to be. The full documentation on customizing the error class is simply:

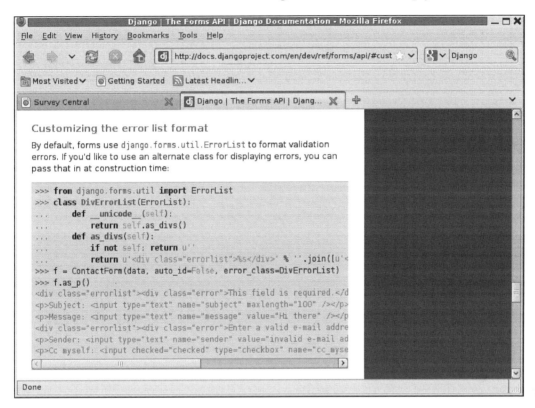

There are a couple of slight differences between what the provided example does and what the `QuestionVoteForm` does. First, the provided example passes the error class as an argument on form creation, and thus it is passed to the form's superclass `__init__`. The `QuestionVoteForm`, on the other hand, manually sets `error_class` after the superclass `__init__` runs.

This seems unlikely to be the cause of the problem, since over-riding values in a subclass __init__ routine, as we have done with QuestoinVoteForm, is a very common idiom. We can check, though, to see if this slight difference causes a problem by attempting the demonstration of use of the custom error_class setting, as shown in the documentation in a Python shell, for the QuestionVoteForm:

```
kmt@lbox:/dj_projects/marketr$ python manage.py shell
Python 2.5.2 (r252:60911, Oct  5 2008, 19:24:49)
[GCC 4.3.2] on linux2
Type "help", "copyright", "credits" or "license" for more information.
(InteractiveConsole)
>>> from survey.forms import QuestionVoteForm
>>> from survey.models import Question
>>> qvf = QuestionVoteForm(Question.objects.get(pk=1), data={})
```

Here we have created a form instance, qvf, for the question with primary key 1 in the database. By passing in an empty data dictionary, we have forced the error condition of a form submitted with no answer value. The documentation shows that using the form's as_p method to display this form should show the error formatted using the form's custom error class. We can check whether that happens for the QuestionVoteForm:

```
>>> qvf.as_p()
u'Please select an answer below:\n<p><label for="id_answer_0">What is your
favorite type of TV show?</label> <ul>\n<li><label for="id_answer_0"><input
type="radio" id="id_answer_0" value="1" name="answer" /> Comedy</label></
li>\n<li><label  for="id_answer_1"><input  type="radio"  id="id_answer_
1"  value="2"  name="answer"  /> Drama</label></li>\n<li><label  for="id_
answer_2"><input type="radio" id="id_answer_2" value="3" name="answer" />
Reality</label></li>\n</ul></p>'

>>>
```

There we see that the as_p method does indeed use the custom error class: there is no HTML unordered list wrapped around the error message. So the error class is being set, and is used when the form is displayed using a routine like as_p.

This leads to the second difference between what the documentation shows and what the survey application code actually does. The `survey/active_survey.html` template does not use `as_p` to display the form. Rather, it individually prints the label for the answer field, errors for the answer field, and then the answer field itself:

```
{% extends "survey/base.html" %}
{% block content %}
<h1>{{ survey.title }}</h1>
<form method="post" action=".">
<div>
{% for qform in qforms %}
    {{ qform.answer.label }}
    {{ qform.answer.errors }}
    {{ qform.answer }}
{% endfor %}
<button type="submit">Submit</button>
</div>
</form>
{% endblock content %}
```

Should that cause the custom error class to not be used for display? You wouldn't think so. Though the documentation only shows the custom error class used with `as_p`, there is no mention there that the custom error class is only used by the convenience display methods such as `as_p`. Such a restriction would be very limiting, since the convenience form display methods are frequently not appropriate for a non-trivial form.

It seems clear that the intent of the `error_class` attribute is to override the error display regardless of the exact way in which a form is output, but it doesn't seem to be working. This is the point where we may begin to strongly suspect a bug in Django instead of some error or misunderstanding of usage in the application code.

Searching for a matching problem report

The next step, then, is to visit the Django website to see if anyone has reported a problem using `error_class`. Choosing the **Code** link from the main Django project page (rightmost of the links across the top of the page) brings up the main page for Django's code tracker:

The Django project uses Trac, which provides an easy-to-use web-based interface for tracking bugs and feature requests. With Trac, bugs and feature requests are reported and tracked in tickets. Specifics of the way in which the Django project has configured Trac, and thus the meaning of the various ticket attribute values, can be found in the Django documentation page on contributing. Specifically, the diagram and descriptions found here: `http://docs.djangoproject.com/en/dev/internals/contributing/#ticket-triage` are very helpful in understanding all of the information associated with a ticket.

What we want to do now is search the Django project tickets for reported problems with the use of `error_class`. One way to do that is to select the **View Tickets** tab and construct an appropriate search. When **View Tickets** is first selected, by default it will show a page listing all non-closed tickets. For example:

The criteria used to generate the report are shown in the box labeled **Filters**. Here we see that the report includes all tickets with any status that is not **closed**, since that is the only **Status** choice that is not checked. In order to get a report that is more useful for what we are trying to research, we need to modify the search criteria in the **Filters** box.

First, we can remove the constraint on the ticket status. We are interested in all reports related to error_class, regardless of ticket status. We can remove the existing constraint on status by clicking the box with a minus sign on the extreme right side of the line that contains the constraint.

Second, we need to add a filter for the search constraint we want to apply. To do this, we select an appropriate choice from the **Add filter** drop-down box. This drop-down box contains a full list of the ticket attributes we could search on, such as **Reporter**, **Owner**, **Status**, and **Component**. Most of these attributes are not relevant for the search we are currently interested in. The one in the list most likely to find what we are looking for is **Summary**.

The ticket summary is the brief description of the problem. We could hope that this summary would include the string error_class for any reports of the problem we have run into with using it. Adding a single filter on **Summary** with a specification that it contains the string error_class will thus hopefully find any relevant tickets. Clicking on the **Update** button to refresh the search results given the new criteria then shows the following:

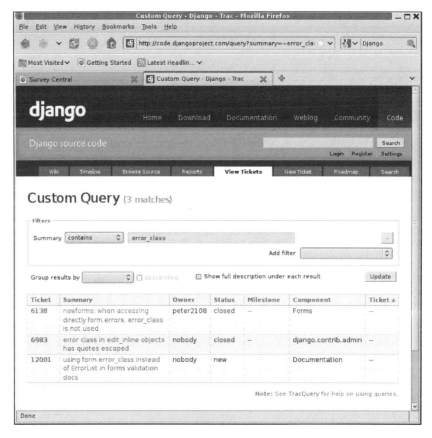

There have been three tickets opened that contain error_class (or error class) in the summary. Two have been closed, one is still open (status **new**). Of the three, based on the displayed summary, the top one sounds like it might be the problem we are seeing with error_class, while the other two do not sound particularly relevant.

We can get more details on a listed problem by clicking on the ticket number or summary, both of which are links to view the full ticket details. Looking at the full details will allow us to verify that it is really the same as what we are seeing, and find out more details on when and why it was closed. In this case, we see the following:

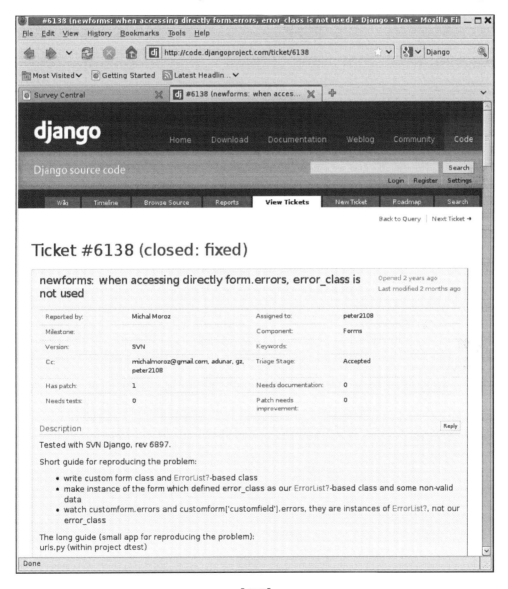

This ticket has a fairly long history—two years between when it was opened and the last activity. The short guide for reproducing the problem does make it sound like exactly the same problem we are seeing with error_class. The resolution of **fixed** listed after the ticket number near the top sounds encouraging, but unfortunately this ticket has no details on what code change was made, and when, to fix the problem. Scrolling all the way down to the tail end of the various comments added to the ticket history, we see that the last few updates are as follows:

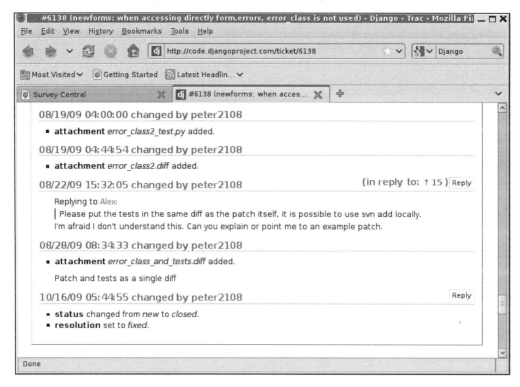

In August of 2009 user **peter2108** was interested in helping move the ticket along by providing patches, including tests, to fix the problem (reading through the full history, the lack of tests in the originally-provided patches was one reason this ticket was open for a long time). Then, on October 16, 2009, **peter2108** closed the ticket with a resolution of **fixed**.

It may not be obvious at first, but this way of closing a ticket is not typical for a ticket that required a Django code change. Normally, when the code change is committed to the Django SVN repository, the ticket number is included in the commit message and the corresponding ticket is automatically updated with a comment including the commit message and a link to the changeset. This automatic process also closes the ticket with a resolution of fixed. This makes it very easy to see exactly what code was changed to fix the problem and when the code change was made.

Sometimes that automatic process fails to run properly, and usually someone will notice when that happens and manually close the ticket, noting which code update fixed the problem. But that's not what happened here either. Rather it looks like **peter2108**, who was interested in seeing the bug fixed, simply noticed that the problem had gone away at some point and closed the ticket as fixed.

We could guess, based on the fact that the same user who was interested in getting the problem fixed in August closed the ticket as fixed in October, that the fix went into the code base sometime between August 28 and October 16. What we'd like, though, is to know for sure when exactly the fix was made, so we could know for sure whether we should already have it in the code we are running, or if updating to the latest release would fix the problem, or if the fix is available only in a version of code pulled directly from the SVN repository.

Looking back at the other two tickets that mention `error_class` in the summary, neither of them are helpful in determining when exactly this problem with `error_class` was fixed, since they describe different problems entirely. How, then, can we locate the information about when exactly the problem we are encountering was fixed? For this case, it turns out that the **View Tickets** type of search is not broad enough to get us the information we are looking for. Fortunately, there's an alternate way of searching the Django tracker that we can use to find the missing information.

Another way to search for a matching problem report

This alternative way of searching is found by clicking on the **Search** tab instead of the **View Tickets** tab. This brings up a page with a single text entry box and three check boxes to control where to search: **Tickets**, **Changesets**, and **Wiki**.

This page provides a much broader and less targeted way of searching. In addition to searching ticket data, changesets and Wiki articles are searched by default as well. Even when those options are turned off, the ticket search alone is broader than what is possible under **View Tickets**. The ticket search from this page covers all of the ticket comments and updates, which cannot be searched under **View Tickets**.

A plus side of using this page to search is it may find relevant results that cannot be found using a **View Tickets** search. A downside of using this page to search is it may find an overwhelming number of irrelevant results, depending on exactly what search terms are entered in the textbox. If that happens you can further limit the results shown by entering more words that must be matched in the textbox, which can help. In this case, though, searching on a string as uncommon as `error_class` is not likely to produce an overwhelming number of results.

To proceed, then, entering `error_class` in the textbox and clicking on the **Search** button leads to the following:

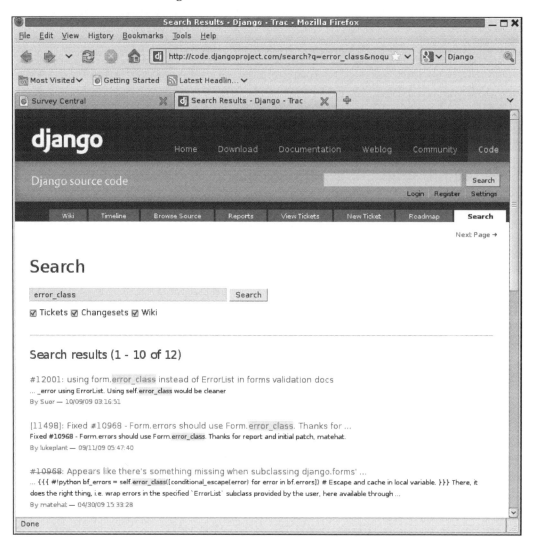

This search does produce more results than the **View Tickets** search—twelve instead of three. The first result listed, ticket **#12001**, is the same as the still-open ticket found by the previous search. The other results from the previous search are also contained in the full list, only further down. But first we can see a result that is a changeset, **[11498]**, which mentions `error_class` in the commit message, and its associated ticket **#10968**. This ticket did not show up in the original search we tried because, though it includes reference to `error_class` in the full description, the string `error_class` is not in the ticket summary.

Clicking through to the details of ticket **#10968** shows that it is a duplicate report of the same problem we have encountered and that was reported in the other ticket we found, **#6138**. Ordinarily when duplicates like this are opened, they are quickly closed as duplicates with a reference to the existing ticket that describes the problem.

However, if nobody realizes a new ticket is a duplicate, then the duplicate ticket may turn out to be the one referenced when the fix is checked into the code base. That's apparently what happened in this case. We can see in the last update to this new ticket the automatically-generated comment added when the fix was committed to the SVN repository:

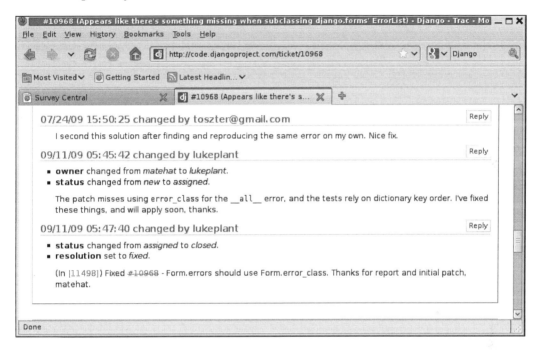

The changeset number in that comment is a link to a detailed description of the changeset. Clicking on it, we see the following:

Here we can see all the detailed information related to this code change: when it was made, who made it, the commit message, the files that were changed (or added or deleted), the specific lines in the files that were changed, and what those changes were. Most of this information is more than we really need to know for the problem we are researching now, but it can come in handy at times. For this problem, what we'd like to know is: what released level of code contains this fix? We'll consider that question next.

Determining the release that contains a fix

For the particular case we are looking at, we can tell, simply based on dates, that the first release containing the fix should be Django 1.1.1. A quick check of the web log on the Django project home page shows that Django 1.1 was released on July 29, 2009 and Django 1.1.1 was released on October 9, 2009. All bug fixes made between those dates should be included in the 1.1.1 release, thus a fix made on September 11, 2009 should be in Django 1.1.1.

Sometimes things may not be so clear. For example, we might be unsure if a code change made on the same day as a release was included in the release or happened just after the release. Alternatively, we might be unsure if a change was classified as a bug fix or a new feature. For such cases, we can check on the revision number of the release and compare it to the revision we are interested in.

Django uses the standard subversion practice of tagging released versions; the tagged release versions can be found under `root/django/tags/releases`. We can navigate down this path by first selecting the **Browse Code** tab and then selecting each path component in turn. Navigating in this way to the 1.1.1 release and clicking on **Revision Log** in the upper-right corner brings up the following page:

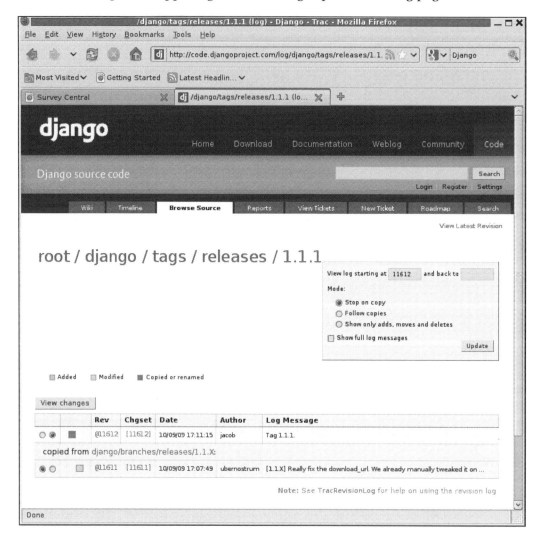

This shows that the 1.1.1 tagged release version was created by copying the 1.1.X release branch. The changeset that created the tag is **[11612]**, higher than the changeset we are interested in (11498), so we'd expect the fix we are concerned with to be in the 1.1.X release.

But wait a minute. Looking at the details of changeset 11498, the files changed were on trunk (`django/trunk/django/forms/forms.py`, for example), not the 1.1.X release branch `django/branches/releases/1.1.X`. If the release was created by copying the 1.1.X branch but the fix was only made to trunk, is it really included in the 1.1.1 release?

The answer is yes. Clicking through the link on this page to the 1.1.X release branch, selecting **Revision Log** for it, and scrolling down to the bottom shows that the 1.1.X release branch was created as a copy of trunk at revision 11500, two revisions past the revision 11498 we are interested in. Thus, when the 1.1.X branch was initially created, it contained the fix we are looking for.

You might wonder why the 1.1.X branch was not created until sometime after September 11, 2009 when the 1.1 release went out in late July. The reason is because once the release branch is created, bug fixes have to be applied in two different places: trunk and the latest release branch. This is slightly more work than having to apply them in only one place (trunk). Creation of the release branch is thus generally delayed for some period of time after a release to allow bug fixes to be made more easily.

This delayed creation of the release branch means that during the time it does not exist, no changes related to new features can be made to trunk, since the release branch must contain only bug fixes, and no new features. That's generally not a problem, though, since right after a release there is little feature work being done. Everyone involved usually needs some time to take a breather and first decide what features might go into the next release. Once some feature work for the next release gets close to needing to be checked in, then the release branch for the previous release is created. From then on, feature work gets checked into trunk while bug fixes get checked in to both trunk and the release branch.

What if a fix hasn't been released yet?

Here we were lucky enough to run into a problem that had already been fixed, and the fix was already available in an officially released version. In any case of a problem like this that is encountered, it should be an easy choice to simply update to the latest micro release to get the fix. As mentioned earlier, it is always recommended to install the latest micro release for the particular major.minor version in use.

But what if the fix we wanted was made sometime after the latest available release? What should we do then? The easy technical answer is to simply check out the latest level of either trunk or the release branch that contains the fix, and run with that code. If the release branch, in particular, is used, there should be no concern about picking up any code instabilities, since the only changes that go into the release branch are bug fixes.

This easy technical answer may, however, run afoul of local policies regarding running only "release level" code. If you are working in an environment with such policies, you may have some additional hurdles to overcome in order to use fixes that have not yet been made available in an official version. The best course to take will likely be determined by factors such as the exact policies you are dealing with, the severity of the problem you have encountered, and the ability to find a workaround in your own code.

What if a fix hasn't been committed yet?

Sometimes when researching a problem the results will show that the problem has been reported, but not yet fixed. How best to proceed then will likely depend on how interested you are in getting involved and contributing to Django, and how close the matching problem report is to being fixed. Details of how to get involved in contributing to Django are beyond the scope of what is covered here, but this section provides some broad guidelines for how to proceed based on your level of interest. If you are interested in contributing, the Django website has details of how to contribute, available at: `http://docs.djangoproject.com/en/dev/internals/` `contributing/`.

If you are not interested in experimenting with code that has not yet been committed to the code base, there will likely not be much you can do besides wait for a fix to be committed. The exception to this would be for problems that are not well understood. In that case, you may be able to provide specific details of the case where you are running into the problem that can help others better understand the problem and develop a fix.

If you are willing to experiment with uncommitted code, you'll likely be able to find a workable solution to the problem you've encountered more quickly. In the best case, you may find that the ticket matching the problem you have encountered already has a working patch attached. It's possible and all you need to do is download it and apply it to your copy of the Django code to resolve the problem.

You'll then have to decide whether you are able to, and comfortable with, deploying your application with a version of Django that has some "custom" fixes applied. If not, you might like to help out in getting the working patch checked into the code base by seeing if there is anything missing (such as tests) that needs to be included before the fix is checked in and if so, supplying the missing bits. In some cases, though, there is nothing missing and all that is needed is time for the fix to make its way into the code base.

If you find a matching ticket with a patch that you try, but it doesn't fix the problem you are experiencing, that is valuable information that would be useful to post to the ticket. You might want to be sure first, though, that your problem is really the same as the one in the ticket you have found. If it's really a slightly different problem, then it might be more appropriate to open a new ticket for the somewhat different problem.

When in doubt, you can always post information in what you think is the matching ticket about the problem you are seeing and how the existing patch doesn't seem to fix it. Someone else following the ticket might then be able to provide feedback on whether your problem is the same and the existing patch is indeed not quite right or whether you are really dealing with a different problem.

In the worst case, you may find a ticket reporting the same problem as you are experiencing but no attached patch to try. That's not very helpful to you, but offers you the most opportunity to contribute. If you have the time and are so inclined, you can delve into the Django code and see if you can come up with a patch that you can post to the ticket to help get the problem fixed.

What if a ticket has been closed without a fix?

Sometimes when researching a problem the results will turn up with a matching report (or multiple reports) that have been closed without any fix being made. There are three different resolutions that might be used in cases like this: invalid, worksforme, and wontfix. How best to proceed will depend on the specifics of the problem report and the resolution used to close the matching problem ticket.

First, the invalid resolution is pretty broad. A ticket might be closed as invalid for many different reasons, including:

- The described problem is not a problem at all but rather some error in the reporter's code or misunderstanding about how some feature is supposed to work.

- The described problem is too vague. For example, if a ticket is opened that provides just an error traceback but no information on how to trigger the traceback, there is not much anyone can do to help track down and fix the problem, so it might well be closed as invalid.

- The described problem is indeed a problem, but the root cause is some code other than Django. If there is nothing that can be done in Django code to fix the problem, the ticket will likely be closed as invalid.

In cases where you find a matching ticket that has been closed as invalid, you should read the comment that was made when the ticket was closed. In cases where the ticket was closed due to lack of information about the problem, and you can provide some of the missing data needed to make progress on fixing the problem, it may be appropriate to re-open the ticket. Otherwise, if you don't understand the explanation for closing, or don't agree with the reason for closing, it's best to start a discussion on one of the mailing lists (discussed in the next section) to get some more feedback on how best to proceed to fix the problem you are encountering.

The worksforme resolution is pretty straightforward; it indicates that the person who closed the ticket could not reproduce the reported problem. It, like invalid, may be used when the original problem report does not really contain enough information to recreate the problem. The missing information may be specifics of the code used to cause the problem, or specifics of the environment (operating system, Python version, deployment specifics) where the problem occurs. If you are able to recreate a problem that has been closed worksforme, and can supply the missing details that would allow someone else to do the same, you should feel free to re-open the ticket and provide that information.

The wontfix resolution is also straightforward. Usually only core committers will close tickets wontfix, and that indicates that a decision has been made by the core team to not fix that particular problem (which will usually be a feature request, not a bug). If you disagree with a wontfix decision or believe that not all of the appropriate information was considered in making the decision, you will not make any forward progress on changing anyone's mind by simply re-opening the ticket. Rather, you will need to bring the issue up on the django-developers mailing list and see if you can get enough consensus from the wider development community to get the wontfix decision reversed.

Tracking down unreported problems

Sometimes when researching a problem no matching reports will turn up. How best to proceed then likely depends on how sure you are that the problem you are encountering is a bug in Django. If you are really sure the problem lies in Django, you can proceed directly to opening a new ticket to report it. If you are not so sure, it is best to get some feedback from the community first. The following sections will describe where to ask questions, present some tips on asking good questions, and describe how to open a new ticket.

Where to ask questions

Clicking on the **Community** link on any Django website page brings up the following:

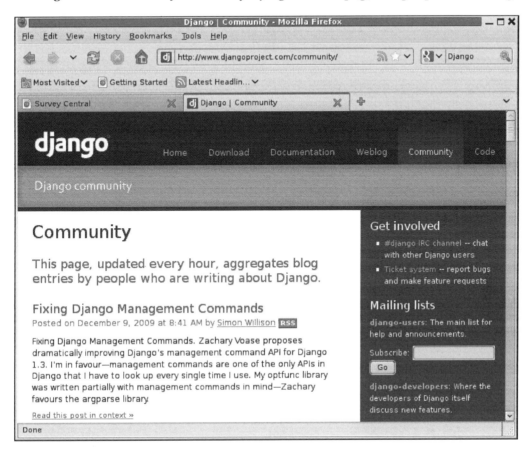

The left side of this page provides links to articles in blogs written by people who discuss Django. While reading such entries is a good way to learn about the community of people using Django, it is the right side of this page that we are interested in right now. Here we see links to ways to interact directly with other members of the Django community.

First in the list is a link to the **#django IRC channel**. (**IRC** stands for **Internet Relay Chat**.) This option provides a chat-type interface to talk to other Django users interactively. This is a good choice for times when you'd like very quick feedback on whatever you'd like to ask about or discuss. It can be difficult, though, to follow a detailed coding discussion in a chat interface. For cases like that, one of the mailing lists is likely a better alternative.

There are two mailing lists, shown next: **django-users** and **django-developers**. The first is for discussions about using Django, the second is for discussions about developing Django itself. If you have encountered a problem that you think, but are not sure, is a problem in Django, django-users is the correct place to post a question about the issue. Members of the Django core development team read and respond to questions on the user's list and will provide feedback on whether the problem should be opened as a ticket or taken to the developer's list for further discussion.

Both of the mailing lists are hosted as Google groups. Each of the group names previously shown is actually a link that you can click to go directly to the Google groups page for the group. From there you can see the list of recent discussions in the group, and read any topics that might be of interest. Google groups also provide a search function, but unfortunately this function does not always work correctly, so searching in the group from the group's page may not produce helpful results.

If you decide you want to post to one of the groups, you will first need to join it. This helps to cut down on spam posted to the groups, since would-be spammers must first join. There are, however, plenty of would-be spammers that do join and attempt to send spam to the lists. Thus, there is also an additional anti-spam measure in place: posts sent by new members are sent through moderation.

This anti-spam measure means that the first post you send to either of these lists may take some time to appear, since it must be manually approved by one of the volunteer moderators. Usually this will not take very long, but it could take up to a few hours. Typically, once a first obviously legitimate post is received from a user, their status is updated to indicate their posts do not need to be moderated, so subsequent posts will appear in the group immediately.

Tips on asking questions that will get good answers

Once you decide to post a question, the next task will be to compose a question in a way that will most likely produce some helpful answers. This section presents some guidance on how to do that.

First, be specific about what you are doing. If you have some code that isn't behaving as you expect, include the code verbatim rather than describing in prose what the code does. Often, it is the detailed specifics of the actual code in use that is key to understanding a problem, and those specifics are easily lost in a prose description of the code.

However, if the code is too lengthy or too wide to be read easily in an e-mail interface that will automatically wrap long lines, it's likely best not to include it in a post. Ideally in a situation like this you would be able to cut the code necessary to recreate the problem down to a manageable size that can be read easily in an e-mail, and post that.

Note that if you do this, it's a good idea to first verify that the cut-down version of the code is both correct (does not have any syntax errors, for example) and exhibits the problem you are asking about. Otherwise, the only responses you get may simply report that the posted code either doesn't work at all or doesn't show the behavior you describe.

If you cannot cut the necessary code down to a manageable size, either because you do not have the time or because cutting it down makes the problem go away, you might try posting the code on some place like dpaste.com and just including a link to it in your question. It is really in your best interest, though, to keep the code needed to demonstrate the problem as short as possible. As the code you post or point to gets longer and longer, fewer and fewer people on the mailing list will take the time to try to understand the problem and help guide you towards a solution.

In addition to being specific about the code you are using, be specific about what you are doing to trigger the errant behavior. Are you observing a problem when you visit one of your own application URLs? When you do something in the admin application? When you try something from a `manage.py` shell? It may seem obvious to you, but it really helps others to recreate the problem if you spell out what you are doing.

Second, be specific about what happens and what you expected to happen instead. "It doesn't work" is not specific. Nor is "it dies", nor "it gives me an error message". Give specifics of what "doesn't work" looks like. A browser page that displays X when you expected Y? An error message that states XYZ? A traceback? In this last case, do include the full traceback in the question, since that provides valuable debugging clues for people who might try to help.

Third, if you mention in the question that your expected behavior is based on what the documentation says, be specific about what documentation, exactly, you are referring to. Django has extensive documentation, including both guide and reference information. Someone reading your question and searching the documentation for what you are referencing may easily find a completely different section and have a hard time following what you are saying. If you provide a specific link to the documentation in question, then misunderstandings are less likely to occur.

A common theme running through all these tips, as you've likely noticed, is: be specific. Yes it takes more work to provide specifics. But a specific question is far more likely to get helpful answers than an imprecise and vague question. If you leave out the specifics, once in a blue moon someone may post an answer that guides you towards a solution. It's far more likely, though, that a vague question will get either no responses, responses asking for specifics, or responses that send you down an entirely wrong path because the responder completely misunderstood the question.

Opening a new ticket to report a problem

If you run into a problem that appears to be an unreported and unfixed bug in Django code, the next step is to open a ticket for it. The process for this is pretty self-explanatory when you select the **New Ticket** tab after clicking on **Code** from the Django home page:

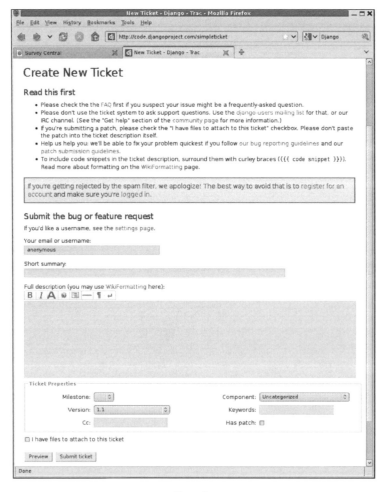

Please do read through the **Read this first** list. Much of the information in that list has been covered earlier in this chapter, but not all. In particular, the last item notes how to mark up submitted code snippets or tracebacks so that they will be formatted properly. The note includes the one type of mark up most frequently left out and also points to the full documentation on how text can be specially formatted. Note that you can check how the formatting will look by selecting the **Preview** button at the bottom—it's always a good idea to try previewing a submission before pressing **Submit**.

Note that the Django Trac installation does allow anonymous ticket submissions and updates. However, it also uses the Akismet spam-filtering service, and this service does sometimes reject non-spam submissions. As noted in the big yellow box, the easiest way to avoid this is to **register for an account** (that text on the page is a link to a page where you can register).

The two most important bits to fill out when opening a new ticket are the short summary and full description. In the short summary, try to include key terms that will make the new ticket show up in likely searches by people encountering the same problem. In the full description, all the advice from the previous section about being specific applies again. If you are opening a ticket after the discussion on one of the mailing lists came to the conclusion that a ticket is a good idea, it's helpful to include a link to that discussion in the problem. However, it is also good to include the basic information about the problem in the ticket description itself as well.

In the information in **Ticket Properties**, you likely don't need to change anything from the default values, excepting **Version** (if you are using a version other than the one displayed) and **Has patch** (if you are going to attach a patch that fixes the problem). You can try to guess the correct **Component** from the list and include some appropriate **Keywords**, but it's not necessary.

Similarly, you can set the **Milestone** to the next release, though that won't really make it any more likely that someone will tackle the problem sooner rather than later. That field is typically only closely watched towards the very tail end of a release to note which bugs absolutely must be fixed before release.

Once you submit a ticket, if you used a login that included an e-mail address, or specified an e-mail address in the field labeled **Your email or username**, updates to the ticket will automatically be e-mailed to the e-mail address specified. So if someone adds a comment to the ticket, you will be notified. An annoying exception to this is the automatically-generated update resulting from a commit to the code base: this does not generate e-mail to the ticket reporter. So, you won't necessarily get notified when the ticket is closed as fixed, but rather will have to check back on its status from the website manually.

Summary

We've now come to the end of discussion of what to do when none of the other debugging techniques covered previously have succeeded in solving some problem. In this chapter, we:

- Encountered a bug that existed in Django 1.1 and caused some of the survey application code to not behave as desired

- Walked through the verification process of tracking down the problem to Django instead of the survey code

- Saw how searching in the Django code tracker revealed the problem was a bug that had been fixed in Django 1.1.1, which provided an easy solution to the problem

- Discussed options for how to proceed when problems are tracked down to bugs with fixes that are either not yet available or not available in official releases

- Described the various community resources that exist for asking questions about behavior that seems puzzling, but doesn't seem to have been reported as a bug

- Discussed tips for writing questions so that they get the desired helpful responses

- Described the process of opening a new ticket to report a problem in Django code

In the next chapter, we will advance to the final stage in developing a Django application: moving to production.

11
When it's Time to Go Live: Moving to Production

The final topic we will cover on the subject of testing and debugging Django applications is the move to production. When the application code is all written, fully tested and debugged, it is time to set up a production web server and make the application accessible to real users. Since the application has been fully tested and debugged during development, this should be straightforward, right? Unfortunately, not always. There are a number of differences between a production web server environment and the Django development server environment. These differences can cause problems during the move to production. In this chapter, we will see what some of these differences are, what types of problems they can cause, and how to overcome them. Specifically, we will:

- Configure an Apache web server with `mod_wsgi` to run the sample `marketr` project.
- Encounter a number of issues during development of the Apache configuration. For each, we will see how to diagnose and address the problem.
- Perform functional stress testing of the application running under Apache to ensure that it operates correctly under load.
- Fix any code errors revealed by the functional stress testing.
- Discuss the possibility of using Apache with `mod_wsgi` during development.

Developing an Apache/mod_wsgi configuration

Ordinarily, the move to production will involve running the code on a machine other than the ones it has been developed on. The production server might be dedicated hardware or resources obtained from a hosting provider. In either case, it is typically entirely separate from the machines used by developers when writing the code. The production server needs to have any of the pre-requisite packages installed (Django and matplotlib, for example, for our sample project). In addition a copy of the application project code, generally extracted from a version control system, needs to be placed on the production server.

For the sake of simplicity in this chapter, though, we are going to configure a production web server on the same machine where we have been developing the code. This will allow us to skip over some of the complexity involved in a real move to production while still experiencing many of the issues that may arise during production deployment. For the most part the issues we will skip over in doing this are not Django-specific, but rather are common issues that need to be dealt with whenever moving any kind of application from development into production. The issues we will encounter will tend to be more Django-specific.

The example deployment environment that will be developed is Apache with mod_wsgi, which is the current recommended environment for deploying Django applications. **WSGI** stands for **Web Server Gateway Interface**. WSGI is a Python standard specification that defines an interface between web servers (Apache, for example) and web applications or frameworks written in Python (Django, for example).

The base Apache web server does not support WSGI. However, Apache's modular structure allows such support to be provided by a plug-in module. Thus, the web server side support for WSGI is provided by mod_wsgi, an Apache module written and actively maintained by Graham Dumpleton. Django itself does implement the application side of the WSGI specification. Thus, there is no need for any additional adapter module between mod_wsgi and Django.

Prior to the development of mod_wsgi, the mod_python module for
Apache was the recommended deployment environment for Django.
Though mod_python is still available and even still in wide use, its
most recent release was over three years ago. The current source code
needs a patch in order to compile with the latest Apache 2.2.X release.
Going forward, more extensive changes will be needed due to changes
in Apache APIs, but there are no active mod_python developers to
make such changes. Given the current moribund state of mod_python
development, I believe it is now a poor choice for Django application
deployment. Therefore, specifics of configuring it are not covered here.
If for some reason you must use mod_python, many of the issues
encountered in this chapter with mod_wsgi apply to mod_python as
well, and the specifics of configuring mod_python are still included in
the Django documentation.

Both Apache and mod_wsgi are readily obtained and easily installed on a variety of
different platforms. Details of installation for these will not be covered. As a general
guide, using your machine's regular package management service to install these
packages is likely the easiest path. If that isn't possible, details of downloading and
installing Apache can be found on the Web at http://httpd.apache.org/ and
the same information for mod_wsgi can be found at http://code.google.com/p/
modwsgi/.

The machine used to develop the sample configuration shown in this chapter
is running Ubuntu, a Debian-based version of Linux. This flavor of Linux has
developed a particular structure for Apache configuration that may not match the
structure used on your own machine. The configuration structure, however, is not
significant. Rather it is the Apache directives contained in the configuration that are
important. If your machine does not follow the Debian structure, you may simply
place the directives shown here in the main Apache configuration file, usually
named httpd.conf.

There are two pieces to the configuration for a WSGI client application running
under Apache with mod_wsgi. First, there is a Python WSGI script that sets up the
environment for and identifies the WSGI client application that will handle requests.
Second, there are the Apache configuration directives that control the operation of
mod_wsgi and direct requests for particular URL paths to mod_wsgi. Creating each
of these for the Django marketr project will be discussed next.

Creating the WSGI script for the marketr project

The WSGI script for a Django project has three responsibilities. First, it must set the Python path to include any paths that are needed by the Django project but are not on the regular system path. In our case, the path to the `martketr` project itself will need to be added to the Python path. All of the other pre-requisite code used by the project has been installed so that it is automatically found under the Python site-packages directory.

Second, the WSGI script must set the `DJANGO_SETTINGS_MODULE` variable in the environment to point to the appropriate settings module. In our case, it will need to be set to point to the `settings.py` file in `/dj_projects/marketr`.

Third, the WSGI script must set the variable `application` to an instance of a callable that implements the WSGI interface. For Django, this interface is provided by `django.core.handlers.wsgi.WSGIHandler`, so the script for the `marketr` project may simply set `application` to an instance of that class. There is nothing specific to the `marketr` project here—this piece of the WSGI script will be the same for all Django projects.

Where should this script go? It might seem natural to place it directly in `/dj_projects/marketr`, along with the `settings.py` and `urls.py` files, since they are all project-level files. However, as mentioned in the `mod_wsgi` documentation, this would be a poor choice. Apache will need to be configured to allow access to files in the directory containing the WSGI script. Thus, it is best to keep the WSGI script in a directory separate from any code files that should not be accessible to website users. (The directory containing `settings.py`, in particular, should never be configured to be accessible to website clients, since it may contain sensitive information such as the database password.)

Therefore, we will create a new directory inside `/dj_projects/marketr` named `apache`, to hold all of the files related to running the project under Apache. Under the `apache` directory, we'll create a `wsgi` directory to hold the WSGI script for the `marketr` project, which we will name `marketr.wsgi`. Based on the three responsibilities previously noted for this script, a first pass at implementing this `/dj_projects/marketr/apache/wsgi/marketr.wsgi` script might be:

```
import os, sys

sys.path = ['/dj_projects/marketr', ] + sys.path
os.environ['DJANGO_SETTINGS_MODULE'] = 'marketr.settings'

import django.core.handlers.wsgi
application = django.core.handlers.wsgi.WSGIHandler()
```

This code adds the `marketr` project directory at the front of the Python system path, sets the `DJANGO_SETTINGS_MODULE` environment variable to `marketr.settings`, and sets `application` to be an instance of the Django-provided callable that implements the WSGI application interface. When `mod_wsgi` is called to respond for a URL path that has been mapped to this script, it will call the appropriate Django code with an environment correctly set so that Django will be able to handle the request. The next step, then, is to develop the Apache configuration that will route requests appropriately to `mod_wsgi` and this script.

Creating an Apache VirtualHost for the marketr project

In order to isolate the Django project from anything else that you might already be using Apache for, we will use an Apache `VirtualHost` tied to port 8080 for the Django configuration. The following directives instruct Apache to listen for requests on port 8080 and define a virtual host to handle those requests:

```
Listen 8080
<VirtualHost *:8080>
    WSGIScriptAlias / /dj_projects/marketr/apache/wsgi/marketr.wsgi
    WSGIDaemonProcess marketr
    WSGIProcessGroup marketr

    # Possible values include: debug, info, notice, warn, error, crit,
    # alert, emerg.
    LogLevel debug

    ErrorLog /dj_projects/marketr/apache/logs/error.log
    CustomLog /dj_projects/marketr/apache/logs/access.log combined
</VirtualHost>
```

Note that this is in no way a complete Apache configuration, but is rather what needs to be added to an existing (or the shipped sample) configuration to support handling requests for the `marketr` project directed at port 8080. Inside the `VirtualHost` container are three directives that control the behavior of `mod_wsgi`, and three that will affect how logging is handled for this virtual host.

The first directive, `WSGIScriptAlias`, is straightforward. It maps all requests matching its first argument, /, to the WSGI script specified in its second argument, `/dj_projects/marketr/apache/wsgi/marketr.wsgi`. The effect of this directive will be to have all requests for this virtual host routed to the `marketr` WSGI script defined in the previous section.

The next two directives, WSGIDaemonProcess and WSGIProcessGroup, instruct mod_wsgi to route requests for this virtual host to an independent group of processes, distinct from the normal Apache child processes used to service requests. This is referred to as running mod_wsgi in daemon mode. By contrast, having mod_wsgi use the normal Apache child processes is referred to as running in embedded mode.

Generally running in daemon mode is preferable (see the mod_wsgi documentation for full details as to why), but this mode is not supported when running Apache on Windows. Thus, if you are using a Windows machine for your Apache server, you will need to omit these two directives from your configuration.

In the directives shown, the WSGIDaemonProcess directive defines a process group named marketr. This directive supports several additional arguments that can be used to control, for example, the number of processes in the group, the number of threads in each process, and the user and group for the processes. None of those arguments have been specified here so mod_wsgi will use its default values. The WSGIProcessGroup directive names the previously-defined marketr group as the one to use for handling requests for this virtual host.

The next directive, LogLevel debug, sets logging to its most verbose setting. A more typical setting for production would be warn, but when just getting started setting something up, it is frequently useful to have the code log as much information as possible, so we will use debug here.

The final two directives, ErrorLog and CustomLog, define error and access logs for this virtual host, distinct from the main Apache error and access logs. This can be convenient to isolate log information related to the new project from any other traffic Apache may be handling. In this case, we have directed Apache to place the logs in a logs directory under the /dj_projects/marketr/apache directory.

Activating the new Apache configuration

Where should the configuration directives from the previous section be placed? As noted earlier, the answer depends on the specifics of how Apache is configured on your machine. For an Apache configuration that consists of a single httpd.conf file, you may simply place the directives at the end of that file. Although that may also work for more structured configurations, it is better to avoid confusion and use the provided structure. Thus, this section will describe how to integrate the definitions previously listed into a Debian-based configuration, since that is the type of machine being used for the example project.

For a Debian-based Apache configuration, the `Listen` directive should be placed in `/etc/apache2/ports.conf`. The `VirtualHost` directive, and all it contains, should be placed in a file under `/etc/apache2/sites-available`. For this example, though, the virtual host configuration has been placed in a file `/dj_projects/marketr/apache/conf/marketr` so that the `/dj_projects` directory can contain complete configuration information for the project. We can make this file also appear in the `sites-available` directory by creating a symbolic link for it:

```
kmt@lbox:/etc/apache2/sites-available$ sudo ln -s /dj_projects/marketr/
apache/conf/marketr
```

Note that general users cannot create or modify files under `/etc/apache2/sites-available`, so the `sudo` command is needed to perform the requested command as a superuser. This is necessary for all commands that modify the Apache configuration or control its operation.

Once the file containing the virtual host configuration is in place in `sites-available`, the `a2ensite` command can be used to enable the new site:

```
kmt@lbox:/etc/apache2/sites-available$ sudo a2ensite marketr
Enabling site marketr.
Run '/etc/init.d/apache2 reload' to activate new configuration!
```

The `a2ensite` command creates a symbolic link in the `/etc/apache2/sites-enabled` directory to the specified file in the `sites-available` directory. There is a companion command, `a2dissite`, that disables a site by removing the symbolic link for it in `sites-enabled`. (Note that you can also manage the symbolic links manually and not use these commands, if you prefer.)

As noted by the output of `a2ensite`, it is necessary to reload Apache in order for the new site configuration to take effect. In this case, since a `Listen` directive was added, a full restart of Apache is required. That is done by running the `/etc/init.d/apache2` command and specifying `restart` as an argument. When we try that, the response is as follows:

The **[fail]** on the right-hand side of the screen does not look good. Something apparently went wrong during restart, but what? The answer is not found in the output of the command used to restart Apache, which only reports success or failure. Rather, the Apache error log contains details of the reason for the failure. Further, for a failure related to server start-up, it will likely be the main Apache error log that contains the detailed information, not a site-specific error log. On this machine, the main Apache error logfile is `/var/log/apache2/error.log`. Looking at the end of that file, we find the following:

```
(2)No such file or directory: apache2: could not open error log file /
dj_projects/marketr/apache/logs/error.log.
```

```
Unable to open logs
```

The problem is that the new virtual host configuration specified a directory for the error logfile that does not exist. Apache will not automatically create the specified directory, thus we need to create it manually. Doing that and again attempting to restart Apache produces a better result:

[OK] certainly looks better than **[fail]**; apparently this time Apache was able to start successfully. We've now gotten to the point where we have a valid Apache configuration, but there may still be some work to do to get a working configuration, as we will see next.

Debugging the new Apache configuration

The next test is to see whether Apache will successfully process a request directed to the new virtual host's port. To do that, let's try to retrieve the project root (home) page from a web browser. The result does not look good:

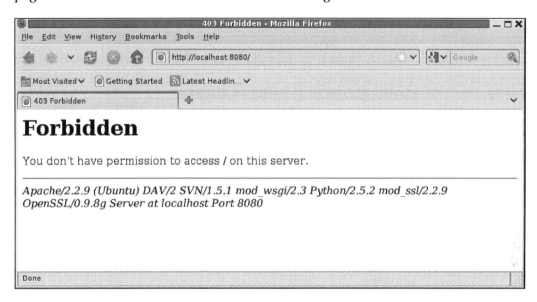

What might be wrong now? In this case, the main Apache error log is silent on the reason for the error. Rather, it is the error log configured for the `marketr` virtual site that provides an indication of the problem. Checking that file, we see that the full content of `/dj_projects/marketr/apache/logs/error.log` is now:

```
[Mon Dec 21 17:59:01 2009] [info] mod_wsgi (pid=18106): Attach
interpreter ''.

[Mon Dec 21 17:59:01 2009] [info] mod_wsgi (pid=18106): Enable monitor
thread in process 'marketr'.

[Mon Dec 21 17:59:01 2009] [debug] mod_wsgi.c(8301): mod_wsgi
(pid=18106): Deadlock timeout is 300.

[Mon Dec 21 17:59:01 2009] [debug] mod_wsgi.c(8304): mod_wsgi
(pid=18106): Inactivity timeout is 0.

[Mon Dec 21 17:59:01 2009] [info] mod_wsgi (pid=18106): Enable deadlock
thread in process 'marketr'.

[Mon Dec 21 17:59:01 2009] [debug] mod_wsgi.c(8449): mod_wsgi
(pid=18106): Starting 15 threads in daemon process 'marketr'.

[Mon Dec 21 17:59:01 2009] [debug] mod_wsgi.c(8455): mod_wsgi
(pid=18106): Starting thread 1 in daemon process 'marketr'.
```

```
[Mon Dec 21 17:59:01 2009] [debug] mod_wsgi.c(8455): mod_wsgi
(pid=18106): Starting thread 2 in daemon process 'marketr'.


[... identical messages for threads 3 through 13 deleted ...]


(pid=18106): Starting thread 14 in daemon process 'marketr'.
[Mon Dec 21 17:59:01 2009] [debug] mod_wsgi.c(8455): mod_wsgi
(pid=18106): Starting thread 15 in daemon process 'marketr'.
[Mon Dec 21 17:59:45 2009] [error] [client 127.0.0.1] client denied by
server configuration: /dj_projects/marketr/apache/wsgi/marketr.wsgi
```

Except for the last one, none of these messages indicate a problem. Rather they are informational and debug level messages logged by mod_wsgi, as requested by the setting of LogLevel debug in the virtual host configuration. These messages show mod_wsgi reporting on various values (deadlock timeout, inactivity timeout) it is using, and show that mod_wsgi started 15 threads in the daemon process marketr. All looks good until the last line, which is an error level message.

The specifics of this last message are not much more helpful than the bare **Forbidden** displayed by the web browser. The message does indicate that the marketr.wsgi script is involved, and that the request is **denied by server configuration**. In this case, the problem is not that the file does not exist, but rather that the server has been configured to not allow access to it.

The cause of this specific problem lies elsewhere in the Apache configuration on this machine, and this is a problem you may or may not encounter depending on your overall Apache configuration. The problem is that this machine's Apache configuration has been set up to deny access to files in all directories except those that are explicitly enabled for access. This type of configuration is good from a security standpoint, but it does make configuration a bit more tedious. In this case, what is needed is a Directory block that allows access to files in the directory containing the marketr.wsgi script:

```
<Directory /dj_projects/marketr/apache/wsgi>
    Order allow,deny
    Allow from all
</Directory>
```

The details of Apache's three-pass access control system is beyond the scope of this book; if you are interested, the Apache documentation describes the process in detail. For our purposes, it is sufficient to note that this Directory block allows all clients to access files in /dj_projets/marketr/apache/wsgi, which should be acceptable and enough to get past the **Forbidden** initially returned by the browser for the marketr project's home page.

The `Directory` block should be placed inside the `VirtualHost` block for the `marketr` project. Changing the configuration requires an Apache restart, after which we can try again to access the project home page. This time we see the following:

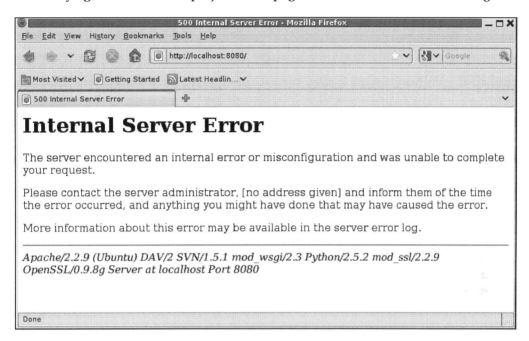

The good news is we got past the **Forbidden** error. The bad news is we did not get much farther. Again the page returned to the browser is of little use in debugging the problem, rather the site's error log is where details of the problem are recorded. This time at the end of the file we find:

```
[Mon Dec 21 18:05:43 2009] [debug] mod_wsgi.c(8455): mod_wsgi
(pid=18441): Starting thread 15 in daemon process 'marketr'.

[Mon Dec 21 18:05:49 2009] [info] mod_wsgi (pid=18441): Create
interpreter 'localhost.localdomain:8080|'.

[Mon Dec 21 18:05:49 2009] [info] [client 127.0.0.1] mod_wsgi (pid=18441,
process='marketr', application='localhost.localdomain:8080|'): Loading
WSGI script '/dj_projects/marketr/apache/wsgi/marketr.wsgi'.

[Mon Dec 21 18:05:49 2009] [error] [client 127.0.0.1] mod_wsgi
(pid=18441): Exception occurred processing WSGI script '/dj_projects/
marketr/apache/wsgi/marketr.wsgi'.

[Mon Dec 21 18:05:49 2009] [error] [client 127.0.0.1] Traceback (most
recent call last):
```

```
[Mon Dec 21 18:05:49 2009] [error] [client 127.0.0.1]    File "/usr/lib/
python2.5/site-packages/django/core/handlers/wsgi.py", line 230, in __
call__

[Mon Dec 21 18:05:49 2009] [error] [client 127.0.0.1]      self.load_
middleware()

[Mon Dec 21 18:05:49 2009] [error] [client 127.0.0.1]    File "/usr/lib/
python2.5/site-packages/django/core/handlers/base.py", line 33, in load_
middleware

[Mon Dec 21 18:05:49 2009] [error] [client 127.0.0.1]      for middleware_
path in settings.MIDDLEWARE_CLASSES:

[Mon Dec 21 18:05:49 2009] [error] [client 127.0.0.1]    File "/usr/lib/
python2.5/site-packages/django/utils/functional.py", line 269, in __
getattr__

[Mon Dec 21 18:05:49 2009] [error] [client 127.0.0.1]      self._setup()

[Mon Dec 21 18:05:49 2009] [error] [client 127.0.0.1]    File "/usr/lib/
python2.5/site-packages/django/conf/__init__.py", line 40, in _setup

[Mon Dec 21 18:05:49 2009] [error] [client 127.0.0.1]      self._wrapped =
Settings(settings_module)

[Mon Dec 21 18:05:49 2009] [error] [client 127.0.0.1]    File "/usr/lib/
python2.5/site-packages/django/conf/__init__.py", line 75, in __init__

[Mon Dec 21 18:05:49 2009] [error] [client 127.0.0.1]      raise
ImportError, "Could not import settings '%s' (Is it on sys.path? Does it
have syntax errors?): %s" % (self.SETTINGS_MODULE, e)

[Mon Dec 21 18:05:49 2009] [error] [client 127.0.0.1] ImportError: Could
not import settings 'marketr.settings' (Is it on sys.path? Does it have
syntax errors?): No module named marketr.settings
```

Clearly, the `marketr.wsgi` script did get used this time, since the traceback shows that Django code has been called. But the environment was not set up entirely correctly, since Django is unable to import the specified `marketr.settings` settings module. This is a commonly-encountered error that is almost always due to one of two things: either the Python path has not been set properly, or the user that the Apache process runs as does not have read access to the settings file (and the directory that contains it).

In this case, a quick check of the permissions on the `/dj_projects/marketr` directory and its files show that they are readable by all:

```
kmt@1box:/dj_projects/marketr$ ls -la
total 56
drwxr-xr-x 7 kmt kmt 4096 2009-12-21 18:42 .
drwxr-Sr-x 3 kmt kmt 4096 2009-12-20 09:46 ..
drwxr-xr-x 5 kmt kmt 4096 2009-12-21 17:58 apache
```

```
drwxr-xr-x 2 kmt kmt 4096 2009-11-22 11:40 coverage_html
drwxr-xr-x 4 kmt kmt 4096 2009-12-20 09:50 gen_utils
-rw-r--r-- 1 kmt kmt    0 2009-11-22 11:40 __init__.py
-rw-r--r-- 1 kmt kmt  130 2009-12-20 09:49 __init__.pyc
-rwxr-xr-x 1 kmt kmt  546 2009-11-22 11:40 manage.py
-rwxr--r-- 1 kmt kmt 5800 2009-12-20 09:50 settings.py
-rw-r--r-- 1 kmt kmt 2675 2009-12-20 09:50 settings.pyc
drwxr-xr-x 3 kmt kmt 4096 2009-12-20 09:50 site_media
drwxr-xr-x 5 kmt kmt 4096 2009-12-20 19:42 survey
-rwxr--r-- 1 kmt kmt  734 2009-11-22 11:40 urls.py
-rw-r--r-- 1 kmt kmt  619 2009-12-20 09:50 urls.pyc
```

Thus, it does not seem likely the problem is related to the ability of the web server process to access the settings.py file. Note, however, if you are running a version of Linux that uses the security-enhanced kernel (SELinux kernel), the permissions information displayed by ls -l may be misleading. This kernel has a complex file access control structure that requires additional configuration (beyond the scope of this book) in order to allow the web server process to access files outside of its own designated area.

In this case, though, the machine is not running the SELinux kernel and the permissions information shows that any process can read the settings.py file. The problem, then, is likely in the path setting. Recall that the path and settings specification in the marketr.wsgi script is:

```
sys.path = ['/dj_projects/marketr', ] + sys.path
os.environ['DJANGO_SETTINGS_MODULE'] = 'marketr.settings'
```

That path does not work to import a settings file specified as marketr.settings because the marketr part has been duplicated in both the path and the module specification. Python, in trying to find the module and using the first element on the path, will attempt to find a file named /dj_projects/marketr/marketr/settings.py. This will fail since the actual file is /dj_projects/marketr/settings.py. Unless /dj_projects alone is on sys.path, Python will not be able to load marketr.settings.

One fix, then, is to include /dj_projects in the path setting:

```
sys.path = ['/dj_projects/marketr', '/dj_projects', ] + sys.path
```

It seems a bit odd, though, to need to add two different items to the path for a single project. Are both really necessary? The first is necessary because throughout the survey application code, for example, we used imports of the form:

```
from survey.models import Survey
from survey.forms import QuestionVoteForm
```

Since `marketr` is not included in those imports, it must be included in an element of the Python path. When running the development server, the `/dj_projects/` `marketr` directory is the current path, which is automatically included in the Python path, so these imports work. When running under Apache, `/dj_projects/marketr` must be included on the path for these imports to work.

Alternatively, we could change all the imports in both the `survey` and `gen_utils` applications to use the form:

```
from marketr.survey.models import Survey
from marketr.survey.forms import QuestionVoteForm
```

This approach, however, ties these applications tightly to the `marketr` project, making it harder to re-use them outside of that one project. I feel it is better practice to make applications independent and not include in their imports the name of the containing project.

What about `/dj_projects`—does that really need to be included in the path? Could we eliminate needing to have it in the path by specifying the settings module as simply `settings` instead of `marketr.settings`? Yes, that would get us past this particular error, but we would quickly hit another similar error when the `ROOT_URLCONF` value in the settings file was processed. `ROOT_URLCONF` also includes `marketr` in its specification:

```
ROOT_URLCONF = 'marketr.urls'
```

We could change that as well, and hope it is the last one, but it is probably easier to just include `/dj_projects` in the path when running under the web server.

You might wonder how `/dj_projects` was included in the path when running under the development server, since the parent of the current directory is not generally included in the Python path the way the current directory is. The answer is that the setup code for the development server places the parent of the project directory in the Python path. This can be helpful to people new to Python when starting out, but often causes confusion in the long run, since it is somewhat surprising behavior to anyone who is not new to Python.

To proceed from this point, however, we will just include /dj_projects as well as /dj_projects/marketr in the Python path, as previously shown. Note that when running mod_wsgi in daemon mode, it is not necessary to reload or restart Apache to get it to pick up changes to the WSGI script. Changing the WSGI script itself is sufficient to cause mod_wsgi to automatically restart its daemon processes. Thus, all we need to do is save the modified file and again try to access the project home page. This time we see the following:

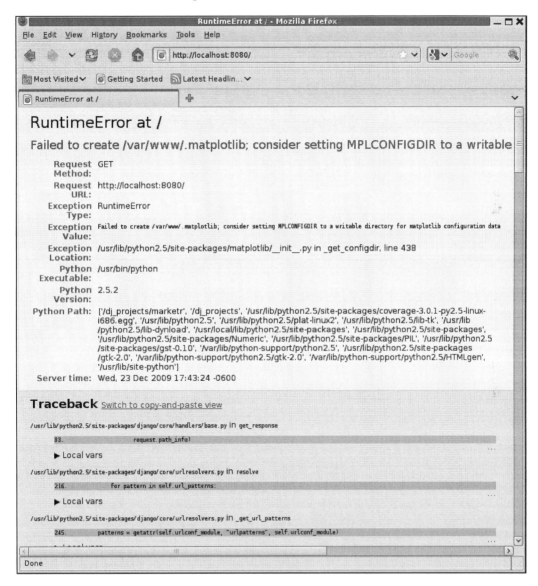

Again, we have good news and bad news. We certainly got further, and the Django code is working well enough to return a debug page, which is encouraging and easier to deal with than having to go search in the Apache error logs for the problem. Unfortunately, the fact that we got a debug page and not the project home page means there is still more that is not quite right in the environment when running under the web server.

This time the exception information indicates that the `matplotlib` code needs write access to a directory for its configuration data. It apparently tried to create a directory named `/var/www/.matplotlib`, and that failed. The message suggests that if an environment variable named `MPLCONFIGDIR` is set to point to a writable directory, we may get past this problem. We can certainly set this environment variable in the `marketr.wsgi` script, just as the `DJANGO_SETTINGS_MODULE` environment variable is set:

```
os.environ['DJANGO_SETTINGS_MODULE'] = 'marketr.settings'
os.environ['MPLCONFIGDIR'] = '/dj_projects/marketr/apache/.matplotlib'
```

We also need to create the directory specified there and make it writeable by the web server process. The easiest way to do this is to simply change the owner of the directory to the user the web server process runs as, which on this machine is `www-data`:

```
kmt@lbox:/dj_projects/marketr/apache$ mkdir .matplotlib
kmt@lbox:/dj_projects/marketr/apache$ sudo chown www-data .matplotlib/
```

Alternatively, the `WSGIDaemonProcess` directive in the virtual host configuration could be changed to specify a different user. But the only user that would have write access, by default, to directories under `/dj_projects` would be my own user, `kmt`, and I would prefer not to have a web server process running with write access to all of my own files. Thus, it is easier to simply let the web server continue to run as `www-data` and explicitly give it permission to access directories as necessary. Note that if you are using SQLite as your database, you will also need to set permissions on the database file so that the Apache process can read and write it.

Have we got past the last problem yet? Saving the changed `marketr.wsgi` file and retrying the project home page brings up the following:

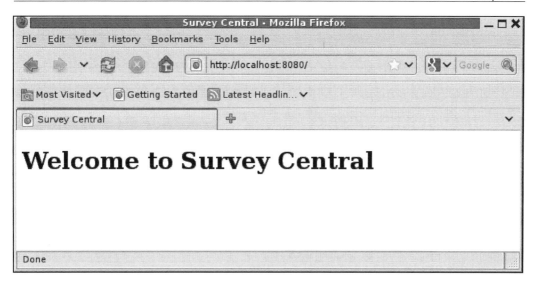

Success at last, of a sort. There are no surveys displayed on the home page because enough time has passed that the one closed `survey` we had been working with has now been closed for too long to be listed. Thus, there is not much of interest to see on the home page. The next natural step in testing is to go to the admin application and change the `closes` date on the survey so that it will appear on the home page. Attempting to do this reveals some configuration we have not yet set up, which will be discussed next.

Configuring Apache to serve static files

Attempting to access the admin application running under Apache, we get:

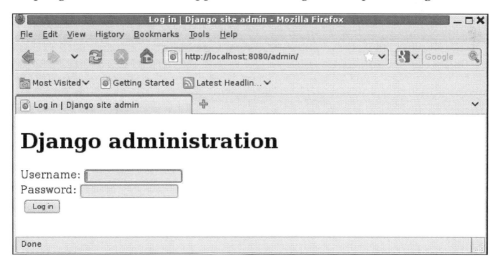

That looks a lot like our sample project pages, bare of any custom styling. But the admin application, unlike our sample project, does have stylesheets it uses, which were correctly loaded when running under the development server. That was done by special-purpose code in the development server. When running under Apache, we need to configure it (or some other web server) to serve the admin application's static files.

How do we do that? All of the admin's static files will be referenced using the same prefix, specified by ADMIN_MEDIA_PREFIX in settings.py. The default value for this setting is /media/. Thus, we need to instruct Apache to serve files with this prefix directly from the admin's media directory tree, instead of routing the request to mod_wsgi and our Django project code.

The Apache directives to accomplish this are (note that though the Alias and Directory lines below are split due to page width constraints, these need to be placed on single lines in the Apache configuration file):

```
Alias /media /usr/lib/python2.5/site-packages/django/contrib/admin/
media/
<Directory /usr/lib/python2.5/site-packages/django/contrib/admin/
media>
    Order allow,deny
    Allow from all
</Directory>
```

The first directive, Alias, sets up a mapping from URL paths that start with /media to the actual files which are located (on this machine) under /usr/lib/python2.5/site-packages/django/contrib/admin/media/. The following Directory block instructs Apache to allow all clients to access files in the directory where the admin media is located. Like the Directory block for the marketr.wsgi script, this is only needed if your Apache configuration has been set up to deny access to all directories by default.

These directives should be placed in the VirtualHost block for the marketr project virtual host. Apache then needs to be reloaded to recognize the configuration changes. Reloading the admin page in the browser then brings up a page with the correct custom styling:

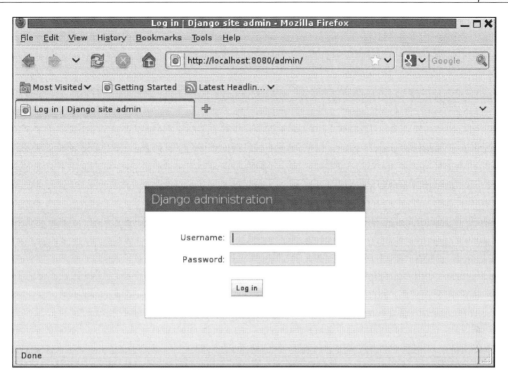

Note, though, it is not only admin that has static files. In *Chapter 9, When You Don't Even Know What to Log: Using Debuggers*, we added some use of static files into the marketr project. Specifically, the image files generated by matplotlib to show survey results are served as static files. These files, unlike the admin media files, were not automatically served by the development server, so we had to add an entry for them in the marketr project urls.py file, specifying that they be served by the Django static server view:

```
(r'^site_media/(.*)$', 'django.views.static.serve',
    {'document_root': settings.MEDIA_ROOT, 'show_indexes': True}),
```

This configuration would still work to serve the files under Apache, but the static server is not recommended for use in production. Besides being a very inefficient way to serve static files, the static server code has not been audited for security. Thus, for production, this URL pattern should be removed from the urls.py file and Apache (or another server) should be configured to serve these files directly.

The directives to get Apache to serve these files are:

```
Alias /site_media /dj_projects/marketr/site_media
<Directory /dj_projects/marketr/site_media>
    Order allow,deny
    Allow from all
</Directory>
```

These are nearly identical to the directives needed for the admin media files, only modified to specify the URL path prefix used for the site media files, and the actual location of those files.

Is that all? Not quite. Unlike the admin media files, the image files used by the marketr project are actually generated on-demand by the marketr project code. If we delete the existing image files and attempt to access the detail page for the completed survey, we will get an error when the web server process attempts to create one of the image files, as the following shows:

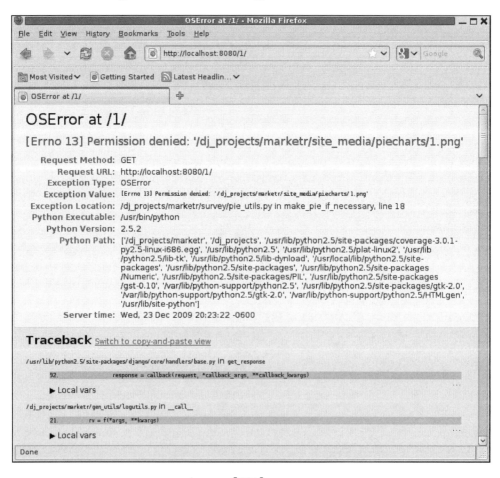

To fix this, the web server code will need write access to the directory containing the files. This can be done by changing the owner of the directory `/dj_projects/marketr/site_media /piecharts` to `www-data`, as was done for the matplotlib configuration directory. After we make that change, attempting to reload the survey detail page shows that the web server is now able to create the image files, as the following shows:

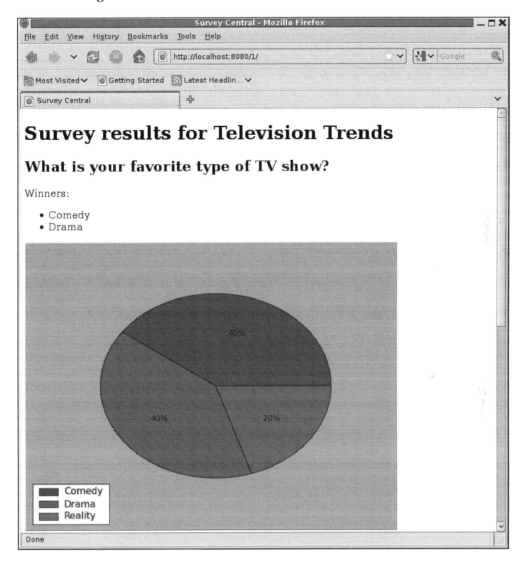

We have now got the project up and running under Apache. Next, we will consider whether there are any additional potential problems we might run into as a result of differences between the development and production web server environments.

Testing multithreaded behavior

In the previous section, we encountered a few environmental differences between running under the development server and running under Apache. Some of these (for example, file permissions and Python path differences) caused problems that had to be overcome before we could get the project functioning properly under Apache. One difference we observed, but have not yet encountered a problem with, is multithreading.

When we checked the error log in the previous section we could see that mod_wsgi had started one process with 15 threads, each ready to handle an incoming request. Multiple requests that arrive at the server nearly simultaneously, then, will be dispatched to different threads for handling, and the steps of their execution may be arbitrarily interleaved in real time. This can never happen with the development server, which is strictly single threaded, ensuring each request is fully processed before processing of the next one is started. It also never happens with any of the test tools covered in the first five chapters, since they too all test in a single-threaded manner.

In Chapter 9 we already noted the need to keep in mind potential multithreading issues. In that chapter, we wrote the code to generate the image files for the display of survey results. The images are generated on-demand when the first request to display the survey is received after the survey has closed. Generating the image and writing it to disk took a perceptible amount of time, and it was fairly obvious that the code needed to properly handle the case where a second request was received for the survey results, but the processing of the first request had not yet completed.

In that chapter, we learned how we could use breakpoints in the debugger to force multiple threads to execute in a particular sequence. In this way, we saw how we could test to ensure that the code behaved properly in whatever worst-case interleaved execution scenarios might arise in a multithreaded environment.

But it is not only operations that take a significant amount of time, such as generating images or writing files, that we need to be concerned with. Under a heavy request load in a multithreaded environment, even the processing of requests that are generally quite quick may get interrupted and interleaved with processing from other requests being handled at the same time. On a multiprocessor machine, it's not even necessary for one request to be interrupted: a second request could be running on a second processor truly simultaneously.

Is there any code in the `marketr` project that might not function properly in a multithreaded environment? Possibly. Generally, the first code to consider for potential multithreading problems is any code that updates data. For the `survey` application, there is one view that updates data on the server: the one that receives and records posted survey results.

Are we sure the survey results recording code will function properly when it is run in a multithreaded environment where many copies of it may be running simultaneously? Since we have not tested it, no, we can't be sure. But now that we have the code running in a multithreaded environment, we can try testing it and see the outcome.

Generating load with siege

Having the code available for testing in a multithreaded environment is only half of what is needed to effectively test multithreaded behavior. The other half is some way of generating many simultaneous requests for the server to process. There are a number of different tools that can be used for this. The one we will use here is called `siege`, a freely available command line tool written by Jeffrey Fulmer. Information on downloading and installing `siege` can be found at `http://www.joedog.org/index/siege-home`.

Once installed, `siege` is very easy to use. The simplest way to call it is to pass a URL on the command line. It will start up several threads and continuously request the passed URL. As it runs, it displays what it is doing and key information about the responses it is receiving. For example:

```
kmt@lbox:/dj_projects/marketr$ siege http://localhost:8080/
** SIEGE 2.66
** Preparing 15 concurrent users for battle.
The server is now under siege...
HTTP/1.1 200     0.06 secs:      986 bytes ==> /
HTTP/1.1 200     0.04 secs:      986 bytes ==> /
HTTP/1.1 200     0.04 secs:      986 bytes ==> /
HTTP/1.1 200     0.02 secs:      986 bytes ==> /
HTTP/1.1 200     0.03 secs:      986 bytes ==> /
HTTP/1.1 200     0.03 secs:      986 bytes ==> /
HTTP/1.1 200     0.03 secs:      986 bytes ==> /
HTTP/1.1 200     0.03 secs:      986 bytes ==> /
HTTP/1.1 200     0.04 secs:      986 bytes ==> /
```

Here we see `siege` called to continuously request the project home page. During startup, it reports its version and prints out how many threads it will be using to make simultaneous requests. The default, as seen here, is 15; the `-c` (for concurrent) command line switch could be used to change that. `Siege` then prints out information about each request it sends. For each, it prints the protocol used (here all `HTTP/1.1`), the response code received (`200`), how long it took for the response to arrive (between `.02` and `.06` seconds), how many bytes in the response (`986`), and finally the URL path for the request.

By default `siege` will keep running until interrupted by *Ctrl-C*. When interrupted, it will stop generating load and report statistics on the results. For example:

```
HTTP/1.1 200     0.11 secs:      986 bytes ==> /
HTTP/1.1 200     0.47 secs:      986 bytes ==> /
^C

Lifting the server siege...       done.
Transactions:                     719 hits
Availability:                  100.00 %
Elapsed time:                   35.02 secs
Data transferred:                0.68 MB
Response time:                   0.21 secs
Transaction rate:               20.53 trans/sec
Throughput:                      0.02 MB/sec
Concurrency:                     4.24
Successful transactions:         719
Failed transactions:               0
Longest transaction:             0.79
Shortest transaction:            0.02
```

The tool made slightly over 700 requests and all received responses, as indicated by the report of 100 percent availability and 0 failed transactions. The performance numbers reported are interesting, but since we are presently running on a development machine with debug still turned on, it is a little early to be reading much into performance numbers. What we really want to check is whether the code that processes survey responses behaves correctly when called in a multithreaded environment under heavy load. We will consider how to do that next.

Load testing the results recording code

How can we use `siege` to test the code that records survey answers? First, we need a survey in the database that is still open and thus will accept posted responses. The easiest way to do this is to use the admin application and change the `closes` date on the existing **Television Trends** survey to be some time in the future. At the same time, we can change the answer counts for all of the answers in the survey to be 0, which will make it easy to tell if all of the responses we generate with `siege` are processed correctly.

Next we need to determine what URL to specify to `siege` to get it to POST valid data for the survey's form. The easiest way to do this is to bring up the page that displays the survey form in a browser and check the HTML source to see what the form fields are named and what the valid values for each are. In this case, the source HTML for the form displayed when we retrieve `http://localhost:8080/1/` is:

```
<form method="post" action=".">

<div>


    What is your favorite type of TV show?


    <ul>
<li><label for="id_answer_0"><input type="radio" id="id_answer_0"
value="1" name="answer" /> Comedy</label></li>

<li><label for="id_answer_1"><input type="radio" id="id_answer_1"
value="2" name="answer" /> Drama</label></li>

<li><label for="id_answer_2"><input type="radio" id="id_answer_2"
value="3" name="answer" /> Reality</label></li>

</ul>


    How many new shows will you try this Fall?


    <ul>
<li><label for="id_1-answer_0"><input type="radio" id="id_1-answer_0"
value="4" name="1-answer" /> Hardly any: I already watch too much TV!</
label></li>

<li><label for="id_1-answer_1"><input type="radio" id="id_1-answer_1"
value="5" name="1-answer" /> Maybe 3-5</label></li>
```

```
<li><label for="id_1-answer_2"><input type="radio" id="id_1-answer_2"
value="6" name="1-answer" /> I&#39;m a TV fiend, I&#39;ll try them all at
least once!</label></li>

</ul>


<button type="submit">Submit</button>

</div>

</form>
```

The form has two radio group inputs, one named `answer` and one named `1-answer`. Valid choices for `answer` are 1, 2, and 3. Valid choices for `1-answer` are 4, 5, and 6. Thus, we want to instruct `siege` to POST to `http://localhost:8080/1/` a value between 1 and 3 for `answer` and between 4 and 6 for `1-answer`. The way to do this, arbitrarily choosing the first choice for both questions, is to specify the URL as `"http://localhost:8080/1/ POST answer=1&1-answer=4"`. Note that the quotes around this URL are needed when passing it as a parameter on the command line due to the spaces and `&` in it.

In order to get a predictable number of requests generated, we can specify the `-r` command line switch, specifying the number of test repetitions. If we leave the default number of concurrent threads at 15 and specify 5 repetitions, at the end of the test we should see that the two chosen answers each have 5*15, or 75 votes. Let's try it:

```
kmt@lbox:/dj_projects/marketr$ siege -r 5 "http://localhost:8080/1/ POST
answer=1&1-answer=4"
** SIEGE 2.66
** Preparing 15 concurrent users for battle.
The server is now under siege...
HTTP/1.1 302     0.12 secs:          0 bytes ==> /1/
HTTP/1.1 302     0.19 secs:          0 bytes ==> /1/
HTTP/1.1 200     0.02 secs:        543 bytes ==> /thanks/1/
HTTP/1.1 302     0.15 secs:          0 bytes ==> /1/
HTTP/1.1 302     0.19 secs:          0 bytes ==> /1/
HTTP/1.1 302     0.37 secs:          0 bytes ==> /1/
HTTP/1.1 200     0.02 secs:        543 bytes ==> /thanks/1/
HTTP/1.1 302     0.30 secs:          0 bytes ==> /1/
```

Here the output is a bit different from the first example. The `survey` application response to a successful POST of a survey response is an HTTP redirect (status 302). The `siege` tool, like a browser, responds to the received redirect by requesting the location specified in the redirect response. The previous output, then, is showing that the POST requests are succeeding, and then the subsequent redirects to the thanks page for the survey are also succeeding.

The tail end of the output for this test run is:

```
HTTP/1.1 302    0.03 secs:         0 bytes ==> /1/
HTTP/1.1 200    0.02 secs:       543 bytes ==> /thanks/1/
HTTP/1.1 200    0.01 secs:       543 bytes ==> /thanks/1/
done.
Transactions:                    150 hits
Availability:                 100.00 %
Elapsed time:                   9.04 secs
Data transferred:               0.04 MB
Response time:                  0.11 secs
Transaction rate:              16.59 trans/sec
Throughput:                     0.00 MB/sec
Concurrency:                    1.85
Successful transactions:         150
Failed transactions:               0
Longest transaction:            0.56
Shortest transaction:           0.01
```

That looks good. The total number of transactions is twice the number of posts requested, indicating that all of the POST requests returned a redirect, so they were all successfully processed. From the client side, then, it appears that the test ran successfully.

But do the vote counts on the server match up to what we expect? Answers 1 (**Comedy**) and 4 (**Hardly any: I already watch too much TV!**) were each posted 75 times, so we expect that they each have 75 votes while all of the other answers have none. Checking the vote count for the first question in the admin application, we see the following:

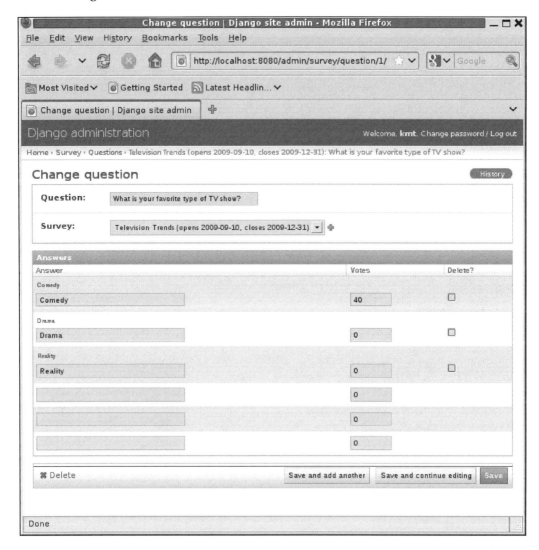

Similarly, checking the second question we see the following:

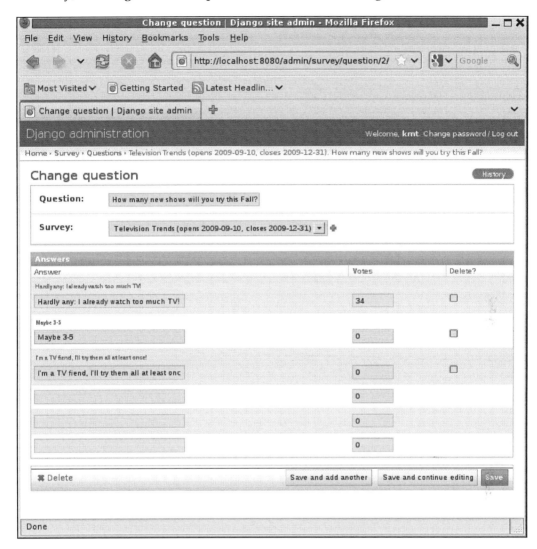

That's not good. While the `votes` values that were supposed to be 0 are all indeed **0**, the two `votes` values that were supposed to be 75 are instead **40** and **34**. Based on the results sent to the client, the server appeared to process all of the requests successfully. Yet clearly many of the votes were not actually recorded. How did that happen? The answer lies in the code that attempts to record posted survey responses, which we will check next.

Fixing the results recording code

Recall that the code which records posted survey answers is in the display_active_survey function in survey/views.py. This code processes both GET and POST requests. In the case of a POST, the code to validate and record the submitted values is:

```
if request.method == 'POST':
    chosen_answers = []
    for qf in qforms:
        if not qf.is_valid():
            logging.debug("form failed validation: %r", qf.errors)
            break;
        chosen_answers.append(qf.cleaned_data['answer'])
    else:
        for answer in chosen_answers:
            answer.votes += 1
            answer.save(force_update=True)
        return HttpResponseRedirect(reverse('survey_thanks',
                                            args=(survey.pk,)))
```

This code runs fine and behaves properly when a single thread runs through it at a time. However, if multiple threads (from the same or different processes) are running through it simultaneously, all trying to increment votes value for the same answers, this code is likely to lose votes. The problem is that retrieving the current votes value, incrementing it, and saving the new value is not atomic. Rather it is done in three distinct steps that may be interleaved with the same steps done by another thread simultaneously.

Consider two threads running concurrently, both attempting to record a vote for the Answer with primary key value 1. (For simplicity, we will assume there is only one question in the survey.) The first thread enters this code and runs through the for qf in qforms loop validating the forms. It is during this loop that the current votes value for the chosen answer will be read from the database. Let's say the value that the first thread reads for the votes value for answer with primary key 1 is 5.

Now, before this first thread is able to finish its work and save an incremented value of 6 for the votes field to the database, a second thread (either through pre-emptive scheduling or multiprocessor execution) enters the for qf in qforms loop. The posted form data this second thread is working with also specifies a vote for the answer with primary key 1. This second thread also reads a current value of 5 for the votes value for this answer. Now we have a problem: two threads, both intending to increment the votes value for the same answer, both read the same existing value, and both will increment that value and save the result. Together the two threads will only cause the votes count to be incremented by one: one of the votes will effectively be lost.

How do we fix this problem? For this simple case of incrementing (or performing some other arithmetic operation on) an existing field's value in the database, it is reasonably easy to avoid the problem. We can slightly change the code in the `for answer in chosen_answers` loop to use a Django `F` expression to describe the desired result for `votes` instead of giving it an explicit numerical value. The changed code looks like this:

```
for answer in chosen_answers:
        from django.db.models import F
        answer.votes = F('votes') + 1
        answer.save(force_update=True)
```

Use of an `F` expression in the value for `votes` will cause Django to construct an UPDATE SQL statement of the form:

```
UPDATE `survey_answer` SET `answer` = Comedy, `question_id` = 1, `votes`
= `survey_answer`.`votes` + 1 WHERE `survey_answer`.`id` = 1
```

This type of UPDATE statement pushes the responsibility of ensuring that the increment operation is atomic onto the database server. That is generally where you want to place such responsibility, since that is exactly what database servers are supposed to do both correctly and efficiently.

If we now save this change to the code, reset all the vote counts to 0, and re-run the `siege` test, the problem will hopefully be gone. Only it is not! Checking the `votes` values again after running the test shows the same behavior: for the two answers that should have values of 75, one value is 43 and the other 39. Why didn't the code change fix the problem?

The problem in this case is that the code change was not seen by the running web server process. When running under Apache with `mod_wsgi`, changes to the Django application code will not automatically cause a reload of the processes that handle requests. Thus, the existing running processes will continue to use the old code. When running in daemon mode, touching the WSGI script will trigger a reload on receipt of the next request. Alternatively, restarting Apache will ensure the new code is loaded. As we will see later in the chapter, it is also possible to code the WSGI script to automatically restart the daemon process when a code change is detected.

For now, since the existing WSGI script does not monitor for source code changes, and since we are running in daemon mode, touching the WSGI script is the easiest way to get the application code change loaded. If we do that, again use the admin application to reset the vote counts to 0, and again try the `siege` test, we see that when the test finishes the votes for the two chosen answers are indeed the correct value, 75.

Additional load testing notes

While we have successfully found and fixed a multithreading problem with the code that receives and records survey results, we have not done enough testing to ensure that the remainder of the application will behave properly in a typical production environment. A full test would involve load testing all views, both in isolation and in combination with each other, and ensures that the server responds correctly. Constructing such a test is beyond the scope of this book, but some notes about the process are included here.

First, for the problem we did find we were fortunate that a very simple code change, namely use of an F expression, was available to easily make the database update atomic. For other situations, Django may or may not provide a simple API to help ensure atomicity of updates. For creating objects, for example, Django does have an atomic get_or_create function. For more complicated situations, such as ones involving updating several values in different objects, there may not be a simple Django API to use to ensure atomicity.

In these cases, it will be necessary to use database support for maintaining data consistency. Some databases provide transactions to help with this, and Django in turn provides an API that allows an application to control transactional behavior. Other databases don't support transactions but do provide lower-level support, such as the ability to lock tables. Django does not provide an API for table locking, but it does allow applications to construct and execute arbitrary (raw) SQL, so an application can still use such functions. The disadvantage of using the raw SQL API is that the application will generally not be portable to a different database.

When setting out to create a new application, then, careful consideration should be given to the kinds of database updates the application will need to perform. If possible, it is best to structure the data so that simple atomic APIs can be used for all updates. If that is not possible, then use of database transactions or lower-level locking support may be required. The range of options available may be restricted by the database in use (if it is predetermined), and likewise the choice of specific technique used for ensuring data consistency may limit the databases on which the application will ultimately be able to run correctly.

Second, while careful consideration and coding will help to ensure no multithreading surprises like the one bug we uncovered, explicit testing for problems like this is a good idea. Unfortunately, it is not something supported by the testing tools covered in the first five chapters, which all focus on verifying correct single-threaded behavior. Thus, some additional work will generally be required to augment the unit testing suite with additional tests that ensure correct behavior (and possibly some minimum level of performance) in a production environment under load. It may not be practical to expect individual developers to routinely run these additional tests, but having them available, and running them before placing any code updates into production, will save headaches in the long run.

Using Apache/mod_wsgi during development

As described throughout this chapter, the switch from using the Django development server to a production server such as Apache with mod_wsgi may run into various snags along the way. Some are easily overcome, others may require more effort. It is often inconvenient to encounter such difficulties late in the development cycle, when there is typically very little time available for making code changes. One way to make the transition smoother is to use a production server configuration during development. This is an idea worth some serious consideration.

One possible objection to using a production server (namely Apache with mod_wsgi) during development is that installing and properly configuring Apache is difficult. Asking individual developers to do this is asking too much of them. Installation, however, is not generally difficult—and most development machines today are easily capable of running Apache without causing any performance impact for other activities.

Configuring Apache can indeed be daunting, since there are many configuration directives and optional modules to consider. However, it is not necessary to become an expert in Apache configuration in order to successfully take a shipped default configuration and modify it to support running a Django application. The result may not be finely tuned for great performance under heavy load, but such tuning is not required for use of the configuration during development testing.

A second objection to using Apache during development may be that it is relatively inconvenient, compared to the development server. The console of the development server provides an easy way to check on what is going on; needing to consult the Apache log files is a bit of a nuisance in comparison. This is true but a very minor inconvenience.

A more serious inconvenience is the need to be sure the running web server processes are restarted in order to pick up code changes during development. It is very easy to get used to the development server's automatic restart, and forget the need to do something (even if it is as simple as touching the WSGI script file) to ensure that the web server is using the latest code.

However, it is in fact possible to set up the WSGI script for a Django project to behave in the same way as the development server. That is, the WSGI script can start up a code monitoring thread that checks for changed Python source files and triggers an automatic reload when necessary. Details of this can be found at `http://code.google.com/p/modwsgi/wiki/ReloadingSourceCode`. Using the code included on that page, an Apache with `mod_wsgi` configuration can be almost as convenient for development as the Django development server.

One remaining convenience of the development server that has not yet been covered is the ability to easily put breakpoints in code and drop into the Python debugger. Even this is possible when running under Apache, but for this Apache does need to be started in a special mode from a console session, so that it has a console to allow the debugger to interact with the user. Details of doing this can be found at `http://code.google.com/p/modwsgi/wiki/DebuggingTechniques`.

In summary, it is quite possible to get nearly all the convenience of the Django development server from an Apache/`mod_wsgi` setup. Using such a configuration during development can help to ease the eventual transition to production, and can be well worth the additional early effort of installing and configuring Apache with `mod_wsgi` on a development machine.

Summary

We have now reached the end of discussing the move to production for a Django application. In this chapter, we:

- Developed a configuration to support running the `marketr` project under Apache with `mod_wsgi`.

- Encountered a number of problems getting the project running under Apache. For each, we saw how to diagnose and fix the issue.

- Considered what additional testing could be done in the new environment, given its ability to run multiple threads concurrently.

- Developed a test for the code that records posted survey responses, and observed that the code did not operate correctly under heavy load in the production environment.

- Fixed the problem found in the results recording code, and discussed other techniques that may be needed to fix more complex multithreading problems.

- Discussed the possibility of using Apache and `mod_wsgi` during development. This configuration can be made nearly as convenient for development as the Django development server, and use of the production setup during development can help reduce the number of problems encountered during the eventual move to production.

Index

**Thank you for buying
Django 1.1 Testing and
Debugging**

Packt Open Source Project Royalties

When we sell a book written on an Open Source project, we pay a royalty directly to that project. Therefore by purchasing Django 1.1 Testing and Debugging, Packt will have given some of the money received to the Django project.

In the long term, we see ourselves and you—customers and readers of our books—as part of the Open Source ecosystem, providing sustainable revenue for the projects we publish on. Our aim at Packt is to establish publishing royalties as an essential part of the service and support a business model that sustains Open Source.

If you're working with an Open Source project that you would like us to publish on, and subsequently pay royalties to, please get in touch with us.

Writing for Packt

We welcome all inquiries from people who are interested in authoring. Book proposals should be sent to author@packtpub.com. If your book idea is still at an early stage and you would like to discuss it first before writing a formal book proposal, contact us; one of our commissioning editors will get in touch with you.

We're not just looking for published authors; if you have strong technical skills but no writing experience, our experienced editors can help you develop a writing career, or simply get some additional reward for your expertise.

About Packt Publishing

Packt, pronounced 'packed', published its first book "Mastering phpMyAdmin for Effective MySQL Management" in April 2004 and subsequently continued to specialize in publishing highly focused books on specific technologies and solutions.

Our books and publications share the experiences of your fellow IT professionals in adapting and customizing today's systems, applications, and frameworks. Our solution-based books give you the knowledge and power to customize the software and technologies you're using to get the job done. Packt books are more specific and less general than the IT books you have seen in the past. Our unique business model allows us to bring you more focused information, giving you more of what you need to know, and less of what you don't.

Packt is a modern, yet unique publishing company, which focuses on producing quality, cutting-edge books for communities of developers, administrators, and newbies alike. For more information, please visit our website: www.PacktPub.com.

Django 1.0 Template Development

ISBN: 978-1-847195-70-8   Paperback: 272 pages

A practical guide to Django template development with custom tags, filters, multiple templates, caching, and more

1. Dive into Django's template system and build your own template

2. Learn to use built-in tags and filters in Django 1.0

3. Practical tips for project setup and template structure

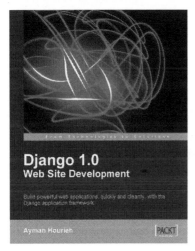

Django 1.0 Website Development

ISBN: 978-1-847196-78-1   Paperback: 272 pages

Build powerful web applications, quickly and cleanly, with the Django application framework

1. Teaches everything you need to create a complete Web 2.0-style web application with Django 1.0

2. Learn rapid development and clean, pragmatic design

3. No knowledge of Django required

4. Packed with examples and screenshots for better understanding

Please check **www.PacktPub.com** for information on our titles

Python Testing: Beginner's Guide

ISBN: 978-1-847198-84-6   Paperback: 256 pages

An easy and convenient approach to testing your powerful Python projects

1. Covers everything you need to test your code in Python

2. Easiest and enjoyable approach to learn Python testing

3. Write, execute, and understand the result of tests in the unit test framework

4. Packed with step-by-step examples and clear explanations

Expert Python Programming

ISBN: 978-1-847194-94-7   Paperback: 372 pages

Best practices for designing, coding, and distributing your Python software

1. Learn Python development best practices from an expert, with detailed coverage of naming and coding conventions

2. Apply object-oriented principles, design patterns, and advanced syntax tricks

3. Manage your code with distributed version control

4. Profile and optimize your code

Please check **www.PacktPub.com** for information on our titles

PUBLISHING

Matplotlib for Python Developers

ISBN: 978-1-847197-90-0   Paperback: 308 pages

Build remarkable publication-quality plots the easy way

1. Create high quality 2D plots by using Matplotlib productively

2. Incremental introduction to Matplotlib, from the ground up to advanced levels

3. Embed Matplotlib in GTK+, Qt, and wxWidgets applications as well as web sites to utilize them in Python applications

4. Deploy Matplotlib in web applications and expose it on the Web using popular web frameworks such as Pylons and Django

Practical Plone 3: A Beginner's Guide to Building Powerful Websites

ISBN: 978-1-847191-78-6   Paperback: 592 pages

1. Get a Plone-based website up and running quickly without dealing with code

2. Beginner's guide with easy-to-follow instructions and screenshots

3. Learn how to make the best use of Plone's out-of-the-box features

4. Customize security, look-and-feel, and many other aspects of Plone

Please check **www.PacktPub.com** for information on our titles

Grok 1.0 Web Development

ISBN: 978-1-847197-48-1   Paperback: 308 pages

Create flexible, agile web applications using the power of Grok—a Python web framework

1. Develop efficient and powerful web applications and web sites from start to finish using Grok, which is based on Zope 3

2. Integrate your applications or web sites with relational databases easily

3. Extend your applications using the power of the Zope Toolkit

4. Easy-to-follow and packed with practical, working code with clear explanations

Learning Website Development with Django

ISBN: 978-1-847193-35-3   Paperback: 264 pages

A beginner's tutorial to building web applications, quickly and cleanly, with the Django application framework

1. Create a complete Web 2.0-style web application with Django

2. Learn rapid development and clean, pragmatic design

3. Build a social bookmarking application

4. No knowledge of Django required

Please check **www.PacktPub.com** for information on our titles

Made in the USA
Lexington, KY
05 December 2011